Stories of Culture and Place

STORIES

of **CULTURE AND PLACE**

An Introduction to Anthropology
SECOND EDITION

Michael G. Kenny and Kirsten Smillie

UNIVERSITY OF TORONTO PRESS

Library and Archives Canada Cataloguing in Publication

Kenny, Michael, 1942–, author
    Stories of culture and place : an introduction to anthropology/Michael
G. Kenny and Kirsten Smillie.—Second edition.

Includes bibliographical references and index.
Issued in print and electronic formats.
ISBN 978-1-4875-9370-4 (softcover).—ISBN 978-1-4875-9371-1(EPUB).—
ISBN 978-1-4875-9372-8 (PDF)

    1. Anthropology—Textbooks.   2. Textbooks.   I. Smillie, Kirsten, 1979–,
author   II. Title.

GN25.K46 2017   301   C2017-903610-6
                                    C2017-903611-4

We welcome comments and suggestions regarding any aspect of our publications—please feel free to contact us at news@utphighereducation.com or visit our Internet site at www.utorontopress.com.

North America   UK, Ireland, and continental Europe
5201 Dufferin Street   NBN International
North York, Ontario, Canada, M3H 5T8 Estover Road, Plymouth, PL6 7PY, UK
                                     ORDERS PHONE: 44 (0) 1752 202301
2250 Military Road   ORDERS FAX: 44 (0) 1752 202333
Tonawanda, New York, USA, 14150   ORDERS E-MAIL: enquiries@nbninternational.com

ORDERS PHONE: 1–800–565–9523
ORDERS FAX: 1–800–221–9985
ORDERS E-MAIL: utpbooks@utpress.utoronto.ca

Every effort has been made to contact copyright holders; in the event of an error or omission, please notify the publisher.

This book is printed on paper containing 100% post-consumer fibre.

The University of Toronto Press acknowledges the financial support for its publishing activities of the Government of Canada through the Canada Book Fund.

Printed in Canada.

Contents

Illustrations

Plates

Maps

Figure

Acknowledgements

We first of all acknowledge Anne Brackenbury, our editor at the University of Toronto Press, for her enthusiasm and encouragement over the course of this project. Fulsome thanks to the team at University of Toronto Press for their input and feedback, and to the anonymous reviewers of the first edition.

Kirsten Smillie would like to thank Dusty, Georgia, and Charlie for all their love and support.

Michael Kenny thanks Angela Tai for being there, and his long-time colleagues in the Department of Sociology and Anthropology at Simon Fraser University for their intellectual stimulation over the years.

Preface

This book aims at providing you with an overview of social and cultural anthropology—its origins, its distinctive methods and concepts, and its place in the contemporary world. Anthropology is a rich and diverse subject, so it's difficult to give a precise definition of just what anthropology *is*. We think this end is far better served by seeing what it *does,* and that is our goal. You can then judge for yourself. However, to get things started, we should at least say the following.

What we now know as anthropology arose out of contact between western Europeans and the strange new worlds that were encountered during the great age of overseas exploration and imperial expansion. Previously unknown societies were "discovered," the true map of the globe outlined, new trade routes established, and colonies founded. It was suddenly a much bigger world, and those events are the prelude to the story we want to tell. In its beginnings, anthropology is inevitably a Eurocentric story, but that would change.

Travelers, empire builders, missionaries, and scholars asked themselves how these new peoples and their unfamiliar customs fit into the broader scheme of things—their place in history, their status as human beings, and the value of their cultures. Anthropology as an academic discipline emerged from attempts to answer questions such as these. Encounters with human diversity provoked reflection and stimulated further inquiry; these new worlds turned out to be incredibly diverse, ranging from small bands of hunter-gatherers to centralized empires.

As for theory, it shapes the questions one thinks worth asking, so theory, observation, and practice are intimately related. Even in the early days it came to be seen that much could be gained by *comparing* societies with one another in a systematic manner—that light could be shed on human nature and history by doing so. Anthropology was in the process of becoming a scientific endeavor, and this entailed the development of methods for analyzing, classifying, and comparing.

The most natural way to go about it was by comparing other societies with one's own. But difference, after all, is in the eye of the beholder! Conceptions about the nature of the non-European world were therefore an inverted mode of self-perception, seeing oneself through *the other*. One expression of this was a tendency to place particular societies on a scale ranging from the "primitive" to the "civilized." This progressive scale had a historical dimension. Europeans imagined that so-called primitive peoples resembled what their own ancestors had been like in the distant past, which, in turn, raised the question of what historical processes were responsible for differentiating peoples, making some more "progressive" and others less so. This scale was a fertile but misguided idea. Be that as it may, so-called primitive peoples were once the distinctive object of anthropological inquiry, studied with the hope of casting light on earlier stages of social evolution, or even on the essence of humanity in its purist, simplest, most natural form. They were seen as a laboratory of human possibility, the beginning point for everything that followed. That is still a common stereotype about our subject, and it's not entirely wrong.

But the world has moved on, and so has the discipline: it has gone global and, as an academic discipline, is now found everywhere with a much broader range of interests than its traditional subject—tribal societies. Contemporary anthropologists regularly turn their research lens on those who are "just like them," and they thus contribute to a better understanding of social issues that plague contemporary times, such as poverty, discrimination, and environmental degradation. Anthropologists are also regularly employed outside the world of academia, in fields including development, health, government, and law. In this text we will explore how the history of anthropology has shaped the discipline into what we see today, and how the lessons learned along the way have contributed to the development of a social science that is relevant, critical, and pertinent to understanding the world we live in. As you will see, some of our examples are taken virtually from yesterday's news. Of course, the world moves on, and what counts as newsworthy moves with it. We encourage you, therefore, to think about contemporary events from an anthropological perspective.

Our Approach

The typical introductory anthropology textbook is fat, heavy, expensive, and attempts a comprehensive overview of the field with many examples illustrating particular issues. Our experience suggests that students (and instructors!) often find such an approach deeply boring, so we have opted for another. For many of you, this may be your first and last formal contact with anthropology. No hard feelings; that's often the case with introductory courses, and then you move on to other things. What we hope to leave you with is a sense of what anthropology is all about and of its relevance to other aspects of life and academic endeavor. But some of you may be stimulated to go on and find out more; if so, all the better.

Given those facts of life, our view is that a few well-chosen examples are better than many superficial ones that can be memorized and quickly forgotten. Therefore, in each chapter we focus on a few specific cases that open up a discussion of the intellectual themes and wider anthropological issues involved. Each chapter of this book will follow a similar mode of presentation: beginning with a statement of what we intend to accomplish, followed by examples and discussion, concluding with a summary of the main points.

Outline

Chapter 1: The Story of Anthropology: The "New" World What anthropology is all about, a few key terms, and a brief overview of sub-disciplines; narratives of three early "first contact" encounters between European explorers and non-Western cultures; an overview of the social evolutionary approach that characterizes much of nineteenth-century anthropological theory.

Chapter 2: History in Context Continues the historical account in Chapter 1; including the twentieth-century British anthropological approach known as "functionalism," and the emergence of "cultural anthropology" in North America.

Chapter 3: Culture Shock Examines the nature of the anthropological experience through examples of life in the **field.**

Chapter 4: Making a Living Anthropological studies of economic life; basic concepts such as exchange and reciprocity; "cultural ecology"; hunting-gathering; ceremonial exchange; working.

Chapter 5: The Ties That Bind: Kinship and the Social Order The importance of the study of kinship to anthropology; how we view and construct human relationships; kinship systems; kinship in our own time.

Chapter 6: Symbol, Myth, and Meaning Culture as a cognitive system; the social construction of the world and our place in it; the problem of language.

Chapter 7: Health, Medicine, and Society The origin and nature of "medical anthropology"; concepts of illness and their practical implications; biomedicine as a cultural system.

Chapter 8: Gender and Social Expectations Problems of definition; biology, sexuality, and gender; gender roles.

Chapter 9: Race, Science, and Human Diversity Why "race" matters; the rise of genetic essentialism; eugenics—taking control of evolution; the anthropological critique of race; race in the post-genomic age.

Chapter 10: The Politics of Culture Human rights; cultural identities and cultural property; alternative histories; land claims; applied anthropology; anthropologists as advocates and activists.

Chapter 11: Anthropology, Cultural Change, and Globalization We've always been global; the global and the local; colonialism; "modernization" and "development"; information technologies old and new; migration; caught between worlds; implications for anthropology as a discipline.

Preface to the Second Edition

The first edition of this book was published in 2015 and very favorably received. Nevertheless everything is capable of improvement. To that end, the University of Toronto Press sought the input of a number of outside reviewers with experience in teaching introductory anthropology who have kindly provided comments on our text. They made some valuable suggestions that we have incorporated into this edition. Our account of the history and development of anthropology follows a more chronological approach than previously, and some new material has been added. It was also thought that the book would benefit from inclusion of chapters on economic life and medical anthropology. This we have done (Chapter 4: Making a Living; Chapter 7: Health, Medicine, and Society). Otherwise the text is largely unchanged, though there have been some rearrangements or abridgements and the chapter sequence has been altered.

Michael G. Kenny
Kirsten Smillie

CHAPTER 1

//

The Story of Anthropology: The "New" World

LEARNING OBJECTIVES

After reading this chapter, students should be able to

- describe the four major sub-fields of anthropology and identify what makes cultural anthropology unique as a discipline;
- identify and explain the key rescarch methods of cultural anthropologists, including participant observation, fieldwork, reflexive thinking;
- outline the historical context that helped give rise to the anthropological perspective on cultural difference;
- explore the relationship between theory and observation of the social world— what is seen and how it's seen;
- explain the difference between the persectives of early colonial explorers and that of anthropology;
- understand concepts like "civilization" and "savagery" in the earlier history of our subject;
- understand the significance of the nature of history and **social evolution** to the development of anthropology;
- understand the "comparative method" and the kinds of insights that can be gained by comparing one society with another;
- explain why the question of "meaning" is important to anthropology, and how difficult the problem of "interpretation" can be;
- outline how Darwin's experiences with the people of Tierra del Fucgo were central to his understanding of social progress;

- describe the "myth of the savage" and its influence on eighteenth-century anthropology, including its biblical origins and interpretations by the philosophers Hobbes and Rousseau;
- discuss how social theorists used observations of peoples such as the Aboriginal Australians and the Fuegians to illustrate social evolutionism; and
- summarize the work of Lewis Henry Morgan and explain what differentiates his theory of social evolutionism from other social evolutionists.

KEY TERMS

archaeology

holistic

linguistic anthropology

physical anthropology

reflexive thinking

social memory

State of Nature

globalization

meaning

interpretation

social evolutionary scale

value

"We cannot escape history"—Abraham Lincoln (1862)

Introduction

Society is a moving target, and anthropology has moved with it, undergoing its own theoretical development in the process. In this chapter, we will provide a brief introduction to the discipline, with some key terms including a description of the four fields, the broad aim of cultural anthropology and the research methods employed. We will then consider the historical background to a number of important trends in anthropological thought, and provide examples of each as they took shape in actual research. We should point out, however, that we're emphasizing the story of how anthropology developed in the English-speaking world, and make relatively little mention of other national traditions.

It is our hope that, by the end, you will have acquired a fair overview of what modern socio-cultural anthropology is all about, and will be in a position to ask anthropological questions yourselves. We seek to illuminate the history and nature of a discipline and to document the emergence of a particular way of seeing. Call it the anthropological perspective. But we won't try to define just what that is. As we said in the Preface, that end is better served by seeing what anthropology *does*—through examples of anthropology in practice.

What Do Anthropologists Do?

What do anthropologists study? And what do they do with their findings? Most popular representations of anthropologists have them digging bones and fossils in exotic locations, or studying secluded tribes in the South Pacific. While both these portrayals are true, they do not begin to describe the diversity of subjects that anthropologists turn their lens on. The term anthropology encompasses four sub-disciplines that, on the surface, appear to have very little in common with one another. What unifies these sub-disciplines, however, is a desire to understand humankind. We will focus exclusively on **social and cultural anthropology**, the study of human culture, social organization, and behavior. Because it is just as useful to know what one is *not* studying as it is to know what one is studying, we will briefly define the three other major areas associated with the discipline.

Physical anthropologists seek to understand human variation, adaptation, and change. Physical anthropology was once preoccupied with questions about the nature of "race," with classifying people according to their perceived physical types and explaining what such differences mean in historical terms. Physical anthropologists have moved on since those days, and, as you'll see, a critique of the concept of race was one of the formative influences on anthropology as it is practiced now. Today's physical anthropologists can be found studying nutritional issues in Africa, examining pre-human fossil remains, or using genomic evidence to reconstruct ancient human migrations. Two sub-fields of physical anthropology include *primatology*, the study of non-human primates and how their behavior and genetic composition compare with those of humans, and *forensic anthropology*, the focus on human skeletal remains found at crime scenes and at the site of accidents. **Archaeology** shares many research interests and methodological approaches with physical anthropology. Broadly speaking, archaeologists study the material remains of past cultures, but not exclusively. "Garbage Archaeologists" on Staten Island near New York City, for example, have been examining the Fresh Kills landfill to understand recent consumption practices and the rate of decomposition of materials. Finally, **linguistic anthropology** explores the relation between culture and language. Linguistic anthropologists explore everything from the structure, origin, and development of languages to the relationship between language and social interaction. Linguistic anthropologists are also interested in exploring how communication is influenced by technology, such as email, social media, cell phones, and text messaging.

The focal points of the four sub-fields of anthropology are clearly very different from one another, and as one might expect, the methods employed to collect, analyze, and interpret these data also vary considerably. Socio-cultural anthropology is primarily regarded as a social science, a classification based upon the type of research questions asked, the research methods used, and the approaches employed to analyze data. Throughout this text, we will explore these research components as they relate to pertinent topics such as gender, race, religion, and **globalization**.

Cultural anthropologists want to know how the elements in a cultural system are related to one another, and how they are expressed in individual lives. When we try to account for the behavior of other people, what we are really asking is: What does their behavior *mean*? What do they intend by it? What institutional structures constrain and direct it? What makes it sensible, rather than just random or crazy? Culture is a system of **meaning**; it provides the standards of **value** through which action is judged and is usually an unconscious, taken-for-granted reality for the people who share it. It is one thing to experience a new city or country, meet new people or try a new activity, and quite another to consider how one will interpret or manage these experiences and findings so that others can make sense of them. For many anthropologists, considering how their own opinions and beliefs influence the way they see the people and activities around them is as important as considering how their participants might view these things. This is called **reflexive thinking**, and in a discipline in which the researcher is the instrument, it is extremely important.

Contemporary anthropologists seek to understand the similarities and differences between human cultures. Deconstructing the social world to fit into neat patterns and simple governing laws, as was the approach of early anthropologists, has largely been abandoned. Anthropologists conduct fieldwork in a specific location or with a specific group of people to gain an understanding of why they behave the way they do. Through **participant observation**, or joining and engaging in the culture and customs of the people who are the focus of one's study over an extended period of time, the anthropologist gains a **holistic** understanding of how the group works. How are social institutions related to one another in society? How does the economy impact the political system, and vice versa? Is religion a prominent feature in society, and why or why not? Is society highly stratified along class lines, or is it fairly egalitarian?

The presence of an anthropologist in a community has a recognized impact on the way in which people act. Any account of an event, issue or group of people is a re-telling by a person who has their own values, beliefs, and experiences that influence what they see and how they see it. No matter how long one stays in the field and gets to know one's participants, one's own life experiences and worldview will affect what one deems important to document and discuss, and what one does not. Many cultural anthropologists will identify how their own life experiences and biases impact their observations.

The best way to gain an understanding of what anthropologists do, and how they do it, is to explore the product of their fieldwork and research. This is often presented as **ethnography**, a theoretically informed description and explanation of a way of life or activity. We will explore a number of ethnographic studies in this book, but before we do, we will consider the origins of the discipline itself, in terms of the philosophical thought that governed the day, the key players who were exploring new and exciting areas of study, and the topics that ignited their interest. In order to understand contemporary anthropology, we must consider the foundation on which the discipline was built.

The New World

This may well be your first encounter with anthropology, and so we begin with stories of three first-contact experiences: that of Captain James Cook of the Royal Navy with the Hawaiians in 1778; of the Canadian fur trader, Simon Fraser, with the Indigenous inhabitants of interior British Columbia during an 1808 journey down the great river that bears his name; and finally that of Charles Darwin's encounter with the Indigenous inhabitants of Tierra del Fuego at the southern tip of South America during the famous voyage of HMS *Beagle* in 1832–35. Encounters such as these altered the course of history.

Cook, Fraser, and Darwin were not anthropologists. The emergence of our subject was in their future. At their best they were meticulous *observers*, and this tells us something about the difference between their perspective and that of modern anthropology. There's little sense of how Indigenous peoples viewed *them*, and what their own world looked like from within. It's mainly a one-sided story that these explorers tell, from a "superior" outsider's perspective. Of course these were travelers who didn't come to stay. True enough, but we will show that this perspective was built into how Europeans of their time saw the world and its history. That would change as anthropology developed as a discipline and as the world changed around it. Broadly speaking, it can be said that the "anthropological perspective" has evolved from observation of "the others" to both collaboration and advocacy with regard to human and environmental rights.

The Islands of Paradise

On Monday, January 19, 1778, Captain James Cook of the Royal Navy unexpectedly came across the Hawaiian Islands during his third Pacific expedition. The first two voyages (1768–71; 1772–75) had been sponsored by the British Royal Society, which was founded in the 1660s to promote the advancement of natural knowledge, and still exists today. These trips made Cook a famous man; their by-product was the expansion of the Empire into Australia and New Zealand. The third voyage was aimed at establishing whether or not there was a usable northwest passage: an ice-free sea-route across northern Canada to the Atlantic Ocean and Europe. This time, commercial interests had a hand in the game, notably the Hudson's Bay Company, which sought to advance its fur trade in the region.

Cook's ships, *Resolution* and *Discovery*, made landfall in Hawai'i on their way up from Tahiti. Their goal was the northwest coast of North America and the Bering Strait. Even though the Spanish had long been sailing the Pacific from Mexico to the Philippines, no Europeans had ever crossed at this latitude. No one knew of the Hawaiians, not even the closely related peoples of Tahiti and the other Polynesian Islands to the south; nor did the Hawaiians know of them, and it is possible that there had been no outside contact for hundreds of years (Beaglehole 1974: 574). Cook first stopped at the island of Kaua'i, these days a popular tourist destination:

> At this time we were in some doubt whether or no the land before [us] was inhabited, this doubt was soon cleared up, by seeing some Canoes coming off

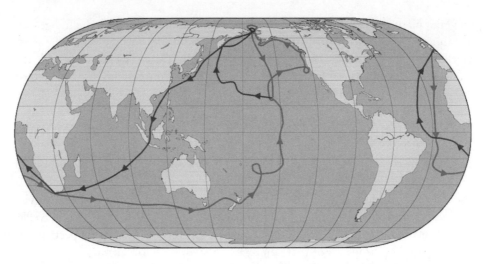

MAP 1.1 Cook's Third Voyage

from the shore towards the Ship.... There were three and four men in each and we were agreeably surprised to find them of the same Nation as the people of Otahiete and the other islands we had lately visited. [...] I never saw Indians so much astonished at the entering of a ship before, their eyes were continually flying from object to object, the wildness of their looks and actions fully express'd their surprise and astonishment at the several new objects before them and evinced that they never had been on board a ship before. (Cook 1967: 263–64)

Cook then went ashore himself near the present town of Waimea, where his statue now stands. He found the Hawaiians very hospitable and ready to trade just about anything for pieces of iron: "The very instant I leaped ashore, they all fell flat on their faces, and remained in that humble posture till I made signs to them to rise.... This, as I afterwards understood, is done to their great chiefs" (Cook 1967: 269). He had encountered a hierarchical society of a type already familiar to him from other Polynesian islands (1967: 284). Noting many similarities of language and culture, Cook asked himself, "How shall we account for this Nation spreading itself so far over this vast ocean? We find them from New Zealand to the south, to these islands to the North and from Easter Island to the Hebrides; an extent of 60° of latitude ... and 83° of longitude ... how much further is not known" (1967: 279).

James Cook was a meticulous observer, with a keen eye for religious practice and other things:

We observed at every Village one or more elevated objects. It proved to be a [*heiau*—a ritual enclosure] which in many respects was like those of Otaheite.... It was 4 feet square at the base and about 20 feet high, the four sides was [*sic*] built of small sticks and branches…. On each side … stood erect some rude carved boards…. At the foot of these were square places, a little sunk below the common level and inclosed with stone, these we understood were graves. About the middle of the [*heiau*] were three of these places in a line, where we were told three chiefs had been buried; before them was another that was oblong, this they called … taboo and gave us clearly to understand that three human sacrifices had been buried there, that is one at the burial of each chief. (1967: 270)

There were two effigies of goddesses in a nearby structure, and the whole place was surrounded with an aura of *taboo*: "sacred, dangerous, set apart"—a term that entered the English language via the Polynesians, its first recorded use by Captain Cook himself in 1777. The British had stumbled into a complex symbolic world of myth and ritual, as became evident when Cook was treated like a god on the Big Island of Hawai'i upon his return from the north Pacific in November 1778.

What happened in the meantime is a story in itself. *Resolution* and *Discovery* departed Kaua'i with an ample supply of fresh water and foodstuffs that they had traded for with the Hawaiians. They reached the coast of North America near the Straits of Juan de Fuca between what is now Washington State and Vancouver Island in British Columbia. Cook missed the strait and sailed up the west coast of the Island to Nootka Sound, where they met the people who now know themselves as the *Nuu-chah-nulth* ("along the mountains and sea"). They lived in houses made of boards, mainly subsisted on the products of the sea, and also had a keen interest in acquiring metal. We will return to them again.

Cook's ships then passed through the Aleutian Islands and circumnavigated the Bering Sea up to the edge of the Arctic ice pack. After encounters with local Indigenous peoples and with Russians on the Siberian side, Cook headed back to Hawai'i before winter set in. This time it was to the Big Island, where the British were astonished to find snow-capped mountains (Mauna Loa, 10,000 ft.; Mauna Kea, 13,000 ft.). They went ashore in Kealakekua Bay, on the famous Kona Coast.

What happened next raises persistent questions about just what sort of being the Hawaiians took James Cook to be. His own diaries become spotty at this point, but they are supplemented by the journals of his officers, in this case by Lieutenant James King of the *Resolution*. Cook had established some degree of rapport with local men of evident importance, who now wanted him to participate in a ceremony:

We landed on the Beech, & were receiv'd by 3 or 4 men who held wands tipt with dogs hair, & who kept repeating a sentence, wherein the word Erono was always mention'd, this is the name by which the Captn has for some time been distinguish'd by the Natives. At the [north] end of this beach is a Village, on the other an oblong pile of Stones & between a grove of Coco nut trees, with a stone wall separating it from the Beech; Not a Soul but those I have mention'd were to be seen on the beach, but close round the huts we saw numbers of the Inhabitants Prostrate, as they were at our first Visit at [Kaua'i]. We were conducted to the top of the pile of stones.... There was a stout Railing all round, on which there were stuck 20 Skulls, the most of which they gave us to understand were those of [Maui] men, whom they had killd on the death of some Chief.... There were 12 Images ranged in a semicircular form & fronting these opposite the Center figure was a [rotten] hog, placed on a stand.... On one side were two wooden Images; between these the Captain was seated.... [The priest] kept repeating in a very quick tone some speeches or prayers, to which the rest responded ... till at last he repeat'd only two or three words at a time & was answer by the Croud repeating the Word Erono. (Cook 1967: 505–6)

The Lieutenant and his Captain were obliged to attempt to eat morsels of the rotten pig. King was mystified by "this long, & rather tiresome ceremony, of which we could only guess at its Object and Meaning, only that it was highly respectful on their parts, & seemed to promise us every assistance they could afford us" (1967: 506–7).

Lieutenant King's puzzlement about what was going on here raises a central anthropological issue: the problem of *meaning* and **interpretation**. How is a ritual of this sort to be understood? What is the nature of a concept such as "taboo"? Who or what was "Erono," and why was Captain Cook associated with this being in the eyes of the Hawaiians? As Cook's biographer wrote, "we may not unnaturally ask ... why Cook should have received such extraordinary notice at this particular island" (1967: 657). We'll return to such questions in Chapter 6.

PLATE 1.1 Hawaiian Temple

These questions take on added force given the unfortunate events that followed. After Captain Cook had been treated virtually like a god, the *Resolution* and *Discovery* took their leave but were forced to return within a week because of a broken mast. This time things didn't go well at all. Cook ended up in a dispute with the locals over the theft of a small boat; he and several others were killed in an attempt to get the boat back. His body was taken inland and dismembered, and his shipmates were only able to retrieve some of the parts. What was left of Captain Cook was put in a coffin and buried at sea in Kealakekua Bay, which had been placed under a do-not-enter taboo by a local lord so as to prevent further hostilities. As Lieutenant King reported, "we now assurd him we were entirely their friends, & as the Erono was buried all recollection of the affair was also buried" (1967: 567). A monument to Captain Cook now stands near where he was killed; it is considered extra-territorial British property.

As for Hawai'i itself, in 1810, the islands were unified into one kingdom by Kamehameha the Great. In 1893, the kingdom was overthrown in a bloodless coup organized by a group of American planters and merchants (see Daws 1968). In 1959, Hawai'i was admitted to the American Union as the 50th state. If you travel around the islands these days you may occasionally see the original Hawaiian flag flying by the roadside. A local man explained that it was to protest the illegal American seizure of the islands and to agitate for the restoration of the kingdom. On his t-shirt was written, "My people killed Captain Cook." Over the years Cook became for some "a symbol of the colonialism, dispossession and oppression that sometimes followed in the wake of his explorations" (Williams 2008: 172). As one radical said, "the best part of Cook's visit was that we killed him … we can defend our honour by declaring that we rid the world of another evil white man" (Williams 2008: 170, 172). In 2015 Native Hawaiian protestors and their allies effectively blocked the construction of a huge telescope at the observatory on the summit of Mauna Kea, which they regard as a sacred mountain; the project may find a new home on the Canary Islands off the west coast of Africa.

Simon Fraser's Journey

River geography was of great interest to fur-traders, such as Simon Fraser. He was born in 1776 in New York State, moved to Quebec as a teenager, and was commissioned by a Montreal-based fur company to search out new opportunities in the far West. He knew about the discoveries of previous expeditions, but what lay between the Prairies and the coast remained unclear. There had been reports of a major river beyond the Rockies, and Fraser undertook to determine whether or not it was in fact the Columbia, which had been partially explored by George Vancouver in 1791–92 and the Lewis and Clark expedition in 1805–06.

Fraser and his party traveled by canoe down that uncharted river in the spring of 1808, encountering numerous Indigenous groups along the way. Fraser regarded himself as "English" and he called his canoemen "Canadians"; they were probably *Métis*, men of mixed French Canadian and Indigenous ancestry. He kept a detailed journal, while Native people living in the vicinity of the present town of Lytton kept alive memories of the first European they had ever seen. The following quote records Fraser's reaction to their encounter.

> At 8 A.M. set out ·... The natives ferried us over a large rapid river [the Stein River]. I obtained, for an awl, a passage to the next village, a distance of three miles through strong rapids. The others who went by land met some of the Indians on the way who were happy to see them. The Indians of this village may be about four hundred souls and some of them appear very old; they live among mountains and enjoy pure air, seem cleanly inclined, and make use of wholesome food. We observed several European articles among them, viz. a copper Tea Kettle, a brass camp kettle, a strip of common blanket, and clothing such as the Cree women wear. These things, we supposed, were brought from out settlement beyond the [Rocky] Mountains. Indeed the Indians made us understand as much.
>
> After having remained some time in this village, the principal chief invited us over the river. We crossed, and he received us at the waterside, where, assisted by several others, he took me by the arms and conducted me in a moment up the hill to the camp where his people were sitting in rows, to the number of twelve hundred; and I had to shake hands with all of them. Then the Great chief made a long harangue, in course of which he pointed to the sun, to the four quarters of the world, and then to us, and then he introduced his father, who was old and blind, and was carried by another man, who also made a harangue of some length. The old man was placed near us, and with some emotion often stretched out both his hands in order to feel ours.
>
> The natives have many chiefs and great men, appear to be good orators, for their manner of delivery is extremely handsome. We had every reason to be thankful for our reception at this place; the Indians shewed us every possible attention and supplied our wants as much as they could. We had salmon, berries, oil and roots in abundance, and our men had six dogs. Our tent was pitched near the camp and we enjoyed peace and security during our stay. (Fraser 1960: 86–87)

In 1900 the story of Fraser's visit was recounted to James Teit, a Scottish immigrant who had married into a local family. Teit was a self-taught anthropologist who became an associate of Professor Franz Boas of Columbia University in New York, and wrote extensively on the interior peoples of the Pacific Northwest. Boas was a central figure in the early history of North American anthropology, and we'll see him again in Chapter 2. The following quotation gives us an Indigenous perspective on Fraser's 1808 account. It was related to Teit by Semalitsa, a woman of the Slaka'pamux First Nation, who was living near the present town of Lytton, BC.

MAP 1.2 The Pacific Northwest: Simon Fraser's Journey

My grandmother told me that when she was a young girl she was playing one day in the summer-time (about the time the service-berries get ripe) near the river beach at the village of [Stein], when she saw two canoes, with red flags hoisted, come downstream. She ran and told her mother, and the people gathered to see the strange sight. Seeing so many people gathered, the canoes put ashore and several men came ashore. Each canoe carried a number of men, and many of them wore strange dresses, and everything about them was strange. Some of the men looked like Indians, and others looked like what we call white men. Among them was a Shuswap chief who acted as interpreter. Our people were not afraid of the strangers, nor were they hostile to them. The strangers produced a large pipe, and had a ceremonial smoke with some of our men. After distributing a few presents, they boarded their canoes and went on to Lytton, where they were presented with food of various kinds, and gave in

PLATE 1.2 James Teit and Lucy Antko

exchange tobacco, beads, and knives. The Lytton chief … went up the east bank of the Fraser, and conducted them to his place with considerable ceremony. All the Lytton people were assembled to meet them, and before they left they had many talks and smokes with the Indians. The Spence's Bridge chief ran on foot all the way [to Lytton] and arrived in time to see the strangers and to deliver a great speech. The Lytton chief at this time was also a great orator. The Spence's Bridge chief was presented with some kind of metal or brass badge, and a hat worn by the leader of the strangers whom the Indians called "The Sun." He was called this because of some kind of shining emblem he wore on his hat or cap, which resembled the symbol of the Sun. The Indians applied names to most of the strangers, all taken from some feature of their appearance or from certain marks or emblems on their clothing. (Wickwire 1994: 8–9)

Fraser had noted unfamiliar cultural practices, such as the speech in which the orator pointed to the sun and the four quarters of the world. He could not know that later generations in the Lytton area would call *him* "The Sun" or that some would remember him as having traveled in company with Coyote, Moon, and Morning Star. "Coyote" was a powerful figure among interior peoples, the trickster-transformer who gave the world its present form and was a central character in many local tales. Some said that Fraser's visit was foretold by prophets, and even that Fraser was *himself* Coyote: "This is the only time Coyote has appeared since the end of the mythological age" (Wickwire 1994: 10). A more recent and quite different account recalls that some member of Fraser's party, perhaps even Fraser himself, had molested a local woman (Wickwire 1994). That is possible of course, but it may also reflect the tensions that have arisen between whites and Indigenous peoples since Fraser's time. History gets rewritten or retold in the light of present circumstances.

When Fraser's party reached the river's mouth, he took latitude measurements and determined that this new river could not be the Columbia, but was well to the north of it. They found that things were tense because of raids by the "Indians of the Sea," and so headed back upriver again. In years to come the peoples Fraser had encountered along the way would be confined to small reserves, a tiny fraction of the territory they had once used freely. The river now bears Fraser's name.

The contrasting stories of Semalitsa and Fraser point to the topic of **social memory**—the social factors affecting recollection and forgetting (see Fentress and Wickham 1992; Connerton 1989). The written accounts of Cook, Fraser, and Darwin are stories too—told from the point of view of a particular time and place and with a particular audience in mind. Sometimes the "truth" of historical accounts is difficult to judge, and a lot may depend on it. In Semalitsa's account we see a process at work whereby long-ago events were assimilated into a First Nations style of storytelling. Memories of events, by being told and retold, change their shape over time. Events happen, but what do they mean? By themselves nothing much, unless a place is found for them in a narrative. It might be tales of heroic deeds, or something as everyday as shared memories of a family holiday. Things that happened long ago or even occurred at entirely different times may get absorbed into one story and take on "mythological" qualities. Much is simply forgotten and lost. The making of "history" can itself be a very political process, and we'll revisit that topic in Chapter 10.

Time Travel

In 1826 the British Admiralty dispatched two ships—the *Adventure* and the *Beagle*—to survey the southern coasts and peninsula of South America. This first voyage of the *Beagle* lasted four years and took its crew to Tierra del Fuego at the far southern tip of the continent. They returned home with four native Fuegians on board, three young men and a girl. Other travelers had encountered Fuegians before, and had formed an unfavorable opinion of them. These hunter-gatherers lived in small and sometimes mutually hostile bands, and subsisted off the products of both sea and land. Robert Fitzroy, captain of the *Beagle*, described them as

"… wrapped in rough skins, with their hair hanging down on all sides, like old thatch, and their skins of a reddish brown colour, smeared over with oil, and very dirty. Naturally petulant and quarrelsome, they are also ever intent upon mischief; fear of punishment alone restraining them; their extremely dirty black hair half hides yet heightens a villainous expression of the worst description of savage features" (Fitzroy 1966, v.1: 216, 319; v.2: 137).

Nevertheless Fitzroy noted that "unwilling as we may be to consider ourselves even remotely descended from human beings in such a state … [Julius] Caesar found the Britons painted and clothed in skins like these Fuegians" (Fitzroy 1966, v.2: 121). After another incident involving the theft of a boat, the British picked up the four Fuegians as hostages, but found it impossible to drop them off again. Robert Fitzroy assumed personal responsibility for their welfare, and vowed to return them on a subsequent trip. His views on their abilities changed for the better with greater familiarity: "During the time which elapsed before we reached England, I had time to see much of my Fuegian companions; and daily became more interested about them as I attained a further acquaintance with their abilities and natural inclinations. Far, very far indeed, were three of the number from deserving to be called savages [he wasn't

PLATE 1.3 Robert Fitzroy

PLATE 1.4 Charles Darwin

so sure about the fourth]. They look forward with pleasure to seeing our country, as well as to returning to their own" (Fitzroy 1966, v.2: 1–2, 6).

In the end he became quite fond of his four guests and saw them as possible cultural ambassadors; they were even introduced to King William IV (Queen Victoria's predecessor) at the monarch's own request. Fitzroy was true to his word, and the Fuegians were returned on the second expedition (there were now only three; the other had died of smallpox in England). This time a 22-year-old Charles Darwin rode along as expedition naturalist on a five-year journey around the world. The role of that trip in the development of Darwin's theory of evolution is well known, and we'll return to it. The immediate product of the expedition was his popular travel narrative, *The Voyage of the Beagle* (originally volume 3 of the official report of the expedition, published in 1839). On Christmas Day, 1832, he first encountered the "savage" Fuegians:

PLATE 1.5 Indigenous Fuegian

The astonishment which I felt on first seeing a party of Fuegians on a wild and broken shore will never be forgotten by me, for the reflection at once rushed into my mind—such were our ancestors. These men were absolutely naked and bedaubed with paint, their long hair was tangled, their mouths frothed with excitement, and their expression was wild, startled, and distrustful. They possessed hardly any arts, and like wild animals lived on what they could catch; they had no government, and were merciless to every one not of their own small tribe. (Darwin 1966: 642)

Viewing such men, one can hardly make oneself believe they are fellow-creatures, and inhabitants of the same world…. The tribes have no government or head, yet each is surrounded by other hostile ones, speaking different dialects; and the cause of their warfare would appear to be the means of subsistence…. Whilst beholding these savages, one asks, whence have they come? What could have tempted, or what change compelled a tribe of men to leave the fine regions of the north, to travel down … the backbone of America, to invent and build canoes, and then to enter on one of the most inhospitable countries within the limits of the globe? (Darwin 1966: 235–37)

But Darwin was also shipmate with the Fuegians whom Fitzroy had adopted, and that gave him occasion to reflect on racial difference and the nature of civilization. That concern stayed with him throughout his life, and he returned to the theme 30 years later in his 1871 book *The Descent of Man*: "The Fuegians rank amongst the lowest barbarians; but I was continually struck with surprise how closely the three natives on board H.M.S. 'Beagle,' who had lived some years in England, and could talk a little English, resembled us in disposition and in most of our mental faculties" (Darwin 1998: 66).

When Fitzroy and Darwin looked at the Fuegians they saw a living image of our remote ancestors. As a devout Christian, Fitzroy turned to Adam and Eve to identify our common parents, and traced the subsequent settlement of the earth back to the events described in Genesis 9–10. Leaving the truth of the biblical narrative aside, what he was trying to get at remains a problem today: the nature and timing of human settlement in the Americas (Fitzroy 1966, v.2: 640–66).

By 1871 Darwin had read widely in the anthropology of his day, and extended his comparison between Fuegians and the English to all the peoples of the world. He concluded that, no matter how different local varieties of humankind may seem on the surface, "the close similarity between the men of all races in tastes, dispositions and habits" shows that all humanity is a single species with similar psychological qualities. Darwin concluded that all humanity had a common origin in the not so distant evolutionary past and branched out into the varieties we see today. Just *how* remained a question.

Racial diversity puzzled him, and Darwin grappled unsuccessfully for a way to explain it. When thinking about the various peoples of the world he saw many superficial differences, but when looking more deeply he found much greater similarities both with regard to physical structure and cultural capacity. The nature of physical and genetic remains an issue for anthropology and evolutionary biology, as does the problem of how the human capacity for culture arose. Many think the concept of "race" has no scientific validity and should be abandoned entirely, but it remains very much a part of our everyday worlds. We'll look at these issues more closely in Chapter 9 and will now turn to the history of socio-cultural anthropology as we understand it today.

Prelude: Back to Nature

Anthropology emerged out of the pre-history described above. An increasing flow of information about human diversity was certainly part of the equation. But there were also philosophical and political questions that European intellectuals believed a comparative and historical approach to human affairs might help them address. One way of getting at these problems was by imagining a primitive "**State of Nature**" before society itself came into being, a world of essentially solitary individuals. By stripping away all the things we think of as features of a "civilized" way of life, perhaps things can be seen as they *really* are. The myth of the "savage" was employed to help distinguish between what is natural and what is artificial in the human condition—a creation of society itself. The German word for "primitive peoples" is *Naturvölker*, "natural peoples; peoples of nature." The French term *sauvage* has similar connotations, "natural; undomesticated" (as in *riz sauvage*, "wild rice"). How such people actually live might cast light on basic questions about human nature and the origin of society. Even now the news media get excited by reports of a previously un-contacted Indigenous group turning up somewhere, usually in Brazil. But of course there is always the danger of projecting pre-conceived attitudes onto these peoples. Widespread interest in them tells us something already.

The Garden of Eden tale in the Hebrew book of Genesis is one version of the State of Nature myth. God gave physical structure to the world and then made the creatures that inhabit it. First came the plants, fish, and animals, then human beings, molded out of the earth itself. Adam and Eve were naked and lived off what nature provided them. But they disobeyed God by eating from the fruit of the Tree of Knowledge and learned that they were naked. The first "cultural" act was therefore the invention of clothing. As punishment for their disobedience, God cursed them and threw them out of the Garden; childbirth, work, death, and patriarchy have been our fate ever since: "By the sweat of your face you shall eat bread until you return to the ground, for out of it you were taken; you are dust, and to dust you shall return" (Genesis 3: 19). History as we know it begins with the exile from Eden, and it's been a pretty bloody affair ever since. Genesis is quite literally a creation story, and explains, like many others of the sort, the emergence of our complex world; it provides an explanation and justification for why things are the way they are.

James Cook was generally level headed, but emotion seems to have gotten the better of him when writing about the Indigenous Australians he met on the coastline of what became New South Wales:

> The Natives of this country ... are of a very dark brown or Chocolate Colour with lank black hair, they are under the common size and seem to be a timorous inoffensive race of Men .... Men women and children go wholy naked. It is said of our first Parents that after they had eat of the forbidden fruit they saw themselves naked and were ashamed; these people are Naked and are not ashame'd; they live chiefly on Fish and wild Fowl and such other articles as the land naturly produceth, for they do not cultivate one foot of it. These people may truly be said to be in the pure state of Nature, and may appear to some to be the most wretched upon Earth: but in reality they are far more happier than ... we Europeans. They live in a Tranquility which is not disturb'd by the inequality of condition, the Earth and Sea of their own accord furnishes them with all things necessary for life. (Cook 1968, v.1: 508–9)

This style of thought is associated with Swiss philosopher Jean-Jacques Rousseau (1712–78), who examined the origins of society and the nature of human inequality. "In order to form a proper judgment of our present state," he imagined a time before

PLATE 1.6 Indigenous Australians

people lived in societies, and speculated about what being raised in such a condition would be like (Rousseau 1992: 13). He concluded that, if people appear to be wicked, it is only because they live in wicked societies based on gross inequalities of wealth and status. In his hands the myth of the State of Nature was used to imagine what a just society would be like if we were free to go back and start again from scratch—to form a democratic social contract based on natural human sympathy and rational self-interest. The implications were revolutionary.

Rousseau was arguing against a very different view associated with the seventeenth-century English political theorist Thomas Hobbes (1588–1679). His image of the "savage" was one of self-centered violence, a war of all against all. This was a very real issue at the time, since he was writing in the wake of the English Civil War of the 1640s, during which the foundations of society had been seriously shaken (think about Syria today, and Rwanda or Bosnia in 1994 and 1995). Hobbes took events of that sort to be the modern equivalent of the violence supposedly typical of primitive society, and summed it all up in a famous passage that resonates to this day:

> [In the State of Nature] there is no place for industry; because the fruit thereof is uncertain: and consequently no culture of the earth; no navigation; no commodious building; no knowledge of the face of the earth; no account of time; no arts; no letters; no society; and which is worst of all, continual fear, and danger of violent death and the life of man, solitary, poor, nasty, brutish, and short. (Hobbes 1962: 100)

The fundamental role of government, and for that matter society itself, is therefore to protect us from one another through the rule of law, backed up by the threat of force exercised by a sovereign ruler. Only then is there any possibility for social progress. This contrast between Hobbes and Rousseau shows that the myth of the savage can be used for exactly opposite ends. Real-world examples can be found to support either position, and both have had an influence on the development of anthropology and social thought more generally. The concept of the "savage" provided an inverted image of the European world itself.

How "primitive" peoples were judged therefore reflected how social theorists and satirical writers regarded the worth of their own societies. If they saw their own societies as progressive in nature, the "savage" represented what had been outgrown and surpassed; if their own societies were seen as unfair and corrupt, then the savage represented primitive simplicity and equality. Looked at either way, a central question becomes how this primitive simplicity gave rise to the complexity and variety the world actually contains. Both logic and history require that we think of hunter-gatherers as the ancestors of us all. They provide an image for setting the zero point of history—a baseline for inquiries into how and why social change has taken place, and to anticipate its future direction.

The Idea of a Social Science

There is no single "scientific method," but there is the underlying hope that seemingly complex phenomena hang together in a law-like way, and that these laws are accessible to our understanding and manipulation. Social life is a complex affair, with many factors all in play at the same time. A nineteenth-century French philosopher named Auguste Comte (1798–1857) coined the term **sociology** to help define the kind of study that social phenomena seemed to call for. His "sociology" included what we now think of as "anthropology." From his point of view, it came last in the historical development of the sciences because it is the most difficult and the hardest to separate from prejudice and superstition. Comte's new science was to be comparative and historical in nature, charting the evolutionary progress of knowledge, while also providing insights into the practical administration of society—a serious concern in an age of revolutions, class division, and chronic social instability.

For anthropology as we know it to emerge, there first had to be an understanding that society *can* and *should* be studied scientifically, using methods that had already been proven fruitful in other areas of inquiry. Comte helped set the stage for this. Physical science provided one model for how it might be done: construct an experiment to test a hypothesis, manipulate the variables, and see what happens. Of course that's difficult with societies, but there are many *natural experiments* already at hand. Humans live in an extraordinary variety of situations, and the variability of these conditions provides many opportunities for comparative research. History does as well—a vast laboratory of human experience.

Biology offered a somewhat different model. Organisms are composed of parts, and the parts must work together to sustain a living creature. There has to be a high degree of functional integration. Is it possible to think of societies in the same way? Individual persons belong to groups such as families, clans, social classes, or some other collective entity. The arrangement of these relationships and groupings constitutes the *social structure*—the anatomy of society. The next step is to observe the system in motion to see how the life of the social organism is (or is not) sustained and changes over time—how the various parts relate to one another in the context of the whole, how they *function* or fail to function together.

Evolutionary concepts add the time dimension, long durations in which historical tendencies have enough room to work themselves out and produce structural change. Darwin's great book *The Origin of Species* (1859) applied this kind of thinking to the animate world; in his vision evolutionary change is slow, incremental, and driven by adaptation to conditions. Nineteenth-century social theorists came up with various evolutionary schemes to classify types of society, and proposed various causal factors to explain how the differences between them arose (Burrow 1968). They were searching for the underlying dynamic of world history and where their own societies stood in relation to it. They wondered what the next steps would be. We wonder what they would have made of globalization and the Internet.

The Evolutionist Paradigm: Edward Tylor and Lewis Henry Morgan

The concept of "primitive society" provided a logical starting point for anthropological speculation and research. The term "primitive" has a double meaning: (1) "primitive" as in "backward," but also (2) "primitive" as in "original," the starting point for some kind of future development. Social evolutionists were very taken by the idea of progress, the sense that history was in fact leading onward and upward and that they had the key to understanding it.

The 1870s and 1880s were a fertile period in the history of our subject. In 1871 Darwin published *The Descent of Man* in which he publically spelled out what he had in fact believed for many years: that humankind has evolved from a more primitive form. But, as we've mentioned, he also emphasized that humanity is essentially one species, no matter how different local varieties may appear. Darwin cited anthropological writers to buttress this point, and mentioned a work entitled *Researches into the Early History of Mankind* (1865) by an Englishman, Edward Burnet Tylor (1832–1917). Darwin commented that "he who will read Mr. Tylor's ... interesting works can hardly fail to be deeply impressed with the close similarity between the men of all races in tastes, dispositions, and habits" (Darwin 1998: 185), something that Darwin had already noted with regard to his Fuegian shipmates on the *Beagle*.

Their stance reflects a lively debate at the time about whether the races of humankind have one origin or several (Stocking 1987). Darwin and Tylor emphasized human similarity rather than difference; in essence it was a plea for human equality. Darwin's own family and associates had a long history of involvement in the British anti-slavery cause (Desmond and Moore 2009). One of Darwin's main concerns in *The Descent of Man* was the nature and origin of human racial difference (see Chapter 9).

Tylor is a central figure in the emergence of anthropology, and what cemented his reputation was a large and wide-ranging book published in the same year as *The Descent of Man*. It was simply entitled *Primitive Culture*, and in its first chapter, "The Science of Culture," Tylor detailed what he thought such a science includes. He begins with a comprehensive definition of *culture* itself:

> Culture, or Civilization, taken in its wide ethnographic sense, is that complex whole which includes knowledge, belief, art, morals, law, custom, and any other capabilities and habits acquired by man as a member of society. The condition of culture among the various societies of mankind, in so far as it is capable of being investigated on general principles is a subject apt for the study of laws of human thought and action. On the one hand, the uniformity which so largely pervades civilization may be ascribed, in great measure, to the uniform action of uniform causes; while on the other hand its various grades may be regarded as stages of development, or evolution, each the outcome of previous history, and about to do its proper part in shaping the history of the future. (Tylor 1903: 1)

That statement packs a lot in: it sets an agenda for his book, but is also a statement of Victorian faith in the power of science and the progressive nature of history. It also makes a crucial assumption about human psychology—"the laws of human thought and action"—namely, that no matter how odd or superstitious the result may seem, humans apprehend the world in similar ways. "We may accept the theory of the unity of mankind as best agreeing with ordinary experience and scientific research" (Tylor 1891: 6). Tylor's definition of "culture" applies to all humanity, not just elites. It's a species characteristic; everyone's got it and, likewise, the potential for further development. The general course of that development has been directed by "the uniform action of uniform causes," a principle that also underpinned Darwin's argument in *The Origin of Species*. Evolutionary change is driven by natural selection: the survival and reproduction of those best adapted to the conditions around them.

The essence of Tylor's method was to identify the origins of various customs and then track their worldwide development. For example, he did personal research on spontaneously developed sign language in schools for the deaf—then drew parallels with the gesture language of primitive peoples. Tylor thought he was witnessing the probable origins of language itself. However, outside of a youthful journey to Mexico, he did no on-the-ground research, or fieldwork in the modern sense, nor did he engage with political or social structural questions. Instead he assembled information from folklore, material culture, mythology, and linguistics and used it as evidence for his evolutionary sequences. The first British academic post "in Anthropology" was created for him at the University of Oxford in 1884.[1] Tylor's legacy to the discipline was his conceptualization of the term *culture*, and his pioneering of the comparative method, an approach taken up by anthropologists who followed.

Lewis Henry Morgan (1818–81) is in the more direct line of development leading to anthropology as it's practiced today (Trautmann 1987). Not only did Morgan come up with a comprehensive evolutionary scheme to explain the advance of civilization, he was highly influential in initiating the anthropological study of kinship (Chapter 5). Morgan was not an academic or a man of letters, but rather a lawyer and businessman in the upstate New York town of Rochester. The crucial influence that led to his research was his interest in the Iroquois and his close friendship with a number of them—one of whom, Eli Parker (1828–95), rose to high rank in the Union Army as an aide to Ulysses S. Grant during the American Civil War. Of course the Iroquois were already well known because of their role in the struggle between Great Britain and France for control of North America. But, by Morgan's time, their power had been broken and the population divided between the United States and Canada as a result of events during the American Revolutionary War.

The first product of Morgan's labors was a sympathetic historical and ethnographic study entitled *The League of the Ho-Dé-No-Sau-Nee, or Iroquois* (1851). As Morgan noted, "Among the Indian nations whose ancient seats were within the limits of our republic, the Iroquois have long continued to occupy the most conspicuous position. They achieved for themselves a more remarkable civil organization, and acquired

PLATE 1.7 Lewis Henry Morgan

a higher degree of influence, than any other race of Indian lineage, except those of Mexico and Peru" (Morgan 1851: 3). In historical times the Iroquois had grown into the powerful Six Nations Confederacy, and Morgan saw this process as analogous to similar events in the early history of Israel, Greece, and Rome. He had read widely in history and political theory, and by 1851 he was already thinking of the Iroquois in terms of the classical Greeks and their republican city-states.

Morgan was also well aware of the great diversity of social organization and social complexity among Native peoples themselves; he had what appeared to be an evolutionary sequence laid out before him—a sequence leading in specific stages from savagery to civilization, with the Iroquois somewhere in between. Morgan assumed, as did Tylor and Darwin, that the working of uniform causes will lead to uniform effects—that societies placed in similar situations will develop in similar ways—and asserted that the Iroquois of recent times lived in much the same way as Europeans once had done:

> Since mankind were one in origin, their career has been essentially one, running in different but uniform channels upon all continents, and very similarly in all the tribes and nations of mankind down the same status of advancement.

It follows that the history and experience of the American Indian tribes represent, more or less nearly, the history and experience of our own remote ancestors when in corresponding conditions. Forming a part of the human record, their institutions, arts, inventions and practical experience possess a high and special value reaching far beyond the Indian race itself. (Morgan 1877: vii)

In his 1851 book Morgan showed how Iroquois social institutions and economic practices are related to one another as parts of a whole. He came to see this problem in broadly theoretical terms and, in his classic work *Ancient Society* (1877), generalized these notions to the entire world by dividing human history into what he called "ethnical periods." The major periods were Savagery, Barbarism, and Civilization, each having internal gradations (lower, middle, upper) characterized by *technological* innovations, particularly those related to food production.

He envisioned intellectual progress as a feedback loop, the brain and mind expanding "with the production of inventions and discoveries" (Morgan 1877: 37). Where a people ended up on the **social evolutionary scale** depended on local circumstances, and so, given the wide variation in local conditions, every position on it save one was represented by "tribes still existing." The only exception was the "lower status of savagery," when "mankind were then living in their original restricted habitat, and subsisting upon fruits and nuts" (1877: 10).

The Iroquois were placed in the "lower status of barbarism," having acquired agriculture, the bow and arrow, and pottery. For our purposes, the most important part of his theory was how he correlated a given stage of evolutionary progression with particular modes of kinship, political organization, and property rights. When the Iroquois were still a free people, they depended on maize cultivation and hunting. Like many tribes of eastern North America they were matrilineal (see Chapter 5). They traced inheritance through the mother's side of the family, lived in communal longhouses, followed complex religious practices, and had a council form of government governed by leaders known as *sachems*. These were hereditary office holders, but they could hold their titles only if judged by their peers to be fit for the job (Morgan 1851: 62–63). As Morgan saw it, the Iroquois had an essentially *republican* social order based upon relative equality of status, not unlike his idealistic vision of the United States itself. Tendencies to despotism were thwarted because power was distributed among the *sachems* and the tribes of the Confederacy.

Morgan thought that the place of a given society as more or less advanced along the evolutionary scale reflected technological innovation. Such progressive changes were accompanied by increasing individualism and erosion of group identities, which in turn were correlated with the rise of individual property rights, patriarchal authority, and monogamous marriage. Therefore the broad sweep of history demonstrates a transition from clan-based societies based on personal relationships to state structures "founded upon territory and upon property" (Morgan 1877: 7). Tribal confederations such as the Iroquois represent a stage in this upward movement. Karl Marx (1818–83) and Friedrich Engels (1820–85) thought highly of Morgan's "materialistic" evolutionary scheme and adapted it in their analysis of the social processes at work in pre-capitalist societies (Marx 1965; Engels 1972).

The Iroquois were taken to illustrate a particular stage in the development of the human spirit. Morgan's scheme was based on what turned out to be a very fruitful and more complex idea: that the various aspects of a society at a given stage of its development *cohere* together as a package: "Each of these periods has a distinct culture and exhibits a mode of life more or less special and peculiar to itself. This ... renders it possible to treat a particular society according to its condition of relative advancement, and to make it a subject of independent study and discussion" (Morgan 1877: 13).

Morgan's sweeping scheme of linear social development proved to be too simplistic an explanation for the diversity of human cultures; history is too complicated to yield to that approach. Nevertheless, Morgan and others were working toward the idea that social institutions are bound to one another in a systematic and law-like way, functioning together to compose a working whole. That perspective underlies the development of fieldwork-based anthropology of the British functionalist school, which we'll consider in the following chapter.

The first contact accounts we've outlined above are the product of the age of European imperial and commercial expansion, in which nations competed with each other for access to the resources then considered valuable—gold, furs, spices, trade routes, sites for new colonies. A by-product of all this activity was an ever-increasing flow of information about the world's peoples, a vast database for what would become anthropology. How this came about is the subject of our next chapter.

But for now let's identify a few themes that have emerged from the discussion thus far:

1   **The Nature of History** An important element in our story is the idea that history has a meaning and a direction. For example, the concept of "evolution" also entails a theory of history—that what we see today has grown out of what came before, that there are reasons for this, and that can be identified by scientific means. Fitzroy and Darwin supposed that their own nations must have arisen from some more primitive condition like that of the Fuegians. The question was how? What is the dynamic that propels some nations in a more progressive direction and leaves others behind? That kind of question—the question of cultural evolution—is central to the nineteenth-century emergence of anthropology as a recognizable and distinct subject. Getting at the answers called for a *comparative method* of approach.

2   **The Problem of Meaning** European travelers were constantly encountering practices that seemed to them strange or barbarous. Observers like James Cook didn't simply write them off, but asked how they fitted into a particular worldview. The concept of *culture* as we understand it today implies the presence of a *system of meaning*, something like a language in which one element

in a sentence only makes sense in relation to others. Concepts such as *taboo* have to be understood in a similar way, in relation to other local cultural elements. More on that in Chapter 6.

3   **Observer Bias** Everyone brings their preconceptions into interpreting what they observe. Our three explorers were embedded in what might be called a "progressive" idea of history—that in some sense they were more "advanced" than the peoples they were observing. Even Simon Fraser, who generally had a very matter-of-fact approach to his encounters with Indigenous peoples, wasn't above referring to them as "savages" when he was having a bad day! This kind of problem is a central one with regard to anthropological method. Everyone has a point of view; it can't be avoided. The trick is to be aware of it and avoid projecting one's own cultural understandings onto others, taking one's own culture as the gold standard through which others are judged. Only in the case of Semalitsa's account of Fraser's visit do we get a sense of local people looking back.

4   **Globalization** James Cook was searching for the Northwest Passage, Fraser for furs, and the *Beagle* expedition for knowledge of the South American coast so as to further British commercial and strategic interests. Those endeavors were enabled by the consolidation and competition of European nation states along with the emergence of financial institutions capable of funding such ventures. They are early episodes in the long process that we now call "globalization," and will be the subject of Chapter 11.

Note

1   Tylor was affiliated with Oxford University's Pitt Rivers Museum of Ethnology. It had been endowed by a British military officer with the wonderful name of General Augustus Lane-Fox Pitt Rivers to house his vast collection of artifacts. These artifacts are displayed by type—musical instruments here, weapons there, and so on—and are arranged in sequences "displayed to show how the same problems have been solved at different times by different peoples" (http://www.prm.ox.ac.uk/pittrivers). The museum itself is a remarkable piece of Victorian architecture, and the displays are still in their original form. You can explore its collection via a virtual tour (http://www.prm.ox.ac.uk/virtualtour). General Pitt Rivers' great-grandson Julian became an anthropologist remembered for his research in Spain and Mexico.

Study Questions

1   What economic and political circumstances led the Europeans to go out in search of the new worlds that we've described? How is this related to the history of globalization?

2   How did what the Europeans found in these new worlds influence their perception of the history of their own societies?

3   How would you go about understanding and interpreting things such as Hawaiian "taboo" practices? What else would you need to know in order to understand them?

4   What changes in society did Charles Darwin believe were necessary for social progress? Give an example.

5   Compare and contrast the political beliefs of Hobbes and Rousseau and explain how the "myth of the savage" can be applied to both extreme understandings of human nature.

6   How does Cook apply Rousseau's concept of the "State of Nature" when describing the Indigenous peoples of Australia?

7   Summarize what Cook and Darwin failed to observe about the complex societies of Indigenous peoples in Australia and the people of Tierra del Fuego. Explain how the "myth of the savage" interfered with their understanding of these peoples.

8   Explain Lewis Henry Morgan's approach to anthropology. What aspect of the social world was he most interested in? Why?

Discussion Questions

1   Discuss the concept of human nature. Given your understanding of human diversity thus far, do you think there is a basic and universal "human nature"? Or is much of what we take to be human nature actually the product of culture and circumstance? Use examples from what you've learned to illustrate your argument.

2   Human curiosity has always been the motive behind anthropology. As the world becomes more accessible through the Internet and affordable travel, we are aware as never before of the diversity that makes up humankind. How might anthropology help in understanding this new world? What future roles do you see for anthropology in the global community?

3   Why did Cook and Darwin fail to see the complexity of the societies they observed?

4   Social context always creates a bias for the observer. How do you think future anthropologists will contextualize the work of today? What biases do you think you might hold in the field?

//

CHAPTER 2

History in Context

LEARNING OBJECTIVES

After reading this chapter, students should be able to

- outline the British school of anthropology and identify its major figures;
- summarize and explain Richards's use of *structural functionalism* and her contributions to anthropological methodology;
- outline the American school of anthropology and identify its major figures;
- describe how the work of Franz Boas helped to move anthropology away from a biological understanding of racial difference and social evolution; and
- summarize Mead's work in Samoa, her methods and findings, and their effect on the discipline of anthropology.

KEY TERMS

diffusion	inductive approach	qualitative research
historical particularism	purposeful sampling	structural functionalism

Introduction

In the last chapter we examined the social and intellectual climate in which anthropology developed as a discipline. If we were to characterize the nineteenth century by the theme of social evolutionism, where societies were thought to pass through stages of development, starting with the "primitive" and ending with the "civilized," the twentieth century would be characterized by the consideration of "culture" over biology in explaining human diversity. In this chapter we will look at the direction that anthropology took at the beginning of the twentieth century. We will briefly examine the development of two prominent schools of thought: the British school, as led by Arthur Reginald Radcliffe-Brown (1881–1955) and Bronislaw Malinowski (1884–1942), and the American school, pioneered by German-born Franz Boas (1858–1942).

Malinowski was instrumental in establishing fieldwork as a main component of anthropological enquiry. We will take a look at the work of one of Malinowski's students, Audrey Richards, to see the structural-functionalist approach applied in a fieldwork setting. Boas, along with many of his students, was influential in dismantling the racist ideology that was used by academics and politicians alike to restrict immigration and maintain racial segregation in America. We will consider Boas's most famous student, Margaret Mead (1901–78), and her best-selling ethnography *Coming of Age in Samoa* to explore how this way of thinking about the world was applied in ethnographic research. Finally, we consider where anthropology sits today as a discipline, both theoretically and methodologically. It is our hope that by gaining an understanding of where anthropology has come from and how the political climate of the time influenced what was deemed important to study, you will better appreciate where anthropology is positioned today. One small caveat before we proceed: we have selected what we believe to be compelling times and figures in the discipline's history. This is by no means intended to be a history of anthropology. Rather, we offer a brief look at some influential figures and approaches to understanding culture and society.

Functionalism

We've used the awkward term "socio-cultural anthropology" to describe what this book is about. The need for such a term stems in part from a kind of split that developed in the early twentieth century between the way anthropology was thought about and practiced in Great Britain and in North America. In both cases a few charismatic personalities set the stage for much of what was to follow: Arthur Reginald Radcliffe-Brown (1881–1955) and Bronislaw Malinowski (1884–1942) in England, and Franz Boas (1858–1942) in North America.

The British version of our subject came to be called "social anthropology" and the North American variant "cultural anthropology." These alternatives were not mutually exclusive, and indeed how could they be? It's more a question of emphasis, and in any event there was a lot of trans-Atlantic interchange between these scholarly communities, such that the distinction became muddled and more or less irrelevant.

The British tended to focus on social institutions, institutional structures, social dynamics, and the relationships between them within given "social systems." Radcliffe-Brown characterized social anthropology as "micro-sociology." Following Boas's lead, the North American approach was more pluralistic: archaeology, linguistics, physical anthropology, and cultural anthropology were often brought together under one tent and taught within one academic department. British social anthropology tended to avoid psychological issues, whereas some of the Americans embraced psychology as a necessary part of the wider picture, seeing that individual psychology, language, and culture are intrinsically related. We'll return to Boas and his students shortly.

The British turned away from speculative social evolutionism and emphasized the status of anthropology as a science, one that should be based on the in-depth ethnographic investigation of living societies. Here a leading figure was A.R. Radcliffe-Brown, who became interested in anthropology while a student at Cambridge University. He was greatly influenced by French sociologist Émile Durkheim (1858–1917), and came to think about society in structural and functional terms (for more on Durkheim see Chapter 6). One result was an innovative ethnography called *The Andaman Islanders* (1922), which was based on his fieldwork with a tribal people in the eastern Indian Ocean. He then shifted his gaze to Australia and concentrated for a time on Indigenous Australian kinship systems. Radcliffe-Brown taught at the University of Chicago in the mid-1930s and was Professor of Social Anthropology at Oxford from 1937 to 1946.

The concept of "system" is at the core of what came to be called "**structural functionalism**"—it's a simple idea, though complex in practice.

> The social life of the community is … defined as the *functioning* of the social structure. The *function* of any recurrent activity, such as the punishment of a crime, or a funeral ceremony, is the part it plays in the social life as a whole and therefore the contribution it makes to the maintenance of the structural continuity. The concept of function. … thus involves the notion of a *structure* consisting of a *set of relations* amongst *unit entities*, the *continuity* of the structure being maintained by a *life-process* made up of the *activities* of the constituent units. (Radcliffe-Brown 1952: 180)

This approach combined analysis and synthesis: identifying the groups and activities ("unit entities") of which a given society is made—clans and lineages for example—and then putting the parts back together again to form a picture of the working whole. Radcliffe-Brown saw cross-cultural generalization as an essential goal, though whether he ever came close to it himself is debatable (Radcliffe-Brown 1957). Nevertheless, his approach took hold among his students on both sides of the Atlantic and guided a great deal of fieldwork, much of it in Africa. A fundamental concern of Radcliffe-Brown's students was with the sources of stability and instability in social systems. Tribal society was the laboratory setting for working through such issues. Societies without chiefs or formal governmental institutions were of special interest because they seemed to be self-regulating, rather than disintegrating into the kind of anarchy that Thomas Hobbes had feared.

Bronislaw Malinowski was the other major figure in the formative period of British social anthropology. He too was a "functionalist," though of a somewhat different variety than Radcliffe-Brown. Malinowski's father was Professor of Slavic Languages at the University of Cracow in Poland, and Malinowski developed a keen interest in language that served him well during his fieldwork in the southwest Pacific, as well as anthropology. In 1910 he began studies at the London School of Economics, to which he would return as a professor himself. His fame was largely derived from "epoch-marking fieldwork" on the Trobriand Islands, which lie off the northeastern coast of New Guinea (Stocking 1995: 255). The major outcome was a study of a system of ceremonial exchange known as *kula*, as described in Malinowski's influential ethnography *Argonauts of the Western Pacific* (1922). We'll take a closer look at Malinowski's fieldwork experiences in Chapter 3 and his analysis of the *kula* in Chapter 4.

Malinowski's theoretical focus—as outlined in his book *A Scientific Theory of Culture* (1944)—was on "basic needs" and how culture as an adaptive mechanism functions to supply them; some of these needs are biological in nature—nutrition,

PLATE 2.1 Bronislaw Malinowski

sexuality, control of aggression, nurturance of the young, care of the aged—while others are seen as intrinsic to culture itself, such as the coordination of activities so as to achieve at least a minimal degree of coherence in social life. Malinowski said that his version of functionalism was "meant primarily to equip the field-worker with a clear perspective and full instructions regarding what to observe and how to record" (Malinowski 1944: 145).

That's all a bit abstract, so a concrete instance of the functionalist approach in action will be helpful at this point. Our example is the work of one of Malinowski's students, Audrey Isabel Richards (1899–1984), who studied with him at the London School of Economics in the 1920s. She applied his method to the letter in her study of food production, distribution, and consumption among the Bemba people of what was then the British Protectorate of Northern Rhodesia (now the independent nation of Zambia). She was in a doubly advantageous situation—treated by influential men as an honored outsider and by women as one of their own. Indeed, her work with women led to *Chisungu*, a groundbreaking study of a female initiation ritual (Richards 1956).

The preamble to the Bemba research was her Ph.D. thesis, which was based on the existing ethnographic literature concerning food practices in southern Africa. It was subsequently published under the very "Malinowskian" title, *Hunger and Work in a Savage Tribe: A Functional Study of Nutrition among the Southern Bantu* (Richards 1948).

Malinowski wrote the preface, in which he noted that Richards was something of an anthropological pioneer, venturing into a field that had never been systematically dealt with before. What he said about Richards's book could apply to the study of food practices anywhere (think of your own friends and family): "[A central motif] in Dr. Richards' book is her thesis that the traditional tribal or cultural attitudes towards food are among the most important cohesive forces in the community, which unite its members to each other and differentiate them from the surrounding tribes. The attitude to food, table manners, customs of common eating—the morals of food, as we might call it, the things permitted, forbidden, and enjoined—all form a complex and developed ideology of food" (Richards 1948: xv).

When Richards arrived in Northern Rhodesia in 1930, the Bemba lived mainly in small villages widely dispersed throughout a deciduous forest with an economy based on shifting cultivation. Her fundamental method was meticulously recording what went on in the daily life around her and making connections between the various facets of what she observed or was told. Like many central African peoples, the Bemba were matrilineal and matrilocal, village residence being determined by kinship established through women. The men of the village generally married in from elsewhere, and a new husband had to spend an extended period of time providing labor for his in-laws. He helped produce raw food for them, while they in turn provided him with cooked meals, a type of arrangement characteristic of social relationships between people of unequal status.

MAP 2.1 Zambia

The Bemba were dependent on one staple crop—finger millet—and suffered from periodic scarcity. The population density was very low, and yet the Bemba were politically fixated on their Paramount Chief, who was seen as having mystical powers with regard to the prosperity of both land and people: "The power of the chief rests ultimately on his people's belief in his supernatural powers over the prosperity of the land and the welfare of his individual subjects. By his inheritance of the guardian spirits of the line of dead chiefs, and his possession of the sacred relics of the tribe, he has power of approach to the tribal deities and he is responsible for the economic rites on which the food-production of these people is thought to depend" (Richards 1939: 25).

Food, of course, was one of Malinowski's "basic needs," but, as Richards found, the value of food went far beyond mere nutrition. It was the general focus and glue of social life; social relationships were created and defined through its production and consumption. By observing how people dealt with and talked about food—which they did incessantly—Richards was arriving at insights into the entire Bemba social order. Food was wealth, and there was little else to be had until the coming of the Europeans and the beginnings of the mining industry. Food meant followers, and much of the power of the Paramount Chief was traditionally based on its re-distribution, particularly in the form of beer:

This giving or receipt of food is part of most economic transactions, and may come to represent a number of human relationships whether between different kinsmen or between subject and chief. For this reason the whole question of handling or dividing food acquires tremendous emotional significance ... and discussions of personalities or legal relationships tend to be ultimately expressed in this idiom.... For us it requires a real effort of imagination to visualize a state of society in which food matters so much and from so many points of view, but this effort is necessary if we are to understand the emotional background of Bemba ideas as to diet. (1939: 45–46)

Richards's use of the term "idiom" is an interesting one; it implies a manner of speech in which one thing is talked about in terms of another. For the Bemba the idiom of food was a largely unconscious way of talking about the *quality* of social relationships, and it contained fundamental notions of justice and reciprocity—"obligations to share and to give," the Bemba version of the Golden Rule (Richards 1939: 200). There were supernatural sanctions to back this up, since a relative who died with a grievance in his or her heart could visit misfortune on those who had provoked it. And if you offend the living, there's always the danger of witchcraft.

This sketch can only hint at the richness of Richards's ethnography. She systematically investigated the kinship system and village structure of the Bemba, their land tenure arrangements, the details of their agricultural practices, the place of ritual, their ideas about the natural world and the nature of chieftainship. How she went about this shows what the "functionalist" approach to social life was capable of, and there are other studies like it from that period. Rather than just recording a collection of unconnected facts, Audrey Richards saw a social system at work, each element related to every other in sometimes very subtle ways. Of course, that is also how she chose to tell her story, and this was not one that could have been told by anthropologists of earlier generations. The anthropological movement known as functionalism was based on a theory of a very particular kind, with a history of its own (Stocking 1984). As always, theory shapes perception.

Richards's work is transitional. In some ways it reads like a study of a more or less isolated and coherent tribe. But, as she knew very well, by the 1930s Bemba society was far from isolated and was in fact becoming increasingly *in*coherent. The very fact that she chose to study nutrition was due in part to Malinowski's influence, but also to concerns that had arisen from within the colonial bureaucracy and the mining industry about the health of the Native population and its suitability as a workforce. Bemba villages were being sucked dry of younger men as they departed for the mines and rapidly growing multiethnic towns of southern Africa. Women, children, and older men were left behind in the villages to live as best they could, supplemented by cash remittances from relatives working in the outside world. Zambia, which became independent from Britain in 1964, is now one of the most urbanized countries in sub-Saharan Africa. Situations like this called for a new style of research, and some social anthropologists shifted their attention to studying life in the new towns.

Things were changing in other respects as well. After studies in Britain, students from the colonial world were undertaking anthropological research back in their home countries. Kofi Busia, one of Radcliffe-Brown's Oxford students, wrote on the political system of his Ashanti people in Ghana, and then served as prime minister of Ghana himself from 1969 to 1972. Another, M.N. Srinivas, returned to India and wrote extensively on caste and social mobility.

Malinowski's student at the London School of Economics, Johnstone (Jomo) Kenyatta, published a study of his Kikuyu people entitled *Facing Mount Kenya* (1938)—again which Malinowski introduced (Kenyatta 1979). It was a functionalist analysis that, among other things, defended female circumcision against the attacks of missionaries and the colonial government. Kenyatta represented this custom as an integral part of Kikuyu culture, an essential female coming-of-age ceremony preparatory to marriage. In our own time such practices are widely condemned as "female genital mutilation." Kenyatta became a nationalist politician and, after spending time in colonial jails, went on in 1963 to become the first president of the independent Republic of Kenya. The students of the founding generation of British social anthropology fanned out to fill academic positions worldwide.

The American School

The growth of anthropology as a distinct subject was a side effect of European imperial expansion. Colonial governments were faced with the question of how to deal with the Indigenous peoples within their domains. Understanding who these peoples were— their cultures, their languages, their histories—was part of the anthropological project from the beginning. Governments were more concerned with how to administer to them. Hence there was a natural tension between those with scholarly interests and the practical realities of the colonial situation. That tension expressed itself in various forms. Sometimes anthropologists worked for government, sometimes they opposed government policy and served as advocates for Indigenous rights, others just continued on with their research while coping as best they could with the situation at hand. In North America this work was regarded as a race against time, given Indigenous depopulation, relocation on reservations, forced acculturation, and language loss.

Anthropology was not yet taught in universities, and research was either undertaken independently, in museums, or in government agencies. An important development during this period was the creation of the Smithsonian Institution in 1846, and the American Museum of Natural History in New York in 1869. A parallel development was the founding of the Geological Survey of the United States (Darnell 1990). The US Geological Survey was the work of Major John Wesley Powell, a dynamic individual who combined a taste for exploration with an interest in American Native peoples, which he pursued during his surveys of the Colorado River region of the Southwest.

In 1879 Powell also became the founding Director of the Bureau of American Ethnology (BAE). The study of Indigenous languages was one of Powell's central interests and an integral part of the Bureau's mission from the start, one that had a considerable impact on the direction of American and Canadian anthropology. Powell, who had been influenced by Morgan, expressed this in his introduction to the first Annual Report of the BAE:

> … all sound anthropologic investigation in the lower states of culture exhibited by tribes of men, as distinguished from nations, must have a firm foundation in language. Customs, laws, governments, institutions, mythologies, religions, and even arts cannot be properly understood without a fundamental knowledge of the languages which express the ideas and thoughts embodied therein. (Powell 1881: xv)

One of the central missions of the early BAE was therefore to document Native languages and to determine their geographical distribution. Such an effort was seen as a key to understanding historical relationships between these peoples. Another way of getting at that question was through the collection of myth and folklore and then looking for recurrent themes that might suggest a historical connection between them. The Bureau helped to support numerous researchers, including James Mooney, who first worked on the myths and medical lore of the eastern Cherokee in North Carolina; another was Franz Boas, who collected masses of ethnographic, linguistic, and folkloric material in a series of trips to the Pacific Northwest. Boas went on to have an instrumental role in establishing anthropology as a discipline taught at colleges and universities across North America.

James Mooney

James Mooney (1861–1921) is one of many researchers who contributed to the work of the Bureau of American Ethnology, but his accomplishments have a continuing political relevance that others do not. He is principally remembered for his extraordinary ethnographic and historical study of the Ghost Dance outbreak of 1890, which led to the infamous battle of Wounded Knee between the Lakota Sioux and the US Army on the Pine Ridge Reservation in South Dakota.

Mooney came from a family of poor Irish immigrants who settled in Indiana. In his earlier years he took a considerable interest in Irish-American politics, but also developed a fascination with Indigenous people. He familiarized himself with the work of Morgan and Powell and, because of Morgan's work on the Iroquois, decided to study the Cherokee, a culturally related people who once had occupied a considerable territory in the southern Appalachian region (Moses 1984: 11). To that end he wrote directly to Powell and eventually managed to wangle an appointment with the BAE. In the 1830s the decision had been made to relocate the majority of Cherokee, and other southeastern tribes, to what was then known as Indian Territory and now as Oklahoma (see Chapter 5 for more on this). The Cherokee group Mooney worked with in North Carolina was therefore just a local remnant of what had once been a much more numerous people. Mooney's first publication on this research, *The Sacred Formulas of the Cherokee*, appeared in the Bureau's annual report for 1885–86.

His second publication—*The Ghost-Dance Religion and the Sioux Outbreak of 1890*—appeared in the report for 1892–93, and is of a very different character. It is over 400 pages long, highly detailed, and describes a number of similar Indigenous protest movements:

> In the fall of 1890 the author was preparing to go to Indian Territory, under the auspices of the Bureau of Ethnology, to continue researches among the Cherokee, when the Ghost dance began to attract attention .... Proceeding directly to the Cheyenne and Arapaho, it soon became evident that there was more in the Ghost dance than had been suspected, with the result that the investigation, to which it had been intended to devote only a few weeks, has extended over a period of more than three years, and might be continued indefinitely, as the dance still exists (in 1896) and is developing new features at every performance. (Mooney 1973: 653)

The battle on Pine Ridge took place in late December, a lopsided affair after which some "200 Indian men, women, and children, with 60 soldiers were lying dead and wounded on the ground." The remaining Lakota fled, and "there can be no question that the pursuit was simply a massacre, where fleeing women, with infants in their arms, were shot down after resistance had ceased and when almost every warrior was stretched dead or dying" (1896: 869). What happened there is seared into memory by photographs of frozen corpses in the snow, and commemorated by a monument that has become a pilgrimage site. In 1973 there was a standoff at Wounded Knee between Indigenous activists and the government, which the protestors accused of treaty violations.

Mooney documents what happened in 1890, and spoke with many of the participants and witnesses on both sides of this affair. But much of the strength of his work is rooted in his account of the origins and nature of the Ghost Dance itself, and how it came to be taken up by the Lakota. Mooney shows how radically things were changing for Indigenous people. The Ghost Dance prophecy arose in western Nevada and spread over much of the interior West, from Indian Territory to Oregon. Word of it came via the railways, telegraph lines, and the mail, joining together peoples who 50 years earlier would not even have known of each other. It was a sign that a common Indigenous identity was taking shape, defined by their relationship to a dominant external power.

The Dance itself originated with a western Paiute visionary named Wovoka (English name, Jack Wilson) who lived in Nevada near the border with California. In 1891 Mooney managed to meet him and learn the story of his "great revelation":

> "the sun died" (was eclipsed) and he fell asleep in the daytime and was taken up to the other world. Here he saw God, with all the people who had died long ago engaged in their old time sports and occupations, all happy and forever young. It was a pleasant land and full of game. After showing him all, God told him he must go back and tell his people they must be good and love one another, have no quarreling and live in peace with the whites … that if they faithfully obeyed his instructions they would at last be reunited with their friends in this other world, where there would be no more death or sickness or old age. He was then given the dance which he was commanded to bring back to his people. (1896: 771–72)

This message was condensed into a widely distributed letter. Learning of the prophecy, a council at Pine Ridge sent a delegation to Nevada to meet Wovoka and learn the dance. It returned in the spring of 1890, apparently with a more radical message than what Mooney later heard from the prophet himself:

> … there was a man near the base of the Sierras who said he was the son of God, who had once been killed by the whites, and who bore on his body the scars of the crucifixion. He had now returned to punish the whites for their wickedness, especially for their injustice toward the Indians. With the coming of the next spring (1891) he would wipe the whites from the face of the earth, and would then resurrect all the dead Indians, bring back the buffalo and other game, and restore the supremacy of the aboriginal race. (1896: 820)

By December gatherings for the Dance were in full swing, accompanied by trances and visions of the dead. Government Indian agents and the army got nervous, and events escalated toward the fight at Wounded Knee. The Lakota ritual leader, Sitting Bull, became involved with this agitation. He was already famous because of his role in what led up to the annihilation in 1876 of General Custer's force at Little Bighorn in Montana. Sitting Bull and his people had fled to Canada after that, but were allowed to return to the United States by a government amnesty. In following years he played a part in Buffalo Bill Cody's Wild West show, but was later attracted to the Ghost Dance movement, which took root on the Standing Rock reserve where he lived. The decision was made to arrest him, and Sitting Bull was killed in a struggle with Lakota policemen on December 15, 1890.

Mooney's book contains a wealth of information about how the ritual was performed, the songs that accompanied it, and the diverse cultural elements that were incorporated into it. His study "has served generations of anthropologists and historians as the fountainhead of evidence about the religion and the Sioux rebellion" (Moses 1984: 93). It also provides a striking example of what is now called a "revitalization movement," an attempt to rebalance or restore a culture under threat (see Chapter 10). By 1890 the Lakota and many other Native peoples had been confined to ever-shrinking reservations or, like the Cherokee, deported to Indian Territory. With the buffalo gone, the Lakota were entirely dependent on the government for rations. "Alienation, cultural decay, and desperation became the themes that bound the characters Mooney wrote of to a common history" (1984: 88). As we write, there is an ongoing confrontation involving local police, the federal government, and residents of the Standing Rock Reservation over a proposed oil pipeline under the Missouri River, which they believe threatens their water supply.

As for Mooney, he continued his work with the Bureau, but became unpopular in some quarters because of his research on the nature and spread of the peyote religion. He encountered the ritual use of this hallucinogenic cactus in 1891 and participated in ceremonials in which the eating of peyote took on a sacramental character akin to the Catholic use of bread and wine. The practice had spread north from Mexico into the American Southwest and beyond. Mooney's attitude toward it aroused official hostility; one government servant complained that:

> … he is openly and avowedly in favor of the use of peyote as a medicine and as the basis of Indian worship and [has] advised and assisted the Indians in securing … a charter for the organization of a peyote church. [He] has advised Indians that peyote is all right and should be used by them as often as they choose. [He] has told the Indians that missionaries have no right to interfere with peyote…. His entire attitude which he openly expressed to the Indians…. is absolutely [opposed] to the efforts of government. (quoted in Moses 1984: 207)

In 1918 the peyote religion crystallized in the form of the Native American Church, which still claims many adherents. It has run into occasional legal hassles over the ritual use of hallucinogens (see Aberle 1982).

Boas and the Boasians

James Mooney and Franz Boas crossed paths occasionally because of their mutual interests and their connection to the Bureau of American Ethnology. Mooney and other Bureau researchers produced an enormous body of valuable ethnographic material, but left little organizational legacy. Boas's impact was another matter altogether.

Boas made contact with Powell and the Bureau in the early 1880s after initiating research among the coastal peoples of British Columbia. He had been attracted to that area through earlier museum research in Germany, which alerted him to the complexity and unique artistic traditions of the region. This led to numerous field trips to the Northwest and his recruitment of local associates to continue this research in his absence. The Bureau under Powell's leadership had an evolutionary focus: "to place the American Indian within the evolutionary development of mankind as a whole" (Darnell 1998: 90). As his research unfolded, Boas largely abandoned that goal in favor of a detailed study of culture, language, and history. So, who was Boas?

Franz Boas was born in 1858 in Germany. He was educated in the fields of physics, mathematics, and geography, and his first research expedition was a geographical investigation of the Inuit on Baffin Island in the 1880s. Boas was forever a scientist at heart, and his early training greatly influenced the meticulous manner in which he collected and analyzed data, whether it was investigating the color of sea water (the subject of his doctoral thesis) or describing the *potlatch* (a system of ceremonial exchange discussed in Chapter 4 and Chapter 10) among the Kwakiutl of the Alert Bay area in British Columbia (who now know themselves as the Kwakwaka'wakw). Where he slightly diverged from his scientific roots, however, was the way in which he formulated his research questions.

Rather than using data to prove a preconceived hypothesis or theory, Boas applied an **inductive approach**, whereby explanation and theory emerged from massive amounts of data that could be collected only through an extended period in the field (Barrett 2000: 55). This differed greatly from the approach taken by evolutionary anthropologists who attempted to "prove" their hypothesis through library research and debate with other academics, rather than collecting their own data via fieldwork. While Boas did not believe in an anthropology devoid of science, he argued strongly for a discipline that subjected scientific "truths" to criticism and further interpretation. Boas's approach is often labeled **historical particularism**, for he considered the unique history of each culture to be influential and central to understanding the present.

Boas was instrumental in dismantling many of the problematic elements associated with social evolutionism. He disagreed with the notion that societies passed through stages of development, such as progressing from matrilineal to patrilineal forms of inheritance and organization. Instead, Boas asserted that each culture or society consisted of elements **diffused** from other cultures. Boas argued that changes in culture did not occur in a single, unilinear process, but instead in "a multiplicity of converging and diverging trends" (Freeman 1983: 30). Cultures could not be ranked in a hierarchy, as hypothesized by the social-evolutionary theorists.

Unlike his evolutionary predecessors who embarked on massive studies that attempted to locate a culture in relation to the development of other societies, Boas argued that a study should be limited to one particular cultural area. He was wary of universal categories and generalizations that attempted to convey scientific truths about groups of people, and instead he stressed the importance of diversity, the individual, and the need to historically contextualize research (Lewis 2001: 447). A strong proponent of cultural relativism, Boas asserted that each culture is unique and should be understood in terms of the beliefs and ideals of that culture and not judged

PLATE 2.2 Franz Boas

according to another. Boas championed a rigorous approach to fieldwork, in which extensive notes and data were collected.

Boas believed that the value in anthropology lay in its ability to break down barriers that prevented a greater understanding between people, and in the consequent lessening of ignorance that would result (Lewis 2001: 450). Boas also strongly believed in social equality, particularly concerning race—as a Jewish German living in the United States, he had experienced racism in society and academia first hand (Lewis 2001). At the heart of much of his work was an attempt to dismantle and deconstruct aspects of early anthropology that served to strengthen scientific theories of biological and racial determinism, such as the idea that certain human "races" were more or less developed than others by virtue of their biological makeup (Mukhopadhyay and Moses 1997: 517).

It was with these goals in mind that Boas published his groundbreaking work *The Mind of Primitive Man* (1911), a book that set out to disprove biological explanations of the superiority of the white race and the consequent inferiority of all others, particularly Africans and Indigenous peoples (see Chapter 9). Boas used anthropometric measurements and statistics to illustrate the large gaps that existed within scientific theories that purported to "prove" the biological differences between races. By 1918, Boas had published over 50 articles on racial and bio-logical issues. He showed how nutrition and access to shelter and clothing affected physical growth and development (Mukhopadhyay and Moses 1997), and how socio-economic class and access to resources affected an individual's ability to thrive in certain environments. While this may seem fairly obvious to us in the twenty-first century, it was somewhat groundbreaking at the time. As with many new ideas that challenge the status quo, Boas's work was not well received by intellectuals and politicians of the day. However, the establishment of the Anthropology Department at Columbia University in 1890 under Boas ensured that his relativistic approach would be institutionalized and perpetuated by his eager American students, many of them women.

By the early 1920s, the "nature versus nurture" debate was at its height, and the positioning of culture and environment against biology was driving a wedge between anthropology and the scientific disciplines. The resulting gap would have profound effects on shaping anthropology into the discipline that exists today. Boas and his students, most notably Margaret Mead (1901–78), Ruth Benedict (1887–1948), and Edward Sapir (1884–1939) were pioneers of a discipline that sought to explain behavior in cultural and environmental terms (Freeman 1983: 48). They represented a major shift in thinking that occurred at the beginning of the twentieth century, when many academics and scientists began to realize that the diversity that character-ized humankind did not represent snapshots of stages of development, but was rather illustrative of the ways in which groups of people adapted to their environments and the social world around them. Late in life, Boas summarized his views on the value of anthropology:

> Anthropology, the science of man, is often held to be a subject that may satisfy our curiosity regarding the early history of mankind, but of no immediate bearing upon problems that confront us. This view has always seemed to me erroneous. Growing up in our own civilization we know little how we ourselves are conditioned by it.... Knowledge of ... conditions of life fundamentally different from our own can help us to obtain a freer view of our own lives.... (quoted in Boas 1966: xii)

We will now take a closer look at the work of Margaret Mead, for it was her classic ethnographic story *Coming of Age in Samoa* (1928) that not only intro-duced anthropology to a mass audience, but also ignited a debate about the valid-ity of observations and ethnographic fieldwork that has continued long after the book's publication.

Margaret Mead

Coming of Age in Samoa was Margaret Mead's first foray into anthropological field-work. At just 23, Mead left the United States under the direction of her advisor Franz Boas to examine the lives of adolescent girls in Samoa. As discussed above, the intel-lectual climate at this time was rife with debates concerning racial determinism and the tension between culture and biology. Mead was intent on exploring this tension through her fieldwork, and she set out to investigate if adolescence was "a time in the life history of every girl child which carries with it symptoms of conflict and stress as surely as it implies a change in the girl's body" (Mead 2001: 136).

Intent on traveling to an "untouched and undiscovered place," Mead was directed by Boas to American Samoa, primarily because of the frequency with which ships called on the island and the possibility of regular contact via written mail. After arriv-ing with a letter from the surgeon-general of the US Navy, Mead decided on the island of Ta'u, one of the three small islands in the Manu'an archipelago and with a population of 600.

Before settling in Ta'u, Mead studied the Samoan language for approximately 10 weeks in the port of Pago Pago. After 10 days living with the family of a county chief, Mead moved herself into the medical dispensary, where she lived with the Holts, local representatives of the naval government in American Samoa and the sole white family

MAP 2.2 Samoa

on the island. The Manu'an people had been governed by the United States for about 21 years, and a government school had been established for at least 10 of those years by the time Mead arrived (Freeman 1983).

Mead selected 50 girls for her study, 11 of whom were children showing "no mammary signs of puberty," 14 of whom would likely mature in the next 18 months, and the balance who were past puberty (Mead 2001: 180). Mead's **purposeful sampling** of her study subjects was based on her assertion that "a detailed investigation will be of more value than a more diffused and general study based upon a less accurate knowledge of a greater number of individuals" (2001: 179). Due to the small number of participants involved and the nature of the data, Mead believed that a **qualitative research** approach was the most suited: "The composite of the background against which the girl acts can be described in accurate and general terms, but her reactions are a function of her own personality and cannot be described without reference to it" (2001: 180). Mead conducted interviews in the Samoan language and used intelligence testing, such as "color-naming, rote memory, opposites, substitution, ball and field, and interpretation" to gain what she believed was an understanding of the mental capacity of the girls (2001: 182). She examined the social organization of the community, including the various roles a girl would likely play and the relationships she would have. This included the differences between boys and girls at various stages of adolescence and young adulthood; the relationships girls established within the household, the community, and with those of the same age group; sex relations within and out of wedlock; and the case of the "deviant" and the consequences of existing on the perimeters of society.

After nine months in the field, Mead returned to the United States with findings in hand. In Samoa, there existed no great behavioral or emotional differences between

PLATE 2.3 Margaret Mead, with Manus Mother and Child

pre-adolescents, adolescents, and young adults. Mead concluded that as the physical and biological development of girls was essentially the same in both Samoa and the United States, the turmoil and distress that American girls experienced were due to the cultural constraints placed upon them by American society. As assumptions concerning the disposition of *all* humans would have to be found true in *all* societies, Mead concluded that the despair and anxiety associated with adolescence was indeed an American cultural construction and not a universally experienced biological stage. Her findings were wholeheartedly supported by Boas and other colleagues.

Mead attributed the Samoan adolescents' seeming emotional calm to their social environment—because they did not establish intense personal relationships, and because they were exposed to all forms of experiences, such as birth, sex, and death at a relatively young age, they were far more accepting of a wider range of "normalcy" than their American counterparts. Mead described what seemed to her as a lack of choice for adolescent girls—because their lives were simple and straightforward, they were not bothered with decisions regarding education, extracurricular activities, career or other lifestyle issues that would contribute to their social status in society. Those who strayed from this easy-going nature were labeled as deviant.

In contrast, American society offered children a plethora of religions, standards of morality and sexual practice, occupations, and family life from which to "choose." The social location of American children played a major role in the breadth of their "choices"—education, class location, and ability all combined to limit and expand their opportunities. The media also played a key role in perpetuating the idea of "endless possibilities," while at the same time disregarding the importance of social class and race. The downfall of American adolescents, Mead asserted, was the sheer plurality of choices in a society that championed "one standard" for all.

Now that we know what Mead's findings are, it is helpful to consider the social context in which she conducted her research. Mead was in Samoa at a time when there existed much opposition by Samoan chiefs to American administration (Gilliam 1993). In addition, the political circumstances of the people under study were often ignored by anthropologists, as was the position of the anthropologist in relation to their participants. Mead's identification with the foreign administration of Samoa never wavered during her time there, a relationship that certainly had an impact on how the Samoan people perceived her (Gilliam 1993). Furthermore, Mead believed the Samoan people to be "simple" and therefore ideal as an easy study subject: "… the anthropologist chooses quite simple peoples, primitive peoples, whose society has never attained the complexity of our own" (Mead 2001: 7). Mead relied on generalizations as a way of characterizing her subjects' "modal" personality type (Feinberg 1988).

By portraying Samoan adolescence as representing one personality type, she could easily contrast this with the anxious and depressed American teen, another personality type. Mead's assumptions most certainly influenced the manner in which she approached and spoke to her participants, and in turn, the way that they spoke and interacted with her. This is not to say that her work is inadequate; rather, by making her assumptions clear we are provided with much-needed context for understanding her conclusions. Mead's approach and her portrayal of non-Western societies were similar to those of most anthropologists conducting research at this time, a fact that has undergone close scrutiny over the last few decades by other anthropologists.

Mead's work greatly contributed to the defeat of biological-determinist thinking in the United States. Her work also illustrated that childhood is not a universal experience and is just as susceptible to environmental and social conditions as other stages of life, a concept widely ignored in the realm of social science until the 1990s. *Coming of Age in Samoa* was an enormously popular book. The American public could not get enough of reading about the carefree and sexually promiscuous lives of exotic South Pacific Islanders, and it continued to be consumed by the public for decades to come. In the realm of academia, however, fellow anthropologist Derek Freeman (1916–2001) launched an attack on Mead's work after her death in 1978, asserting that Mead's conclusions on female adolescent sexuality were all wrong, and that her informants had essentially "duped" her. Freeman's criticism of Mead's work has been widely critiqued within academia and provides an interesting snapshot of how two people can observe and interpret the lives of others in vastly different ways.

Despite the criticism, Mead's contribution to illuminating one of the basic tenets of anthropological research—the power of research to increase understanding between diverse groups of people—cannot be ignored. As Mead herself said, "Realizing that our own ways are not humanly inevitable nor God-ordained, but are the fruit of a long and turbulent history, we may well examine in turn all of our institutions, thrown into strong relief against the history of other civilizations, and weighing them in the balance, be not afraid to find them wanting" (Mead 2001: 160).

Mead went on to have a very high-profile career as a respected, if controversial, anthropologist—she was a professor at The New School, Columbia University (1954–78) and Fordham University (1968–70), was the executive secretary of the National Research Council's Committee on Food Habits during World War II, and served as curator of ethnology at the American Museum of Natural History from 1946 to 1969. Her research in later years continued to consider child-rearing practices and was greatly influenced by the field of psychology. She wrote for popular periodicals and often appeared in the media as a liberal cultural guru, and was among many other things a staunch opponent of the Vietnam War. Margaret Mead died of pancreatic cancer in 1978.

A World of Villages

As you've seen, our subject in its earlier days was preoccupied with more or less small-scale "primitive" or "tribal" societies. But, by the time researchers got to them, peoples like the Bemba, Iroquois, Trobrianders, Kwakiutl, and Samoans were in fact far from isolated, and had already been exposed for some time to outside influence and the dominance of external powers. It was recognized that if anthropology aspired to be the study of humankind, then it was missing out on where the majority of human- ity actually lived—in agricultural villages that were themselves incorporated in wider societies and caught up in an ever-accelerating pace of social change: in India, China, Japan, Africa, Latin America, the Middle East, and the rural or peripheral parts of Europe and North America. Therefore social change itself became a topic for investiga- tion in the context of research into village social structure.

Shortly after Margaret Mead set off for Samoa, Robert Redfield (1897–1958) began his fieldwork in Tepoztlan, a village in the state of Morelos, some 50 miles south of Mexico City. Redfield became interested in anthropology at the University of Chicago, which was already a center for urban sociology, in part through the influence of his father-in-law, Robert Park, who studied immigration, urban geography, and race relations. Chicago had grown explosively in the last years of the nineteenth century, attracting many immigrants from southern and eastern Europe, and after World War I increasing numbers of African Americans. Redfield's early work was with Sicilians and Mexicans in Chicago itself. A trip to Mexico shifted his attention southward (Cole and Eggan 1959).

Places like Chicago represent one pole of what we now call "modernization," the other being the rural communities and small towns that these new populations had left behind. What was happening in Chicago is comparable to the economic and cultural processes set in motion by the growth of Mexico City, which is now one of the largest urban concentrations in the world. Redfield was a witness to that process in Tepoztlan, and the book that resulted from his experiences, *Tepoztlan: A Mexican Village* (1930), has had a wide influence on village studies. Redfield was influenced by Radcliffe-Brown who had a low opinion of the Boasian approach and argued that, if social anthropology were to become a science, it had to think comparatively and look for cross-cultural regularities—or, as Redfield (1930: 10) put it, "to study social processes as such rather than to rest content with the mere description of cultures." Redfield sought to generalize his findings in Tepotzlan to the analysis of what was, and still remains, an ongoing global phenomenon.

Tepoztlan in the 1920s was an Indigenous community of about 4,000 people in which the local language—Nahuatl, the language of the Aztecs—was spoken by everyone, who to different degrees were also bilingual in Spanish. It is a pre-Spanish settlement and the remains of an Aztec temple are on the mountain above it. However, the forms and rituals of Spanish Catholicism had largely displaced the old religion, and Tepoztlan came to resemble another Mexican or southern European village. As in the rest of Mexico, corn was the staple crop. The town surrounded a square central plaza and an imposing stone-built church; in the 1920s there were as yet no proper roads, and the only way in or out was on foot or pack animal. The plaza was the site of a twice-weekly market, in which craft articles and produce were offered for sale, along with a few products brought in by traders or acquired by local people in Mexico City. There were a few shops around the plaza featuring such goods, and a couple of bakers making bread with wheat flour imported from the city.

While the villagers live by agriculture, the village lives by trade. It is essentially a market, and the central *plaza*, where occur the periodic markets attended by people from other villages and where are situated all the public buildings and private dwellings of size and importance, dominates and affords a focus for the town. The village, like Mexico itself, has a center and a periphery. (1930: 19)

The town was divided into sections—*barrios*—and each had its own patron saint, whose image was kept in a local chapel and venerated in a ritual cycle hosted by the various *barrios* over the course of the year. Beyond this, all the villages in the region were bound together in a system defined by the scheduling of their markets and the saints' *fiestas*. "A strong feeling of group solidarity develops, and not a little feeling of competition, each village priding itself on the merits of its *santo* and the splendor of its *fiesta*.... The *santo* is the symbol of the collective spirit of the *barrio*" (1930: 65, 78). Redfield viewed the social structure of Tepoztlan as a kind of federation, probably dating back to pre-Spanish times (1930: 82). He analyzed the village in terms of the geographical, economic, and sociological factors that shape its everyday life, and found it to be divided at some levels but unified at others. Each *barrio* had its own identity in opposition to the other *barrios*, but the community as a whole had a distinct identity in relation to the outside world, which it expressed in dramatic and rather drunken rituals that reenacted the imagined history of the village. This is a conventional "functionalist" style of analysis, perhaps reflecting Radcliffe-Brown's influence.

Redfield was interested in a more general issue: the economic and cultural processes of social change. The subtitle of his book is *A Study of Folk Life*. By "folk" Redfield meant people who "enjoy a common stock of tradition; they are the carriers of a culture. This culture preserves its continuity from generation to generation without depending upon the printed page" (1930: 2). It involves a shared understanding of how the world works, as expressed in folk songs, folklore, and common values transmitted via oral tradition (1930: 173). Though Redfield found Tepoztlan to have qualities "much like isolated, illiterate peasant peoples everywhere," there were changes afoot influenced by the culture of urban Mexico and the country's turbulent recent history. One of Tepoztlan's local heroes was the radical agrarian reformer Emiliano Zapata, who had been martyred during the civil war of 1910–20.

In Redfield's time the rural-urban distinction was expressed in the dress styles of those who had more familiarity with city ways, as opposed to their less sophisticated fellow villagers. It was also evident in a creeping spread of new technologies such as crank-operated phonographs, the cultural influence of elite liberal progressive values, and growing internal class divisions in which shopkeepers became money-lenders. Folk songs lost popularity to pop songs. "The ways of the city diffuse outward from the central *plaza*" (1930: 219), another expression of Redfield's observation that, like Mexico as a whole, Tepoztlan was marked by a tension between the center and the periphery. Redfield thought of Tepoztlan as a village "in between" the rural and urban worlds.

To the extent that Tepoztlan is economically and mentally self-sufficient, to the extent that its social heritage is local and is transmitted without the use of writing, to the extent that all knowledge is intimate and personal and is closely associated with the ancient habitat of the people, the community resembles a primitive tribe. But to the degree that Tepoztlan conceives itself as a part of the outside world, and that the Tepoztecans define their personal problems in terms of modern city civilization, it is unlike a tribal society. The Tepoztecans are primarily Tepoztecans, but they are also Mexicans (Redfield 1930: 217)

That was the mid-1920s. In our own day, Tepoztlan has some 14,000 residents and gets its most important income from a tourist trade attracted by its dramatic setting, the Aztec temple, and proximity to Mexico City. What were once local crafts have become tourist art sold in the plaza. According to the Mexico Tourism Board, "the town that is sheltered by Tepozteco Hill is a land of magic, artisanry, an unbeatable climate, relaxation, and, above all, a certain indescribable energy and mood that will recharge anyone's batteries."[1]

Robert Redfield regarded his relatively brief study of Tepoztlan as more exploratory than definitive. Seventeen years later another anthropologist, Oscar Lewis (1914–1970), returned for another go at it and to see how things had changed since Redfield's time. The result was *Life in a Mexican Village: Tepoztlan Restudied* (Lewis 1951). This was a much more detailed study than Redfield's but, like Redfield's, was aimed at situating Tepoztlan and the changes it was undergoing in the context of its region and Mexico as a whole. Lewis found that

in physical appearance [the village] had changed but little. Once off the highway which runs to the plaza, there were the same unpaved streets and adobe houses, the barrio chapels, the people carrying water to their homes from the nearest fountain…. But signs of change could also be seen. There were the new asphalt road, the buses, the tourist cars, the Coca-Cola and aspirin signs … the new stores and poolrooms in the plaza, and a few women with bobbed hair and high-heeled shoes. (1951: xii-xiii)

Reading Redfield and Lewis together makes for an interesting comparison.[2] Broadly speaking Redfield had focused on the internal functional balance of the community, whereas Lewis emphasized class division, poverty, and conflict. Redfield himself commented on the differences between their two studies, and wondered if "the greater part of the explanation for the difference between the two reports on this matter of Tepoztecan life and character is to be found in differences between the two investigators" (Redfield 1960: 135; Lewis 1951: 428–40). His emphasis on the personal equation identifies a problem that is inherent in the ethnographic method, in which the researcher is in fact the research instrument. We've mentioned the principle that "theory shapes perception." The truth of this notion is evident in the contrast between these two men. Perhaps they saw much the same thing, but saw it in a different way.

As for Redfield himself, he went on to a study of a Maya community in the Yucatan, and Lewis went to India. Their works represent a growing body of research on what Redfield called "little communities." There are many studies of this sort: from pre-Revolutionary China, to India, the Balkans, Europe, and North America itself. Anthropology was broadening the traditional scope of its subject matter to include small-scale social groupings of many kinds: urban neighborhoods, scientific laboratories, street gangs, political parties, right-to-life advocates, gun clubs, environmental activists, agricultural co-ops, undocumented foreign workers, and many more. We will give an account of some of them in the chapters that follow.

Mention of the personal equation in anthropological research brings us to the nature of the anthropological experience itself, and that is the subject of our next chapter: Culture Shock. You'll again encounter Bronislaw Malinowski, who left a remarkable uncensored diary of his thoughts and feelings while in the Trobriands. You'll also meet Elizabeth Fernea who accompanied her husband Robert during fieldwork in a southern Iraqi Arab village in the 1950s. What took the Ferneas there was Robert's research for his doctorate at the University of Chicago. Elizabeth ended up doing fieldwork of her own, which, given the conservative nature of rural society, was completely impossible for men—gaining access to the world of Arab women.

Notes

1 http://www.visitmexico.com/en/magicaltowns/center-region/tepoztlan
2 Redfield was drawn to anthropology by Fay-Cooper Cole, who founded the Chicago department and had been a student of Boas at Columbia; Lewis was converted to anthropology by Ruth Benedict, also of Columbia and another of Boas's students.

Study Questions

1 Compare and contrast the British and the American schools of anthropology using examples from the work of Malinowski, Richards, Boas, and Mead.
2 Explain the *structural functionalism* approach to anthropology by discussing the work of Audrey Richards among the Bemba in what is now Zambia.
3 Explain Boas's anthropological approach, and identify how it is different from that of evolutionary anthropologists.
4 Describe Margaret Mead's theoretical and methodological approach to studying adolescent girls in Samoa.
5 Describe how Mead's findings from Samoa influenced the discipline of anthropology and our understanding of human diversity.
6 Summarize the criticism of Mead's work from a contemporary perspective.

Discussion Questions

1   How did Boas's approach to understanding human diversity help to dispel quasi-scientific biological explanations concerning the superiority of the white race? How does Boas's work inform your current understanding of race and diversity?

2   Considering the origins of anthropology, discuss the role of anthropologists in the "developing world," and how this role has changed since the work of Richards and Mead. What contribution can anthropologists today make to international development and global health?

3   The nature versus nurture debate rages on today. Given what you've learned about the role anthropology has played in framing the debate, discuss the issue using examples from this text and your other areas of experience and knowledge.

4   What is the relationship between the individual and the wider society? How do our social circumstances affect who we are as people? Consider the person you are today; do you think you would be different if you had grown up in a different place, among different people, or even in a different environment?

//

CHAPTER 3

Culture Shock

LEARNING OBJECTIVES

After reading this chapter, students should be able to

- identify and explain the key research methods of cultural anthropologists, including participant observation, fieldwork, and reflexive thinking;
- distinguish between *culture shock* and *ethnocentrism* and understand these terms in relation to the larger concepts of cultural relativism and moral relativism;
- define the term *ethnography* and describe the ethnographies of Malinowski, Fernea, and Small;
- understand the ethical implications of anthropology, the role of reflexive thinking, and how social position and category influence the work of the researcher;
- compare and contrast the comparative method and inductive approach, using examples from major researchers; and
- explain how the concepts of unity and diversity are related to the question of human nature and how this affects the work of anthropologists.

KEY TERMS

comparative method	culture shock	holistic approach
cultural relativism	ethnocentrism	inductive approach
culture	ethnography	participant observation

Introduction

The experience of an anthropologist's first day in the field shares many of the same characteristics as that of an explorer—feelings of isolation, uncertainty, and wonderment at the people, customs, and location unfolding before them. The difference, however, is the objective of these excursions: the explorer seeks a better understanding of geography in order to establish trade routes and other profitable endeavors; the anthropologist sets out in the field to gain a better understanding of the people who inhabit a particular space—their attitudes, behaviors, customs, and beliefs (or **culture**), and how they interact with others around them, whether in a neighboring town or a country on the other side of the world. The term "anthropology" is derived from the Greek words for "man" or "humanity" (*anthropos*) and "knowledge" (*logos*): "knowledge of humanity." As we hope to show in the following discussions, the study of humanity that we call anthropology is as diverse and complex as its subject matter. What unifies the discipline, however, is a commitment to a cross-cultural perspective, to thinking about society in a comparative and global manner. What this commitment means in practice is that anthropologists investigate social life by participating in it—by being there in real situations and observing from a theoretically informed perspective.

The focus of this chapter is the ethnographic experience. While **ethnography** is often defined as the systematic study of people and cultures, the lived experience of the anthropologist collecting this data is often messy and tumultuous. People's lives tend not to fit into neat categories, and gaining an understanding of their culture and society can be overwhelming, to say the least. We will consider three very different accounts of ethnographic fieldwork from three anthropologists. The first is from Bronislaw Malinowski and his pioneering ethnographic study *Argonauts of the Western Pacific*. The second ethnography by Elizabeth Warnock Fernea recounts her experience in a small isolated village in Iraq in the mid-1950s, before the 1958 overthrow of the British-established monarch. While *Guest of the Sheik* was written and published over 50 years ago, Fernea's description of her experience arriving late at night to the village and slowly getting to know the people and customs of her new home remains a relevant and compelling read. The third anthropologist whose work we will consider is Rebekah Nathan (a pseudonym), a professor of anthropology in the United States who went "undercover" as a freshman at the university where she taught. While these experiences are very different, we bring your attention to the notion of being on the outside looking in. You can likely relate to this feeling—have you ever traveled to a country where the language spoken was not your own? Have you ever moved to a new town or city where you knew very few people? Think about your first day of school or of a new job—did you find yourself wondering where to sit and who you would talk to over lunch?

PLATE 3.1 Anthropologist Charlotte Whitby-Coles in India

Experiencing the Field

Bronislaw Malinowski

If you were to ask a random selection of anthropologists which ethnographic works they consider the most important to the development of the discipline, Malinowski's *Argonauts of the Western Pacific* would probably make the top five. One reason for this is its intriguing subject matter—an analysis of a system of ceremonial exchange known as the *kula*, which was conducted over great distances in sophisticated sailing canoes. The subtitle is *An Account of Native Enterprise and Adventure in the Archipelagoes of Melanesian New Guinea*. Malinowski also wants to tell us a romantic tale of adventure, in which the ethnographer comes across as an adventurer himself, one who goes off to exotic places and brings back important insights about the human condition.

The part of Poland in which Malinowski grew up was then part of the Austro-Hungarian Empire, ruled from Vienna. His father was a professor of Slavic languages and folklore at the University of Cracow, and the study of language also became an important aspect of Malinowski's career. At university Malinowski studied physics and philosophy, but along the way he became interested in anthropology and undertook graduate work at the London School of Economics (see Stocking 1995: 244–97; Young 2004). This led to an opportunity to go off to Australia and then to New Guinea, where he engaged in fieldwork in 1915–18 along the south coast of the main island, and in the Trobriand chain off to its northeast. The Trobrianders are yam-farmers, pig-raisers, fishermen, and traders, part of the wider "Melanesian" cultural and linguistic community in New Guinea and its adjoining island chains. World War I was under way—this "accursed war," as he called it. As Malinowski was born in Poland, he was technically "an enemy alien," but the Australian authorities let him continue with his work anyway. And he had met the daughter of a professor at the University of Melbourne, Elsie Masson, who—as his diary shows—he thought about obsessively while in the field. So … what was it like "out there"?

> Imagine yourself suddenly set down surrounded by all your gear, alone on a tropical beach close to a native village. Since you take up your abode in the compound of some neighbouring white man, trader or missionary, you have nothing to do, but to start at once on your ethnographic work. Imagine further that you are a beginner, without previous experience, with nothing to guide you and no one to help you…. This exactly describes my first initiation into field work on the south coast of New Guinea. I well remember the long visits I paid to the villages during the first weeks; the feeling of hopelessness and despair after many obstinate but futile attempts had entirely failed to bring me into real touch with the natives, or supply me with any material. Imagine yourself then, making your first entry into the village…. Some natives flock around you, especially if they smell tobacco. Others, the more dignified and elderly, remain seated where they are. (Malinowski 1922: 4)

Of course the diary adds another dimension to this account. He was, as he says, troubled by "lecherous thoughts." Troubled quite a lot actually, since—in addition to the young woman in Melbourne—he thought about many others as well, both white and native. Malinowski was also a hypochondriac, constantly worried about his state of health, and occasionally down with what seems to have been bouts of malaria. This is a typical entry on a bad day, and they were many:

> Monday, November 26th, 1917: Yesterday I had what is usually called *an attack of feverishness, a touch of fever*. Physical and mental sluggishness. Yesterday, for instance, I felt no desire and was not strong enough to take a walk, not even around the island. Nor have I the energy to get to work, not even to write letters to E.R.M. [in Melbourne] or look over my ethnographic notes. Moreover, I am extremely *irritable* and the yells of the boys and other noises get horribly on my nerves. Resistance to lecherous thoughts weaker. Tendency to read *rubbish*; I leaf through a magazine…. (Malinowski 1967: 131)

But he also had good days:

> April 19th, 1918: I was very tired and I could not think straight. I took a walk along the sandy, stony beach, then walked back. The bonfire cast flickering

lights on the pastel-colored background of palms, night fell. Once again upsurge of joy at this open, free existence amidst a fabulous landscape, under exotic conditions, a real picnic based on actual work. I also had the real joy of creative work, of overcoming obstacles, new horizons opening up; misty forms take on contours, before me I see the road going onward and upward.... I came back late and slept well—oh yes, on my way back I went to the pool and delighted in the view of trees, water, and moonlight. It's a pity that I may leave this forever. I want to write about all this to E.R.M.... (1967: 257–58)

The diary also shows what he wanted to make out of his complex experiences, as on June 6, 1918: "I analyzed the nature of my ambition. An ambition stemming from my love of work, intoxication with my own work—*romance of one's own life*.... When I think of my work, or works, or the revolution I want to effect in social anthropology—this is a truly creative ambition" (1967: 289). In a mood like this, he found it hard to concentrate: "external ambitions keep crawling over me like lice," for example getting elected to the prestigious British Royal Society and being able to put F.R.S. (Fellow of the Royal Society) after his name (1967: 291).

There are also occasional references to the *kula* and how to establish some sort of order in the information he was collecting. He reflected on the relation between theory and observation and noted that "we cannot speak of objectively existing facts: theory creates facts"—in other words, without a framework to put them in, "facts" by themselves are meaningless (1967: 114). Malinowski noted that the Trobrianders have a practical approach to everyday affairs and are not in a position to see their society as a whole, as a set of related social institutions, values, and activities. That is the ethnographer's job, and he set out to do it for the *kula*, always keeping the "final goal" in mind: "to grasp the native's point of view, his relation to life, to realize *his* vision of *his* world" (Malinowski 1922: 25).

Argonauts of the Western Pacific was the result. Its title is taken from the ancient Greek epic of the hero Jason, who, to regain his rightful throne, must steal and bring back the golden fleece from the statue of a mythical ram. He assembles a crew, and they go off to find the fleece in a ship named the *Argo*. Many adventures follow. The Trobrianders also ventured off in search of valuable items—the decorative arm-shells and necklaces known as *vaygu'a*. *Argonauts* is a book about economics, about concepts of *value*—what it is that makes these things valuable in the eyes of the Trobrianders, and hence worth going to great lengths to obtain.

Malinowski set out to document the structure of this social institution, how "it welds together a considerable number of tribes, and it embraces a vast complex of activities, interconnected, and playing into one another, so as to form one organic whole" (1922: 63). This greater whole includes myth and magic. Malinowski had found that every important social undertaking had a magical element. He collected a great amount of material on the use of magic in ensuring the success of canoe building and the long-distance ceremonial trading it made possible. He had a gift for languages, and paid close attention to magical spells as a kind of poetry, which he analyzed in detail in later works (Malinowski 1966). His method was to create an ethnographic picture of a society through detailed analysis of what he took to be a pivotal aspect of Trobriand culture.

And the Trobrianders themselves; what of them? Malinowski mentions many of his informants, but these people do not emerge as full human beings. Their value seems to have been mainly restricted to the information they could provide him. When he was successful in his work he thought well of them—"*native life and native society* had come to seem almost enough to me" (Malinowski 1967: 195). When he encountered difficulties, he grew more negative. On April 24, 1918, he recorded a "hatred for bronze-colored skin, combined with depression, a desire to 'sit down and cry,' and a furious longing '*to get out of this.*' For all that, I decide to resist and work today— '*business as usual*'" (1967: 261).

In the end, Malinowski got his golden fleece, and he was rewarded with considerable fame and a professorship at the London School of Economics, where he had a central role in educating the next generation of British anthropologists. In large measure he was actually successful in bringing off the "revolution in social anthropology" that he yearned for in his diary. He did indeed marry Elsie Masson, but he was never elected to the Royal Society.

Elizabeth Fernea

Elizabeth Warnock Fernea set out for a small isolated village in Iraq in 1956. She was going to join her husband, Robert Fernea, who was conducting two years of fieldwork in the village of El Nahra to complete his doctoral degree in social anthropology (R. Fernea 1970). Elizabeth Fernea was not an anthropologist, but despite a lack of formal training she had a keen eye for observation, a curiosity for learning, and an ability to "slip between countries and cultures with ease, never fully belonging but always at home" (Hassan 2001). Pairing these qualities with the fact that she was due to spend two years in an isolated village, Fernea became a skilled ethnographer and, most importantly, gained access to a group that her husband would never have had the opportunity to approach: the women of the village. Despite being game for this exciting adventure, Fernea had a difficult time when she first arrived in the village.

Fernea and her husband arrived in the village late at night, covered in mud and exhausted from their bumpy travels. Her heart fell as her husband opened the door to their new home: mud walls, a dirt floor covered in reed mats, a ceiling infested with birds, and trash and clothing littering the floor. Her husband had been there for three months and was clearly not much for keeping house. As she noted, "This wasn't what the romantic, roving life should be at all …" (E. Fernea 1969: 14). While Fernea eventually settled into her new lodgings, a more difficult task was adapting to the social organization of the village and gaining acceptance by the women.

MAP 3.1 Iraq

At the time the book was written, men and women lived in segregation in El Nahra. When in public, women donned an *abayah*, a head-to-toe veil. They only removed this in the presence of their husbands and other women. It was expected that when doing errands around town one would bring little attention to oneself, and whenever possible the task should be done by servants, children or husbands. Shopping at the market was done by only those women of the lowest status. When visiting a household, women would sit with the women, and men with the men. These customs seemed strange to Fernea at first. She asserted before arriving in the village that she would not wear an abayah, telling her husband that "if they can't take me as I am—if we have to make artificial gestures to prove we are human beings too—what's the point?" (E. Fernea 1969: 6). After a few days of traveling unveiled and being the focus of much unwanted staring, Fernea reconsidered her hastiness. Perhaps blending in would not be such an "artificial gesture" after all.

As her time in the village passed, Fernea gained a better understanding of women's roles in society. While at first she noticed only the restrictions and limitations that seemed to confine women to the private sphere, after time she began to see the different ways that women exercised control and authority. She learned the high importance placed on female friendship and companionship in the village. Women spent hours together and called on one another regularly—their social life may have taken place behind closed doors, but it was extremely rich and active. She learned of the negotiation of public space, of how the bridge connecting the neighborhoods to the village center had originally been built slightly removed from the center so that women could come and go undetected by men sitting in coffee shops or stores. The outer walls of homes had essentially no windows to provide complete privacy for women, but inside those walls open-air courtyards were found. She also learned of women's role in the family—in choosing a marriage partner for their sons, and how, in some cases, they negotiated the introduction of second and third wives to their own families. She also attended weddings and religious ceremonies and learned of the rituals and customs that governed these occasions.

While Fernea was gaining insight into the social organization of society, she was becoming increasingly frustrated with her slow progress in establishing personal relationships. When she first arrived in Iraq, her Arabic was basic at best. While she frequently visited the women in the village, she always had the suspicion that they were talking *about* her: "Were they talking about me or not? What errors in etiquette or custom had I committed? What in heaven's name were they *saying?* My uneasiness grew in this atmosphere of half hearing and part understanding" (1969: 70). After a particularly bad episode when a number of women visited her home, poked fun at her cooking, and implied she was a bad housekeeper, Fernea was surprised at how hurt and lonely these encounters were making her feel: "Six months before, I would not have believed that I could be so upset at being accused of laziness and incompetence by a group of illiterate tribal ladies…. It had now become important to me to be accepted by these people as a woman and a human being" (1969: 77).

Fernea was experiencing **culture shock**, or the feelings of confusion and insecurity that arise from living in a new culture or surroundings. Experiencing culture shock is not unique to anthropologists; you may have had your own culture shock experiences throughout your life. People are accustomed to believing that their own way of doing things—speaking, eating, dancing, dressing, worshipping, etc.—is the *best* way of doing things. After all, we have spent our whole life learning these activities, so it is not unreasonable to think that when presented with a different approach, people are surprised and taken off guard. There is a distinction, however, between the feelings of culture shock and those of **ethnocentrism**. Ethnocentrism is judging other cultures by the standards and values of one's own. There exist varying degrees of ethnocentrism: the mildest form we all exhibit by virtue of being raised in a particular social environment; the most severe form can be extremely harmful and can manifest as prejudice and racism. Ethnocentrism has appeared in some serious and world-altering ways: European colonizers not only explored and extracted wealth from countries all over the world, but also imposed their culture and way of life on the people that they encountered, as did (and, some say, continue to do) Christian missionaries. Can you think of any current events that are characterized by an ethnocentric mentality?

Cultural relativism is the idea that one should suspend moral judgment and assumption in order to appreciate and understand a culture on its own terms, rather than in comparison to one's own. While in the field, this is central to anthropologists' ability to move forward from their state of culture shock and gain an understanding of what is going on around them. The concept of cultural relativism, however, is complex. At its best, cultural relativism encourages engagement with and consideration of new ways of doing things—judgment is put on hold, as much as possible, until an understanding of what is going on is reached. At its worst, cultural relativity can lead to moral relativity, which makes it difficult for us to say that actions or behaviors that may be harmful to certain individuals are wrong. Anthropologists grapple with their sense of professionalism in the field as they do not want to judge a people according to their own values and ideals; however, at the same time, they must consider the issue of human rights and the idea that just because an act is deemed "cultural" does not make it free from criticism or even outrage. People view this position as an uncertain foundation for morality and political action, and anthropologists must walk a fine line between relativism on the one hand and ethnocentric judgments on the other. While there exists no instruction book on how to react to questionable behaviors and actions, there are now international agreements, such as the United Nations *Universal Declaration of Human Rights*, that define morality and human rights in absolute terms, regardless of culture. As you can imagine, this in itself is controversial.

For example, in the pages of her ethnography, Fernea recounts conversations where the discussion turned to beatings at the hands of one's husband. Never does Fernea voice her opinion about this matter, either to the women with whom she is speaking or in her narrative on the page. Given your understanding of cultural relativism, does an anthropologist have a moral obligation to speak up for human rights, or is it more important to gain an understanding of a behavior before any action is taken? Can you think of a time when you judged a situation without fully understanding it? What could you pay attention to in order to get a sense of what this event was all about? What pushes this situation beyond the parameters of "cultural" and into the realm of a human rights issue? As anthropologists, we can collect data and report the wonderful and the tragic in order to increase our understanding of human diversity.

Fernea's ethnography is an interesting and rich read—by the end of her two years in the village she had established many strong relationships and friendships. She went on to have a long career in academia and anthropology. In 1997, she published her last book, *In Search of Islamic Feminism: One Woman's Global Journey*, a personal account of women in a number of Islamic societies from Turkey to Egypt. Fernea died at the age of 81 in 2008.

We will now move on to our final ethnographic example, *My Freshman Year*, to consider the practice of conducting anthropology in one's own backyard. First, we will discuss the tension between directing the anthropological research lens abroad and focusing it locally. Next, we will consider the research methods used by Cathy Small, aka Rebekah Nathan, during her fieldwork at the university where she was employed as a professor, and some of the ethical implications that arose as a result of her covert approach to conducting fieldwork.

Collecting, Organizing, and Analyzing:
Research Methods for Understanding the Social World

Anthropologists are social scientists—like other scientists, they pose a research question and determine what research methods to employ to capture data that will answer their carefully constructed question. Unlike a biologist or a chemist, however, anthropologists do not study in a lab, but on the street, in people's homes, in the classroom, or anywhere that people spend their time and go about their daily lives. This is not a closed and controlled setting like one would find in a laboratory. Due to the dynamic nature of the social world, anthropologists are skillful at adapting to their surroundings. This is all part of the joys and frustrations of fieldwork, and as we saw with Fernea's experience in Iraq, it may take some time before meaningful relationships are formed.

In order to fully acknowledge that the social world in which we live affects the way in which we view the world, we must consider how our own social position informs our actions, our beliefs, and our worldview. What do we mean by social position? Consider a few of the most obvious social categories that we use to understand those around us—gender, ethnicity, class, age, sexuality, ability, to name a few. Now consider what these categories mean to you and your own life—some of them may be very straightforward, some of them might not. How might one's social position influence what one deems interesting or important to study, and how one presents one's research? Because anthropologists are *their own research instrument*, it has become increasingly common for anthropologists over the last 20 years to reflect on their own position in relation to that of their research participants.

In Your Own Backyard: Turning the Lens

The experience of Cathy Small, aka Rebekah Nathan, conducting fieldwork among freshman university students in the United States offers a look at a relatively recent move in anthropology to conduct research in one's own "backyard." As a result of anthropology's colonial past, the discipline became the center of much criticism and critique during the 1970s and 1980s, no less than by anthropologists themselves. Why was this? The constant focus on those who were *not* of western European background was called into question—what gave anthropologists the right to travel to a distant land, document, observe, and make conclusions about a group of people, and then publish this information for professional gain in a setting far removed from the locale in which it was based? What benefit was the interaction bringing to those being studied? And was there not great diversity everywhere, including one's own locale, without traveling across the world to observe and draw conclusions about others? This shift within the discipline reflects a realization that the prospect of studying the exotic "Other" is becoming increasingly problematic due, in part, to the continual self-reflection that the discipline has been undergoing over the last 50 years (Dyck 2000). For the most part, however, anthropology remains a discipline that is largely associated with regional specialization, culturally and spatially removed from the researcher's "home turf " (Amit 2000; Caputo 1995; Dyck 2000).

The term "native" anthropologist refers to those who study "their own"—that is, their own culture/ethnicity/community. As an "insider," there is an assumption that one will have greater and more intimate access to people's lives, and that this access will offer a more authentic portrayal than if the anthropologist hailed from a foreign land. This is not an obscure notion—as a local, you would know what types of food are eaten at which celebrations; the major holidays and traditions and who of the community is the most involved; the location of popular meeting places; what political party holds the most power, etc. Some may argue that it may in fact be *more* challenging to be an insider and be aware of the nuances and commonalities of the everyday that we take for granted. Being an "insider," however, is far more complex than simply speaking the same language, living in the same community, or being committed to the same cause. In reality, our identities are constantly shifting, and how (and with whom) we identify at one time in our life will likely be very different at other times. Kirin Narayan, an anthropologist who conducts research in her home country of India, discusses why the "native" title is both problematic and outdated: "The loci along which we are aligned with or set apart from those whom we study are multiple and in flux. Factors such as education, gender, sexual orientation, class, race, or sheer duration of contacts may at different times outweigh the cultural identity we associate with insider or outsider status" (Narayan 1993: 672). Think about your own identity—does it change depending on who you are around? Is it different around parents and your grandparents than it is around your university friends? Are you interested in the same things as you were 10 years ago? Our identities are not static but rather are influenced by experience—whom we meet, what we have seen, and what we have done.

As a cultural anthropologist, Cathy Small spent much of her professional life overseas conducting fieldwork in the traditional sense, that is, with people with whom she had very little in common. For three decades, Small conducted her research with the Polynesian society in the kingdom of Tonga in the southwest Pacific. Small found that upon her return to the US, her experiences abroad had forced her to turn a critical eye on her own culture: "On your return from another world, things once unnoticed—our reliance on date books, for instance—seem glaring; what was a daily routine can resurface as an exotic American custom" (Nathan 2005: 1). A professor for over 15 years, Small began to feel as though she did not understand her students. Their behaviors and attitudes no longer made sense to her. She decided to investigate the lives of this now "foreign" group and to go "undercover" as a student on her own campus, which she refers to as "AnyU." Small registered as a freshman under the name Rebekah Nathan, moved into the freshman dorm, and took classes from professors she did not know. She did not tell her fellow students her profession or background, explaining only to those who asked that she was a writer. For one academic year, she lived as a student, attending classes, completing assignments, and waiting in line with the other dorm residents for showers in the morning.

Small employed a number of research methods during her year as a student. **Participant observation** was a major component of her work. She participated in dorm social activities, such as the orientation weekend before classes started, and movie and games nights organized to increase student morale. As a student, she was required to complete readings and assignments and to participate in class discussions. She became privy to the discussions of students sitting in the lecture hall simply because she was sitting *with* them rather than in front of them as a professor. She took notes about what was going on around her, including conversations in the cafeteria, in the classroom, and in shared spaces in the dorm. She posted questions on pieces of paper in the women's bathroom and recorded the responses. She documented the content displayed on students' dorm room doors: Who was featured in the photographs? What did the slogans say? Did people have a wipe board for messages or not? She also conducted formal interviews with individual students.

Before beginning a program of research, scientists formulate a hypothesis, or a research statement that the study aims to prove. Anthropologists also formulate a research question; however, their research is less likely to *prove* a hypothesis than to offer an interpretation and understanding of the issue. This can be done in many ways. The traditional approach is the **comparative method**, or considering how a particular theory fares when applied cross-culturally. The comparative method directs the anthropologist to collect information about the local factors that shape human action and perception. Small considered the college experience in the United States as "a rite of passage": "these are the rituals that shepherd individuals and groups from one stage in the life cycle to another" (Nathan 2005: 146). Small states that it is during these stages that people who may have different social status become equals while experiencing a new way of life: "undergraduate culture itself becomes this liminal communal space where students bond with one another, sometimes for life, and, amid rules of suspended normality and often hardship, explore their identities, wrestle with their parents' world, and wonder about their future" (2005: 147). Anthropologists have observed and written about these liminal spaces all over the world—rites of passage have been examined in small-scale hunter-gatherer societies as well as in large industrial societies. It is in these spaces that people challenge cultural norms, roles, and rules and where creativity and social change can be ignited. By comparing rites of passage cross-culturally, we see not only the power of social norms and values to have an impact on behavior, but also the profound diversity of human culture.

Another approach positions the actions and beliefs of those under study as central to determining what is important to be observed and documented, and what is not. This **inductive approach** favors what the people themselves have to say about their lives—understanding these subjective meanings is central to understanding the way in which people make sense of their world. A very well-known example of this type of research is Clifford Geertz's work in Bali studying illegal cockfights, recounted in the essay *Deep Play: Notes on the Balinese Cockfight*. Geertz investigated illegal cockfighting in a small Balinese town—why did people engage in such a high-stakes game? What significance did this immensely popular social gathering have to the locals?

Geertz begins his account with a story about a situation in which he and his wife had found themselves—being caught up in a police raid on a cockfight, which the Indonesian government had banned as a wasteful and primitive custom. The anthropologists fled from the police just like everyone else, and this was the ice-breaker. Before then, they had been treated by the locals as though they didn't exist: "As we wandered around, uncertain, wistful, eager to please, people seemed to look right through us with a gaze focused several yards behind us on some more actual stone or tree" (Geertz 1973: 412). Their actions during the raid made them real. It turned out that the local people had been acutely aware of these exotic strangers all along, but their code of etiquette blocked overt expression of curiosity. After the raid, "the next morning the village was a completely different world for us. Not only were we no longer invisible we were suddenly the center of all attention, the object of a great outpouring of warmth, interest, and most especially, amusement" (1973: 416).

Geertz now found it easier to get information about the cockfight and many other aspects of Balinese society. He was interested in the role of symbols in society. Through "thick description," or a close examination and analysis of individual cases, Geertz interpreted the symbols of a culture through an explanation of people's behavior, and the context in which this behavior occurred (Barrett 2000: 32). Geertz's close observations led to an interpretation of cockfighting in which the process and act of gambling encompassed the social relationships of the village, including family and non-family relationships. Geertz also illustrated that the *cock* is a symbol of powerful men in Balinese society, and that the double entendre of the word exists in the Balinese language as it does in English. This approach makes less use of cross-cultural comparisons and generalizations, because local knowledge makes sense only when considered in the context from which it was created.

As Geertz (1973: 10) notes, "What the ethnographer is in fact faced with ... is a multiplicity of complex conceptual structures ... which are at once strange, irregular, and inexplicit and which [the ethnographer] must contrive somehow first to grasp and then to render." Analysis of the cockfight was a way for Geertz to get at broader cultural themes and to explore their relationship to one another. Through examination of very particular events, he sought to arrive at general conclusions about the nature of Balinese society. He found that "the cockfight ... is fundamentally a dramatization of status concerns. Its function … is interpretive: it is a Balinese reading of Balinese experience, a story that they tell themselves about themselves" (1973: 437, 448).

That, in any case, is Geertz's interpretation. Other approaches are possible, depending on the anthropologist's background and theoretical goal. Consider what South African anthropologist Max Gluckman brought to the analysis of the opening of a newly constructed bridge in Zululand in the late 1930s. He begins, as Geertz did, with his immediate experience of a particular event: "In 1938 I was living in the homestead of Chief's Deputy Matolana Mdwandwe, thirteen miles from the European magistracy and village of Nongoma and two miles from the Mapopoma store. I awoke at sunrise … and prepared to leave for Nongoma to attend the opening of a bridge in the neighbouring district of Mahlabatini" (Gluckman 1958: 2). The ceremony at the bridge was staged by the white-dominated local government. It was meant to connect the area to the administrative headquarters and the local maternity hospital—and to promote a moral bond between the African population and the government, even though the society as a whole was rigidly segregated into white and black, "two categories that must not mix, like castes in India" (1958: 12). The participants were white officials, the Zulu workmen who built the bridge, Christian missionaries, influential local tribesmen, and a representative of the Zulu royal family. And of course there was the anthropologist himself, who—being white, but living with Zulu and speaking their language—was acutely aware of his ambiguous status: "I, as an anthropologist, was in a position to become an intimate friend of Zulu as other Europeans could not, and this I did in virtue of a special type of social relationship, recognized as such by both races. Yet I could never quite overcome the social distance between us" (1958: 19).

In the ceremony itself, the white Native Commissioner drove his car across the bridge followed by a Zulu in full warrior dress. Having officially opened the bridge by breaking the tape, the Europeans went into their own tent for tea and cakes while the Zulu celebrated with local beer and feasted on roast meat. One of the Europeans was a labor recruiter for the gold mines, whose presence indicates the wider economic context of the encounter at the bridge.

Gluckman exploited his experience to comment on the "color bar," on the use of traditional ritual forms by both sides in this affair, and on how the two parties were both joined with and yet divided from each other because of their different roles in this social drama. Gluckman then went on to situate what he had seen in the historical context of South African race relations and the rise of the mining industry with its insatiable demand for cheap native labor. He saw this ceremony as an event that "crystallized" aspects "of the social structure and institutions of present day Zululand" (1958: 12). For Gluckman the concept of a "social situation" was an organizing principle, in that the analysis of such situations "reveals the underlying system of relationships" within the social structure of the community (1958: 9).

Geertz and Gluckman both examined events that they observed in the course of their fieldwork, but they did it in different ways and for different ends. Geertz was after the "deep" cultural elements expressed in the cockfight; Gluckman was interested in the interplay between race, class, and group organization in a divided society—a more "sociological" approach than Geertz's. In fact, Geertz knew a great deal about Balinese social organization—the kinship system for example—and wrote about it extensively elsewhere, but in his account of the cockfight he chose to highlight how such events fit in with other aspects of the culture. His aim was to achieve a **holistic** understanding of the Balinese world.

Likewise, Gluckman was well attuned to the nuances of both Zulu and white South African culture, but he represented what he saw in relation to the contextual demands of a particular social situation, in which—for a moment in time—the two came together at the bridge. Whereas Geertz saw Balinese culture as a thing in itself with its own internal integrity, Gluckman situated his analysis in relation to the expansion of European power and the spread of global capitalism into southern Africa. These are not mutually exclusive approaches. They do, however, represent different theoretical orientations originating in distinctive British and American anthropological traditions that we'll have more to say about later. What we wish to emphasize here is how both Geertz and Gluckman used particular events to inductively arrive at general conclusions about the societies they were studying.

Ethical Considerations in Anthropological Research

All research studies must go through a review process, usually conducted by an ethics review board at the university where the researcher is employed, to ensure that the research proposed is ethical and will not bring harm to the participants. The nature of anthropological fieldwork is such that researchers are frequently working and likely living closely with their research participants in often intimate and candid situations. A degree of trust must be established by all parties in order for this relationship to be fruitful. Consequently, there is a great responsibility on the part of anthropologists to present their research in a manner that does not bring harm or humiliation to participants. In much anthropological research, research is carried out with participants who are socially marginalized, meaning that for reasons such as income level, sexual preference, ethnicity, gender, age, ability, etc., people tend to be excluded by the wider society and may find it difficult to fully participate in the social world around them. As anthropologists are often educated and of the middle class, their social position calls into question the right and ability of an individual to accurately portray another's experiences. With this in mind, it is important to think about the relationship of the researcher to their participants.

Small's fieldwork adds another layer to this complex relationship because she did not disclose to those around her *why* she had returned to university and was living in a freshman dorm, unless they specifically asked (and according to her, only one person did). This is not standard practice for anthropologists; Small's methodological approach received criticism and ignited debate within the academic community regarding her somewhat "covert" study. Small admits that she was surprised to find herself asking whether or not the observational data she had collected—observations and conversations she overheard in class or the halls when she was in her student "role"—could be ethically reported: "I realized that my level of comfort and certainty was shifting with the depth and quality of my relationships and with the lived concreteness of seeing the data in their human context, that is, as incidents, stories and conversations attached to real people and real encounters" (Nathan 2005: 164). Small recounts her experience running into a former classmate once she returned to her regular position as an anthropology professor: "We exchanged warm 'how you doin?' small talk. Then my friend asked where I was headed. 'To class' I answered. 'What is it?' she asked. 'Oh, an anthropology class ... actually I'm teaching it.' 'No kidding!?' she exclaimed. 'How did you get to do that? I want to take it!' 'Well,' I answered sheepishly, 'it's cause I'm actually a professor too. I was a student last year to do some research, but now I'm back to being a professor.' 'I can't believe that,' she responded and then paused. 'I feel fooled'" (Nathan 2005: 167).

While reporting people's conversations and day-to-day activities is certainly an activity fraught with ethical questions, in the end Small's study posed little risk for those she was observing. This issue is complicated when the anthropologist is in a more volatile situation—for example, in 2007, anthropologists were employed in Afghanistan by the US military to collect information from Afghani people. The intent was to increase understanding between the soldiers and the citizens; however, this information could be used for many purposes other than for what it was originally intended. This created a great debate, both within academia and outside, about the ethical position of an anthropologist who conducts this type of research. The fundamental question was posed: "Who should anthropological research serve—those paying the salary, or those under study" (Rhode 2007)? We will encounter these issues again in later chapters in the text.

If, generally speaking, anthropological research aims to break down barriers of understanding between groups of people, a logical next step is to consider just how profound those differences are. As a species, how much of who we are is biological, and how much is socially learned? In the next and final section of this chapter we will consider the themes of unity and diversity, and the meaning of these concepts from an anthropological approach.

Unity and Diversity

Unity and diversity are important themes that have been considered by anthropologists since the discipline's inception, and are related to key questions about who we are as a species. On the one hand is the diversity of cultures across the span of world history and geographical space. On the other is the question of human nature—what underlying factors enable culture to exist in the first place? Perhaps one of the most fundamental questions in anthropological enquiry concerns what it means to be human. Are there shared characteristics and beliefs that are fundamental, regardless of specific cultural traditions and values? Are there fundamental similarities that unite us as humans or, as social beings, does our learned behavior negate or make obsolete the question? Are the differences between males and females rooted in biology or culture, or in some complex mix of the two? How is it possible that some humans can be responsible for the genocide in Central Africa and Bosnia, while others can become the saintly figures of various religious traditions? These questions are complex and do not have simple answers. Through anthropological research, however, aspects of these issues are investigated, usually on a local and individual level. As we have seen, anthropologists encounter and experience these issues first hand via their fieldwork.

Consider the concept of unity as it relates to Fernea's research in Iraq. As a woman, Fernea gained almost instant access to the other women of the community, a group her husband had not met and would in fact never meet. She was invited into their homes, asked to have tea and eat food and to participate in hobbies such as embroidery. This was simply because she shared their social position in society—as a woman. Their relationship, at least superficially, was characterized by a sense of unity gained by being members of the same group. As we know, however, it took some time for Fernea to develop true relationships with any of the women. Their social backgrounds—culture, education, upbringing, religion, etc.—were so different that the women in El Nahra found it difficult to relate to Fernea in the beginning. Simply being a woman was not enough to bridge the cultural gap that separated them. Classifying a group according to one characteristic, whether it is gender, race, age or ethnicity is problematic, for it ignores the great diversity within these groups. Classifying all the women of El Nahra into one group neglects the powerful roles of family heritage and social class. Anthropologists, particularly feminist anthropologists, have been very critical of generalizations made within and across groups (McGee and Warms 1996).

Small encountered the concepts of "diversity" and "community" during her fieldwork at AnyU. Those who identify as part of a community are announcing their membership in a particular group and, to varying degrees, a sense of unity among members exists. Establishing a "community" is advertised by college administrators as key to engaging freshman students in the college "experience." At AnyU, great lengths were taken to create a community-like atmosphere. One example was a seminar course that all freshman students were required to take. A novel was chosen, students were to meet in small groups to engage in debate and discussion (led by a professor), and then they were introduced to the author at the end of the course. This course was cancelled, however, after many attempts at offering it were met with a lack of enthusiasm and engagement. Through this experience, the university learned that *requiring* students to establish a community (in this case, the community of freshman students) was not a successful strategy. Small observed that real networks of engagement among students had more to do with shared experiences that occurred *before* college, as well as with demographic factors such as race, religion, and class (Nathan 2005: 47). Removing the element of choice to engage in a group goes against the fundamental individualism that is a cherished value in America. Small observed students struggling with this, particularly when they were encouraged to join in one of the many extracurricular activities or clubs offered at the university. While students voiced their interest in participating and may have even intended to join, they would "resist the claims that community makes on their schedule and resources in the name of individualism, spontaneity, freedom, and choice" (2005: 47). Small characterizes this as the "American way"—students are conflicted about wanting to be part of an entity that provides a sense of belonging, but are hesitant to give up their freedom.

While community is advertised as a key component of university life, so too is diversity. University administrators hope that students will engage with those from a different background, and that part of the learning experience in college that takes place outside of the classroom will lead to an increase in understanding between diverse groups of people. Small's discussions with international students, however, suggest that the notion of acceptance and understanding was not something that American university students had wholeheartedly embraced. International students talked of the friendly manner of American students—they would say hello and suggest getting together sometime, and then would never hear from them again. International students also discussed the lack of interest that many American students showed toward learning about home countries, as well as their lack of knowledge about other parts of the world. Small concludes that as with efforts to establish "community," embracing diversity is not something that comes easily to students who have been educated over their lifetime about the centrality of American culture and way of life.

Unity and diversity are complex concepts because along with being abstract, they also relate to fundamental questions about how we live and organize ourselves. In order to understand them in a specific context, we must look to how individuals experience them. This is the goal of the anthropologist. What Malinowski, Fernea, and Small illustrate through their research is that "culture"—whether in an isolated village in Iraq or a university campus in the US—cannot be fully understood in bits and pieces. Rather, the components of culture, such as social organization, gender, and ethnicity, can be understood only when contextualized within the society in which they occur.

Conclusion

In this chapter we have introduced and defined a number of foundational anthropological concepts, as well as methodological and theoretical approaches. Through different examples of ethnographic fieldwork, we have explored some of the challenges and successes associated with anthropological research, such as the experience of culture shock and the challenges associated with developing new relationships with individuals whom one is observing and studying. While anthropologists often study those that they do not know and ways of life that they are not familiar with, a fundamental goal of much anthropological research is to break down barriers of understanding between groups of people. Ethical issues associated with how anthropologists conduct research and what is done with their findings have long been explored, debated, and critiqued. Rather than threatening the legitimacy of the discipline, however, these debates have required that those who practice anthropology remain vigilant, reflective, and adaptable.

Study Questions

1   Define *reflexive thinking* as it relates to our discussion of "native" anthropology, and explain the purpose of employing reflexive thinking while in the field.
2   Explain the terms *culture shock, ethnocentrism*, and *cultural relativism* using examples from the work of Fernea.
3   Compare and contrast the inductive approach as used by Geertz in Bali and Gluckman in South Africa.
4   How does Small's work at AnyU differ from that of Malinowski in the Trobriand Islands and Fernea in Iraq? Outline the ethical implications of this difference.
5   Define the term "native" anthropologist. Outline the origins of this term and the limitations it places on so-called native researchers.
6   Describe the concepts of *unity* and *diversity* and use examples to explain how they can coexist within the same context.

Discussion Questions

1   Describe the history of anthropology in terms of Eurocentrism, and discuss how the field has changed since the days when explorers first began to observe "primitive" cultures.
2   Consider the concept of cultural relativism and how it relates to moral relativism. Discuss how relativism influences the ethics of anthropology. Consider recent current events that might cause you, the researcher, to question the appropriateness of cultural relativism. Do you think that anything is universally wrong? When do you think an observer, such as a researcher or journalist, should intercede? If there are moral absolutes, when should anthropologists become activists?
3   Fernea gained access to a segment of the community closed to her husband, the trained anthropologist, by nature of belonging to a particular category: women, and more specifically, wives. What does this suggest about the limitations of anthropological research in general, and the body of knowledge we have about women in society?

CHAPTER 4

//

Making a Living

LEARNING OBJECTIVES

After reading this chapter, students should be able to

- learn how to think about economic systems "anthropologically;"
- see such systems in their environmental contexts;
- think about how exchange works in establishing social bonds;
- identify how gift-giving or receiving defines the quality of personal relationships;
- analyze the factors affecting equality and inequality in economic relations; and
- identify the influence of gender in the productive process.

KEY TERMS

cultural ecology

division of labor

exchange

gender

gift

globalization

hunter-gatherers

kinship

kula

mode of production

money

potlatch

primitive communism

reciprocity

State of Nature

the Market

Introduction

"Making a living" is a large topic, and "economic anthropology" is a major branch of our subject.[1] When we survey the adaptations that humans have made to the world around us, we encounter a vast range of possibilities: **hunter-gatherers**, wet-rice farmers, dry-rice farmers, slash-and-burn cultivators, nut collectors, banana growers, fishers, herders, peasants, factory and service workers, agribusiness corporations … the list goes on. But with more and more of humanity living in urban conglomerates, a connection to the natural world that makes it all possible becomes increasingly tenuous and largely invisible. Ever increasing populations now "work" for a living in the context of globalized money-based economies. It wasn't always like this. Not so long ago the production, distribution, and consumption of food were the primary concerns of humankind.

Origins

Hunter-gatherers have figured large in the anthropological and public imagination. In part this is because of the "State of Nature" myth mentioned in Chapter 1, but also because this is how the human story actually begins—very likely in southern and eastern Africa. The question naturally arises of what, if anything, the lifestyles of recent hunter-gatherers can teach us about the circumstances in which humanity evolved. That question has several dimensions: (1) the environmental opportunities and constraints shaping a particular way of life; (2) the technologies of food production, preparation, and storage; (3) how people deal with basic biological facts such as sexuality, the tending of children, and the care of the infirm; (4) the division of labor and the allocation of resources within particular communities; (5) relations between groups; (6) exchange, kinship, and conflict.

Such questions lead on to consideration of the moral ideas that sustain these societies (or *any* society, for that matter). They pertain to the rules and social practices governing reciprocity—basic ideas concerning justice and fairness, who counts as a good person or a bad one, who is in and who is out. Exchange is a central anthropological theme, and the basis for economic life as we usually conceive of it. The analysis of exchange is in turn associated with the problem of *value*—the factors that go into deciding what something is worth. Evolutionary theorists wonder how the moral notions and social practices associated with exchange and value arose in the first place. The underlying issue is just what—in comparison to other social species—makes us distinctively *human*. We'll come back to that shortly, but first—through a few examples—we will take a look at how anthropologists have studied the relationship between environment, society, and economy.

Our first example is from the Great Basin region of western North America, the second and third are from Tanzania in eastern Africa and Botswana in the far south, respectively. These cases, though half a world apart, have significant parallels.

Life on the Margins

Julian Steward (1902–72) was a second-generation Boasian, a student of Alfred Kroeber who established the Anthropology Department at the University of California, Berkeley. Kroeber himself had earned his Columbia Ph.D. under Boas in 1901 and became an authority on the Indigenous peoples of California.[2] Steward first encountered the Great Basin region while at a boy's school in the east of the state, where he became an avid outdoorsman. His later research under Kroeber focused on determining the boundaries of Indigenous groups in the interior high desert, which embraces parts of Oregon, Idaho, Nevada, Utah, and California (Clemmer et al. 1999). It's a challenging environment, and was sparsely inhabited when the Americans arrived in the nineteenth century. Steward's familiarity with this landscape led him to examine how the problems it presented to Indigenous groups affected the patterns of their social life. To get at these issues he came up with the concept of *cultural ecology*, an influential notion that embraces the five dimensions mentioned above, while remaining sensitive to the nuances of particular cases (Steward 1972: 30–42). He emphasized that along with environmental constraints, cultural factors and local history need to be considered in understanding any particular case.

The basin-and-range country that interested Steward is dominated by long parallel mountains trending north-south and separated by deep valleys. The basins are dryer than the ranges, which are high enough to capture enough rainfall to support a sparse forest cover of juniper and piñon pines, the source of highly nutritious pine-nuts when the cones open in late fall. Water collects in pans in the lowlands fed by seasonal streams, but both dry up toward the end of summer. The major fauna consists of rodents (notably jack rabbits), antelope, deer, and the occasional mountain sheep. However, plants and seeds of various sorts constituted the major subsistence base for the Paiute inhabitants of the region:

> All the plant and animal foods had in common the extremely important characteristic that the place and quantity of their occurrence from year to year were unpredictable, owing largely to variations in rainfall. A locality might be very fertile one year and attract large numbers of families but offer little food for several years thereafter. Few localities had foods in sufficient quantity and reliability to permit permanent settlements. Throughout most of the area, the families were concerned predominantly with warding off potential starvation by moving from place to place. These movements were determined by reports from friends or relatives about the probable quantities of food to be had. Families from different localities would assemble at places where food was temporarily plentiful, but, owing to the impossibility of storing large quantities of food for the future, they soon dispersed to seek elsewhere. (1972: 105)

Given this dispersed pattern and the sporadic or seasonal nature of available resources there was no sense of land ownership. The land itself was essentially common property. Whoever was exploiting it at a given moment had possession of what they found, but no permanent rights beyond that. Nor were there chiefs, though well-regarded individuals could exercise leadership in collective activities such as rabbit or antelope drives. There were also shamans who, while in trance, diagnosed and prescribed cures for illness, but had no particular authority otherwise.

As with other hunter-gatherers there was a pronounced sexual division of labor, with women mainly engaged in gathering and men with hunting, though with some degree of overlap between the two. Marriage was economically fundamental, in that cooperative labor was essential for survival and, of course, the rearing of children. Intermarriage was the glue that created a wider social order through networks of sharing and reciprocity. You will see in Chapter 5 that kinship systems can take quite an elaborate form with lineages and clans functioning as political groups. The Paiute had none of this, and kin relationships were essentially bilateral and flexible with no emphasis on a particular line of descent. As Steward saw it:

> These marital and kinship ties were the knots of the social fabric ... but they did not constitute sociocultural frontiers. Marriage was contracted most often between families in contact with one another, but it was not governed by territorial or political units. While it united strands in the netlike fabric of society ... it could not consolidate or integrate local groups in a political, social, or economic sense. To the contrary, it cut across local boundaries, making interfamilial ties diffuse and thus actually militating against band or community development. (1972: 119)

He made that argument in the context of a larger one about the factors affecting the evolution of political society. The Great Basin Paiute served as his baseline, and he sought the elements that were conducive or not to the development of more elaborate social arrangements such as clans, economically based social hierarchies, and political centralization. The circumstances of Paiute life favored equality and reciprocity; concepts of ownership were very rudimentary because there really wasn't much worth owning. The kind of society that Steward described has been characterized as "**primitive communism**," and it isn't far off what Darwin thought he was seeing among the Fuegians.

Nor is it far off what ethnographers have found among the San of the Kalahari region of southern Africa and the Hadza of Tanzania.[3] These peoples have been of particular interest because they live in the general region where modern humanity is thought to have originated, and also speak unique but unrelated languages that may have deep historical roots. No one supposes that these peoples are relics of the ancestral human population itself. However, it is reasoned that their environment and way of life must be similar to how things once were in those parts of Africa, and therefore can tell us something about the evolutionary forces that were then at work to make us what we are today (Marlowe 2010: 17).

A noted physical anthropologist has observed that "the human gathering-hunting ways are based on language, technology, social patterns, and, especially, reciprocity" (Washburn 1976: xv). As with the Paiute, ethnographic studies of the African hunter-gatherers emphasize the egalitarian nature of these societies, the small sizes of their bands, their flexible social arrangements, and the opportunistic nature of resource exploitation within a variable environment. For example, settlement patterns in these semi-arid regions are determined by the presence of water and game; in the dry season humans and animals concentrate near permanent water sources, while in the wet season both disperse. As it was with the Paiute, the land and its products are free goods. The Hadza

> … assert no rights over land and its ungarnered resources. Any individual may live wherever he likes and may hunt animals, collect roots, berries and honey and draw water anywhere in Hadza country without any sort of restriction. Not only do the Hadza not parcel out their land and its resources among themselves, they do not even seek to restrict the use of the land they occupy to members of their own tribe. (Woodburn 1968: 50)

What also comes across clearly in the ethnography is the importance of the sexual division of labor and the contribution of the gathering activities of women to overall caloric intake (see Dahlberg 1981). A recent ethnographer of the Hadza reckons that women may be responsible for 60 per cent of the total. Canadian anthropologist, Richard Lee, who spent many years working with the San of Botswana, found the same pattern.

> Vegetable foods comprise from 60–80 per cent of the total diet by weight, and collecting involves two or three days of work per woman per week. The men also collect plants and small animals but their major contribution to the diet is the hunting of medium and large game. The men are conscientious but not particularly successful hunters; although men's and women's work input is roughly equivalent in terms of man-day of effort, the women provide two to three times as much food by weight as the men. (Lee 1968: 33)

Male hunting activities are nevertheless very important, though in a different way. Meat is valued for its own sake, but—unlike the mainly vegetable products that women bring into camp on a daily basis—it tends to be shared more widely. Given that life takes place in public, monopolizing anything is difficult. The overall effect of such publicity is an "inability to dominate others and resist sharing" (Marlowe 2010: 252). "The Hadza expect others to give them food, so food-sharing is common. Surely this is partly due to egalitarianism, but it is also partly responsible for creating egalitarianism" (2010: 237). As Lee (1968: 41) says, "it would be theoretically possible for the [San] to survive entirely on vegetable foods, but life would be boring indeed without the excitement of meat feasts." We might think of these redistributive practices as a kind of generalized reciprocity.

These researchers were reminded of the "State of Nature" myth, and the contrast between Jean-Jacques Rousseau and Thomas Hobbes that we mentioned in Chapter 1. Lee, for instance, finds that the San didn't live badly at all, managing to get by successfully and more or less peacefully in what seems to us to be a difficult environment (see Chapter 7 below): "Life in the state of nature is not necessarily, nasty, brutish, and short. It is likely that an even more substantial subsistence base would have been characteristic of these hunters and gatherers in the past, when they had the pick of African habitats to choose from" (1968: 43). In the conclusion to his Hadza ethnography, Frank Marlowe (2010: 286) remarks that "the foraging lifestyle is not as Hobbes imagined: nasty, brutish, and short. Rather it is to a great extent peaceful, healthy, and fulfilling. That is not to say it is the idyllic existence conjured up by Rousseau's noble savage.... The views of Hobbes and Rousseau are both too extreme."

Research with hunter-gatherers is valuable for its own sake, especially given the tenuous situation of such peoples today. The Hadza and San live in close proximity to encroaching African farmers and herders. The San, who are most exposed to the farm economy, have undergone a "pervasive ideological shift ... away from the egalitarianism of the hunters and toward the pursuit of wealth and social status through the possession of cattle, small stock, and money" (Guenther 1976: 131). Indigenous Australians were all hunter-gatherers before the coming of the Europeans and had been for tens of thousands of years, but now have been largely swamped and marginalized by the immigrants with their farms, cattle stations, mines, and great coastal cities. The Paiute established early relationships with American miners and ranchers, and mainly live on small reservations now. The hunting-gathering way of life is fast disappearing, and yet this was how all of humanity lived for the better part of its existence.

The emphasis on reciprocity and sharing in the literature on these peoples is very striking; such findings lead to questions about the evolutionary origins of the cognitive and behavioral capacities that enable such practices. This is an area in which speculation can run riot, since it involves the reconstruction of events and processes that unfolded a very long time ago. Among other things, Charles Darwin was interested in social behavior and instinct, and believed that if whatever underlies such traits is heritable, then it should be subject to the forces of natural selection just like anything else. In *The Descent of Man* he speculated about the origin and development of the moral sense in early human society, and his ideas set the terms for a debate that continues to the present. The gist of his argument is that social selection *within* groups might have led to the development of pro-social traits that gave certain early human populations an evolutionary edge over their rivals (Darwin 1998: 100–38; Boehm 2012). He thought that competition *between* groups would then have led to the rise of some and the extinction of others.[4] That can be argued, but one thing we can say for sure is that sharing, reciprocity, and the sexual division of labor were essential factors in the human story.

The Power in Things

If "primitive communism" was indeed humankind's original economic system, it is a marginal niche now. Historians, archaeologists, and anthropologists have long been concerned with mapping the roads that led to other possibilities, and constructed various developmental schemes to describe and explain what has occurred. Archaeologists, for instance, have attempted to chart the steps that led from scattered settlements of hunter-gatherers, to the origins of plant and animal domestication, to the appearance of village settlements, and the eventual emergence of centralized state structures in the Middle East, India, China, Central America, and elsewhere. Long-distance trade and the invention of money to facilitate it have been important factors in some cases, as have innovations such as irrigation that have allowed for increasing concentrations of population. In the Middle East some of the earliest written documents take the form of merchants' account ledgers on clay tablets.

Exchange is clearly important to all these stories, but it's a long way from early communal economies to the emergence of the money-based systems of our own time. Anthropologists have classified types of exchange, investigated how they work, and the kinds of historical transformations they have given rise to. Money itself is an interesting thing, especially if you don't have enough of it. But just what kind of thing is "it"? Money, like everything else, has a history. Many kinds of things have filled that role: cowrie shells, brass rods, gold coins, or whatever. In the Lake Victoria area of East Africa even packets of salt—the cheapest of commodities now, but in pre-industrial times hard to obtain—once served as a token of exchange in local markets; of course it really wasn't suitable as a true currency, in that it was likely to eventually end up in someone's stew. At present money may not take physical form at all, and instead have a ghostly existence as a string of digital numbers in cyberspace.

The original essence of money—whatever the form—was the use of symbolic objects to mediate exchange relationships. The seventeenth-century British philosopher John Locke (1632–1704) thought the invention of money was a crucial development in human progress, because it allowed wealth to be stored in concentrated form and transferred when and wherever needed. It also facilitated the creation of a class hierarchy, and with that a desire to emulate the rich, which Locke thought was a good thing in that it stimulated the desire to get ahead. Darwin thought it was precisely this that the Fuegians were lacking and which accounted for their stagnation.

Money is particularly useful in mediating exchange between strangers, but there has to be approximate agreement about just what such a token is "worth": how much of X is worth how much of Y—how many packets of salt equals a goat, for example. But monetary exchange is not the only kind. Barter is also a way to move goods and services around (as in swap-meets). Gift exchange is another. We all know something about this and suppose that it occurs to acknowledge, reinforce, or create a personal relationship in a way that money cannot. But was there ever a free gift? Love is important, but so is debt. Gifts imply return gifts—"to give, to receive, to reciprocate"—and form the subject of a famous essay by the French ethnologist Marcel Mauss: *The Gift: The Form and Reason for Exchange in Archaic Societies*, which we will discuss further in Chapter 5.

When dealing with such topics, standard introductory textbooks tend to cite (as Mauss did) two systems of exchange prominent in the earlier history of our subject: the Pacific Northwest Coast potlatch as described by Boas and the *kula* of the Trobriands as described by Malinowski. We won't be going into great detail about either of these, and instead will focus on what such institutions tell us about the nature of *value*.[5] But a few details are necessary first. Both *potlatch* and *kula* are systems of competitive gift-giving in which the prestige of individuals and groups is involved.

The institution of the potlatch was (and is) widely spread among Northwest Coast peoples. Boas describes its fundamental principle through his work among the *Kwakwa̱ka̱wakw* (Kwakiutl) of British Columbia, who like other coastal peoples, were able to generate considerable surpluses due to the richness of their marine environment. The potlatch was a way of acquiring rank or celebrating significant events through feasting and the distribution of goods. "The underlying principle is that of the interest-bearing investment of property" (Boas 1966: 77).

> Possession of wealth is considered honorable.... But it is not as much the possession of wealth as the ability to give great festivals which makes wealth a desirable object.... The man's name acquires greater weight in the councils of the tribe and greater renown among the whole people, as he is able to distribute more and more property at each subsequent festival. (1966: 79)

These ceremonies might be held to publicize some important event in the life of an individual and his community, such as taking on a new title or erecting a ceremonial pole. The grandeur of the occasion served to dramatize the prestige of the host group in relation to rivals who then found it necessary to up the game when it was time for them to reciprocate. Embossed copper plates were one of the most significant indicators of wealth and had a large role in potlatch exchanges. But they didn't have a fixed value in relation to other wealth items; instead that depended "upon the amount of property given away in the festival at which the copper is sold" (1966: 82).

The way Boas describes it, the entire enterprise was inflationary, and outside input such as Hudson's Bay Company blankets were one factor in driving that process. For this reason, and with the intent of eliminating practices thought to interfere with the goal of assimilation, the Canadian government of the day outlawed the institution as a wasteful extravagance that distracted the people from getting ahead in the new colonial economic order: "Strenuous measures should be adopted to put a stop to the heathenish custom known as the 'potlatch'.... It produces indigence, thriftlessness, and habits of roaming about which prevents home association and is inconsistent with all progress" (LaViolette 1961: 38). The ban stayed in place from 1884 to 1951, but was widely circumvented (see Cole and Chaikin 1990; Loo 1992). The potlatch remains a vital institution among Northwest Coast Indigenous peoples to this day—as a marker of important events and celebration of collective identity.

Boas wasn't inclined to abstract theorizing and, as we've said, his ethnographic writings have a descriptive character. On the other hand Malinowski had definite theoretical and methodological goals, and the outcome was an extraordinarily rich and suggestive analysis that has had an enormous effect on the development of our subject. So, what then is the *kula*, and what wider message did Malinowski derive from his findings?

As mentioned in Chapter 2, the Trobriand Islands are part of the wider Melanesian cultural sphere, which embraces the big island of New Guinea and adjoining island groups. The entire area has been fascinating to anthropologists interested in exchange because of the presence of institutions such as the *kula*—regional trading networks deploying high prestige items such as pigs and shell ornaments. Formal institutions of chieftainship and rank were lacking, with the exception of the chiefly class among the Trobrianders. Men generally competed as individuals, or as representatives of their kin groups, to gain renown through success at organizing ceremonial exchanges involving the wider society. By that means they became recognized as "big men." The practice was similar to potlatch in that respect:

> The Kula is a form of exchange, of extensive, inter-tribal character; it is carried on by communities inhabiting a wide ring of islands, which form a closed circuit. Along this route, articles of two kinds and these two kinds only, are constantly travelling in opposite directions. In the direction of the hands of a clock, moves constantly one of these kinds—long necklaces of red shell .... In the opposite direction moves the other kind—bracelets of white shell. Each of these articles, as it travels in its own direction on the closed circuit, meets on the way articles of the other class, and is constantly being exchanged for them. Every movement of the Kula articles, every detail of the transactions is fixed and regulated by a set of traditional rules and conventions, and some acts of the Kula are accompanied by an elaborate magical ritual and public ceremonies. (Malinowski 1984: 81; originally published 1922)

A participant in *kula* has partners with whom he is in an ideally permanent relationship, "one of the special bonds which unite two men into one of the standing relations of mutual exchange of gifts and services so characteristic of these natives" (1984: 91). "Once in the Kula, always in the Kula" (1984: 83). The imagery is one of marriage, the armshells "conceived as a female principle, and the necklaces as the male" (1984: 356). They come together in a productive relationship when exchanged, but their only fate is to be passed on again around the circuit; these valuables are possessed but not owned. "Giving for the sake of giving is one of the most important features of Trobriand sociology," since by this means social ties are created and maintained and prestige enhanced (1984: 175).

This was certainly not a "communistic" society, and in fact it was capable of generating significant surpluses, particularly in yams, the staple food. Chiefs were in a good position to profit, since they tended to be polygynous and therefore had access to a larger workforce than the average person. Nevertheless, "the main symptom of being powerful is to be wealthy, and of wealth is to be generous. Meanness, indeed is the most despised vice, and the only thing about which the natives have strong moral views, while generosity is the essence of goodness" (1984: 97).

> ... *the whole tribal life is permeated by a constant give and take*; that every ceremony, every legal and customary act is done to the accompaniment of material gift and counter gift; that wealth, given and taken, is one of the main instruments of social organization, of the power of the chief, of the bonds of kinship, and of relationship in law. (1984: 167)

The *kula* items—the *vaygu'a*—themselves have no functional use beyond their display, though their ceremonial exchange may be accompanied by "secondary" trade in more everyday items. Where then does the value of such things come from? Malinowski finds parallels in how we regard family heirlooms or historically important artifacts like the British Crown Jewels (which are, of course, unique and "priceless"—a condensed history of the Monarchy). "Every really good Kula article has its individual name, round each there is a sort of history and romance in the traditions of the natives" (1984: 89). Much of their value derives from memories of the exchanges in which they've taken part and the risky overseas ventures that were necessary to acquire them. There's a lot magic in these things. Malinowski was reminded of sporting trophies like the Stanley Cup, "objects which are kept for a time only by the winning party, whether a group or an individual. Though held only in trust, only for a period, though never used in any utilitarian way, yet the holders get from them a special type of pleasure by the mere fact of owning them, of being entitled to them" (1984: 95).

Malinowski emphasized that these items don't resemble or function as money, "except that both money and *vaygu'a* represent condensed wealth. *Vaygu'a* is never used as a medium or exchange or as a measure of value.... Each piece of *vaygu'a* of the Kula type has one main object throughout its existence—to be possessed and exchanged" (1984: 511). He concluded that "the Kula presents to us a new type of phenomenon, lying on the borderland between the commercial and the ceremonial" (1984: 513).

Potlatching Comes to New York

If the practices we've mentioned above seem a bit strange and exotic, consider what goes on in the high-end Western art market. Here's an example reported by the *New York Times* in 2015:

In an overheated art market where anything seems possible, a painting of an outstretched nude woman by the early-20th-century artist Amedeo Modigliani sold on Monday night for $170.4 million with fees to Liu Yiqian, a former taxi driver turned billionaire art collector, in a packed sales room at Christie's. It was the second-highest price paid for an artwork at auction. The painting became the 10th work of art to reach nine figures under the hammer. The bidding was palpably tense, with six people vying for the lot, and it took nine minutes to sell, with the winning bid coming from the phone. Mr. Liu, who with his wife Wang Wei is among China's most visible art collectors, confirmed on Tuesday that he is the buyer. He said he planned to bring the work back to Shanghai, where he and his wife have two private museums.[6]

This is merely one among many of the extraordinary and seemingly ever-increasing prices that sales of "classic" art such as the Modigliani can command. As the story suggests, this market is international, and a Picasso sold in this manner might just as well end up on a wall in Dubai as in some Western capital (or, since bidding may take place anonymously, in some place unknown). It can be a risky business however, since not all high-end art proves to be the real thing, as in a 2017 item, also from the *Times*:

Sotheby's has filed a lawsuit related to the sale of works originally attributed to European old master painters that it now says are forgeries. On Monday, the auction house announced that it had initiated proceedings in the English High Court against ... a London art dealer ... and a collector to recover the profits of a 2011 private sale of a Frans Hals painting, "Portrait of a Gentleman," which it subsequently declared was a fake. Sotheby's said that the evidence that it is fake is "unequivocal," because it found a modern synthetic pigment throughout the paint layer.[7]

The sellers of this alleged forgery received $10.75 million for it, which Sotheby's reimbursed to the buyer upon discovery of the fraud. As you can see, "authenticity" is an important issue and may take advanced sleuthing to resolve. A further risk is that investing in this market can be a convenient avenue for money laundering, thus exposing the sellers' agents to legal trouble.[8]

A few companies dominate this market: the British firms of Christie's (founded 1766) and Sotheby's (founded 1744) are the most prominent. Each has branches in London and New York. What the dealers term "primitive" or "tribal" art is also put up for sale through such agents, which is of particular interest to anthropologists—first because of the concept of the "primitive" itself, and second for how the market actually functions.

Of course, art from Indigenous groups has had a considerable impact on the development of Western art itself—on Modigliani, Gauguin, the Surrealists, and Picasso among others. In part this is due to the unfamiliar and suggestive abstract shapes that non-Western art may take, but also to the notion that somehow these productions are closer to the unconscious mythic roots of all art. This is not just a matter of taste—there are serious ethical issues involved. These artifacts were taken from elsewhere, usually in a colonial context, and frequently acquired by uncertain means. And, with respect to market value, there is again the question of authenticity, a central concern in determining price at auction. "Authentic" articles must carry a pedigree along with them that proves where they came from and specifies their original ethnographic setting (for an overview see Price 1989).

Anthropologists tend to turn up in odd places, auctions of primitive art among them. There's something particularly satisfying about reversing the ethnographic lens in order to witness Western art dealers and collectors fighting over high-value cultural property. This is what Haidy Geismar of the University of London did when investigating auctions of non-Western, pre-colonial art at Christie's New York (Geismar 2001). She asks just how the final sale price is determined, and charts the route from when an object was originally offered for auction to where it finally ends up. It turns out to be quite a complicated business, with a considerable backstory preceding the auction itself. "For the purposes of auction, the history of each item begins upon its entry into the market. An object's 'biography' becomes one of Euro-American ownership and exchange, primarily between dealers, museums and private collectors" (2001: 26).

Like a potlatch copper or Trobriand *vaygu'a*, knowledge of this history is essential. "Ideas about value are socially manipulated around objects, over several events (not just the sale) to fix a price" (Geismar 2001: 29), such as the research conducted by the auction house, the publication of handsome catalogs like the glossy books that appear after prominent museum exhibitions, and the pre-auction displays so that the artifacts themselves may be seen. "The 'best' pieces are always the oldest," and therefore the identities of the original artists usually remain unknown (2001: 32). As with the conventional art market, the value of such an object is affected by the transactions it's entered into in the past; asking prices may be set by what someone was willing to pay for it in the past. But achieving the *final* selling price isn't a foolproof process, and one dealer remarked that "it is like the opposite of the antiques road-show mentality, where everything you thought was junk may be worth something. Here are things we think are worth something and a lot of it is junk" (2001: 39).

"The auction sale is a theatrical production of price, created by market agents, that includes material artifacts as well as persons. It is a performance, complete with stage, lighting, object-props, catalogue-scripts, and noisy interactive audience—a well-practiced pantomime of price" (2001: 43). A pantomime, it might be added, in which the prestige of sellers, buyers, and auctioneers is at risk in a high-stakes game.

Working

It should not surprise you that "the anthropology of work" is a sub-discipline of our field. The Society for the Anthropology of Work is a unit of the American

Anthropological Association, and publishes its own journal, *Anthropology of Work Review*.[9]

We all know something about "work." Most of us will spend our active lives "working"—usually for someone else or an organization of some kind. We have labor power or particular skills that we offer in exchange for the money that gives us access to the things we need to get by and hopefully prosper. But what determines the value of labor? Perhaps it's set by a remote set of economic forces known as "**The Market**"—in this case the labor market. The market itself functions within an even higher-level abstraction known as "The Economy." It's all very obscure, though the practical implications of the workings of these abstract forces are painfully obvious down on the ground.

But there are many kinds of work relationships, ranging from slavery to self-employment. Titles of a few articles in the *Review* will suggest the range of possible topics:

Making Trash into Treasure: Struggles for Autonomy on a Brazilian Garbage Dump

Labor and the Urban Landscape: Mobility, Risk, and Possibility among Syrian Delivery Workers in Beirut

The Ties That Bind: Mexicana Caretakers and Aging Americans Construct Kinship

Anthropology's great strength is its commitment to deal with life on the ground as it's lived and experienced. Actually going out to look at work in farm fields, food processing plants, factory floors, hotels, convenience stores, and hospital emergency rooms gives a perspective often obscured by social distance, rhetoric, and prejudice.

You're probably aware that the question of undocumented foreign workers has been a hot-button political issue in the United States. This topic is a natural for ethnographic investigation, though it's a sensitive one ethically given that researchers will frequently be encountering illegal activity. Agriculture is one sector where this question is most acute, given a heavy dependence on Hispanic immigrants for both field labor and food processing. There has been a huge undocumented presence there for years, accompanied by the growth of long-standing, but legally marginal, communities of Mexicans and Central Americans. Given the current political emphasis on documentation, backed up by the threat of deportation, they have become still more marginal as their status has been increasingly criminalized. Privately run but government-subsidized prisons for deportees are a growth industry in a society well known for mass incarceration.

> There has been general agreement in labor migration scholarship that mass unauthorized migration is not an accident, but rather supplies an important type of labor with a distinct role in globalized capitalist economies. The legal vulnerability of unauthorized workers renders them "superexploitable," and their labor can be manipulated to undermine organizing efforts and suppress the wages of unskilled workers in postindustrial economies. (Gomberg-Muñoz 2016: 3)

Sarah Horton, an anthropologist at the Denver campus of the University of Colorado, has investigated this phenomenon in California's Central Valley, the source of the vegetables and other agricultural products supplying much of the North American market. We are probably all complicit in the situation that she describes.

Horton goes into the formal legal requirements for hiring agricultural labor. For growers this takes the form of requiring evidence of legal status in the form of Social Security cards or some equivalent. She finds that the bosses are not necessarily all that concerned once the basic legal formalities are taken care of. In interviewing field workers and their immediate supervisors, she discovered that there are considerable numbers of "ghost workers" who are actually using someone else's documentation, in which there is a "thriving black market" (Horton 2016: 14). "Migrants with legal status often use 'identity loan' as a money-making venture; they exploit legally prohibited workers' need for valid documents" (2016: 15). Though California has regulations governing working hours, undocumented laborers may use this technique to work a seven-day week; the practice is "so common that Sunday is universally known among the Valley's farmworkers as 'el dia del fantasma,' or 'the day of the ghost' (2016: 18).

People who came north to escape poverty, and who may have families and have lived in the US for years, find themselves caught in an exploitative situation that they can't complain about for fear of being found out and deported. Attempts on the federal level to regularize the status of such people have gone nowhere. It all works to the advantage of the growers with regard to lowering labor costs:

> As new federal and state laws have increasingly produced unauthorized migrants as prototypical "criminal anti-citizens" who undermine the security of the homeland, immigration enforcement has shifted from policing the nation's borders to increasingly scrutinizing its interior…. As the border has migrated inwards, spaces of everyday life—including workplaces, homes, and neighborhoods—have become subjected to intensified policing on an unprecedented scale. (2016: 20)

In a study of a very different work environment Evin Rodkey of Casper College investigates what happens to some citizens of the Dominican Republic once they are deported from the US for minor criminal offenses, such as drug violations (there are three-quarters of a million Dominicans in New York City alone). Rodkey (2016: 34) wanted to find out "what happens when a 'deportable' labor force becomes a deported workforce." To that end Rodkey took a job in a call-center in Santo Domingo, the capital of the Dominican Republic, and spent a good deal of time hanging out with fellow employees. Many Dominicans have been in the United States for a long time and are highly Americanized, with good English language skills and local cultural knowledge. These skills plus low wage rates also make India and the Philippines desirable locations for such companies; this fact makes call centers a highly competitive industry, since the potential work force has been globalized as well. Deported Mexican farm laborers don't have these options.

> … the globalized call center industry harnesses the labor of long-term U.S. residents expelled from the country—people deemed unfit to live within the borders of the United States, but whose labor is desired by U.S. companies abroad—to cultivate a flexible and culturally suitable labor pool. Deportees who are stigmatized and considered unemployable in most industries, rely on the call centers for both employment and cultural connections to their long-term home—the United States. (2016: 34)

The call-center where the anthropologist worked served an American-based television service provider, and the Dominican employees spent their days helping customers with their issues. Nevertheless they had to keep up a friendly and sympathetic front and come across as American as possible, even to the point of saying they were based in Miami.[10] "In this competitive industry, even characteristics of a call center workforce that may appear unimportant, such as workers' familiarity with the U.S. baseball season, can create a competitive edge for the company" (2016: 36). As one of Rodkey's informants put it:

> You gotta sweet talk 'em; you gotta make them feel like so they understand you and not get agitated, because they get really mad, depending on how you come about it. But if you tell them in a certain way with a nice-toned voice, and they will do actually exactly what you told them. And it will get fixed, hopefully. Working in the call center is hard. You got people on top of you, they think if you don't see it, they think it's your fault. You know, it's hard to convince people to buy something. It ain't an easy job, believe me. (2016: 40)

The irony of all this wasn't lost on the ethnographer. These call center workers "are born in the Dominican Republic, raised in the United States, banished to the Dominican Republic, where they work for a U.S. company located in the Dominican Republic, using skills gained from growing up in the United States" (2016: 41). Rodkey asked one deportee whether he considered himself an American, and was told, "I thought I was until I got deported."

Our examples point toward the larger considerations that underlie the analysis of all economic systems. Broadly speaking we've been talking about "modes of production": technological abilities, the organization of the productive process, the distribution of goods and services, and the exchange relationships that accomplish it—all interacting in complex ways. Julian Steward's concept of *cultural ecology* suggests that we must also take into account the overall environmental context in which the productive process takes place. The hunter-gatherers represent a case in which there is very little specialization and everyone possesses much the same skills. There is little division of labor, the constraints steering everyday life are fairly obvious, and relative social equality is the norm. Our own societies fall at the other end of that scale: knowledge is specialized, the remote economic forces steering the productive process are far from obvious, and social relations are profoundly hierarchical and unequal. The ethnographic question is how life seems to those who actually live within a given social system: how social values, family life, and our relationship to nature play out in the real world. We also need to consider how social relations and concepts of value are defined in the process of exchange. As we said at the beginning, "economic anthropology" is a big topic.

Notes

1   The Society for Economic Anthropology is one of the sections of the American Anthropological Association (AAA): http://econanthro.org/. A number of other units within the AAA are concerned with related issues, such as the environment, agriculture, work, and nutrition.

2   Alfred Kroeber and his wife Theodora were the parents of the renowned science-fiction and fantasy writer, Ursula Kroeber Le Guin. Le Guin's fiction often adopts an "anthropological" stance, commenting on earthly society through imagining an alien world where things are done quite differently. In the same way activist anthropologists such as Margaret Mead and Ruth Benedict used their accounts of actual "alien worlds" as a way of commenting on the US of their day, and to make a Boasian case for tolerance and understanding.

3   The term "Bushman" was formerly applied to these peoples, but became viewed as sexist and racist. "San" is the general term in use now.

4   The fate of the European Neanderthals is still a lively topic of debate among paleo-anthropologists and human geneticists. Were they done in by the ancestors of modern humans moving north from Africa; were they forced into marginal niches and slowly died out; or did the two in fact interbreed and—as the geneticists think—leave their marks within the genomes of their descendant populations today?

5   There is a large literature on both these topics; however, the work of Boas and Malinowski established the framework for subsequent discussion, critique, and additional field research. Here we're only providing a sketch.

6   http://www.nytimes.com/2015/11/10/arts/with-170-4-million-sale-at-auction-modigliani-work-joins-rarefied-nine-figure-club.html?emc=eta1

7   http://www.nytimes.com/2017/02/07/arts/design/sothebys-forgery-lawsuits.html?emc=eta1

8   http://www.nytimes.com/2017/02/19/arts/design/has-the-art-market-become-an-unwitting-partner-in-crime.html?emc=eta1

9   http://saw.americananthro.org

10   One of us had a conversation about the weather with a pleasant young woman working in a call center in Manila before getting into dealing with a broken Sears washing machine in western Canada.

Study Questions

1   What is "cultural ecology" and how did Julian Steward apply this concept in practice?
2   What is the sexual division of labor? Give examples.
3   What is the relationship between kinship and the processes of production and distribution? How would we investigate that question in different cultural settings?
4   What are *potlatch* and *kula*? How do they resemble one another with regard to defining social status?
5   Compare the productive process in hunter-gatherer society to that revealed by studies of migrant labor.

Discussion Questions

1   Are gifts ever free?
2   Analyze some social occasion in which gift-giving or gift-receiving takes place.
3   Consider your own work experience in anthropological terms, applying the concept of "**mode of production**" to what you see before you. What kind of work is it and what forces shape the personal relationships that develop within that work environment?
4   What aspects of family life are affected by exchange relationships?
5   How are gender hierarchies established and defined within the workplace?

CHAPTER 5

//

The Ties That Bind: Kinship and the Social Order

LEARNING OBJECTIVES

After reading this chapter, students should be able to

- understand the concept of kinship and the role kinship systems play in anthropology;
- understand how in-vitro fertilization highlights Euro-American social and cultural beliefs about kinship;
- discuss the myth of the family in Western culture and understand its biblical origins;
- explain the role of marriage in society and the concepts of endogamy, polygyny, bridewealth, bride-service, and dowry;
- explain the meaning of descent and identify the differences between matrilineal and patrilineal systems; and
- understand the difference between genetic identity and social-cultural identity as it relates to kinship.

KEY TERMS

bride-service	endogamy	matrilineage
bridewealth	kinship	patrilineage
descent	kinship systems	polygyny
dowry	marriage	rite of passage

Introduction

The cross-cultural study of **kinship** and **kinship systems** has been a central anthropological topic at least since the time of Lewis Henry Morgan. Why is this so? The primary reason is because early anthropology chose to concentrate on "primitive" societies. Many of these lacked the social institutions—bureaucratic government, money-based economies, formal law, etc.—that Western observers were accustomed to. It came to be perceived that, where such institutions are lacking, "kinship" serves as an integrating force, an all-purpose social glue: "blood kinship" provides the basis for the formation of cohesive groups, marriage establishes cross-generational connections between them, and bonds of affection and complex economic relationships hold it all together. These perceptions were coupled with the evolutionary assumption that "the family" must have been the earliest form of human association, from which all later forms are derived.

Anthropologists and social historians have documented the worldwide range of practices relating to kinship, marriage, and the family. As always, the first impulse was to collect and classify, and then to interpret what was found—as Morgan did—in evolutionary terms. We saw in Chapter 1 that this impulse gave way to detailed ethnographic studies of social systems in their own terms and how they function on the ground.[1] But, given all the diversity that was revealed, even *defining* "kinship" and "the family" proves a difficult order.

The anthropological study of kinship is a game that nearly everyone can play, since most of us have known kin. We invite you, therefore, to think about your own family and its history in light of the discussion to follow. In this chapter we will identify certain key questions that have emerged from these efforts, look back on the history of the subject, and examine how the study of kinship is unfolding in our own rapidly changing world.

We start with an example from our own time that explores the social implications of revolutionary developments in reproductive technology—the role of genetic, social, and cultural factors in shaping who we think we are. We then turn to the ancient world and the biblical saga of Abraham, Sarah, Hagar, Ishmael, and Isaac, which is a tale about preserving the continuity of a family under threat of extinction. This old story is historically important and contains elements that have been widely observed by anthropologists in the field. It has implications for Jewish and Arab identity and for the Palestinian-Israeli conflict that echo down to our own day.

These examples lead to some general remarks on social structure and the nature of kinship. Finally we bring all this together by describing an important case recently argued before the US Supreme Court concerning the adoption of an Indigenous child by Euro-American foster parents. Once more the issue is social identity and cultural integrity. As you will see, it's all very political.

What Is "The Family"?

The first baby created through in vitro fertilization (IVF) was born in 1978, accompanied by media hype about "test tube babies" and a good deal of public hand-wringing over doctors "playing God." This outcome was the result of the long and patient efforts of an English doctor, Robert Edwards (1925–2013), to find a way to fertilize a human egg outside of the body and then to implant it successfully in the uterus. In 2010 his efforts were rewarded with a Nobel Prize in Medicine. At the Nobel ceremony a colleague celebrated him for "transforming the intellectual landscape not just of gynaecology, but also of ethics and social anthropology."[2] The mention of "social anthropology" in this context is interesting. The speaker was referring to the fact that anthropologists can now be found working in IVF clinics and other medical locales, attempting to understand the implications of these new technologies at a local and personal level (Franklin and McKinnon 2001). Consider the following situation that Dr. Edwards's work made possible.

In 2013 a story entitled "What Makes a Jewish Mother" appeared in the *New York Times*. A Jewish couple decided rather late in life that they wished to have a child. The prospective mother, Caren Chesler, was 42 at the time, and she reported that "three years later, I finally accepted that it wasn't going to happen naturally. We narrowed our options to two: use eggs donated by another woman, or adopt."[3] They opted for the former, which meant they would follow the IVF procedure, using eggs from an anonymous donor fertilized with the husband's sperm. "A year and a half later … I gave birth to our son, Eddie. Weighing 7 pounds, 7 ounces, he was the spit and image of my husband. Some said he had my eyes, but I knew that couldn't be true. He has none of my genetic material. It bothered me, but I told myself nature is only half the equation. I would contribute greatly on the nurture front. And of course our baby would be Jewish, given that I am. Under Jewish law, a baby's religious identity is determined by his mother. Or so I thought.…"

Experts on Jewish family law were divided on the issue. The fact that the egg came from an unknown donor raised problems about whether Eddie was "really" Jewish or would have to go through a ritual conversion to Judaism. So here we have a complex debate, rooted in a deep religious tradition, about the relation between *social identity* and *genetic identity*. Which do we think is more important in determining who a person *really* is? This is a tricky problem that could not have arisen in this form before the emergence of modern genetics and the invention of IVF. How puzzling it can become is seen in the case of older women who, with the help of IVF and hormone treatments, become surrogate mothers for their infertile daughters, thus becoming the birth mothers of their own grandchildren.

Such questions go beyond these particular cases. For example, conflicts have arisen over whether persons conceived through anonymous sperm donation have a natural *right* to know who their genetic "father" is. Likewise, some adoptees find it impossible to rest easy until they learn who their *real* parents are. Hidden within such debates are cultural assumptions concerning the nature of kinship.

In the 1960s, anthropologist David Schneider and his colleagues undertook an extensive ethnographic study of American ideas about relatedness. They found that kinship "by blood" was seen as being of paramount importance in defining relationship:

> In American cultural conception, kinship is defined as biogenetic. This definition says that kinship is whatever the biogenetic relationship is. If science discovers new facts about biogenetic relationship, then that is what kinship is and was all along, although it may not have been known at the time. Hence, the real, true, verifiable facts of nature are what the cultural formulation is. And the real, true, objective facts of science … are that each parent provides one-half of his child's biogenetic constitution. The relationship which is "real" or "true" or "blood" or "by birth" can never be severed, whatever its legal position. Legal rights may be lost but the blood relationship cannot be lost. It is culturally defined as being an objective fact of nature, of fundamental significance and capable of having profound effects, and its nature cannot be terminated or changed. (Schneider 1980: 23–24; see also Schneider 1984: 72)

Schneider already had experience of another society—the Yap Islanders in the western Pacific—with a very different take on what constitutes "kinship" (Schneider 1984). He had found that some key relationships, such as that between "father" and "child," were not defined by "blood," but by the services that people do for one another—an exchange relationship and not a blood relationship (1984: 72, 121). There are societies in which what we think of as "kinship" is defined by the sharing of food—by "common belonging" (Sahlins 2013: 6, 22). In these cases "kinship" is created in practice, not laid down in advance by some essential quality that people are thought to share.

Schneider knew that in many societies the two biological parents are held to have an unequal role in procreation, and to contribute quite *different* psychological and physical qualities to their offspring: for example, the man the bone and the woman the blood. There are cases in which the male is thought to have little or nothing to do with conception, and others in which the woman is seen as merely an incubator for the husband's seed. These notions reflect broader structural features and cultural assumptions of the societies concerned.

From his comparative perspective David Schneider was able to speak to fellow Americans about a usually taken-for-granted reality as though it were actually foreign and exotic. A more recent study of British attitudes about the social implications of IVF arrived at similar conclusions by similar means:

> The priority that Euro-Americans … put on the bodily process of procreation is rather special to them. Indeed, a point of debate in anthropology is that

while everywhere social arrangements attend to the production and rearing of children, it is not the case that everywhere the facts of procreation are taken to be of prime significance. Where they are, then the circumstances of birth confer an identity on the child. For Euro-Americans there is no getting around the tie that exists with those persons whose genetic substances combined at the child's conception. This is taken as a fact of life. (Strathern 1992: 14)

We would add that the circumstances of conception also confer an identity on the early-stage embryo, even if it hasn't yet been implanted. This problem is evident in political attempts in the United States to get fetuses defined as "persons" in a legal sense, and hence abortion classified as murder. That question extends to what should be done with frozen embryos in IVF clinics that could—in principle—become full human beings. In other words, do embryos have "rights"? In an odd legal case early in the days of IVF it was debated whether an embryo stored in an Australian clinic whose American "parents" had been killed in a plane crash would have inheritance rights if it were brought to term through a surrogate mother.[4] As IVF has become more widely used, issues have also arisen over "orphan" embryos—surplus frozen embryos abandoned by their creators and left behind in the storage vaults of IVF clinics without instructions about what to do with them.

Questions such as these have no obvious answers, and their outcomes arise from complex interactions between culture, religion, politics, the legal system, and perceptions of what best serves the common good.

Returning to Caren Chesler's problem, the matrilineal inheritance of identity is surprising at first sight given the patriarchal values so evident in the Hebrew Bible, and the fact that the scriptures mention a number of Jewish men having children by non-Jewish women, children who went on to become important figures in ancient Israel. The reasons for this change are obscure but in the early days may have had something to do with the consequences of intermarriage between Jewish women and non-Jewish men; in any event, this practice is not found in all branches of Judaism, but its implications were of concern to Ms. Chesler. Faced with this dilemma, she relied on her heart: "The other night, I was making dinner and my husband had taken our son for a walk. After about half an hour, I heard our screen door opening and the patter of toddler feet running toward the kitchen. 'Muh-MAH!' Eddie said as he ran into my arms. I should have just asked my son who his mother is. He's known all along."

The Power of Myth

Our second example is also about social identity, but in a quite different context. The story of Abraham's family comes from the biblical book of Genesis; it has parallels with the findings of modern anthropological research on family structure, inheritance, and group formation.

For those unfamiliar with the Bible, the Genesis narrative is the first in a group of five texts that outline the formation of the Jewish people and the revealing of laws to govern them. Thinking back to his fieldwork in the Trobriand Islands, Bronislaw Malinowski (1954: 100, 116) observed that "myth … in its living form, is not merely a story told but a reality lived … believed to have once happened in primeval times, and continuing ever since to influence the world and human destinies. The story of origin literally contains the legal charter of the community." The Genesis narrative is a story of just this kind.

You are no doubt familiar with the story of Noah, the great flood, and the ark. One of Noah's sons was Shem, the ancestor of Abraham. God singled out Abraham for a special destiny and promised, "I will make of you a great nation, and I will bless you … and in you all the families of the earth shall be blessed" (Gen. 12: 2–3). However, Abraham's wife, Sarah, was barren—a terrible fate for both of them. But Sarah saw a way out: she had an Egyptian slave-girl named Hagar, and she told her husband, "'you see that the Lord has prevented me from bearing children; go in to my slave-girl; it may be that I shall obtain children by her' … and gave her to her husband Abraham as a wife" (Gen. 16: 2–3).[5] This was a surrogacy relationship; Hagar was to bear Abraham's children in Sarah's name so that the family line could carry on.

Hagar conceived, but she held Sarah in low esteem because of her infertility. Sarah perceived this and abused Hagar, who fled into the wilderness where she encountered the Lord, who promised that she too would be the mother of a great nation: "Hagar bore Abraham a son; and Abraham named his son, whom Hagar bore, Ishmael" (Gen. 16: 15). In the passages that follow, the Lord makes a "covenant" with Abraham, a kind of legal contract in which all good things are promised to them if Abraham and his descendants follow the Lord faithfully. The sign of the covenant is to be male circumcision. The text does not explain why that particular mark was chosen (other references indicate an association with purity), but this ceremony remains a central feature of male Jewish identity and is also the majority practice among Muslims. It is a pivotal **rite of passage**, a sign of incorporation into the community and identification with it: "Any uncircumcised male who is not circumcised in the flesh of his foreskin shall be cut off from his people; he has broken my covenant" (Gen. 17: 14).

But Abraham still did not have a legitimate son of his own; the Lord promised him that Sarah—in spite of advancing age—would bear one, and that he should be called Isaac. Abraham asked that Ishmael not be forgotten, and the Lord replied, "I have heard you; I will bless him and make him fruitful and exceedingly numerous…. But my covenant I will establish with Isaac." There were further adventures, and Sarah eventually produced a son. But tension remained high between Hagar and Sarah, who demanded that her husband "cast out this slave woman with her son; for the son of this slave woman shall not inherit along with my son Isaac." Abraham was conflicted, but he was reassured by the Lord that the descendants of Ishmael would also prosper.

So Hagar and her son were sent off, and again they wandered in the wilderness (always a sign of transitional status) where they nearly died of thirst. Hagar prayed,

"Do not let me look on the death of the child," and a well of water was revealed to her. "God was with the boy, and he grew up; he lived in the wilderness, and became an expert with the bow. He lived in the wilderness of Paran; and his mother got a wife for him from the land of Egypt" (Gen. 21: 20–21).

We are told that when Abraham died, Ishmael and Isaac laid him to rest in "the cave of Machpelah" where Sarah was also interred. Ishmael's part in this story concludes with an account of what groups descended from him. The Hebrew writings then go silent about him save for the occasional mention of "Ishmaelites," desert peoples, presumably the ancestors of the migratory Bedouin Arab tribes. The main narrative shifts its attention to Isaac and his descendants, from whom the Jewish people are derived.

Arab tradition has quite a different emphasis. Ishmael and Hagar are here seen as instrumental in finding the holy spring that became the site of Mecca; Ishmael himself is regarded as an ancestor of the Prophet Muhammad. Whether Isaac or Ishmael was Abraham's favored son became and remains a matter of debate.

Continuing the Family Line

A number of themes run through this story, most obviously the stress on family continuity—a problem that comes up a number of times in the Hebrew writings. It has also been widely noted by anthropologists who have worked in lineage-based societies. Inheritance is a central factor. What happens when a family is in danger of dying out or the property is in danger of being lost to outsiders because there is no legitimate heir? The early Hebrews got around this by marrying *within* the family— "**endogamous**" marriages—preferably with a father's brother's child.[6]

This may seem rather close to incest, but it has the virtue of keeping property within the broader political and economic group—the **patrilineage** as a whole.[7] The Hebrew scriptures attribute this practice to a ruling of the prophet Moses: "Every daughter who possesses an inheritance in any tribe of the Israelites shall marry one from the clan of her father's tribe, so that all Israelites may continue to possess their ancestral inheritance" (Numbers 36: 8).

Similar practices remain widespread in many Middle Eastern, North African, and West Asian societies—among them the Iraqi Arabs with whom Robert and Elizabeth Fernea worked (see Chapter 3). Arranged parallel-cousin marriage is reported among British Pakistanis; the intent of such alliances is to sustain and strengthen ties between the branches of the family in Britain and Pakistan. The family of the Prophet Muhammad also exhibits such a pattern: his daughter, Fatima, married her paternal cousin, Ali—Muhammad's father's brother's son. The descendants of this marriage proved to be extraordinarily important in the history of Islam, and disagreements over their status are at the root of the current divisions in the Muslim world between the Sunni and Shi'a branches of the faith. Marriage between a daughter and a male cousin

PLATE 5.1 Cave of the Patriarchs

was also not uncommon in Victorian England when property issues were involved. Moreover, cousin marriage was virtually the norm among European royalty.

When one sees how the characters in the Genesis story interacted, it is easy to identify with the real-world dilemmas that they faced. Our own soap operas explore similar themes. But there's more to it than this superficial level. The story of the parentage and separation of Isaac and Ishmael also accounts for the origin of major political, cultural, and geographical groupings. It's an example of the processes of family life being mapped onto an interpretation of history.

The family grows and divides along natural lines of tension. For example, co-wives in a **polygynous** household—a household in which there is one husband and multiple wives—may suspect one another of witchcraft. Half-brothers descended from the same father but different mothers may be rivals for the father's inheritance, which leads to quarreling and dispersal of the family. Such tales account for perceived similarities and differences—and political distance—between the groups held to be descended from the founding ancestor. It is impossible to judge their historical truth, and from our point of view it doesn't matter. These "genealogical charters" serve to validate claims to land, power, status, or anything else of social value. Such ancient narratives have been used to back up rival claims in the modern Middle East.

Old stories can have a long afterlife. "The cave of Machpelah"—where Abraham, Sarah, and other biblical figures were said to be buried—is now contained in the Cave of the Patriarchs, which is in the city of Hebron in the West Bank, an area administered by the Palestinian Authority. It has been fought over in various conflicts and is currently maintained by the organization responsible for Muslim holy sites. The site is honored by both Jews and Muslims, who nevertheless must use separate entrances. How we think about kinship has an impact on how we understand history itself and our place in it.

The Nature of Kinship Systems

Social practices like those described above direct our attention toward the "structural" factors involved in the study of kinship. What do we mean by "structure"? Generally the term refers to a larger whole made up of interdependent parts; it could be the "structure" of a language, a body, a building, an economy, or a society. Much anthropological effort has been devoted to unpacking the structure of kinship systems. But all one sees in the field is what people do, or say they do, along with the physical contexts in which they do it. We need to keep in mind that "structures" and "systems" are abstract concepts used to organize and interpret the complex information produced in the course of ethnographic fieldwork.

British social anthropologist A.R. Radcliffe-Brown (see Chapter 2) had a considerable role in the development of kinship studies (see Fortes 1969). He worked up from the smallest and most local parts of a system toward a consideration of the greater whole, a "tribe," perhaps, or some other higher-level social formation: "… a complex unity, an organized whole" (Radcliffe-Brown 1952: 53). As we've seen, this way of thinking led to a large ethnographic literature, much of it on Africa, which attempted to show how the parts of such systems work in an integrated fashion and result in a more or less orderly society. Audrey Richards's writings on the Bemba (see also Chapter 2) are an example. Radcliffe-Brown put it this way in his introduction to an influential collection of essays entitled *African Systems of Kinship and Marriage* (1950):

> A system of kinship and marriage can be looked at as an arrangement which enables persons to live together and co-operate with one another in an orderly social life. For any particular system as it exists at a certain time we can make a study of how it works. To do this we have to consider how it links persons together by convergence of interest and sentiment and how it controls and limits those conflicts that are always possible as the result of divergence of sentiment or interest. In reference to any feature of a system we can ask how it contributes to the working of the system. This is what is meant by speaking of its social function. (Radcliffe-Brown 1950: 3)

In these African societies and many others, ties of kinship and marriage served to form and bind together politically significant groups. Kinship, economics, and politics

A BROWN STUDY

PLATE 5.2 A.R. Radcliffe-Brown

were entangled with one another, which made it possible to think about these relationships in functional terms.[8] For example, if conflict were to arise between descent groups, ties of marriage between them might serve to damp it down, thus contributing to overall social stability. This approach would not be directly relevant in Euro-North American society, where kin groups such as lineages and clans do not generally function in a political capacity. For the most part we live in much more "individualized" societies.

Kinship and the Gift

Ties of kinship are also ties of moral and economic obligation. There are many formal and informal ways of establishing such bonds: adoption, surrogacy, common-law relationships, and—of course—marriage.

Marriage is a classic rite of passage, often involving complex ceremonies and intricate economic transactions. In North America, marriage is now largely a matter of personal choice theoretically based on "love." It's not as popular as it once was; currently in the US and Canada only about 50 per cent of adults are married, and less traditional arrangements are on the rise. In other societies marriage remains a profoundly social act—an affair between groups, not individuals. The ties established between groups by marriage are both political and economic and can span generations. Gift giving of one kind or another is a common feature of these relationships. It is an aspect of what the French ethnologist Marcel Mauss (1872–1950), in his well-known essay *The Gift*, called a "total social phenomenon," in which "all kinds of institutions are given expression at one and the same time—religious, juridical, and moral, which relate to both politics and the family ... production and consumption" (Mauss 1990: 3).

Exchanges involving **bridewealth**, **bride-service**, or **dowry** are frequently found in these contexts. In the case of bridewealth, valuable property is transferred from the family of the man to that of his prospective bride. The Nuer people of South Sudan were put on the anthropological map by the work of another British social anthropologist, E.E. Evans-Pritchard (1902–73).[9] They are a patrilineal society economically based on cattle herding, similar to ancient Israel in some respects. Marriage establishes bonds between lineages that are defined by the transfer of bridewealth in the form of cattle and with definite but negotiable rules about who should get what. Marriage ceremonies are "important public events in Nuer life. A whole district attends them, the mere coming together of so many people making marriage a memorable event. Neighbours thus bear witness to the creation of new social ties and by their presence sanction them" (Evans-Pritchard 1951: 59). Dances are held, speeches are made, and a lot of beer is drunk. You may well have attended large and expensive formal weddings of just this sort!

But what happens if a man dies childless? One option is "ghost marriage." A relative of the dead man may act in his place, and marry a wife to the dead man's name, with bridewealth being transferred in the usual way. The relative takes on the normal role of husband but "the legal husband is the ghost in whose name the bridewealth was paid and the ritual of matrimony was performed." It is the ghost's name that will be remembered in the family genealogy, not that of the biological father. "The woman is ... the wife of a ghost, and her children are ... children of a ghost" (1951: 110). Genealogies are thus not always what they seem.

The principle of bride-service is simple enough: a man works for his in-laws in return for their daughter. We've mentioned the case of the Bemba, but there is another striking example of this practice in the Hebrew writings. The story of Jacob, son of Isaac, continues the narrative we've outlined above.

Isaac wishes to maintain the integrity of the family line through cousin-marriage, and instructs Jacob to journey to the home of his mother's brother, Laban. He encounters Laban's daughter, Rachel, and is much charmed by her. Laban agrees to a marriage if Jacob agrees to work for him for seven years. This he does, and a marriage takes place. However, after it's consummated it turns out that his father-in-law has played a trick on him and in the dark substituted Rachel's older sister, Leah. Laban explains that he did this because in his country the senior sister should marry first. But he promises that, if Jacob works for him another seven years, he can have Rachel as well. Jacob finally ends up married to two sisters who are also his maternal cousins, and who, along with Jacob, become the ancestors of the tribes of Israel. These tribes are unified into one nation because of their common father, but are divided from each other because of descent from different mothers. As myth often does, this kind of story explains large-scale structural arrangements through the recounting of an intimate family drama.

Dowry refers to property that accompanies a woman into the marriage relationship—a kind of pre-inheritance that in an ideal world would be passed on to her offspring. How much property is involved depends on the status and importance of the marriage. Getting together a considerable dowry is one way for the bride's family to move up in the world, and a good deal of public display may be involved in bringing it off. Such practices are well known in India, and to some extent among migrant Indian communities elsewhere. Indeed, families with high-value professional-class sons may hold out for a considerable dowry before they will agree to a marriage:

> In India, almost all marriages are arranged. Even among the educated middle classes in modern, urban India, marriage is as much a concern of the families as it is of the individuals. So customary is the practice of arranged marriage that there is a special name for a marriage which is not arranged: It is called a "love match." Dowry, which although illegal, has become a more pressing issue in the consumer conscious society of contemporary urban India. In many cases, where a groom's family is not satisfied with the amount of dowry a bride brings to her marriage, the young bride will be constantly harassed to get her parents to give more. (Nanda 2000: 196; 203–4)

But that's not the only side of the story. At the beginning of her fieldwork in India, American anthropologist Serena Nanda at first found herself baffled by the readiness of many middle-class Indians to accept a marital choice negotiated by their families. However,

> … during months of meeting many young Indian people, both male and female … I saw arranged marriages in a different light. I also saw the importance of the family in Indian life and realized that a couple who took their marriage into their own hands was taking a big risk, particularly if their families were irreconcilably opposed to the match. In a country where every important resource in life—a job, a house, a social circle—is gained through family connections, it seems foolhardy to cut oneself off from a supportive social network and depend solely on one person for happiness and success. (2000: 198)

India, of course, is large and diverse, as are Africa and North America. There are great differences of class, religion, and ethnicity in all three. There is no single pattern of marriage and family life that applies universally to any of them. Social institutions such as these depend on history, cultural context, and economics, and simple formulations are always going to be misleading if applied too loosely.

Descent

In the course of his extensive research among Indigenous peoples, Lewis Henry Morgan had found that "the American Indians always speak to each other, when related, by the term of relationship, and never by the personal name of the individual addressed. In familiar intercourse, and in formal salutation, they invariably address each other by the exact relationship of consanguinity [kinship by blood] or affinity [kinship through marriage] in which they stand related. I have put the question direct to native Indians of more than 50 different nations, in most cases at their villages or encampments, and the affirmance of this usage has been the same in every instance. Over and over again it has been confirmed by personal observation" (Morgan 1871: 132).

Clearly these relationship terms were of great social importance, and Morgan aimed at working out the details of the systems in use by the various North American tribes. His approach was influenced by his early experience with the Iroquois, where he found that their way of classifying relationships was quite different from that of Euro-Americans and was an aspect of their **matrilineal** social order: "Not the least remarkable among their institutions, was that which confined the transmission of all titles, rights and property in the female line to the exclusion of the male. It is strangely unlike the canons of descent adopted by civilized nations ..." (Morgan 1851: 84).

Early seventeenth-century European explorers and settlers in North America soon became aware of this unfamiliar way of reckoning kinship among the eastern tribes. The Virginia Colony was the first permanent English settlement in the New World, and Captain John Smith (of Pocahontas fame; see Chapter 9 for more on this episode) took careful note of the Native inhabitants and geography in the vicinity of the Jamestown settlement. He found that these people had a paramount chief named Powhatan, and a number of dependent sub-chiefs in surrounding villages. Smith described their dwellings, their religious practices, and their mode of **descent**. Powhatan's "kingdoms descend not to his sonnes nor children, but first to his brethren, whereof he hath 3 ... and after their decease to his sisters. First to the eldest sister, and to the rest, and after them to the heires male or female of the eldest sister, but never to the heires of the males" (Smith 1624: 38).

Matrilineal descent was the norm over a vast area: from Lake Huron in the north, to Florida in the south, and west to the Mississippi. He may have exaggerated a bit, but a Catholic missionary writing in New France in 1724 noted the extraordinarily high status of women among the Iroquois:

It is they who really maintain the tribe, the nobility of blood, the genealogical tree, the order of generations and conservation of the families. In them resides all the real authority: the lands, fields and all their harvest belong to them.... They arrange the marriages; the children are under their authority; and the order of succession is founded on their blood. The men, on the contrary, are entirely isolated and limited to themselves. Their children are strangers to them. Everything perishes with them. A woman alone gives continuity to the household. (Lafitau 1974: 69)

The discovery of such practices came as a great surprise. Everything then known to the Europeans suggested that a patriarchal form of inheritance and family life was the natural human condition. And yet the Iroquois, Huron, and kindred peoples in eastern North America were divided up into matrilineal totemic clans—going under names such as Wolf, Bear, Turtle, and Heron. Office-holders inherited their titles, not from their fathers, but from their mother's brothers, or equivalent relatives on the maternal side. Iroquois clans, and those of numerous other peoples, were divided up into two opposed hereditary groups; members of one grouping of clans (Bear, Wolf, Beaver, Turtle) intermarried with the members of the other group (Deer, Snipe, Heron, Hawk), but they could not marry within their own (Morgan 1877: 90).[10] There were other complementary relationships of this sort between the two halves of the tribe, expressed in ritual and accounted for by myth.

Morgan and others came to believe that matrilineality was the *earliest* form of human kinship organization; this became the collective wisdom of their day concerning the evolution of the family. The reason they thought so is simple: you generally know who your biological mother is, but paternity is more uncertain. Morgan also came to realize that Indigenous kinship systems differ considerably from one another. He wondered if the distribution of such systems could be used to chart the global history of ethnic migration. Following this logic, similar systems should imply a common historical origin. The result of those labors was an innovative book with an impressive title: *Systems of Consanguinity and Affinity of the Human Family* (1871). It is based on his own research and information provided by foreign correspondents.

The method was straightforward. Morgan asked his informants about terms in the local languages that correspond to English kin-terms such as "mother," "father," "cousin," "aunt," "uncle," "grandfather," "grandmother," and so on. It was found, for example, that Iroquois terminology distinguishes the mother's from the father's side of the family in a way that English does not. In English the siblings of one's mother and father are "aunts" and "uncles" regardless of which side of the family they are on; likewise all their children are lumped together as "cousins," *whatever their sex*. On the other hand, the Iroquois terms equate mother with mother's sisters, and father with father's brothers; their children are referred to by the same terms as one's own siblings. Thus a mother's sister's daughter is referred to by the same term as one's own sister.

FIGURE 5.1 Iroquois Kinship

Mother's brothers and father's sisters are referred to by different terms than mother's sisters and father's brothers. What we call "cousins" are *distinguished by sex.*

These linguistic practices reflect a generalized principle whereby all the members of one's own matrilineal clan and of one's own generation could be spoken of using the same terms as those used for "brothers" and "sisters"—in other words, it expresses a collective identity reckoned through women (see Figure 5.1).

Given facts of this kind, Morgan made a speculative leap and concluded that if entire groups referred to one another as brothers and sisters, this reflected a bygone practice of group-marriage. The idea was that, if one calls entire collections of people by the same terms as one's own biological siblings, then this is a linguistic relic of a time in which groups of siblings in the parental generation married (and could have sex with) one another collectively. Morgan's mistake was simple: he projected Western ideas about *biological* kinship onto the quite different systems of kin classification that his comparative research was turning up.

In time, in fact, some of Morgan's other theories came to be seen as misguided. He had indeed determined that many societies classify relatives as "marriageable" or "unmarriageable." But marriageability certainly doesn't correlate to group sex, and never did. Terms like these reflect group identities of individuals as members of clans and lineages—in other words, they reflect local social structure. As the earlier preoccupation with social evolution faded away, anthropologists became more concerned with analyzing such systems on the ground, and produced a large literature in doing so. Kinship systems were classified into types, and much effort went into investigating relationships between the elements in such systems. Works such as Radcliffe-Brown's *African Systems of Kinship and Marriage* are an expression of this endeavor.

For example, the question of how mode of descent affects relations between the genders and between generations has been long been an anthropological theme—a classical application of the comparative method. If a male child doesn't inherit anything worthwhile from his father, and instead inherits from his mother's brother, how does this affect the authority patterns and emotional tone of family life? How do these factors affect who lives with whom and relationships between family groups? What are relations like between same- and opposite-sex siblings? How does marriage work in societies of different types? Do women fare better in matrilineal societies?[11]

Specialized anthropological works on kinship go into more detail about this kind of thing, and as you see it's a vast topic. But we'll now move on to explore in a little more detail the relationship between kinship and politically charged issues concerning social identity.

Defining Kin: Legal Implications

The case with which we began this chapter pertained to who is regarded as "really" Jewish. As Caren Chesler found out, there may be no clear-cut answer to a question like that. We'd broaden the question to ask: Who is really *anything*? What determines how people get categorized, including the slots we place *ourselves* in—say on a census form that asks for our race or ethnicity? Of course the application of kinship terminology is one way of doing this; after all, it's a scheme of social classification. But anthropological research has shown that how such schemes work in practice can be a slippery business—in other words, it may depend on social context and relate to pragmatic interests such as claims to resources. "Kinship" imposes moral and practical burdens on us, which sometimes can weigh very heavily and which we'd rather avoid if possible. Some relatives get remembered, but many more are eventually forgotten or ignored. Genealogical memory is highly selective.

During the Nazi period in Germany, the answer to the question "Who is a Jew?" could have fatal consequences. This problem was particularly evident in cases of mixed marriages—in which the social identity of the offspring was at issue. Just how "Jewish" did one have to be before racially discriminatory legislation kicked in? Relative proportions of Jewish "blood" also determined who could and couldn't marry. Legal criteria for deciding these things were laid out in the 1935 "Law for the Protection of German Blood and German Honor," which "was designed to separate Jews from non-Jews in the sphere of reproductive and familial relations" (Proctor 1988: 132). These measures were based on the belief that Jews are a "race" with unchangeable and inferior moral characteristics relative to those of Aryan Germans.

The other side of this story is the question of who has an automatic right to citizenship in the State of Israel. When Israel was created in 1948, its founders wanted to make it a refuge and secure home for Jews everywhere, and to do that the question of "Who is a Jew?" was answered in very broad terms by the 1950 "Law of Return." The criteria were social and historical, not racial, and only religious in a secondary way: "For the purposes of this Law, 'Jew' means a person who was born of a Jewish mother or has become converted to Judaism and who is not a member of another religion."[12] By this definition, one could be an atheist and not engage in Jewish ritual life at all, and still be certifiably Jewish. However, the application of the Law has led to a lot of problems in particular cases. Specific answers to the identity question can have serious practical implications.

The same is true elsewhere, such as deciding just *who* is an American Indian, a native Hawaiian, an Indigenous Australian, or an Indigenous Canadian. As in the Israeli case, the answer determines who has legal rights to a particular political identity and access to significant resources. Canada, the United States, and Australia have parallel histories with regard to the treatment of Native peoples. Similar moral, political, and economic issues have arisen as a result. All three went to considerable lengths to induce or compel Indigenous peoples to become "civilized" and assimilate to the European-derived mainstreams. Pressures of this sort existed in any event, in that Native peoples ended up as relatively small and powerless minorities in what had once been their own countries.[13]

Governments, churches, and private agencies all bent themselves to the task of converting the local "savages" to "civilization." Their methods focused on religion, language, economics, education, and family life. Since civilization was associated with private property, tribal peoples had to be decoupled from the communal economies that had historically sustained them (see Chapter 4). More radical approaches involved segregating them from their families and their languages altogether. In Canada this led to the rise of the residential school system, run by the churches and still the focus of grievance on the part of Indigenous peoples, who call what the state was trying to do to them "cultural genocide" (see Miller 1996).

In the United States the most radical social experiment was the removal of many Indigenous groups from their original homes and their forced resettlement in Indian Territory, which eventually became the state of Oklahoma. The intent was to settle Indigenous people down, teach them how to farm, and give them agricultural land in the form of private allotments. This was supposed to teach personal responsibility and how to function as responsible progressive citizens. Schooling was also part of the mix. Over time, significant numbers of Indigenous children were taken from their families as well, and adopted by white foster parents. The picture in Australia was much the same, and those treated in this manner are now known as "The Stolen Generation." In 2008 the Government of Australia apologized to Indigenous peoples for the treatment they had received. But our topic is kinship, and a recent case argued before the Supreme Court of the United States brings together a number of the themes in this chapter.

Baby Veronica

It is known as the "Baby Veronica" case, the name of a child caught up in a complex custody dispute in South Carolina. It "has stirred powerful emotional responses from child welfare groups, adoptive parents and Indian tribes."[14] The basic facts are as follows.

Veronica's biological mother and father were residents of Oklahoma. They had not married, though they had intended to. However, the relationship ended before this happened, and the mother (who is of Hispanic descent) decided to put her child up for adoption through a private agency. A couple in South Carolina was chosen as adoptive parents. The biological father, who is Indigenous had relinquished his parental rights, but he later claimed that he was unaware that the child was going to be put up for adoption rather than being raised by her birth mother. He then sued in South Carolina for possession of the child, citing the 1978 Federal Indian Child Welfare Act, which states that "it is the policy of this Nation to protect the best interests of Indian children and to promote the stability and security of Indian tribes and families by the establishment of minimum Federal standards for the removal of Indian children from their families and the placement of such children in foster or adoptive homes which will reflect the unique values of Indian culture."[15]

The Supreme Court of South Carolina decided that, even though the father had never had possession of the child, the federal act applies here, since he is in fact a registered member of the Cherokee Nation and desired to raise the child himself.[16] He also took and passed a genetic paternity test. Baby Veronica was therefore given over to him and they went back to Oklahoma. But the decision was highly controversial and on appeal made its way up to the US Supreme Court, which reversed the South Carolina decision and ordered the return of the child to her adoptive parents. The preamble to the US Supreme Court decision summarized the view of the majority of Justices: "This case is about a little girl [Veronica] who is classified as an Indian because she is 1.2% (3/256) Cherokee. Because [she] is classified in this way, the South Carolina Supreme Court held that certain provisions of the federal Indian Child Welfare Act of 1978 required her to be taken, at the age of 27 months, from the only parents she had ever known [who are non-Indian] and handed over to her biological father, who had attempted to relinquish his parental rights and who had no prior contact with the child."[17]

As always in anthropology, we have to consider the overall context that frames events such as these. There are three key elements involved in this one: the relation of this case to the Indian Child Welfare Act, the status of the biological father and his child as members of the Cherokee Nation, and the troubled history of Indigenous-White relations that we mentioned in the previous section.

The Cherokee are by origin a matrilineal southeastern people, first encountered by the Europeans in what are now North Carolina, Georgia, Alabama, and Tennessee. They were organized under a government of their own during the British colonial period and the early years of the American Republic. Encroachment on their territory by white settlers led to political pressures for their removal from the region, and in 1838–39 they were "induced" to relocate to Indian Territory. Some 16,000 of them made the trek, along what is remembered as "The Trail of Tears": "It was not a friendly removal. It was ugly and unwarranted. For too many Cherokees, it was deadly.... It also meant the continued loss of tribal knowledge and traditions. It is important that we never forget what happened to our people on the Trail of Tears. It was indeed our holocaust" (Perdue and Green 2005: 184, 185; see also Perdue and Green 2007).

Relations between the Cherokee and the colonial powers were defined by treaty. The United States regarded the Cherokee as a separate though dependent nation until

1907, when Indian Territory became Oklahoma. The Cherokee tribal government was then dissolved and tribal lands allotted to Cherokee individuals as their personal property. These holdings were recorded name by name on a document known as the Dawes Roll. However, in 1976 the Supreme Court decided that the status of the Cherokee as a sovereign nation had *not* in fact been terminated at the time of the allotment. The tribal government was reconstituted, and Veronica's father is currently a member in good standing of the Cherokee Nation, which, like Israel, defines eligibility broadly: "To be eligible for Cherokee Nation citizenship, individuals must provide documents connecting them to an enrolled direct ancestor who is listed on the Dawes Roll with a blood degree. Tribal Citizenship is traced through natural parents."[18]

The proportion of Cherokee "blood" doesn't matter, as long as there is a proven connection to a lineal male or female relative on the Dawes Roll (a great-grandfather

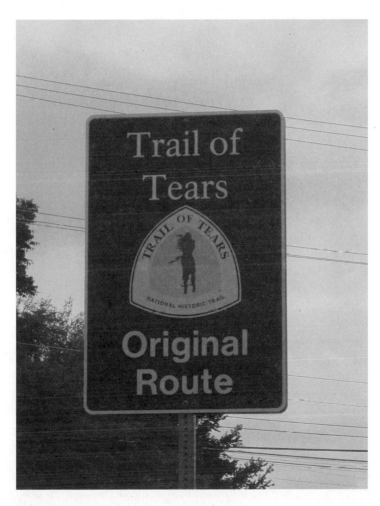

PLATE 5.3 Trail of Tears

or grandmother, say). Given this liberal definition, the original population of 16,000 Cherokee settlers has grown into a population of about 320,000 Cherokees today—the largest Indigenous tribe in the United States. In the US, the criteria for tribal membership are established by the tribes themselves, although not all are as liberal as the Cherokee. The same is true for First Nations bands in Canada, and for Indigenous Australians as well.[19] If economic issues are involved—such as income from tribal enterprises—the more citizens or band members there are, the less there is to go around, and so a more restrictive definition may seem the best course. Deciding who's in and who's out can get very political.

Note that the US Supreme Court decision emphasizes how *little* Indigenous ancestry Baby Veronica has (3/256th). It was also pointed out that neither biological parent had ever lived on a reservation. The implication is that—in the majority view—she and her father have minimal Indigenous cultural heritage and therefore that the Cherokee Nation has little to lose through her adoption. The Court did not dispute that Veronica and her father are tribal members; but the majority of justices concluded that the welfare of the child and the unusual circumstances of the case outweighed the rights of the biological father and fall outside the limits of what the Indian Child Welfare Act had intended.

It was a split decision (5 to 4). A dissenting justice cited previous Supreme Court cases in support of the rights of Veronica's biological father: "A natural parent's desire for and right to the companionship, care, custody, and management of his or her children is an interest far more precious than any property right." The dissenter also cited the Indian Child Welfare Act: "there is no resource that is more vital to the continued existence and integrity of Indian tribes than their children."

This affair has already come before the Cherokee Tribal Court, which *also* claims jurisdiction in such matters. Temporary custody was granted to the paternal grandparents and the father's present wife; Veronica went to live with them on tribal land. The adoptive parents tried to regain the child, and South Carolina was helping them do it. She was returned to her adoptive parents in September 2013. As one observer put it, "from a legal point of view, this case is just a mess."[20] Perhaps, but it's an interesting mess!

Conclusion

It should be apparent by now that there's nothing self-evident about concepts such as kinship, marriage, family, and blood relationship. These are all cultural constructs that have to be understood in their own terms and in relation to local circumstances. There is always the danger of projecting one's own sense of what is natural and proper onto the ways of others.

Consider the factors highlighted by the Baby Veronica case and our other examples above:

- Kinship is not a fact of nature, but a matter of social convention, and there are many ways of defining it.
- Kinship systems are flexible schemes of social classification intimately related to the structure and history of the wider society.
- Our case studies reveal complex tensions between *social* and *genetic identity*.
- They suggest the various ways in which community boundaries are created and maintained, and the challenges that can arise in ambiguous situations.
- Each case also involves controversies over "rights": to inheritance, to children, to group membership, to life itself.
- And each shows how political the whole business can be. What are the local ideas about the nature of conception, gestation, and childbirth? What are the respective roles of male and female seen to be?
- The nature of marriage and other types of union is also brought into question. How are male and female brought together for the purpose of legitimate procreation? What kinds of relationships arise between their respective families? Are exchange and gift-giving involved (bridewealth, dowry, bride-service, etc.)? What ceremonies mark such events?
- A lot of anthropological ink has been spilled on the "incest taboo." What principles govern who can marry or have sex with whom? What kinds of persons are included, and what kind excluded from this sort of relationship?
- Children are also an important consideration. What wider groups do children belong to by virtue of who their parents are? What "rights" do they have (to nourishment, to love, to inheritance, etc.)? What obligations do they have in return?
- And finally, the very nature of "kin" and "family" are subject to debate. Who counts as kin, and what kind of kin? What broader structural arrangements are these families a part of, how is the family defined, and what ritual practices sustain a sense of collective identity?

All these questions can be asked of the world right around us. As mentioned in the introduction to this chapter, we invite you to think about your own circumstances in light of this discussion.

Notes

1   See Fox (1967) for a useful overview.
2   See http://www.nobelprize.org/nobel_prizes/medicine/laureates/2010/edwards_lecture.pdf.
3   See http://well.blogs.nytimes.com/2013/06/03/what-makes-a-jewish-mother/.
4   See http://www.nytimes.com/1984/06/21/us/new-issue-in-embryo-case-raised-over-use-of-donor.html. At the time there were only about 500 people world-wide who had been conceived through IVF; now there are an estimated five million.

5   Biblical quotations are from the *New Oxford Annotated Bible*, 3rd ed. (New York: Oxford University Press, 1991).

6   The technical term for this arrangement is "patrilateral parallel cousin marriage." Parallel cousins are the children of parents' siblings of the same sex as the parent: i.e., mother's sister's children and father's brother's children. "Cross cousins" are children of parents' siblings of the opposite sex: mother's brother's children and father's sister's children.

7   There are indications in the text that Sarah was in fact Abraham's half-sister. First-cousin marriage is banned or restricted in a number of US states, but not in Canada or Europe.

8   Radcliffe-Brown also had an influence on the development of North American anthropology through his teaching at the University of Chicago. See Eggan (1955). See also Chapter 2 above.

9   See Evans-Pritchard (1940). You will meet him again in Chapter 6 via his research on witchcraft. As for the Nuer, they are currently caught up in a complex ethnic and political dispute in the newly formed Republic of South Sudan.

10 We prefer to avoid professional jargon, but should mention that the Iroquois clans practiced what is termed exogamy. In other words marriage had to take place *outside* of one's own group; the opposite would be endogamy, in which there is a requirement or at least a preference to marry *within*. The division of the clans into *two* complementary sections is known as a moiety system and has been found in various parts of the world.

11 For a comparative study of matrilineal kinship systems in relation to other types, see Schneider and Gough (1962). See also Richards (1950).

12 See http://www.mfa.gov.il/mfa/mfa-archive/1950-1959/pages/law%200f%20 return%205710-1950.aspx.

13 The question of "ownership" is a big one, and we will examine it in Chapter 10.

14 See http://www.nytimes.com/2013/06/26/us/justices-order-return-of-indian-child-to-adoptive-parents.html.

15 See http://www.nicwa.org/Indian_Child_Welfare_Act/ICWA.pdf.

16 In the United States, Indian affairs are exclusively a federal matter.

17 For the decision, see http://www.supremecourt.gov/opinions/12pdf/12-399_q86b.pdf.

18 See http://www.cherokee.org/Services/TribalCitizenship.aspx. There are also criteria for cases of adoption within the Tribe.

19 There is no single term used to describe Indigenous peoples, and different terminology is used in the United States, Canada, Central and South America, and Australia. When describing a people, the most respectful pratice is to use terms that they themselves use. For example, in Canada, some groups use the term First Nation such as the Aamjiwnaang First nation, while others use the term nation, such as the Squamish First Nation. Whenever, we have described Indigenous peoples by referring to their specific identities such as the Gitskan

and the Wet'suwet'en. When referring more broadly, we use the term Indigenous.

20   See http://www.tulsaworld.com/archives/biological-father-of-baby-veronica-files-appeal-with-oklahoma-supreme/article_389a51b1-567a-56c8-ae89-d2585ef82342.html.

Study Questions

1   Using the example of Caren Chesler and her family, explain the tension between social identity and genetic identity.

2   Summarize the concepts of family structure, endogamy, inheritance, and group formation using the biblical stories of Sarah, Hagar, Rachel, and Leah as examples.

3   Describe Radcliffe-Brown's approach to studying kinship and outline his contribution to anthropology.

4   Explain the concept of marriage and its role within kinship systems from the perspective of "the gift" and descent.

5   Outline the matrilineal form of descent among the tribes of North America. Explain how Europeans interpreted these kinship systems and why Morgan's Western ideas about biological kinship were inappropriate in this context.

6   Using the example of Baby Veronica, compare and contrast the genetic and social understandings of kinship and explain how cultural beliefs impact whom one identifies as kin.

Discussion Questions

1   Why was kinship deemed such an important area of study by early anthropologists? Do you think kinship remains an important area of study?

2   Consider the paired terms matrilineal vs. patrilineal and matriarchy vs. patriarchy. What is the difference between *matrilineal* and *matriarchal*? Discuss why matrilineal societies can still be considered patriarchal.

3   Given what you've learned about kinship systems, discuss why marriage is becoming less common in the Western world.

4   Think about your family in terms of kinship. How does your "family" define who counts as "kin" and what kind of kin? What ritual practices sustain a sense of collective identity?

CHAPTER 6

//

Symbol, Myth, and Meaning

LEARNING OBJECTIVES

After reading this chapter, students should be able to

- discuss the concept of culture as a system of meaning and understand why the definition of culture is so disputed;
- define the term *habitus* and explain the relationship between culture and bodily techniques as discussed by Mauss;
- summarize the work of Benedict and her perception of culture and cultural patterns;
- discuss how the understanding of culture is related to an understanding of language;
- outline the study of witchcraft by Evans-Pritchard and how his work illustrates the concept of paradigm;
- discuss Durkheim's work and his use of the term *mana*; and
- summarize Luhrmann's ethnographic work on the American evangelical community.

KEY TERMS

culture	*habitus*	sociocentric theory
epistemology	*mana*	
ethnology	paradigm	

Introduction

Try to imagine what it would be like for a child to grow up without other human beings around. Would such a child really be very human at all? Accounts of "wild children"—even of children raised by wolves—have turned up from time to time, though the facts are usually in dispute. For example, one such child—who came to be known as "The Wild Boy of Aveyron"—was discovered in southern France in the early years of the nineteenth century. Until his capture, he had been wandering around the forest, occasionally stealing food from farmers. The doctor who was granted legal custody of this boy was particularly interested in his ability to acquire language, which turned out to be very limited (the renowned French director François Truffaut made a film in 1970 called *L'enfant sauvage–The Wild Child* about the episode).

This case and a handful of others that have emerged over the last century were of great interest to the general public because they seemed to cast light on what human nature might be like "in the raw." So much of our cultural knowledge passes as ordinary common sense that we usually don't think much about it. Only when we are faced with different ways of doing things do we become conscious of the rules of the game, particularly the ones we don't understand properly. Learning another language is a good example. Some of you probably know very well, or your parents know, what it's like when you move from a place where a different language is spoken into the world of English-speaking Canada or the US. A language is a form of life. And it's not only the language: our interactions with people of different cultures may also be based on quite different assumptions about how to act and what kind of person to be.

As the French anthropologist Claude Lévi-Strauss (1908–2009) put it, society is the natural human condition (Lévi-Strauss 1969). We need society to become fully human. It is a biological necessity: our nervous system will not develop properly without social stimulation. But, as Edward Tylor showed, we are also cultural beings, living in a world full of meaning. If **culture** is a system of meaning, then on some level there *must* be rules and conventions or else social life would be chaotic. Of course, sometimes it does seem chaotic, and we shouldn't conceive of cultural rules as rigid—cultures are not clearly defined objects with perfectly clear outlines. Cultures are sets of practices and attitudes that are very complex, particularly in this day of mass media and migration, and the notion that specific cultures are associated with specific geographical locations is no longer entirely relevant.

Reconsidering the Culture Concept

Despite the centrality of the concept of culture to anthropology there continues to be much debate over developing a definition. The word has been described as one of the two or three most complex in the English language. As of the early 1950s, there existed over 150 definitions (Wright 1998)! Some view culture as rules that help govern people's actions and beliefs and unite them as a community or a society, while others view culture as the material things that are specific to particular areas. You might think of food, language, dress, family relationships, mourning rituals, or any other actions and beliefs that dictate a way of life for a group of people. Most recent definitions of culture seem to favor an approach that focuses on the sharing of ideals and values, and how people interpret experience and behaviors. Terre Satterfield, an anthropologist whose ethnography we will consider in Chapter 10, considers culture as a "multi-origined and multi-faceted resource" from which individuals draw—it is not a force that directs an individual's behavior, but a collection of ideas, behaviors, and beliefs that inform the way an individual lives (Satterfield 2002: 6). These cultural resources, such as symbols and meanings, manifest themselves in the everyday actions of groups who share a cultural identity. These definitions of culture, as well as the one given by Tylor and the hundreds that came after it, are necessarily broad and extremely general. In the following section we will not spend much time discussing what is or is not cultural, or what the best way to define it might be. Rather, we will examine some of the issues and concerns that have emerged as a result of the use of the word to define certain people, objects, and beliefs.

Cultural anthropologists are interested in examining the local and specific situations of a group of people. Implicit in this interest is a desire to learn about the individual—that is, what they actually do, say, and believe rather than what they *say* they do, say or believe. Of course, all of this is a matter of interpretation, and it is up to researchers to make clear how their own beliefs or experiences might influence their interpretation of an event or a group of people. What fascinates anthropologists is considering how people act within their own social world—while it is true that there are social rules and regulations that influence how people act and what they believe, it is important that we consider the agency, or power, of individuals to behave in a way that may contradict the social rules and norms of their society. Culture does not bind individuals but rather provides "a network of choices" in which the individual chooses, subconsciously or not, how he or she will believe or act (Yengoyan 1986: 396). Cultural symbols and traditions are extremely powerful and relevant to understanding the world. What is essential, however, is that we pay attention to the diversity that exists *within* these communities, groups, or locales so that we do not assume that generalizations are factual representations of people.

Determining a definition of culture might seem very theoretical and irrelevant to your daily life—in fact, what purpose does defining a concept serve? The reality is that the way we view culture has many political and social consequences, as we will see repeatedly throughout the book. How we define culture affects people at all levels of society—from the local context of the family and the community to the realms of national and international politics. In this chapter we explore some of the ways in which anthropologists have engaged that topic. First we will show that our everyday lives are full of symbolic significance, much of which—like the air we breathe—we're totally unconscious of until forced to think about it. How do we go about interpreting complex cultural phenomena?

As discussed in Chapter 2, Ruth Benedict was one of Franz Boas's early students, a close friend of Margaret Mead, and author of the anthropological bestseller *Patterns of Culture* (1934; see Benedict 1959). We will briefly look at her role in establishing and popularizing the modern culture concept. We'll then explore the idea that culture can be thought of as an open arena in which meaning is dynamically created in the flow of life and therefore can be studied objectively "in the field." As examples we will use a "classic" study of witchcraft beliefs in action, as well as a recent account of the process of religious conversion. In conclusion we briefly revisit the death of Captain James Cook. Just why did he die? How are we to make sense of a fatal encounter between an eighteenth-century British explorer and Native Hawaiians in the midst of one of their religious festivals? The Hawaiian episode raises questions about the relation between culture, myth, history, and the interpretive process.

We should also say what we're *not* going to do. Our topic is vast, and there are many ways of approaching it. The formal study of language is certainly an important aspect of the subject, and a vital part of anthropology, but given our ethnographic focus we will have little to say about language as such. On the other hand, culture is often seen as being *like* a language—elements set in meaningful relationship with one another—and this a metaphor well worth exploring.

Nor will we be dealing to any great degree with the analysis of "myth." This too is an important area, and we should at least take note of an anthropological movement known as structuralism (not to be confused with British structural-functionalism). It is associated with the French anthropologist Claude Lévi-Strauss, mentioned above; one of the central features of this approach, which is based on linguistic theory, is an attempt to unpack the formal logical structure of myth in order to get at underlying universal properties of human thought.

Comprehending Others

If understanding those around us, and even ourselves, can be difficult, then other cultures and times present an even more formidable problem. It has been said that "the past is a foreign country: they do things differently there." Reality doesn't come to us straight on: the world is always understood from a human point of view, and that is always partial. How could it be otherwise? We may try to imagine what it's like to be a dog, a bee, or an extraterrestrial being, but our own standpoint is where we must begin. This is an issue that anthropology has always faced—that of translation between different cultural worlds. Meaning is embedded in language, but also in behavior, and that is where we start.

You are probably aware of the condition known as *autism spectrum disorder*, typified, though to different degrees, by some kind of impairment in the capacity to function as a social being.

Oliver Sacks (1933–2015) was a neurologist and best-selling science writer; the central feature of his work is the attempt to understand neuropsychiatric disorder from *within*—to know as best we can what it's like to *live in* such a world.[1] One of his best-known essays is about Temple Grandin, a well-known figure who has been very successful in educating the public about autism through the telling of her own story (in 2010 a film was made about her life starring actor Claire Danes). She finds animals easier to understand than human beings, has had a successful career as a professor of Animal Science, and is an advocate for both animal and autistic rights. Sacks met with Grandin and heard her story firsthand. He learned that she has trouble understanding the nuances of personal interaction. These difficulties "seemed to arise from her failure to empathize ... to follow the intricate play of motive and intention. She said that she could understand 'simple, strong, universal' emotions but was stumped by more complex emotions and the games people play. 'Much of the time,' she said, 'I feel like an anthropologist on Mars'" (Sacks 1995: 259). For Grandin, "normal" people are the Martians. We live in a social world in which much goes unspoken and usually remains at the fringes of consciousness. And yet it clearly is meaningful; just imagine what you would think if you were talking to someone whose face was devoid of expression and who did not use body language. Try it yourself and see how long you can hold out! We will have more to say about meaning and context in the sections below.

Techniques of the Body

Marcel Mauss (1872–1950) was a French **ethnologist** and nephew of the great social theorist Émile Durkheim (1858–1917), to whom we'll return shortly. Though an armchair scholar and not an ethnographer, Mauss was a keen observer of the world around him and ranged widely in the search for common denominators underlying the diversity of human customs. As you've seen, Mauss is remembered for his essay *The Gift*. Another thing that caught his attention was cross-cultural difference in bodily style and deportment. He called these "the techniques of the body": "A kind of revelation came to me in hospital. I was ill in New York. I wondered where previously I had seen girls walking as my nurses walked. I had the time to think about it. At last I realized that it was at the cinema. Returning to France, I noticed how common this gait was, especially in Paris: the girls were French and they too were walking in this way. In fact, American walking fashions had begun to arrive over here, thanks to the cinema. This was an idea I could generalize" (Mauss 2006: 80).

And generalize it he did. Mauss had been in the French army in World War I and had served with English and Australian troops. He noted differences in bodily style between the English and Australians, and between both of them and the French. He wondered how this had come about, and so he was led to reflect on the cultural history of the societies in question and on the social situations in which particular bodily mannerisms are called for. In 1935 he asked a lecture audience to "look for a moment at ourselves. Everything in us all is under command. I am a lecturer for you: you can tell it from my sitting posture and my voice, and you are listening to me seated and in silence. We have a set of permissible or impermissible, natural or unnatural attitudes. Thus we should attribute different values to the act of staring fixedly: a symbol of politeness in the army, and of rudeness in everyday life" (Mauss 2006: 83).

Mauss went through a long list of bodily techniques: gender and age differences in deportment, variations in athletic styles, use of the hands, eating, sexual positions, ways of giving birth and holding infants, marching, sleeping, dancing, being at rest, etc. Some peoples squat, others sit, some stand on one leg: "the whole of Nilotic Africa … is populated by men who rest in the fields like storks. Some manage to rest on one foot without a pole, others lean on a stick. These resting techniques form real characteristics of civilisations, common to a large number of them, to whole families of peoples" (2006: 88).

Mauss used a Latin term—**habitus**—to cover the meaningful yet unconscious activity that pervades our daily lives (see Hall 1959, 1966). You don't have to look far to find it in your own. Just think about "table" manners, but bear in mind that not everyone uses tables, and some may eat with their hands (probably only the *right* hand) rather than with forks or chopsticks. The point of much childhood education is to make all of this "second nature." Anthropological and historical studies of *habitus* seek to restore that lost world to consciousness and expose the hidden processes behind it

PLATE 6.1 Marcel Mauss

(see Hall 1959, 1966). Audrey Richards's study of the Bemba (see Chapter 2) touches on this theme, as well as that of "the gift"—the ritual significance of preparing, giving, and receiving food.[2]

Etiquette is another word for this kind of thing, and in North America the "bible" of etiquette has long been Emily Post's book of the same name, first published in 1922 and now in its eighteenth edition:

PLATE 6.2 A Dinka Man: South Sudan

Etiquette must, if it is to be of more than trifling use, include ethics as well as manners. Certainly what one is, is of far greater importance than what one appears to be. A knowledge of etiquette is of course essential to one's decent behavior, just as clothing is essential to one's decent appearance; and precisely as one wears the latter without being self-conscious of having on shoes and perhaps gloves, one who has good manners is equally unselfconscious in the observance of etiquette, the precepts of which must be so thoroughly absorbed as to make their observance a matter of instinct rather than of conscious obedience. (Post 1922: 8)[3]

Marcel Mauss couldn't have put it better. But he was well aware of how culturally relative this whole business is, and Post was not. The sub-text of her book is social class and the gender relations that go with it. The evolution of Western table manners and other aspects of *proper* behavior is a story about the democratization of European aristocratic values—part of the unconscious background to the way in which many of us in North America behave every day. China has its own history in this regard, as do Japan and other parts of the world.

The message here is that culture and history are mixed up in everything we do: how we act; how we dress; how we evaluate personal appearance; our preferred colors; notions of hygiene; the foods we eat (and don't); ideas about age, ethnicity, race, gender, and physical disability; health, illness, and healing; and much else besides. The challenge is learning how to read the code.

Culture Goes Public

The term "culture" suggests something—my culture, your culture—that is our unique and valuable heritage. In fact, this way of looking at things owes a great deal to the influence of early-twentieth-century cultural anthropology, and most particularly to the influence of Franz Boas (1858–1942) and his students. As mentioned above, Ruth Benedict (1887–1948) was one of these students, and her *Patterns of Culture* is a foundational work of North American anthropology. It was this book, more than any other, that popularized the modern culture concept. Her aim—like Margaret Mead's—was to get her largely American readership to think more clearly about their own society by presenting examples of very different ways of doing things. Throughout her career she was, like other Boasians, also a critic of racism and the race concept.

Benedict was a published poet and conceived of culture in terms of form, theme, configuration, and pattern—as being made up of related elements in much the same way as language itself is, or a poem, or an artistic style. She compared cultural traits with the fundamental meaningful units of a spoken language (phonemes): the human vocal apparatus can produce an indefinite number of sounds, but a given language selects only a few of them and places them in a particular order in relation to one

PLATE 6.3 Ruth Benedict

another. Meaningful speech is the result. It's the same, Benedict (1959: 23) thought, with culture: "It is in cultural life as it is in speech; selection is the prime necessity." Out of a vast range of possibility, a given culture selects only some elements for emphasis (see Darnell 2001: 191–200).

As a more recent anthropologist put it, the analysis of culture is "not an experimental science in search of law, but an interpretive one in search of meaning" (Geertz 1973: 5). However, that assertion leaves hanging the problem of validity. How are we to decide whether a particular interpretation is satisfying, that it fits the evidence and feels "right"? Interpretation involves the search for relationships between cultural elements. Benedict believed that so-called primitive cultures allow such patterns to be seen with greater clarity than in complex modern societies: "They are a laboratory in which we may study the diversity of human institutions. With their comparative isolation, many primitive regions have had centuries in which to elaborate the cultural themes they have made their own…. It is the only laboratory of social forms that we have or shall have" (Benedict 1959: 17). She thought that if a society has been left in relative isolation for long enough, it would tend to assume a more or less stable and integrated form, and to impress itself upon the very psyches of the people who share it: "A culture, like an individual, is a more or less consistent pattern of thought and action" (1959: 46). Following this logic, along with a given cultural pattern there should also be a preferred personality type.

It was also recognized that some people just don't fit in, and Benedict had a good deal to say about their fate. The deviant "is the representative of that arc of human capacities that is not capitalized in his culture. In proportion as his civilization has committed itself to a direction alien to him, he will be the sufferer" (1959: 25). She had "homosexuals" particularly in mind, but she noted that how sexuality is regarded varies considerably from society to society along that great "arc" of human possibility (Benedict 1959: 262–65; see also Foucault 1988, 1990). For example, some Native North American societies had an honored role for the *berdache*—cross-dressing men. Benedict was also familiar with the highly elaborate artistic traditions, myths, and formal ritual practices of the town-dwelling Puebloan peoples of the American Southwest. She thought that they are all connected together as expressions of an underlying pattern that turns up in every facet of life: a culture "whose delight is in formality and whose way of life is the way of measure and of sobriety" (Benedict 1959: 129).

The other case studies in *Patterns of Culture* receive similar treatment, but Benedict's most satisfying study of a cultural pattern came in her last major work, *The Chrysanthemum and the Sword* (1946), which wasn't about a "primitive" society at all, but about Japan. It was written during World War II and had been commissioned by the government to help Americans understand their exotic adversary. Since Benedict couldn't actually visit Japan, she used published historical and ethnographic sources, novels, memoirs, local informants in New York, and Japanese art—particularly cinema—to get at the inner logic of Japanese culture. She saw the way the Japanese conducted their war not "as a military problem but as a cultural problem" (Benedict 2005: 5). Japanese soldiers would rather die than surrender.

She found that she had to consider history, religion, family life, and fundamental concepts governing social relationships, particularly concepts relating to indebtedness and social hierarchy—what we owe to others and what they owe to us: "righteousness in Japan depends upon recognition of one's place in the great network of mutual indebtedness that embraces both one's forebears and one's contemporaries" (2005: 98–99). It is as if the Japanese had taken the principle of reciprocity to its greatest extreme: each person calculating the favor given and received and being deeply anxious about whether there is an even balance. Failure results in loss of face and in deep shame that in some cases can only be counterbalanced by suicide.

Benedict placed one Japanese word—*on*—at the core of her analysis. She impressionistically defined the word as "a load, an indebtedness, a burden, which one carries as best one may" (2005: 99). In her view, the Japanese saw no gift as free, and therefore they went to great lengths to avoid situations that might create imbalance. An elaborate and formal code of manners suppresses self-assertion for the sake of smooth social relations. Bowing correctly is an element in this pattern of etiquette—of *habitus*. Respect has degrees, and getting it right is as important as it is difficult. The truly successful person is one who knows how to balance all the obligations that emerge in social life, in addition to those that one is born with, such as obligations to one's parents: "The tensions that are thus generated are enormous, and they express themselves in a high level of aspiration which has made Japan … a great power in the world. But these tensions are a heavy strain upon the individual" (2005: 293).

Patterns of Culture and *The Chrysanthemum and the Sword* were not based on Benedict's own fieldwork; her examples have a static quality and have been criticized for it. We see what Benedict takes to be the patterns, but not the living societies themselves, actual people in real situations. These works are quite old now; both anthropology and the world have moved on. Nevertheless, her books provided an important example of how to go about engaging in cultural analysis. But it should be remembered that "cultures" are abstractions and never reveal themselves directly; their contents and themes are a matter of interpretation. The culture concept, as we now understand it, arose out of the study of relatively isolated tribal societies. But what about vast "multicultural" societies such as Canada, the United States, and the globalized world of the Internet? Social formations like these are of a different order entirely. Anthropologists work in local contexts, while keeping in mind the global processes that surround them. You will learn more about the current status of the culture concept in our next chapter. Meanwhile, we will consider the importance of context itself.

PLATE 6.4 President Obama and Emperor Akihito

Meaning in Context

We've said that culture is sometimes compared to language. Of course, language itself is an *aspect* of culture, but this analogy has much broader implications. Any ordinary language has a lexicon and a grammar: a vocabulary and some general and usually unconscious principles that guide the formation of meaningful utterances. From this point of view culture and history are behind everything that we say, or even *can* say. But there's more to it than this. "Meaning" is context-dependent: if you want to know what someone *really means* by what they say or do, the overall situation must be taken into account. Meaning, in other words, has a sociological dimension.

Bronislaw Malinowski (1884–1942) was very interested in language and collected many Native texts during his fieldwork in the southwest Pacific; many of these related to magical practices and were very obscure, metaphorical, and difficult to translate. In keeping with his brand of functionalism, he focused on what such utterances were aimed at actually accomplishing: getting yams to grow, getting canoes to sail successfully, keeping enemies at bay, etc. As he put it, "a statement, spoken in real life, is never detached from the situation in which it has been uttered. For each verbal statement ... has the aim and function of expressing some thought or feeling actual at that moment and in that situation" (Malinowski 1947: 307; see Malinowski 1954). It is part of the ongoing flow of social life, and its meaning depends on where it stands in relation both to local circumstances and to the wider cultural pattern. That is all a bit abstract, so a couple of examples will help to illustrate the principle.

Who's the Witch?

Sir Edward Evans-Pritchard (1902–73) was a contemporary of Audrey Richards and, like her, had been a student at the London School of Economics, where he inevitably came under Malinowski's influence. E-P (as he was known) didn't much like Malinowski; nevertheless, he applied a contextual approach to the understanding of witchcraft beliefs among the Azande, a people who overlap the borders of what are now the Republic of South Sudan, the Central African Republic, and the Democratic Republic of the Congo. The product of this research was his classic study *Witchcraft, Oracles and Magic among the Azande* (1937). In addition to an ethnographic contribution to what had been a neglected subject, the book is philosophically important because of the **epistemological** questions it raises—questions about social experience and the limits of knowledge.

It's fair to say that E-P wrote *the* book on witchcraft; after him the entire subject appeared in a different light. What was earlier dismissed as primitive superstition could now be viewed as a rational approach to the world, once the underlying premises were understood (see Wilson 1970). Evans-Pritchard presented the Azande as not all that different from ourselves. He said that his interpretations emerged from what Zande people did and thought about the difficult situations they frequently found themselves in—chronic illness, the problems of getting by in economically marginal conditions, the envy, jealousy, and petty quarrels of village life: matters of life and death to them. Underlying all this was the assumption that most misfortune can be accounted for by human ill-will. However, E-P stressed that this does not mean that the Azande have no clue about natural causes, but merely that they add another element—witchcraft—to their explanation of misfortune. This doesn't mean that Zande beliefs about witchcraft were *true*, but they were reasonable under the circumstances. This is true of all anthropological studies of religion or belief—the aim is to understand both what these beliefs mean to the people who value them, and what role they play in society.

In 1937, Zande witchcraft was held to be due to an intrinsic "mystical" power that some people had, perhaps even without knowing it. Where we might see fate or bad luck, the Azande suspected the hostility of those close by—neighbors, even family members: "In a study of Zande witchcraft, we must bear in mind, firstly, that the notion is a function of situations of misfortune, and, secondly, that it is a function of personal relations" (Evans-Pritchard 1937: 106). In other words, it is a function of

PLATE 6.5 Sir Edward Evans-Pritchard

context. Unlike earlier times in Europe where there was a well-developed theology of witchcraft, in Zandeland in the 1930s there was only the application of specific ideas in specific circumstances, such as particular cases of illness or crop failure; they had no Devil, no general principle of "evil" to explain witchcraft, and not much of an idea about God either. In Europe the presence of absolute concepts such as "good" and "evil," or God and the Devil, helped to account for the ferocity of witchcraft prosecutions; witches violated the cosmic order itself. Azande were only interested in sniffing out particular witches. Nevertheless, even without such concepts, Zande witchcraft beliefs contained an implicit moral philosophy—about what kind of person it's good to be, about the circumstances that generate ill-will, and about what it takes to maintain or restore social balance. They had a **sociocentric theory** of why bad things happen: looking for causes internal to society, rather than to impersonal notions such as fate or physical causality.

Coping with misfortune therefore involves determining *who* is behind it and bringing the matter out into the open. That is where Zande "oracles" came in. These were technical procedures that could sniff out the truth, most famously the "poison oracle," which worked by putting poison down a chicken's gullet and posing yes-or-no questions to it, for example: "if X is innocent chicken live, if X is guilty chicken die," and so on. The poison itself, extracted from a forest plant, was regarded as an impartial judge: "If you press a Zande to explain how the poison oracle can see far-off things he will say that its *mbisimo*, its soul, sees them." However, "in saying that the poison oracle has a *mbisimo* Zande means little more than 'it does something' or, as we could say, 'it is dynamic.' You ask them how it works and they reply, 'It has a soul.' If you were to ask them how they know it has a 'soul,' they would reply that they know because it works" (1937: 320–21).

Evans-Pritchard filled his notebooks with observations like these from everyday life; he also sought out the experts—so-called witch doctors and the oracle specialists. He used his observations to ask some profound questions about different systems of thought and how to bridge them. As he said, we are

> not content to know bare facts but seek to discover uniformities in them and to relate one fact to another. Only by so doing can we understand Zande beliefs and compare them with our own. Is Zande thought so different from ours that we can only describe their speech and actions without comprehending them, or is it essentially like our own though expressed in an idiom to which we are unaccustomed? What are the motives of Zande behavior? What are their notions of reality? How are these motives and notions expressed in custom? … I have always asked myself "How?" rather than "Why?" I have tried to explain a fact by citing other facts from the same culture and by noting interdependencies between facts.… My interpretations are contained in the facts themselves, for I have described the facts in such a way that the interpretations emerge as part of the description. (Evans-Pritchard 1937: 4–5)

So let us take a particular case. Someone is suspected of witchcraft; this possibility is based on the assumption that witchcraft is *real* and operates in a certain way, perhaps even as an expression of *unconscious* hostility. When put together systematically, such facts indicate patterns of stress in the community and point toward the *kinds* of people likely to come under suspicion (which could be either men or women). Suspicion is one thing, proof another, and so we turn to an oracle to settle the matter. If the answer seems straightforward, then an accusation is made and the supposedly guilty party is warned to back off and make compensation. However, no one freely *admits* to witchcraft, and so it's all really a question of perspective and always contains an element of ambiguity. Such events reveal the sociological dynamics of the society in question, and historians have used that insight to explore witchcraft in the European past, using records of court proceedings and other written sources.

Evans-Pritchard approached his problem "by noting interdependencies between facts." These facts emerged in particular situations or in response to specific questions. As noted above, there was no theology of witchcraft; no Zande could put things together in the way E-P did in his book, or for that matter in any other way. They had a tendency to reason in a circle when challenged to explain their worldview. Their approach was practical, not theoretical. Is witchcraft at work? If yes, what do we do about it? It proved difficult to get them to consider, much less question, the assumptions that guided their day-to-day activities.

And here's the philosophical issue. We talk today about "thinking outside the box." What we mean by this is getting beyond our conventional way of doing things and acting in an innovative and creative manner. But what if we don't know that we're *in* a box? The situation that Evans-Pritchard describes is something like that. He stood outside the Zande world looking in; witchcraft was real enough for the Azande, but *for him* witchcraft did not and could not exist in some ultimately real sense. The universe as he understood it just doesn't work that way; it doesn't have forces that operate in the same way that witchcraft operates, though it has invisible forces of other kinds (gravity, electricity, etc).

Why couldn't the Azande see the flaws in their own reasoning? Their oracles sometimes contradicted each other; a verdict of witchcraft might be given, accepted by the accused, rituals performed, and the patient died anyway; medicines and magic were used to alleviate suffering, but the suffering continued. On the other hand, sometimes such measures seemed to work. As with us, most illness episodes ended with the patient getting better, no matter what was done about it in the meantime. Success counts much more than failure. Failure could be explained away, but *success* always validated the Zande way of doing things:

> Witchcraft, oracles, and magic form an intellectually coherent system. Each explains and proves the other. Death is proof of witchcraft. It is avenged by magic. The achievement of vengeance-magic is proved by the poison oracle.... Azande often observe that a medicine is unsuccessful, but they do

not generalize their observations. Contradictions between their beliefs are not noticed by the Azande because the beliefs are not all present at the same time but function in different situations. They are therefore not brought into opposition. (Evans-Pritchard 1937: 475)

The Azande appear to have been stuck inside a particular worldview, a **paradigm** full of unconscious assumptions about how the world works. We owe the popularity of this concept to the historian and philosopher of science Thomas Kuhn (1922–96), who—in his famous book *The Structure of Scientific Revolutions* (Kuhn 1962; see Kuhn 1970)—examined how scientific theories constrain and shape knowledge. But, as his title implies, he was also interested in analyzing the circumstances that lead to thinking *outside* the box—resulting in a *paradigm shift*. He suggested that after such a thing happens there is a sense in which we now live in a *different world* than we did before. The outlines of the box have changed. With the onset of colonial rule, missionaries and British government servants made it their business to change the outlines of the Zande world, in order, among other things, to convince these people that witchcraft is unreal.

Belief Is the Least of It

It's not easy to see a process that is usually evident only after the fact, but anthropologists are sometimes in a position to witness and even experience something like this personally. The missionaries of various faiths are professional paradigm shifters. They aim to change people and the societies of which they are a part for the sake of some greater good—personal salvation, social justice, political assimilation, or whatever it might be. There have been anthropological studies of missionaries themselves, which only seems fair.

However, what we're concerned with here is how one process—the conversion experience—plays out in individual lives. Our example comes from a contemporary anthropologist, Tanya Luhrmann (b. 1959), who has worked among American evangelical Christians in order to understand what conversion is like, how it comes about, and what changes it leads to. But first some background.

In 1912 the great French sociologist Émile Durkheim published a highly influential book concerning the origin and nature of religion. It is called *The Elementary Forms of Religious Life*,[4] and it is one of the foundational works of social anthropology. The title is significant: by "elementary forms" Durkheim meant the most basic, the common denominator underlying *all* religious belief and practice ("primitive" in the sense of "original"). His method was anthropological. He reasoned that, if we could examine the "simplest" human society now known and study its religion, insight could be gained into the nature of religion in general. His example was Indigenous Australia.

Like Lewis Henry Morgan (1818–81) and many others of that time, Durkheim was a social evolutionist. And, like others, he believed that the Australians were at the bottom of the social evolutionary scale. He correlated social structure with religious practice. As we've mentioned, the Indigenous peoples were organized into totemic clans, each clan being symbolically identified with a living creature. In those days, a clan-based social system was seen as the structurally simplest form of human society, all others having evolved out of this basic form. Likewise totemism was seen as the simplest religion. But Australian clans were not isolated entities; they were part of wider societies based on precise marriage rules and elaborate ceremonials. Durkheim found that the Indigenous peoples used their own social life to provide a model for the universe in general. Human groups, animal species, and the natural landscape were brought together into a unified symbolic system of belief and practice, and all accounted for in stories about the journeys of the Dawn Beings (Durkheim and Mauss 1965).

PLATE 6.6 Émile Durkheim

Throughout his sociological career Durkheim pursued one consistent theme: the nature of the moral bond that ties people together into communities. His focus was not on *belief* but on religious *practice*, and he found the answer to the problem of religious origins to lie in religious *feeling*. It is essentially a social-psychological theory: the psychology of crowds. By 1912 there was already a good deal of ethnographic material available on Indigenous Australian religion and ritual (see Stocking 1995: 84–98). The early ethnographers had seen that much Indigenous ritual was accompanied by great emotional displays. Durkheim maintained that when people act collectively in groups, they feel the presence of a life-enhancing power that is experienced as originating outside themselves (think of emotionally charged religious rituals, political rallies, rock concerts, etc.). Following this logic, the sense of transcendental power doesn't come from beyond the world at all, but from within us as members of society.

But this is a sociological perspective, and "primitive" peoples (like most of us, most of the time) aren't in a position to see things this way; instead they *project* the emotions they experience in collective ritual onto their totemic symbols. Those symbols are then experienced as the *source* of the power their worshippers feel. Durkheim appropriated a Polynesian word—***mana***—to characterize this free-floating power, which he found to be "the distinguishing characteristic of any sacred being" (Durkheim 1995: 59). Something like this power is present no matter whether the object in question is a totem, the flag of a modern nation state, or any other symbol that inspires and articulates collective action. Living persons can also seem to contain such power: Polynesian royalty, the Queen, the Dalai Lama, the Pope—any charismatic source of spiritual authority.

As Durkheim said, "the whole social world seems populated with forces that in reality exist only in our minds. We know what the flag is for the soldier, but in itself it is only a bit of cloth" (1995: 228). Likewise, the totem symbol is the flag of the clan, even though to an outsider it's only a carved stick. For Durkheim these are all constructs of our collective imagination and—as a sociologist—he wanted to know how they arise and what gives them their power. But there's a problem here: since he was concerned with group dynamics and religious expression, Durkheim did not really consider the "insiders' perspective": that of the Indigenous Australians themselves. Of course, he was an armchair scholar and the sources he consulted didn't consider this perspective either. Even though the sources are often good on a descriptive level, they are from the perspective of an outsider looking in. The problem boils down to the question of what it is like to actually *live* in an Indigenous world in which "man, society and nature, and past, present and future, are at one together within a unitary system" (see Stanner 1979).

Much more could be said about Durkheim, but let's return to Tanya Luhrmann, who did indeed try to see the evangelical world from within. When discussing her work we are not referring to a distant land or time, but to something around us that is of great present-day social and personal importance. A considerable portion of the

American adult population identify as evangelical Christians. The evangelical component in the Canadian religious scene is less prominent, but still significant.

As we have seen, anthropology is engaged in mediating between cultural worlds. In this case, Luhrmann set out to bridge a cultural divide—an "abyss" as she sees it—between evangelicals and those who know little about them. This divide is often seen in terms of the so-called culture wars—"conservatives" on one side and "liberals" on the other. The debate is fueled by hot-button political and moral issues such as gay marriage, abortion, and evolution versus divine creation. Luhrmann's intent was to get beneath the stereotypes and find out what the evangelical world looks like from within:

> The tool of an anthropologists' trade is careful observation—participant observation, a kind of naturalist's craft in which one watches what people do and listens to what they say and infers from that how they come to see and know their world.... I watched and I listened, and I tried to understand as an outsider how an insider to this evangelical world was able to experience God as real. Members of these churches became my friends and confidants. I liked them. I thought they liked me. They knew I was an anthropologist, and as they came to know me, they became comfortable talking with me at length about God. I have sought to understand what they said. (Luhrmann 2012: xx)

The outcome was her 2012 book *When God Talks Back: Understanding the American Evangelical Relationship with God*. She recognized that the evangelical community is huge and diverse, so she focused on one rapidly growing segment of it that emphasizes establishing a personal relationship with God—not as judge but as a friend and companion, though one who sometimes dishes out tough love: "God answers every prayer, but sometimes the answer is no" (2012: 270). Her fieldwork took place in a number of churches in Chicago and Southern California, where her informants often expressed "an intense desire to experience personally a God who is as present now as when Christ walked among his followers in Galilee" (2012: 13).

Evangelical Christianity is *experiential*: feeling should accompany belief. The roots of this religious tradition go back to the Protestant Reformation and, before that, to the earliest days of the Church. Conversion experiences are actively sought, and the imagery is that of *rebirth*: "Very truly I tell you, no one can see the kingdom of God unless they are born again.... The wind blows wherever it pleases. You hear its sound, but you cannot tell where it comes from or where it is going. So it is with everyone born of the Spirit" (John 3: 3–8). Luhrmann therefore didn't think it was enough just to understand what her informants were telling her, but also to make an attempt to feel what they felt (see Luhrmann 2013). It's an unusual stance, because strictly speaking she wasn't a believer at all. This is where Durkheim enters the story. As discussed above, he gave priority to religious practice and placed belief in a secondary role. Such a view is the reverse of how we usually think about such things, but it is consistent with Durkheim's emphasis on ritual and the emotional bonds of community life.

Luhrmann followed Durkheim's lead and investigated the social contexts in which church members develop the sense that divine power is at work among and within them (Luhrmann 2012: 279). Of course, they had to profess belief in certain things as well, particularly the truth of the Christian Bible. The focus of their practice was making the stories in the Bible come alive in their own lives—bringing past and present together in real time. They did this through Bible readings, spiritual retreats, Christian-oriented self-help books, testifying before one another in church, and above all in prayer. It could become very emotional: "people often talk about the Holy Spirit as if it is substance, as if it flows through the body like water through a chute.... People describe feeling a great surge of power running through their bodies" (2012: 12, 146). Indeed, Luhrmann found herself weeping when the people around her wept. Church members learned to interpret some subjective experiences as God speaking back to them, and certain events as being due to God's direct intervention in worldly events. As one informant put it, "patterns and coincidences are not random.... A huge part of hearing God, for me, is just being able to recognize patterns" (2012: 56–57). Correlation becomes cause; you pray and something significant happens; your prayer is seen as helping to bring the event about—this is evidence that God was listening, and that becomes a story worth telling to others. Experience reinforces belief, and vice versa.

Certain experiences seemed to come from "somewhere else":[5] "The central principle was identifying the 'not-me' experience: a thought or image or sensation that one felt was not one's own. If a thought felt spontaneous and unsought, it was more likely to be identified as God's" (2012: 67). Luhrmann suspended whatever disbelief she may have felt, and followed along with her informants and friends in all of this. In the end she found herself somewhere between cultural worlds: "I began to understand parts of the church teaching not just as so many intellectual doctrinal commitments but as having an emotional logic of their own" (2012: 325). "For these Christians, religion is not about explaining reality but about transforming it: making it possible to trust that the world is good, despite ample evidence to the contrary" (2012: 295):

> Knowing God involves training, and it involves interpretation. Each faith … forms its own culture, its own way of seeing the world, and as people acquire the knowledge and the practices through which they come to know that God, the most intimate aspects of the way they experience their everyday world change. Those who learn to take God seriously do not simply interpret the world differently from those who have not done so. They have different evidence for what is true. In some deep and fundamental way, as a result of their practices, they live in different worlds. (Luhrmann 2012: 226)

The Dying and Reborn God

Luhrmann's informants sought to incorporate the teachings of an ancient text into their daily lives. This occurred on an individual psychological level, and also within the rituals of their communities. Much anthropological effort has gone into exploring processes of this sort.

When we go back and examine what happened to Captain Cook (see Chapter 1), it's evident that the Hawaiians interpreted his arrival in terms of their own mythic understandings about the world. Cook's ships arrived from the Bering Sea in late 1778 during the Hawaiian New Year festival, the time after the winter solstice when the rains come to the Big Island and the days start to grow longer. His presence was associated with the god Lono, and he was honored accordingly. When the *Resolution* and *Discovery* appeared off the north end of the island, the image of Lono was being carried around the island in a clockwise direction, stopping at each coastal community along the way: "The season of Lono's passage, period of winter rains, is the transition from 'the dying time of the year' to the time when 'bearing things become fruitful'" (Sahlins 1985: 115). Cook's ships followed the same course and finally ended up at Kealakekua Bay where the king was also in residence. Everything seemed to fit the association of Cook with Lono.

He and his crew were treated royally, and—as we see from Lieutenant King's account—Cook himself went along with the role he was assigned. In a sense Cook *became* the god: "a form of the god who makes the earth bear fruit for mankind: a seminal god, patron of the peaceful and agricultural arts" (Sahlins 1985: 131). The British soon left to resume their explorations on the Northwest Coast. That was also an appropriate moment—close to the same time that the king of Hawai'i was to ceremonially open the agricultural year, accompanied by human sacrifice. Cook's movements still corresponded with the ritual cycle, but the weather intervened, the foremast on the *Resolution* was broken, and the ships returned to the Bay. That was not an opportune time at all: "Unlike his arrival, his return was generally unintelligible and unwanted.... And things fell apart" (Sahlins 1995: 79).

After the fight on the beach, Cook's body was dismembered, only some of the parts recovered for burial at sea. Before they left for a second time, the British were mystified by questions the Hawaiians asked about whether Lono would return again the following year. Evidently the idea of a dying and reborn god was a familiar notion to them. Missionaries later reported that "the relics of Cook were ... worshipped in a temple of rono ... of whom the people had a notion that the British navigator was the representative, if not the incarnation of him" (Sahlins 1985: 102). In his history of the Hawaiian Islands, Daws writes, "It was a curious fate for him to have suffered.... Natives at Kealakekua Bay and elsewhere looked back on Cook's death with a mixture of genuine sorrow and mournful relish, the kind of feeling shared by people who have survived a great catastrophe and cannot stop talking about it. Even as late as [the mid-nineteenth century], old Hawaiians would claim to have seen Cook killed, and even after that, storytellers could command fascinated audiences for their tales of the return of Lono long ago" (Daws 1968: 24).

In 1820 the first missionaries—Protestants from New England—arrived in Hawai'i, stimulated by what they had heard of the Islands and by Native Hawaiians whom they had met in Boston. They went about preaching the gospel, and by 1822 they had built a church in Kailua on the Big Island, which stands to this day. They were particularly concerned about sexual immorality, especially the famous *hula* dance that had been such a part of the celebrations surrounding the god Lono. The Kingdom of Hawai'i became officially Christian and the old taboos were abolished; in time the Native Hawaiian population came to be greatly outnumbered by immigrants from many parts of the world, and the Kingdom itself was overthrown by the Americans. This illustrates that history can shift its meaning depending on one's perspective. Also in Chapter 1 we mentioned the Hawaiian gentleman who was giving out pamphlets protesting what he took to be the illegal American occupation of the islands. Recall that on his t-shirt were the words "My people killed Captain Cook." Here Cook was no longer considered a god, but rather associated with the beginnings of foreign domination.

Conclusion

It's good to keep in mind the very broad definition of "culture" advanced by Edward Burnett Tylor: "that complex whole which includes knowledge, belief, art, morals, law, custom, and any other capabilities and habits acquired by man as a member of society." His definition points to the truth of Lévi-Strauss's comment that society is the natural human condition. Subtract all of the things in Tylor's list and ask yourself what would be left over? Seen in this way, *all* human societies are "civilized," no matter how different they may appear on the surface.

Of course Tylor's definition is too broad to be of practical use. It does, however, call attention to the wide range of phenomena that anthropologists have been concerned with. But when we focus in more closely we need sharper concepts, and this chapter has explored some of the ways in which the culture concept has been applied to specific problems—from "techniques of the body" to Japanese etiquette, Zande witchcraft, and the death of Captain Cook.

Chapter 10 continues this discussion and expands it to look at other aspects of what the culture concept is used for—both by anthropologists and in society at large. We will be taking a close look at several cases in which the culture concept has been used politically. Though anthropologists are largely responsible for its development and elaboration, this notion is now public property. And it's not a *neutral* concept, some kind of disembodied abstraction. The culture concept evolved in response to particular circumstances of time and place, and in large measure this had a political aim—to show that all human beings are in this world together, that we are all civilized beings, and—as Darwin thought—that we are all one species under the skin.

Notes

1   One of Sacks's essays, *Awakenings*, was used as the basis for a 1990 film with Robert de Niro, Robin Williams, and Julie Kavner. It tells the story of what happens when a patient in a catatonic state is restored to consciousness after years "away."

2   The French anthropologist Pierre Bourdieu (1930–2002) made much use of the concept of *habitus*, which he regarded as an "embodied competence" that becomes manifest in the flow of social life and in the context of particular situations (Bourdieu 1977).

3   There is an entertaining YouTube video of Miss Post speaking on this subject in 1947, along with examples of what and what not to do at the dinner table: http://www.youtube.com/watch?v=HAPcnZAJanE.

4   *Les Formes élémentaires de la vie religieuse.* As we pointed out in Chapter 1, the term "sociology" was invented by the French philosopher and historian of science Auguste Comte (1798–1857). Durkheim's brand of sociology included what we now think of as socio-cultural anthropology. Also see Chapter 2 for his influence on the development of social anthropology.

5   Experiences that seem to come from outside the conscious self led Sigmund Freud (1856–1939) to invent psychoanalysis. It is a method of symbolic interpretation, finding meaning beneath what often seems like nonsense. Dreams are one example, as are delusions and hallucinations at the other end of the spectrum. There is also a considerable anthropological literature on spirit-possession phenomena in which a person may seemingly be "taken over" by an external being. Anthropologists have looked into the social circumstances of the possessed, and the procedures that lead to the identification of the troubling spirit.

Study Questions

1   Summarize the various definitions of culture referenced in this chapter.
2   Temple Grandin once said that she feels like an "anthropologist on Mars." Explain how autism spectrum disorder might lead her to use this metaphor.
3   What did Mauss mean by the terms *bodily techniques* and *habitus*? Use examples from the text and from your own culture to illustrate these terms.
4   Explain how etiquette and the concept of *the gift* are related to Mauss's concept of *habitus*, using examples from the text.
5   Outline Benedict's perspective on cultural patterns and explain why she believed so-called primitive societies were central to understanding cultural patterns.

6   Explain how our understanding of language can be used to understand culture as a system of meaning.

7   Summarize Evans-Pritchard's findings on Zande witchcraft and oracles. Explain how this worldview is considered sociocentric.

8   Outline Durkheim's study of religious practice. Why did he focus on religious *practice* rather than *belief*? What is meant by the term *mana*?

9   How did Luhrmann's study of American Evangelicals differ from other anthropological studies of religion? Compare and contrast her methods and findings with those of Evans-Pritchard and Durkheim.

Discussion Questions

1   Why is defining culture important to society? Why is it such a difficult concept to define? What is meant by the phrase "society is the natural human condition"?

2   Benedict's major works were not based on fieldwork. Evans-Pritchard and Durkheim studied culture from the position of outsiders. Luhrmann became a member of the community she studied, but was not a true believer. How valid and accurate can an outsider's portrait of a culture be? Can we ever really define, describe, or explain another culture fully, or even our own?

3   Consider the assertion that with the advancement of science and technology, the place of religion and religious beliefs will gradually fade away. Do you think this is the case? Why or why not?

CHAPTER 7

Health, Medicine, and Society

LEARNING OBJECTIVES

At the end of this chapter, students should be able to

- describe the relationship between subsistence and health through the example of the Ju/'hoansi people;
- define medical anthropology and explain when it emerged as a sub-discipline;
- describe the short-falls of a traditional medical anthropological approach to understanding health and illness;
- explain the difference between applied medical anthropology and theoretical medical anthropology;
- define interpretive medical anthropology;
- explain the three bodies approach and how it challenged the paradigm of traditional medical anthropology;
- summarize the malaria case study and identify the objective of this research;
- define bio-cultural anthropology;
- describe how a bio-cultural approach led to an understanding of sickle cell anemia in Liberia;
- define critical medical anthropology and discuss this approach in relation to the study of the cholera epidemic in Venezuela; and
- describe the differences and similarities between interpretive medical anthropology, bio-cultural anthropology, and critical medical anthropology.

KEY TERMS

applied medical
    anthropology
bio-cultural approach
Cartesian dualism

critical approach
interpretive approach
medical anthropology
medicalization

theoretical medical
    anthropology
universal health care

Introduction

In this chapter we will introduce different contemporary anthropological approaches to understanding health and illness. Health is a predominant social category in all societies: how we define well-being and illness, how we go about maintaining and treating different conditions, who society considers an expert in the field, and what type of information we base our understandings on are all cultural constructs that vary drastically from one society to the next, and are areas of study that anthropologists have long been interested in. Through a number of examples and ethnographic studies, we will explore how anthropologists approach the study of health, and how their research of the local contributes to a critical and informed understanding of health on a global scale. The ethnographies that we will consider illustrate how the anthropologists' theoretical starting point informs the methods they use to collect data, the data they collect, how it is analyzed, and of course, the conclusions they make. Remember—theory steers perception.

Emergence of a Sub-Discipline

Medical anthropology is a sub-field of anthropology that has become increasingly prominent over the last three decades. It employs anthropological theory and method in exploring understandings of health and health care from a cross-cultural perspective. According to the Society for Medical Anthropology, "Medical anthropologists examine how the health of individuals, larger social formations, and the environment are affected by interrelationships between humans and other species; cultural norms and social institutions; micro and macro politics; and forces of globalization as each of these affects local worlds." Anthropologists have been interested in health and illness since the inception of the discipline. A popular area of study for many early anthropologists was considering the characteristics and health status of societies from different systems of organization, whether a band, tribe, chiefdom or industrial nation-state.

One of the most often-cited examples of this research is that exploring the hunter-gatherer way of life of the Ju/'hoansi people of the Kalahari Desert in southern Africa. Despite living in the harsh conditions of the Kalahari desert, the Ju/'hoansi spent only 20 hours per week foraging to establish a diet that was high in protein, fiber, fruits and vegetables and low in carbohydrates, sugar and fat (Cashdan 1989). The nutritional quality of the Ju/'hoansi's diet surpassed the nutritional quality of diets found in "wealthier" agricultural and industrial countries. As you might imagine, they enjoyed excellent fitness due to the large number of kilometers covered while collecting food and hunting. They also lived in a fairly egalitarian society where men and women enjoyed equal status. Their lives were not without health risks, however. Hunting was a dangerous activity, and encounters with wild animals were frequent. As foragers, the Ju/'hoansi were required to move frequently so as not to exhaust their food sources, which was all but impossible for those who were elderly or ill. Today, there are only around 1,400 Ju/'hoansi left, and they continue to live on their ancestral land which is now Namibia (Pfaffe 2003). A century of colonialism, occupation and development schemes have left the Ju/'hoansi in a depressed state that bears little resemblance to what some anthropologists had titled "the original affluent society." As is evident here, health is a component of social life that is directly related to and reliant upon other social categories, including class, gender, and social organization.

Medical anthropology as a sub-field did not emerge until the aftermath of World War II, when a heightened awareness of world-wide suffering and ill-health swept Europe and North America. With this awareness came a sense of responsibility and hope that advances in biomedicine could at least control and at best eliminate major health crises. The role of the medical anthropologist in this effort was to partner with international organizations such as the World Health Organization (WHO) and UNICEF to show the world "the effectiveness of biomedicine and modern public health methods (e.g., the health value of boiling water before drinking it), while addressing contextual and cultural barriers to change, [so that] people would readily adopt new ways and the threat of many diseases would begin to diminish" (Singer and Erickson 2011: 1). Ethnographic data that was once viewed as interesting and descriptive now proved invaluable to organizations attempting to implement health programs or interventions (Sobo 2011). Donald Joralemon describes an early example of ethnographic work in Guatemala, where efforts to implement a child nutrition program sponsored by the WHO, the Pan American Sanitary Bureau and the Institute of Nutrition of Central America and Panama (INCAP) were failing. Joralemon writes:

> Local ethnographic work revealed that community members interpreted INCAP as a communist organization, a very serious assessment given the country's right-wing ruling class and its violent anticommunism campaigns. They also considered the project's requirement that children have blood samples taken as detrimental to their health. Guatemalan Indians believe that blood is a non-regenerative vital fluid, so the samples were seen as a permanent loss of strength. In addition, the idea that outsiders would wish to fatten up the children of the village was linked to popular mythology, dating back to the time of the conquest, that whites capture Indian children to eat them. There were many good reasons, from the viewpoint of the villagers, to keep children out of the program. (Joralemon 2016: 9)

Unfortunately, 70 years after this first swell of enthusiasm, the majority of the world's population continues to experience extreme health disparities with limited access to treatment and care, with the most poor and marginalized suffering from malnutrition and infectious diseases. Meanwhile, the United States and other wealthy countries have experienced a growth in life expectancy of nearly 30 years (Biehl and Petryna 2013).

Why did the efforts of those early medical anthropologists fall so short? Health is multifaceted and complex, yet the approach taken by these anthropologists operated on somewhat simplistic assumptions about "belief" and "culture." A heightened awareness of the power of culture and belief diverted the attention of those working in the field (anthropologist and other) away from structural issues such as poverty and discrimination. The assumption that people act in a manner solely directed by their belief system fails to recognize the impact of powerful external forces. For example, a community with strong beliefs around the connection between sorcery and illness in children may see the need for medical interventions (be they biomedical or community based), but to receive this help would require walking 5 kilometers to the nearest clinic. While belief in a particular health system influences how one treats illness, the issue of access plays a significant role in the ability to receive care.

While qualitative methods such as interviews and observations used to collect illness narratives are effective in understanding ill health and suffering, these narratives are not static and unchanging, and will be expressed differently depending on the context and the audience. People do not explicitly or uniformly describe their values and belief systems (Pool and Geissler 2005). For example, a college student might wake up one morning with a headache, vomiting, and exhaustion. To the professor of the class he is missing, the person might claim that he came down with a mysterious stomach bug rumored to be making its way through the dormitories. To his older brother whom he was supposed to meet for lunch, the student may make reference to having a few drinks the night before as well as the mysterious stomach bug ripping through the dorm. To his friends who accompanied him to the pub, no explanation for the illness may be needed. To understand the complexity of health and illness requires an investment in time and patience, and many early (and contemporary, for that matter) applied approaches were simply not rigorous enough to gain a thorough understanding of these multi-dimensional narratives. Finally, these early forays into the field by medical anthropologists were directed by the assumption that *belief* is not based in truth, unlike a biomedical understanding, which is anchored in fact. The biomedical approach was regarded as the standard to which everything else was measured and compared.

Early medical anthropologists believed that an abbreviated use of tried and true anthropological methods, including short stints of fieldwork and interviews, would give them the required knowledge to fully understand a people's relationship to health, and that this understanding would provide the missing link to implementing life-saving treatment and interventions (Pool and Geissler 2005). This "add anthropologist and stir" approach was inadequate to fully understand the complex structural, social, and political forces interacting to shape population health. Insights into the shortcomings of early applied medical anthropology have shaped the development of the in-demand sub-discipline over the last 50 years, and remain relevant to those practicing in the field today.

Contemporary Medical Anthropology

Today, medical anthropology is characterized by two dominant approaches that, while distinct in their focus, share the objective of an improved understanding of how people think about health and illness, and access care and support when in need. **Applied medical anthropology** operates with the goal of improving the health outcomes of a group, usually in collaboration with biomedical health practitioners. This stream is closely related to the early endeavors discussed above, albeit with an expanded understanding of the importance of structural and political forces. It remains a rapidly growing and in-demand field, particularly by non-governmental organizations (NGOs) doing work in the field of global health. **Theoretical medical anthropology**, on the other hand, aims to understand the how and why of medical systems in a particular context. The focus is less on collaboration with biomedical clinicians and more on investigating the worldview and actions of the people and practitioners, and the overall health system of particular communities. This is not to say that applied medical anthropologists do not seek an in-depth understanding of the belief systems and political landscape of the community with whom they are working, or that theoretical medical anthropologists do not support improved health outcomes of those they are studying. Rather, what distinguishes these approaches is their focus of inquiry, which we will explore in more detail below.

There are an array of theoretical perspectives that medical anthropologists subscribe to, and in the remainder of this chapter, we will consider three different studies informed by **interpretive, bio-cultural, and critical approaches**. As we have stated before, our choice of inclusion represents our interest as anthropologists, and is not meant to be a representation of the field of medical anthropology. Other theoretical approaches include ecological, evolutionary and ethno-medicine, and are well worth investigating through other sources.

Interpretive Medical Anthropology

An interpretive approach to medical anthropology considers how cultural beliefs and perceptions influence people's health and treatment of illness. Because anthropologists are their own research tool, they must be aware of how their own cultural beliefs may skew their interpretations of what they see unfolding before them or hear being described. Medical anthropology as a sub-discipline emerged largely from Western educated anthropologists, and as such, the discipline itself was formed along cultural lines anchored in a biomedical paradigm. This paradigm is informed by a **Cartesian dualism** whereby the mind and the body are separate entities. The Cartesian dualism has its roots in seventeenth-century philosophy and regards the body as a machine with individual parts that must operate together in order for the body to "work." The mind is but one component of that machine. This paradigm is culturally constructed, and far from universally shared.

Biomedicine, a branch of medicine that applies biology and physiology to understanding the body, is the dominant approach to investigating the health and disease of populations in Westernized countries. This epistemology is located firmly in the "hard" sciences, drawing on biology, anatomy, microbiology, genetics, and other related scientific fields to understand how the body works and what happens to the body when illness occurs. Among Western societies, biomedicine is the gold standard for maintaining society's health, and has led to thousands of medical breakthroughs that have improved the lives of millions, from the development and application of vaccinations to the elimination and control of the spread of disease, to the mending of broken limbs, to the use of radiation and chemotherapy to treat cancer.

Like all epistemologies, however, biomedicine is the product of the culture (beliefs, knowledge, etc.) and the time in which it is produced. A review of the discipline's past illustrates that this approach is as prone to misunderstanding and cultural bias as other approaches to understanding health. For example, during the Victorian era, female hysteria was a common medical diagnosis believed to be the result of women's inability to cope with the stress of modern life. The list of symptoms was long and all encompassing, meaning almost any ailment would fit the diagnosis. Symptoms included nervousness, sexual desire, loss of sexual desire, insomnia, shortness of breath and a tendency to cause trouble (Maines 1998), among others. The treatments were as varied as the symptoms, and ranged from admittance to "insane asylums" to surgical hysterectomy (Fugh-Berman 1998). The practitioners of the day, however, believed that this was a serious medical condition requiring intervention and treatments. Needless to say, today's medical experts no longer believe "female hysteria" is a medical condition.

Medical anthropologists Nancy Scheper-Hughes and Margaret Lock argue that medical anthropology has been significantly shaped by a biomedical discourse. The biomedical approach is considered the norm by which other approaches—often classified as "beliefs"—are judged (Farmer and Good 1991). In their seminal work, *The Mindful Body: A Prolegomenon to Future Work in Medical Anthropology*, Scheper-Hughes and Lock call for a deconstruction of how the body and health are conceptualized in order to challenge the biomedical perspective that they assert the discipline relies upon.

In this interpretive approach, Scheper-Hughes and Lock are not attempting to improve a specific health outcome in conjunction with medical practitioners. The purpose of *The Mindful Body* is to suggest a paradigm for use by medical anthropologists that draws attention to *different* conceptualizations of the body, an approach that does not use a biomedical perspective as a comparator, but rather views biomedicine as one of many ways of understanding health and illness. To truly understand how people experience health, illness and the body, one must suspend assumptions about science and challenge notions of the Cartesian divide. Scheper-Hughes and Lock label this approach "Three Bodies," which we summarize below using examples from Western (as many of our readers will relate) and non-Western perspectives:

- **The Individual Body**—how "I" experience my body, which will be different when in good health and when in poor health. The Zinacanteco people from the Chiapas highlands in Mexico regard a person's "soul as having 13 divisible parts. Each time a person 'loses' one or more parts he or she becomes ill and a curing ceremony is held to retrieve the missing pieces" (Scheper-Hughes and Lock 1987). This is a very different perspective from a Western worldview, where illness occurs either in the body (physical) or in the mind (mental). People experience of health and illness and how they describe this experience is directly related to their conceptualization of the body, whether this is made up of 2 components or 13.
- **The Social Body**—the body is a symbol of social and structural relationships. Many cultures view nature, the body, and the dead as continually interacting and interrelated. Scheper-Hughes and Lock write that "[the body] is dependent on and vulnerable to the feelings, wishes, and actions of others, including spirits and dead ancestors. The body is not understood as a vast and complex machine, but rather as a miscro-cosm [*sic*] of the universe" (1987: 21). For example, the Subanen community in the Southern Philippines interprets the occurrence of natural disasters as punishment from the *Supreme Being* for the community members' failure to protect the lands' natural resources (Quilo et al. 2015). A relationship exists between the living body, the dead, and the environment. In contrast, Western narratives of the human body rely on descriptions that invoke machinery and production—individuals often describe themselves as "run down" and needing to "recharge." Rarely are references made to the individual body or ancestors when an earthquake hits a metropolitan area such as San Francisco.
- **The Body Politic**—the body is disciplined and controlled by social institutions; society produces the bodies that are needed to protect a certain way of life. For example, beginning in 1880, the Canadian government sponsored residential schools that Indigenous children were forced to attend, leaving their families and communities and suffering extreme physical, sexual, and mental abuse. The purpose of these schools was to assimilate Indigenous children into European-Canadian culture. The writings of French philosopher Michel Foucault probe the power dynamics between the state (i.e., through

institutions such as the prison system, hospitals, and schools) and the bodies of its citizens, and how the state serves to create and control these bodies through institutions and policies.

An interpretive approach to understanding health and illness begins with the person conducting the research, and insists that they consider their own personal and cultural assumptions about health and the body. The Three Bodies framework described above is not created with the intent of improving medication adherence for children with asthma, or better maternal outcomes for women in Kenya; rather, its purpose is to challenge anthropologists in the field to pay attention to the multitude of social relationships, cultural assumptions and beliefs, and economic and political factors that shape health and illness. Only then can anthropologists fully understand what they observe in front of them. This knowledge can then be used to inform the development of health education campaigns or adherence interventions. In the example that follows, we will see how interviews with mothers in Tanzania about their experience with children's fever illustrate a conceptualization of the individual and social body. An enhanced understanding of health in this context can then inform health education campaigns and strategies.

Malaria

In order to gain an understanding of how the wide range of social, economic, and cultural forces have impacted a community's health, research that positions the experiences and beliefs of people themselves at the forefront of analysis is key. Those dedicated to the field of global health face seemingly insurmountable obstacles in attempting to improve health conditions in low-income countries. While philanthropic organizations such as the Bill and Melinda Gates Foundation and the US President's Emergency Plan for AIDS Relief (PEPFAR) have pumped millions of dollars into research, programs, interventions, and health facilities, the health crises facing the world's poorest nations continue to loom large.

Medical interventions and policies based on scientific evidence have emerged as central strategies used by international organizations to assist in improving global health (Behague et al. 2009). There remains a gap, however, between the context in which this evidence is produced and the local reality for which it is intended. There is no doubt that scientific research is essential for illustrating the effectiveness of an intervention in a controlled setting; these situations, however, often bear little or no resemblance to the local context in which the intervention is to occur. The "inadequate translation of public health knowledge into effective action" as a result of clashing social and cultural beliefs is thus a major barrier to improving global health (Hahn and Inhorn 2009).

The process of implementing an intervention or a program involves the interaction of a number of cultural and social systems, including the local people, the social institutions on a local and national level, the researchers, clinicians, and staff who are there to implement the intervention, as well as funding agencies, NGOs, and local and foreign governments (Janes and Corbett 2009). Anthropologists are well versed in attending to how these social systems interact and, ideally, coexist in a manner that facilitates the best understanding of issues. The importance of designing culturally acceptable prevention and treatment strategies is perhaps best illustrated when we consider the case of malaria, a disease that is avoidable and curable through simple interventions, yet continues to kill millions of people in low- and middle-income countries.

The biomedical explanation of malaria is a disease "caused by a parasite that commonly infects a certain type of mosquito which feeds on humans" (Centers for Disease Control and Prevention [CDC] 2017). According to the WHO, "half of the world's population—3.3 billion people living in 109 countries—are at risk for malaria. In 2000, malaria caused between 350–500 million illnesses and more than one million deaths" (World Health Organization [WHO] 2008: 2). As one scholar writes, this number is the equivalent of "filling seven Boeing 747s with children, and then crashing them, every day" (Attaran et al. 2000: 730). Health costs associated with the disease include both personal and public expenditures: "In some heavy-burden countries, the disease accounts for up to 40% of public health expenditures, 30% to 50% of inpatient hospital admissions and up to 60% of outpatient health clinic visits" (WHO 2015). The toll on the economy in low- to mid-income countries as a result of infection is substantial: death and illness due to malaria cut economic growth rates by as much as 1.3 per cent in countries with high disease rates. Malaria disproportionately affects the marginalized and poor who cannot afford treatment or who have limited access to health care.

Once a person develops malaria, early diagnosis and treatment are central to reducing the risk of illness and death (WHO 2015). While drug therapies exist, the widespread parasite resistance to these drugs is making malaria control increasingly difficult (WHO 2015; Maslove et al. 2009). Prevention of malaria is therefore key to effective malaria control. Prevention strategies focus on reducing the transmission of disease through the use of mosquito nets treated with insecticide (an approach effectively tested), and indoor residual spraying of insecticides (Woelk et al. 2009). The success of efforts to reduce malaria is difficult to assess as there has been poor planning of major initiatives (Attaran et al. 2000), a lack of baseline data (Attaran et al. 2000), and unreliable data on incidence and mortality rates (Kamat 2009). Despite this uncertainty, research funds continue to be directed into treatment and prevention strategies—for example, since 2000 the Bill and Melinda Gates Foundation has donated nearly $250 million (McCoy et al. 2009: 1645). Attention to how individual communities understand the disease and consequently perceive treatment and prevention strategies remains neglected. One anthropologist writes:

> In order to assist the community in selecting and designing appropriate and potentially successful control programs, it is necessary to understand the

context of the disease in the community. This context includes the community characteristics, the community perception of the nature and etiology of the illness and its symptoms, and health seeking behaviour for prevention and treatment, including the use of traditional and cosmopolitan medications.... Programs which take local concerns into account are more likely to be successful (and sustainable) than those that adopt a simple strategy for providing information. (Helitzer-Allen, Kendall, and Wirima, cited in Kamat 2009: 37)

Cultural understandings of illness dictate how individuals protect themselves, when they will seek care, and to whom they will turn. Access to care, understandings of disease and prevention methods, and practices around seeking treatment are dictated by socio-cultural factors. Anthropologist Vinay Kamat (2009) conducted ethnographic research in Mbande, a peri-urban village in Tanzania, to understand caregivers' decision-making processes in seeking malaria treatment for their young children. Through interviews with 45 village women, Kamat learned of local explanations for what causes *degedege*, "the indigenous name for a much feared life threatening illness that in many cases people do not associate with malaria fever" (2009: 43). The characteristics of *degedege* resemble the characteristics of cerebral malaria, the type of malaria that kills the majority of children. Kamat provides a description of *degedege* as told to him by women and the local elders in the village:

The Kiswahili word *degedege* literally translates into English as "bird bird." In coastal Tanzania, among the Zaramo people in particular, the illness is believed to be caused by a coastal spirit (*mdudu shetani*) that takes the form of a bird that casts its shadow on vulnerable children on moonlit nights. Children who come under the bird's shadow subsequently become seriously ill, develop convulsions, and in many cases succumb to the illness and die....

In the dominant local cultural model of fever, if *homa ya kawaida* is left untreated, it may lead to *homa kali*, which in turn, if untreated, may lead to *homa ya malaria*. Finally, if malarial fever is not successfully treated, it may lead to *degedege*—although some informants said that *degedege* is a distinct illness with an etiology that is not related to malaria. They believed that the illness is not an advanced stage of malarial infection but an illness that is caused by "spirits." While most mothers I interviewed shared the cultural understandings of the etiology of *degedege*, there was considerable variation and flexibility in how they interpreted the taxonomy of fevers and the trajectory of the illness or the "ultimate" cause of the illness....

In Mbande, people consider "bad luck" or "God's will" to render particular children to be more vulnerable than others to *degedege*. Thus, when asked why some children are more prone to contracting *degedege* than others, the majority of the people in the village responded that it was just "God's wish" or "God's work" (*kazi ya mungu*) and that it was due to witchcraft (*uchawu*), sorcery (*kurogwa*), or someone's evil actions. This etiological belief significantly influences their acceptance of the fatal outcomes of the illness. Interviews with key informants and with local *waganga* who are known for their expertise in diagnosing and treating cases of *degedege* suggested that there is a general agreement that the illness is caused by a "spirit bird." (Kamat 2009: 45)

As this section illustrates, the local understanding of *degedege* is very different from the biomedical understanding of malaria. When local understandings of how illness occurs do not reflect the biomedical approaches that inform the actions of clinicians, NGOs and public health agencies, the result is a clash of values and beliefs that can stand in the way of effective control efforts. Furthermore, people's decision-making processes and health-seeking behavior are influenced by far more than just an understanding of disease. Kamat used a holistic approach that contextualized the socio-economic world of the residents of Mbande to understand the barriers and facilitators associated with accessing care. He describes the political manner in which the village came to exist (a consequence of relocation and then campaigning by a local leader to create a township distinct from already existing ones), the development of an all-weather road that brought in waves of migrants from northern Tanzania and led to a resulting shortage of land, the ethnic identification of the people in the village, and, finally, the economic activities of its citizens.

These factors directly affect the access to and delivery of health services, such as the availability of medicines, the distance that citizens have to travel to reach the municipal dispensary, the number and availability of trained medical officers and nurses, the number and availability of traditional healers and local pharmacies, and the number of people that these health clinics, both biomedical and traditional, must serve. As a great number of children infected with malaria die because they do not get prompt medical attention, these factors have a direct impact on malaria control efforts (Kamat 2009).

Kamat concludes that even if more efficacious anti-malarial treatments were readily available in Mbande, mothers would continue to delay bringing their children to a health facility because they believe they are dealing with an "ordinary" illness that does not require medical attention immediately. To facilitate early treatment, Kamat suggests that local dispensary staff must be able to effectively communicate the severity of the symptoms of malaria and the importance of early treatment to mothers. This is a conclusion shared by other anthropologists conducting malaria research. Muela and her colleagues (1998) illustrate that in some areas where there is fairly good access to biomedical clinics, a recurring bout of malaria after an individual has received biomedical care is often interpreted as the result of witchcraft or sorcery. While information, education, and communication campaigns can be effective in changing local knowledge about malaria symptoms and treatments, this does not necessarily translate into changed behavior (Muela, Ribera, and Tanner 1998). Despite the fact that knowledge regarding malaria symptoms and treatment of these symptoms was well known by members of the community where Muela and her associates conducted their fieldwork, they repeatedly witnessed individuals acting in a way that seemed to contradict the information they had so recently received.

Simply expecting that knowledge produced in a context far removed from everyday realities will immediately lead to changed behavior neglects the power of culture in informing worldviews and values. Recognizing the importance of local knowledge regarding health, illness, and treatment, and the manner in which this knowledge interacts with biomedical approaches, can lead to a better understanding of how best to target behaviors that may have an impact on malaria prevention and treatment strategies. This is the first step, however, and must be considered as integral to malaria education and prevention strategies as the clinical research that determines the efficacy of a vaccine or intervention.

Bio-cultural Anthropology

Bio-cultural anthropology investigates the complex relationship between biology, culture, ecology, and history. Bio-cultural anthropologists view human biological variability as a function of adaptation to the environment with a specific focus on how socio-cultural environments shape this adaptation (Khongsdier 2007). The aim of this approach is not, as Singer and Erickson (2011: ix) state, "to reduce health and illness to biological terms and mechanisms; rather, it is to see human biology and health as inherently social and cultural."

One of the most well-known examples of a bio-cultural approach is the work of Frank Livingstone on the evolution of sickle cell trait in West Africa in the 1950s. Sickle cell anemia is an inherited form of anemia where there are not enough healthy red blood cells to carry adequate oxygen throughout the body. Healthy red blood cells are flexible and round, but in those who have sickle cell anemia, the cells are rigid and shaped like crescent moons. They can get stuck in small blood vessels, which can slow or block blood flow and oxygen to other parts of the body (Mayo Clinic 2016). Researchers wondered why this hereditary disease was continuing to appear despite its usually fatal consequences. It was soon discovered that this type of anemia could provide a protective advantage against malaria in individuals, but only if the gene was inherited from one parent. The sickle shaped cells were screened through the spleen along with the parasites, which were destroyed. As these individuals did not contract malaria, this favorable adaptation thrived and the sickling trait became more prominent in the population. For those that inherited the gene from both parents, however, full-blown sickle cell anemia was the result, which most often led to death in childhood.

Livingstone set out to understand the effects of "sickling" on child growth in Liberia, a country in western Africa with high rates of malaria. According to Livingstone's understanding of the prevalence of sickle cell anemia, the sickle cell gene should have been in high frequency among the population. However, to Livingstone's surprise, it was virtually absent! How could this be the case? In order to understand what was going on, Livingstone conducted research that combined biology (genetics and evolutionary theory) and anthropology (archaeology, linguistics, subsistence regimes and settlement practices) (Vitzthum, Fix, Livingstone 2006).

The field of genetics has taught us that adaptive genes increase in frequency very slowly—it could take hundreds or even thousands of years to reach an equilibrium frequency where the advantageous effect would become apparent. Livingstone decided to shift his focus from genetics to consider the history of malaria and when it first arrived in Liberia (Vitzthum, Fix, and Livingstone 2006). This shift led him to consider the subsistence practices of Liberians and how these practices changed the natural environment. This type of mosquito requires stagnant, sun-lit pools of water to breed, an environment that is not found in the heavily forested areas that would have been the natural landscape of the country before agriculture was adopted. Livingstone learned that several groups in this population were late adopters of agriculture, and had lived hunter-gatherer lifestyles in forested regions. The advantage that the sickle cell gene would have provided against malaria would not have been needed as the environmental conditions were not optimal for this type of mosquito. Since the population had adopted agriculture as their dominant form of subsistence and cleared the forest to create optimal breeding ground for mosquitoes, they had become susceptible to malaria (Vitzthum, Fix, and Livingstone 2006). Livingstone's work explored the interaction between sickle cell anemia and culture, and explained the link to population growth, agriculture expansion, the prevalence of *Plasmodium falciparun* malaria and the evolution of the sickle cell gene in West Africa (Khongsdier 2007).

This example of bio-cultural anthropology illustrates the effectiveness of a multi-disciplinary approach to understanding a population-wide biological condition. As you will recall from Chapter 1, anthropology was originally established as a four-field discipline consisting of cultural, biological, archaeological, and linguistic subfields. Anthropologists were encouraged to study and train in all four fields so that an integrated and holistic understanding of human life would emerge. Over the last 50 years, each of these fields has developed into a distinct area of study that, depending on where one is located geographically, is likely conducted in silos, an approach that reflects the layout of this book. At the turn of this century, however, a renewed sense of interest in embracing a multi-disciplinary approach has emerged, particularly as the world becomes increasingly linked through the increased flow of people, ideas, and knowledge. The incorporation of a critical perspective into a bio-cultural approach is increasingly acknowledged, particularly as a heightened awareness of the role of social relations on resource production and distribution emerges. Recognizing how history and social inequalities shape access to resources and services, as well as how human behavior adapts to and changes the physical environment, can lead to answers about human health that remain outside the scope of a strictly biological approach.

Critical Medical Anthropology

Critical medical anthropology considers how illness, as described by those in a particular context, represents or misrepresents power relations within society to serve the interests of those in power (Farmer and Good 1991). As Farmer and Good write, "Forms of suffering grounded in social relations can be defined as illness, medicalized and brought under the authority of the medical profession and the state. Thus symptoms of hunger or disease that result from poverty, whether among the North American poor or the impoverished cane cutters of Brazil, are medicalized, treated as a condition of individual bodies—diarrhea, TB, nerves or stress, rather than a collective concern" (1991: 146). Through the **medicalization** of illness resulting from social circumstances, little, if any, attention is paid to the structural issues that have brought about the health issue, and all attention is directed to the individual person and their ailment. Critical medical anthropologists redirect that focus, and ask whose interests are being served and protected by the medicalization of social problems.

Let us focus our anthropological lens on Canada, a country overflowing with wealth, opportunity, and **universal health care**.[1] In 2007, documentary film maker Michael Moore profiled the Canadian health care system as an eye-opening alternative to the for-profit US system that leaves millions of people uninsured and vulnerable. While represented as an idealized utopia in the film, the reality is that all Canadians do not experience the health care system in the same way. Indigenous people in Canada have, as a group, poorer health outcomes than non-Indigenous Canadians. If we restrict our analysis only to health outcome data, we see that Indigenous populations suffer from higher rates of chronic conditions such as diabetes, from rates of tuberculosis that are five times higher than in the general population, and from HIV incidence rates (i.e., new infections) that are 2.7 times higher than people of other ethnicities (Public Health Agency of Canada 2014). Indigenous adults are also more than twice as likely to die from avoidable causes as non-Indigenous Canadians. So what is going on? Are Indigenous people simply more prone to falling ill? Of course not. We need to expand our scope and look to other social and contextual issues that impact health.

The history of residential schools in Canada and the forced separation of children from their families continue to impact generations of Indigenous peoples. A study published in 2015 concludes that racism within the health care system is pervasive and a major contributing factor to the health disparities experienced by Indigenous communities (Allan and Smylie 2015). The study described how Indigenous people experience racism from the health care workers that attend to them. As a result, many avoid the health care system as much as possible. When they must seek care, many people described how they would strategize on how to deal with the racism before they even entered the clinic. Dr. Nadine Carron, Canada's first female Indigenous surgeon, described how she often sees people in her exam room who avoid dealing with the health care system all together because of the inherent racism and discrimination that they face. Dr. Carron explains: "It's not just the skill of the knife or the scalpel. It's not just what you hear with the stethoscope. It's not just being able to read the X-ray or get a spec CT scan. It's pulling that all together so you can communicate that in a culturally safe environment, so that anyone of any background feels comfortable coming in to your office, to your clinic, to your hospital."[2]

The Cedar Project, led by medical anthropologist Patricia Spittal,[3] is an example of a critical approach that acknowledges the historical legacy of colonialism. Dr. Spittal and her team employ a mixed-methods approach to the study of health and addiction in young Indigenous people. This multi-year, multi-site study includes interviews, focus groups, epidemiology and blood samples from over 800 participants who are HIV positive, Hepatitis C positive, or at risk. Findings from this ongoing study have contributed to an understanding of young Indigenous people's health that is not limited to health outcomes, but highlights resiliency and coping strategies employed by the Indigenous research participants. The knowledge gained through this multi-methods research can contribute to the establishment of culturally safe health care for one of the most marginalized groups in Canada.

In addition to conducting research in Canada, critical medical anthropologists frequently turn their focus to the field of global health, where the interplay of governments, NGOs of all scale, funding organizations, private and public interests, and citizens create a complex landscape that mediates access to health care and services. Most global health organizations have their head offices in high-income countries, with strong links to the middle- and low-income countries in need of support. Caught up in this matrix of policies, objectives, and budgets are the citizens themselves. By investigating personal accounts of how individuals experience inequality in their every-day lives, access technology and care, and confront the public policies of their governments and own and external, anthropologists see the lived reality of what has become the field of global health. By focusing on individual narratives, the danger of glossing over lived experience and favoring statistics and aggregate health data is mitigated. João Biehl and Adriana Petryna (2013: 5) write that critical anthropologists have a "shared respect for the dignity and singularity of the people with whom we work, and our close attention to the ways in which their own struggles and visions of themselves and others create holes in dominant theories and interventions…. Their plights and travails demand intense listening and continuous attention."

Many critical anthropologists are unconvinced by an approach to improve health that focuses solely on technology and interventions, for this fails to acknowledge the social factors that influence health outcomes. When individual health behavior is emphasized without consideration of law, politics and violence, the responsibility of the government in providing health services is overshadowed by the behavior of individuals, many of whom are existing in survival mode. Biehl and Petryna describe how the global health landscape has shifted with the addition of private sector interests who favor disease-specific and technologically oriented interventions over investment in the public health system. The result, they argue, is a situation where the concerns and interests of donors supersede the well-being of recipients (2013). "The human populations that constitute the subjects of health and development plans are not just the source of problems or so-called cultural obstacles. Their experiential and practical knowledge, all too readily dismissed by the champions of quick technical fixes and measurable, generalizable results, can transform paradigms and may well provide the keys to effective solutions" (2013: 14).

We will now turn to an ethnographic study exploring the cholera outbreak in Venezuela in 1992–93. Medical anthropologist Charles Briggs and physician Clara Mantini-Briggs employed a critical approach to understand the epidemic. They focused on the actions and discourses employed by the Venezuelan government, the individual actors that made up the health care system, the media response, and of course, the individuals at the center of the epidemic. Their book, *Stories in the Time of Cholera: Racial Profiling during a Medical Nightmare*, illustrates how the complex interplay of neoliberal economics and globalization influenced the actions of the Venezuelan government in the late 1980s and 1990s, which in turn enacted racist policies to control the movement of Indigenous populations who were struggling to escape the deadly disease (Briggs and Mantini-Briggs 2002).

Cholera

The WHO defines cholera as an "acute diarrheal infection caused by ingestion of food or water contaminated with the bacterium *Vibrio cholerae*. Cholera remains a global threat to public health and an indicator of inequity and lack of social development. Researchers have estimated that every year, there are roughly 1.3 to 4.0 million cases, and 21 000 to 143 000 deaths worldwide due to cholera" (WHO 2016). While the majority of people infected with *V. cholerae* do not develop any symptoms, a minority develop diarrhea with severe dehydration that, if left untreated, can lead to death within hours. You might notice the enormous range in the reported cases and deaths listed in the definition—this is due to limitations in surveillance systems and an unwillingness to report rates out of fear of impacts on trade and tourism. Transmission is closely linked to inadequate access to clean water and sanitation facilities, and as such, is often found in overcrowded areas such as refugee camps. Cholera is easily treated through administration of an oral rehydration solution; however, rapid access to treatment is essential for it to be effective.

In 1992 and 1993, cholera was responsible for the deaths of approximately 500 people in Venezuela. Between 1993 and 1995, anthropologist Charles Briggs and physician Clara Mantini-Briggs conducted 15 months of intensive fieldwork in the region. The Delta Amacuro state is located in the eastern region of Venezuela. The state is bordered by the Gulf of Paria and the Atlantic Ocean, and is the home of the Orinoco Delta, a vast fan-shaped area split into numerous distributaries which make their way to the sea. The region is home to the Indigenous Warao, who maintain their own language and speak Spanish. Warao translates as *the boat people*, a fitting description for their reliance on canoes for transportation, fishing, and trade. The Warao live mostly in the rural regions, with non-Indigenous Venezuelans occupying the urban areas of the state. The Delta Amacuro is one of the poorest states in Venezuela, particularly the regions occupied by the Warao.

Charles Briggs had worked in the Delta Amacuro since 1985 conducting research on the social dimensions of the predominant language used in the area at that time—Warao—and how it interacted with Spanish. Back in the United States, he received word from friends and colleagues in the field of a possible outbreak. When he traveled to the area a few months later, he was horrified by what he found. Clara Mantini-Briggs worked as a public health physician in the capital of Delta Amacuro for four months before the outbreak occurred, and played a central role in directing efforts against the epidemic. The two met when Charles Briggs returned to assist in setting up health education and treatment programs in the area. When it became apparent that little else was being done to combat the epidemic, the two researchers began working together to collect as much information as possible. They interviewed 99 people living in the area, and attempted to speak with all medical personnel that had close contact with cholera patients. They interviewed ministry of health officials in Caracas, officials in the US Embassy, and representatives from other

MAP 7.1 Venezuela

government agencies in Venezuela. They traveled to New York, Washington, Geneva, and Bangladesh to understand how cholera research is conducted, and how policies are created at the international level. Interviews were conducted in English, Spanish and Warao, and were recorded whenever possible. They also attended meetings and conferences where cholera was discussed, and sifted through regional and national newspapers, official reports and publications, manuals, flyers and photographs. Their aim was not only to gather information so that they could understand what had happened during the epidemic, but also to develop and deliver a health education program that focused on preventing future outbreaks in a region where health conditions were among the worst in the country. The questions that guided their research included:

- Which stories became part of official statements by regional, national, and international public health authorities?
- Which accounts of cholera made it into the regional and national press?
- How were explanations of cholera morbidity and mortality—who gets infected and who dies—retold in policy statements?
- And how were stories that provided alternative explanations kept from circulating or denied legitimacy?

While Briggs is a medical anthropologist and Mantini-Briggs a physician, the questions guiding their research are not focused on understanding how the Indigenous population described and realized cholera, or how these explanations supported or contradicted biomedical explanations. Rather, their focus is at a macro level with an attempt to understand how stories about cholera are communicated, legitimized, and represented nationally and internationally. Through this lens, they begin their analysis of how the representation of the Indigenous population and the circulation of these stories shaped access to health services in Delta Amacuro.

The response of the Venezuelan government to the epidemic was vastly criticized by both national and international stakeholders. Briggs and Mantini-Briggs describes the warning signs and alerts sounded by those in the delta before the epidemic began, and how they largely went unanswered until a full-blown disaster was underway. They describe the response by the government as relying on constructions of modernity and characterizations of Indigenous peoples that portrayed them as being incapable of adopting modern medicine and hygiene. The government relied on a discourse that linked poverty and a lack of education around proper sanitation with the epidemic, thereby transferring the blame from themselves and their inability to provide basic services, such as health care, sanitation, access to clean water, or relevant health education that could have prevented the catastrophe from occurring. It was the fault of the Indigenous peoples for drinking contaminated water, for practicing "traditional medicine" and ignoring biomedical care, and for not having sanitary toileting practices. Stated one official, "the problem with the Gaujiros [Indigenous group] is that they

EVITAR EL COLERA
ES TAREA DE TODOS

PLATE 7.1 Cover of a *Ministerio de Sanidad y Asistencia Social* (MSAS) Health Education Pamphlet on Cholera

don't permit preventive treatment. Their customs, their culture, makes the work very difficult. They delay seeking treatment because they prefer their own medical rituals. These deaths in some way follow from sociocultural factors" (Briggs and Mantini-Briggs 2002: 42). By telling the story in this way, the government was able to defend their public institutions, whose legitimacy was questioned as a result of the epidemic. When the media began printing stories and pictures of Indigenous people dying, public health officials looked for a scapegoat, which they found in the very victims of the epidemic.

From the government's standpoint, their role was to conduct surveillance on those falling ill, and to provide public health education. Briggs displays a few examples of the brochures that were circulated among different populations at the time of the epidemic. The first produced by the Ministry of Health and Social Development, was intended for "general"—that is, *criollo* or non-Indigenous populations—distribution and contained drawings representing a well-dressed, smiling, light-skinned family consisting of parents and child. "Each recommendation was accompanied by images: well-groomed, smiling children posing in front of a stove in a middle-class kitchen, a woman cooking and cleaning, a man spraying for insects and carrying out trash" (2002: 113). While the majority of non-Indigenous Venezuelans are working-class and were not reflected in the images on the brochure, they were the target audience. In stark contrast is the pamphlet prepared by the Guardia Nacional for distribution in the delta. The pamphlet contains an image of a well-groomed physician looking the reader directly in the eye and sporting an army uniform. This is juxtaposed to the drawings of "nearly naked, beaded *indigenas*, who are shown defecating in the open, vomiting, and living in filthy circumstances" (2002: 115). These drawings do not resemble anyone living in the region—the haircuts and loincloths are distinctly out of place, not to mention the fact that many people classified as Indigenous are nurses, physicians and teachers, and live in enclosed houses with metal roofs. As Briggs writes, "These depictions supported existing Venezuelan images of *indigenas* and created a stark contrast between the polished, professional and confident *criollo* physician, who produces the messages of modernity, and the poor, dirty helpless *indigenas*, whose lives depend on their ability to listen and to follow his direction" (2002: 115).

The government used the discourse of *culture* (traditional medicine, cooking practices, etc.) as evidence of the Indigenous peoples' inability to learn. Here was an education campaign providing important information about how to protect oneself against cholera; yet the culture and habits of the Indigenous people remained unchanged. Those who are capable of learning from the campaign—i.e., non-Indigenous—were

PLATE 7.2 Drawings That Appeared Side by Side in a Health Education Pamphlet by the Venezuelan National Guard

not at-risk of cholera, and thus the majority of Venezuelans were excused from partici-pating in prevention efforts.

The use of narratives and photographs to convey information and describe the lives of the poor, if done so uncritically, has the potential to perpetuate stereotypes and mis-information about Indigenous peoples. Heart-wrenching images of a woman cradling her dead child and a row of beds in a makeshift cholera clinic convey the horror of the situation and the urgent need for help. At the same time, however, these images are in stark contrast to the cleanly dressed and sharply focused government officials and public health authorities addressing the public and providing information about the epidemic. The images of the sick and desperate came to represent all Indigenous people in the delta, as there were no images of the Indigenous nurses tending to the ill and dying, or friends and neighbors who transported the sick in their canoes and boats to makeshift clinics at all hours of the day and night. While the government was criticized by the public who consumed these images, it was not because they had failed to ensure access to services and health care, but for failing to save the helpless *indigenas* (Briggs and Mantini-Briggs 2002: 136).

Critical medical anthropologists, as Biehl and Petryna stated, recognize the personal stories of their research participants and how they live and experience globalization and neoliberal policies on a daily basis. *Stories in the Time of Cholera* includes many of these narratives, and effectively portrays the horror of living in a place where limited access to sanitation facilities and clean water has deadly consequences. The aim of the book, with its recounting of illness narratives and critiques of government policies and education campaigns, is to disrupt the circulation of stories that foster racism and blame, and instead promote critical thinking around the politics of health. Charles Briggs (2013: xvii) states that "assertions regarding cultural difference—the idea that poor people and individuals representing marginalized communities think and act differently and cannot embrace modern hygiene and medicine—increasingly shape institutional practices that permit or even multiply unnecessary and unconscionable deaths from disease."

Conclusion

In this chapter we explored medical anthropology, an increasingly in-demand sub-discipline that emerged in the aftermath of World War II. Since its inception, medical anthropologists have come to understand the complexity of health and illness, and the manner in which understandings and realizations of these concepts are intricately woven with other facets of social life. Health, like other prominent social catego-ries, is not something that can be fully understood by brief stints of fieldwork or a few interviews with locals. Anthropologists came to realize that prolonged field-work, with attention to historical events and processes, political forces, the economy and, of course, cultural beliefs and values, was central to understanding how health and illness were realized in a particular society. We explored interpretive, bio-cultural, and critical approaches through ethnographic cases in Tanzania of mothers whose children had shown signs of malaria, through the disease sickle cell anemia and its surprising absence in Liberia in the 1950s, and through a cholera outbreak in Venezuala in the late 1990s that took the lives of over 500 people. Each of the anthropologists leading these studies employed a different theoretical perspective, and as such, focused their lens on different elements of society, including cultural beliefs and interpretations of illness; biological, historical, and economic dimensions; and national and international policies regulating discourse and response to disease. While their focus was diverse, they share a common goal of gaining a better understanding of a population's health, and importantly, offer insight for how this enhanced understanding can inform health programs and interventions and, often, awareness of inequality.

Notes

1   A health care system that provides care and financial protection to all citizens of a particular country. It is organized around providing a specified package of benefits to all members of a society with the end goal of providing financial risk protection, improved access to health services, and improved health outcomes (World Health Organization 2010*)*.

2   http://www.cbc.ca/news/health/dr-nadine-caron-indigenous-surgeon-health-1.3887752

3   http://www.cheos.ubc.ca/people/patricia-spittal/

Study Questions

1. Using the example of the Ju'/hoansi people, describe the relationship between subsistence and health.

2   How did the international political situation contribute to the development of medical anthropology as a sub-discipline? What were the lessons learned by these early anthropologists?

3   Explain the Three Bodies approach and how it challenged the paradigm of traditional medical anthropology.

4   Using the example of malaria and *degedege*, explain why implementing a public health initiative is so complex, and how anthropological research may assist in this endeavor.

5   Describe a bio-cultural approach to medical anthropology, and explain how this approach led to an understanding of sickle cell anemia in Liberia.

6   Define critical medical anthropology and explain how anthropologists Charles Briggs and Clara Mantini-Briggs approached the study of the cholera epidemic in Venezuela through this theoretical lens.

7   Describe the differences and similarities between the three theoretical approaches discussed in this chapter.

Discussion Questions

1   Medical anthropologists often do extensive fieldwork in one setting rather than survey research in multiple or large-scale settings. Why do you think this is the case, and what are the implications for the questions under study?
2   What does it mean to say that health and illness are socially constructed?
3   What might a biomedical clinician learn from a medical anthropologist, and vice versa?

CHAPTER 8

//

Gender and Social Expectations

LEARNING OBJECTIVES

After reading this chapter, students should be able to

- identify the differences between gender, sex, and sexuality;
- understand gender as a social construct in contrast to the concept of biological determinism, and the social systems that contribute to that construct;
- discuss the importance of a holistic approach to the study of gender;
- outline and discuss the work of Thorne and Pascoe among American youth and explain the use of *feminist* and *queer theoretical approaches*;
- summarize Fong's methods and findings surrounding China's one-child policy and the effect on singleton daughters in urban areas; and
- outline Nanda's study of the *hijras* in India and discuss the value of a cross-cultural approach to studying gender.

KEY TERMS

biological determinism	gender	patriarchy
caste	gender role	queer theory
feminist theoretical perspective	hetero-masculinity	trans
	interpretive perspective	

Introduction

In this chapter we will explore how **gender** is realized in relation to the social organization of society. What do we mean by gender? The usual answer is to say that sex is a matter of biology and that gender is socially constructed—a set of local ideas related in some way to the biological "fact" of sex. Ideas about gender distinction, however, are not everywhere the same—there is diversity in attitudes and practices. Some cultural traditions, such as those found in regions of India, have a place for a gender that is neither male nor female. This role is not defined in terms of a contrast between "female" and "male," but is rather a matter of degree, of "more" or "less." In North American society, we often remark that some men are more masculine than others and some women more feminine. What does it mean to say so, and what does it tell us about our own cultural values?

Masculinity and femininity are *social* constructions that must be considered alongside other social categories such as childhood, adolescence, adulthood, and old age. Gender identity varies across an individual's life course—babies, children, and the elderly tend to be regarded differently than when they are in the prime of their reproductive years. Anthropologists consider such issues on the basis of their ethnographic experiences, and their observations have had a great impact on North American public consciousness.

Biologically speaking, we have two primary sexes and several possibilities that stand outside of these two options (inter-sexed individuals with characteristics of both sexes; people with a surplus of X or Y chromosomes). Until quite recently, the nature of sexual identity and reproduction was pretty much a mystery to everyone, and in certain ways it still is. The way the collective imagination tries to explain the mysteries of sexuality relates to the broader structure of society, including the distribution of power within it. In studying gender, we are on the track of deeper issues involving the social definition of personhood, which in turn relates to worldview, religion, economics, and law. These are not just academic concerns: they are extremely important on both individual and societal levels, and they are fought over every day in legal courts around the world.

In this chapter we will explore gender and sexuality by considering how these social categories are realized within a particular cultural context. This chapter is heavy on ethnographic case studies, for we feel that gaining a better understanding of a somewhat abstract category such as gender (as well as kinship, race, and religion) is best accomplished through the exploration of how these categories are actually embodied and experienced in the daily lives of individuals around the world. Through case studies, we will see how anthropologists have applied theory to their observations and data, what methods they have used to collect data and arrive at their conclusions, and the significance of this knowledge to how we think about society.

We will begin by considering how gender is learned in a North American context through two ethnographic examples that explore gender from within the American educational system. Barrie Thorne's *Gender Play* considers how elementary school children learn gender behaviors, while C.J. Pascoe investigates masculinity and sexuality in an American high school in her ethnography, *Dude, You're a Fag*. Both authors employ a feminist theoretical perspective to make sense of their observations and data. We will consider how this theoretical perspective shapes the perceptions of each author. We will continue our discussion by looking at how China's one-child policy has impacted urban "singleton" daughters born after the policy was implemented. While Vanessa Fong's research demonstrates how gender norms and behaviors have been transformed as a result of the rapid industrialization of the Chinese economy, she also illustrates that cultural understandings of gender are closely related to kinship relations and obligations. Finally, we will conclude our discussion of gender and sexuality by exploring Serena Nanda's ethnography *Neither Man nor Woman*. Nanda's cross-cultural analysis of gender roles employs a comparative approach to "explain alternative gender roles by correlating their presence with other cultural characteristics" (Nanda 1999: 145). A comparative approach operates on the assumption that understanding gender roles in a particular society requires the consideration of other social factors, such as social hierarchy and religion. A cross-cultural analysis that is informed by an interpretive perspective allows for an investigation that does not simplify social systems or discount the people within them, but gives space for the complexity of each situation to be fully considered.

We "Do" Gender

In many Western societies, the term **gender role** is used to describe the seemingly different sets of actions and behaviors associated with girls and boys, men and women. Gender is most often conceived as dichotomous and simply an extension of biological sex. Despite the frequency with which we hear that women are "naturally" (i.e., biologically) more nurturing and better at raising children, while men are "naturally" more ambitious and better at occupying the most powerful positions in the workforce, these roles are cultural constructs. These roles are not universal because they are not biological. Notions of **biological determinism**, in which there is a direct correlation between cultural characteristics regarding gender (or race, or class) with biological traits, has been largely disproved. This way of thinking is continually reinforced and perpetuated by everyday conversations and actions that, however subconsciously, serve to reinforce the idea that girls and boys behave in specific ways that are pre-determined at birth. One need only look cross-culturally to find examples of gender roles that do not fit what many in the West take for granted as "natural." For example, in much of rural Thailand, the difference in physical size between men and women is minimal, the clothing they wear is very similar, and both perform agricultural tasks that are often interchangeable (Miller, Van Esterik, and Van Esterik 2001). While gender roles exist, they are not the same as those found in Euro-Western cultures, which one would assume they would be if gender were in fact biological.

We "learn" how to be male and female through the social acts that make up the everyday, such as interacting with our family, meeting people and developing friendships, attending school, being employed, watching television and movies, etc. Within minutes of being born, we are wrapped in pink or blue blankets and our education begins. As sociologist Barrie Thorne (1994: 5) states, "gender is not something one passively 'is' or 'has' … we 'do' gender." Of course, people are not mindless drones who go about their lives accepting everything they are taught—far from it. The idea that we are socialized into behaving a certain way can become very problematic if we do not consider the agency of the individual. Otherwise, people would be nothing more than inactive bodies with little or no control over their own behavior and beliefs. Culturally defined behaviors and beliefs are very powerful; however, we must be cognizant of the fact that there are many exceptions to these rules.

So how do we go about understanding gender? We continually return to the statement that theory steers perception. Understanding the social organization and relationships of a community or society, whether one is focusing on gender, the economy, politics or religion, requires that anthropologists have a method of organizing their thoughts and observations theoretically so that they don't emerge from the field with a mass of notes that remains, well, a mass of notes! How they make sense of these ideas and observations is dependent on their theoretical perspective.

Anthropology conducted from a **feminist theoretical perspective** operates on the assumption that all social relations and the knowledge of these relations are gendered. Gender, therefore, must be considered alongside class, race, and age as a fundamental social category. Feminists argue that knowledge of the social world has traditionally been taught and learned from a male-centered perspective, and women's experiences, positions, and beliefs have been marginalized and ignored. Women's experiences are extremely diverse, and issues such as class position and ethnicity affect a woman's experience of the world around her. It is therefore not enough to simply consider all women as victims of oppression simply because they are women; rather, the specific circumstances and social position of the woman herself must always be considered. An Australian corporate executive will have a very different experience of employment than that of a Peruvian rural farmer. Simply being a woman does not unite them in a shared oppression, and ignoring individual circumstances overlooks the class and race oppression that many women experience. Feminist anthropologists desire to reshape how knowledge is gathered and interpreted; simply including women in the scope of study does not qualify as a feminist approach.

Feminist research is characterized by a desire to empower women and eliminate oppression, and such research is conducted for the purpose of enacting social change. Moreover, the relationship between the researcher and researched is open and subjective, and the quest for objectivity is considered impossible. Feminism is characterized by a multiplicity of sub-fields, including liberal, radical, and Marxist feminism, to name just a few. We will consider two ethnographic examples of research conducted through a feminist lens on the topic of gender.

Gender on the Playground

Barrie Thorne explored gender norms and behaviors by employing a feminist perspective during her ethnographic fieldwork in an elementary school in California in the late 1970s and early 1980s. While this research was conducted over 30 years ago, Thorne provides valuable insight into the various ways in which children "learn" to be boys and girls in the public education system. Thorne's approach to studying children was distinctive, for rather than *observing* kids and *talking* to the teachers and other adults in the school, Thorne both observed and talked to the children themselves. As a result, her findings highlight a number of misleading assumptions about gender behavior in kids that we will explore below. Her approach also exemplifies the importance of two central anthropological tenets—an individual's experience and context.

Observing children for the purpose of understanding how gender is realized and constructed has long been an interest of social science researchers, perhaps because children represent a group that has yet to be fully formed or shaped by the social world around them. In much of this social-scientific and developmental psychology research, children are regarded as adults in the making (James and Prout 1997; Caputo 1995). Their behavior and attitudes are examined with an eye to the future—how will this behavior affect their development in later years? Discussions in the media illustrate that this is a topic that continues to ignite passionate debate. For example, retail giant J.Crew was the focus of such debate when, in April 2011, company president Jenna Lyons posed for a photo with her five year-old son while painting his toenails fluorescent pink. Conservative pundits raged with claims that Lyons was participating in "blatant propaganda celebrating transgendered children," while others rushed to her defense, proclaiming that painting toenails had nothing to do with sexuality. *Forbes* online magazine covered the story, and it sparked debates in print and television media for days (Phillips 2011). Clearly, gender identity and behavior in children is a hot topic in the Western world.

Thorne positions her young research participants as a group who "act, resist, rework and create; they influence adults as well as being influenced by them" (Thorne 1994: 3). She challenges adults (i.e., teachers and parents, etc.) to consider children's actions as important in the present, and to recognize that they are not simply passive recipients of socialization. To do this requires an awareness of how one's assumptions and stereotypes inform understandings of gendered behavior in children. Parents and other adults tend to exhibit a phenomenon labeled by sociologist Michael Messner as "believing is seeing"—individuals choose what they would like to believe is true rather than allowing what they see to inform their beliefs.

To many teachers and parents that Thorne spoke with, instances that did not fit within a stereotype were regarded as exceptions to the "rule" of gendered behavior rather than evidence of there being many ways to behave as a girl or boy. An often-cited example of the fundamental differences between girls and boys is how they seem to play with those of the same sex. This research, primarily from the field of developmental psychology, has been explained both by evolutionary arguments (Pellegrini 2009) and socialization (Fabes, Martin, and Hanish 2003; Hoffmann and Powlishta 2001; Maccoby 1998; Maccoby and Jacklin 1987). Thorne observed this in many instances on the playground and in the classroom, such as kids scrambling over one another to be in line with other girls and boys: "Once when the recess bell had rung and they began to line up for the return to class, a boy came over and stood at the end of a row of girls. This evoked widespread teasing—'John's in the girls' line'; 'Look at that girl over there'—that quickly sent him to the row of boys" (Thorne 1994: 40).

Thorne considers the research on sex segregation and play against her own observations and interpretations of the data. She finds existing explanations found in the literature to be problematic as they rarely account for exceptions, something that she was continually struck with during her time in the schools—the existing theories simply fell short in explaining the behavior that she witnessed before her. One such example became evident to her as she was *talking* with kids about friendships. Thorne learned that *who* kids play with and identify as friends changes depending on the context and situation—who they hang out with in school and why is not always the same as who they hang out with on the weekends, at church, at baseball, etc. She writes: "When I stood on the Ashton playground talking with Melanie, a sixth-grader, I learned of a boy–girl friendship that went underground in school. After Jack walked by without even glancing at her, Melanie whispered to me, 'He's one of my best friends.' 'But you didn't even nod or say hello to each other,' I said. 'Oh,' she replied, 'we're friends in our neighbourhood and at church, but at school we pretend not to know each other so we won't get teased'" (1994: 50).

Girls socializing with other girls on the playground is but one example of friendship; rather than describing this behavior as gendered (i.e., all girls act this way, all boys act that way), Thorne illustrates instead that this is just one example in a specific context. As the dynamic of school is different from the dynamic of the neighborhood, the way kids identify with one another also changes. Researchers tend to conduct their observational studies in schools because working within the realm of an institution is inherently easier than approaching individual families and asking if they can be observed in their home or their neighborhood. When findings from one context are generalized to all contexts, however, the complexity of the situation is lost and grand generalizations emerge, such as the belief that girls and boys play differently and therefore prefer to exclusively socialize with those of the same sex. What are also lost are the voices of the kids themselves, that is, if they were even asked in the first place.

Thorne conveys an understanding of gender that is not fixed and static, but rather fluid and situational. Gender behavior does not follow a set of strict rules informed by what is appropriate for a boy or a girl and what is not; rather, this behavior is flexible and changes depending on the situation, context, and company. Thorne observed many instances of girls and boys enacting and challenging typical gender roles. For example, she writes that "day after day on the Ashton playground I noticed that Evan, a first-grade boy, sat on the stairs and avidly watched girls play jump rope, his head and eyes turning around in synchrony with the rope. Once when a group of girls were deciding who would jump and who would twirl (the less desirable position), Evan recognized a means of access to the game and offered, 'I'll swing it.' Julia responded, 'No way, you don't know how to do it, to swing it. You gotta be a girl.' He left without protest" (1994: 45). Sometimes these instances were a result of the rules of the classroom, such as when one teacher assigned seating in her classroom and mixed boys and girls at each table. Here, the girls and boys worked together on class projects and were much more cooperative than the girls and boys in another class that were allowed to pick their own seats. In the latter class, the girls ended up on one side and the boys on the other to create an atmosphere of girls versus boys. No comments were made about the ability of the girls and boys to work together as peers, but for the class segregated by gender, the teacher frequently used the threat of "not having a boys' side and a girls' side" in order to gain quiet and control in the classroom (1994: 37).

To conceive of gender roles as binary and oppositional fails to acknowledge the diversity that exists within these categories, and the desire of many to live outside of them. For the physical and boisterous girl and the boy who sits quietly to be regarded as peculiar simply because they do not "fit" with gender stereotypes places limitations on kids, something we will explore in more detail when we consider Pascoe's work in the next example.

As a feminist scholar, Thorne desires to effect social change related to the hierarchical and unequal relationships between men and women that are inscribed by

PLATE 8.1 Children in Gender-Specific Hallowe'en Costumes

constructions of gender. Thorne did not simply observe children for the sake of research, but did so with the hope that educators would read her work and think critically about how they organize their classrooms and talk to girls and boys, much on the model of Margaret Mead and her research with adolescent girls in Samoa. Her recommendations focus on how educators can rethink their teaching approaches to challenge assumptions that girls are better students than boys, and that boys have more energy than girls. For example, she notes the importance of challenging the notion that play that perpetuates aggressive masculine behavior is innate and simply a case of "boys being boys."

Creating an environment where children are free to try on and experiment with a diversity of roles is central to challenging the assumption that girls and boys must behave in certain ways. Thorne argues for the importance of continuing to resist and question stereotypical ideas of femininity, masculinity, and social arrangements that are rooted in patriarchal beliefs concerning the "natural" order of things: "A more complex understanding of the dynamics of gender, of tensions and contradictions, and of the hopeful moments that lie within present arrangements, can help broaden our sense of the possible" (1994: 173).

Gender Grows Up

If we fast forward over 20 years, we are presented with another ethnographic exploration of gender, this time one that takes place in an American high school in 2003. C.J. Pascoe conducted fieldwork in a racially diverse California high school with the intent of exploring two socially constructed categories, sexuality and masculinity, which Pascoe asserts are fundamentally linked. Over 18 months, Pascoe conducted ethnographic fieldwork among students in their classrooms, common spaces, and at school events. She conducted over 50 formal interviews with students, faculty, and administrators, and countless other "informal" interviews that took the form of conversation. Like Thorne, Pascoe employs a feminist approach to understanding gender. She also investigates sexuality, in which she employs **queer theory**. How do these theories differ, and what can they tell us about how teenagers identify and live their lives?

Like feminism, queer theory challenges the "assumed naturalness of the social order"—that is, that heterosexuality is a concrete and static category that is natural, and that all other sexual identities, desires, and discourses are not. Queer theory "moves beyond traditional categories such as male/female, masculine/feminine, and straight/gay to focus instead on the instability of these categories. That is, we might think of 'heterosexual' and 'homosexual' as stable, opposing, and discrete identities, but really they are fraught with internal contradictions. To this end, queer theory emphasizes multiple identities ..." (Pascoe 2011: 11).

Pascoe regards sexuality as she does gender—as an "organizing principle of social life," and not simply in reference to an individual's sexual identity. Traditionally, sexuality has been thought of in terms of private, individual acts; however, social science research has illustrated that the meanings we associate with terms and categories such as "gay," "straight," or "bisexual" have implications that reach far beyond closed doors. Take the controversial issue of gay marriage in Canada and the United States. This issue illustrates the significance the public assigns to how individuals define their sexual identity. In Canada, up until 1999 heterosexual couples were awarded rights and benefits from the state that same-sex couples were not. This was officially changed when marital benefits were extended to all co-habiting couples that met the definition of a common-law partnership, whether the relationship was same-sex or not. In the United States, each of the 50 states is responsible for its own marriage laws; however, on June 26, 2015, the Supreme Court ruled that the Constitution allows for same-sex couples to marry. Prior to this ruling, 37 states and the District of Columbia had legalized same-sex marriage. As you will see in the next chapter, debates in the United States about legalizing gay marriage revisit past arguments about interracial marriage, given that some states then allowed it and some did not. The debate around marriage exemplifies how sexuality is a central organizing structure in society, and that institutions, such as the government and the courts, play a role in how we organize sexual life and produce sexual knowledge.

Pascoe considers how the high school, as a social institution much like the government, contributes to our understanding and realization of sexuality and masculinity. By putting sexuality front and center, Pascoe examines how students, faculty, and administrators at this high school created, challenged, and supported expectations around the presumed naturalness of heterosexuality. Some of these activities were seemingly mundane and harmless, such as a feature in the school yearbook that highlighted "best of" categories for girls and boys in each grade. Pictures of boy–girl pairings were placed in categories such as "best dressed," "biggest flake," "best smile," "best looking," and "best couple." There were no pairings of two girls or two boys in this section, a fact that points to the presumed "naturalness" of heterosexual pairings.

Popular school events such as school dances, where public displays of sexuality were much more explicit, showed a contrast between a desire to control student sexuality on the one hand, and a desire to encourage it on the other. Pascoe describes how there were very clear rules around "dancing inappropriately" at these events, and one teacher told her how they were instructed to "'keep our eyes on the chairs.' Surprised, I asked her, 'why the chairs?' She explained, 'Boys like to sit on the chairs and then the girls stand up and dance for them'" (Pascoe 2007: 42). At the same dance, however, scantily clad girls and fully clothed boys screamed the lyrics to rapper Nelly singing "It's getting' hot in here / So take off all your clothes" and chanted in unison the word "ho" when the DJ turned down the volume on the chorus of a Tupac Shakur song. Pascoe observed two vice-principals joking with a male and female student as they left early, "You two going to a hotel or what?" (2007: 43). All of these instances served as venues for performing and proving heterosexual identities—"while the staff were concerned with students' sexuality, they also, to some extent, encouraged it through sponsoring these types of rituals and joking around with students" (2007: 43). The staff were less concerned with policing the "gender inequality fostered by such heterosexuality," such as the fact that the teachers appeared to have no problem allowing students to chant the word "ho" at the tops of their lungs (2007: 43).

What Pascoe finds problematic is not that students were exploring their sexuality within the walls of an institution; rather, it is that heterosexuality and a very specific type of masculinity were the *only* options supported by the high school. Holding a girlfriend's hand in public, caring about the appearance of one's clothing, or dating someone of the same sex did not align with the ideals of "**hetero-masculinity**." The consequence of exhibiting these behaviors was at best to be ignored and, at worst, to experience intense harassment and violence. Pascoe tells the story of Ricky, "a lithe, white junior with a shy smile and downcast eyes, [who] frequently sported multicolored hair extensions, mascara, and sometimes a skirt. An extremely talented dancer, he often starred in the school's dance shows and choreographed assemblies" (2007: 65). Ricky was often the subject of abuse and ridicule, at the hands of both other male students and teachers. While the insults and threats he heard from students were overt, many of the teachers did little to protect him or to punish the perpetrators. Ricky used an example of being beaten up in middle school to illustrate the attitudes of many of his teachers: "They gave them a two-day suspension and they kind of kept an eye on me. That's all they could do. The PE coach was very racist and very homophobic. He was just like 'faggot this' and 'faggot that.' I did not feel comfortable in the locker room and I asked him if I could go somewhere else to change, and he said, 'No, you can change here'" (Pascoe 2007: 67). As a non-heterosexual youth who did not conform to a masculine gender role, Ricky was unable to ever break free of the "fag" label. As a result of this relentless and intense bullying, Ricky dropped out of high school.

Dude, You're a Fag is a title clearly meant to elicit a reaction in readers. The frequent use of the word "fag" by her research participants led Pascoe to theorize that "becoming a fag has as much to do with failing at the masculine tasks of competence, heterosexual prowess and strength, or in any way revealing weakness or femininity as it does with a [homo]sexual identity" (Pascoe 2011: 54). Pascoe illustrates through a number of ethnographic examples that it was not only those males who identified as gay or bisexual, such as Ricky, that were subject to bullying—it was any male whose behavior was perceived to be outside of the established masculine gender role. The difference was the manner in which these boys were able to shrug off the fag label, and how this was dependent on their ability to perform the masculine gender role. When she asked a student named Ben what kinds of things boys are called fags for, Ben answered, "Anything … literally anything. Like you were trying to turn a wrench the wrong way, 'Dude, you're a fag.' If a piece of meat drops out of your sandwich, 'You fag!'" (Pascoe 2007: 57). Ben's comments illustrate that the term has just as much to do with being incompetent and therefore unmasculine as it does with anything sexual. For this reason, focusing *only* on concepts of sexuality to understand homophobia neglects how the construction of masculinity contributes to the belief that heterosexuality is the norm.

Whether or not you find this type of research interesting, you may be asking yourself "what does it matter?" With so many other social issues in contemporary society, does it really matter how boys and girls in an American high school understand masculinity and sexuality? Pascoe provides a compelling argument that attention to the construction of these social categories certainly does matter. Pascoe positions her work in relation to the tragic instances of cyber and face-to-face bullying that led to a number of male adolescents taking their own lives in the United States. These cases have been largely classified as instances of homophobia, where boys and young men were teased and taunted because of their presumed or actual sexual preference. Pascoe believes, however, that these cases are as much about stepping outside the traditional definitions of masculinity, however slight, as they are about homophobia:

> Evidence in several of the cases indicates that their [the victims'] (mildly) non-normative gendered behavior (such as enjoying schoolwork or drama class) was just as likely to turn them into targets as were their sexual identities .... That these cases exist, however few, illustrates how serious the problems are around the contemporary making of masculine identities—and that we need to start thinking about the ways in which young males come to think of themselves and others as masculine. (Pascoe 2011: xi)

So what does Pascoe suggest society do to counteract this activity? As her work is informed by both feminist and queer theory approaches, her ultimate goal is to challenge the status quo. She asserts that students who are subject to harassment, such as gay, lesbian, bisexual, and **trans** students, need legal protection. Teachers and administrators must be educated as to what constitutes harassment, and must in turn educate those students who are observed exhibiting this type of behavior. In order to change the way we think, disciplinary action is not enough—education is key, as is critically examining curriculum and student events that do not allow for the expression of sexuality and gender roles that are not "hetero-normative." At the center of both Pascoe's and Thorne's work is the assertion that talking to individuals about their experiences will lead to a better understanding of how kids and teens realize their gender and sexual identities. While talking to adults and situating research within an institution allows for access and a safe environment through which kids can be approached, it is always important to remember that labels and identities are often context- and situation-dependent.

We have spent a fair amount of time discussing gender and sexuality as it relates to North American culture, primarily because this is where most of our readers hail from. To learn to think critically about one's own culture is one of the greatest contributions of cultural anthropology—deconstructing what we think of as normal and natural illustrates that these behaviors are learned and culturally dependent. Next we will consider how policy related to a nation's birth rate has significant consequences on how gender roles are perceived and experienced in the family specifically, and in society as a whole.

Gender and Social Organization: The Family and the Economy

The construction of gender roles and behaviors has a significant impact on how the social world is organized. While Thorne and Pascoe have offered ethnographic portraits of how kids experience gender in the school system, another realm where gender norms are extremely important is within the family. In what ways are the expectations placed on children by their family related to gender norms, and how do these expectations shift when significant social changes impact the role of women in society? Understanding social organization requires a holistic approach: our lives are not organized by categories titled "gender," "economy" or "religion," but instead are a product of these interrelated roles, beliefs, and behaviors. The ways in which people think about gender roles are influenced by the political, social, and economic climate of the time and directly impact family relationships and social institutions such as schools and the workplace.

Anthropologist Vanessa Fong considers how China's one-child policy has had an impact upon urban-born daughters. China's first official population-control campaign was implemented in 1970, when families were encouraged to have no more than two children. It was not until 1978, when the government set a population target of 1.2 billion people or under by the year 2000, that the one-child policy was officially enforced. The approach was successful in curbing the birth rate: "in 1970, when population control policies began, China's total fertility rate was six births per woman; in 1980, two years after the start of the one-child policy, China's total fertility rate was down to two births per woman" (Fong 2002: 1099). The policy led to enormous international backlash, particularly from the United States. Fong notes that much of the literature exploring the effects of the policy highlights the negative impact on women, detailing instances of forced sterilizations and abortions, and of the blame placed upon women who had daughters instead of sons in a culture where male children were traditionally more valued than females. The preference for male children has had a very real impact on the make-up of urban Chinese society. Demographically speaking, China has a skewed gender ratio with more males than females, the cause of which may have been female infanticide, abandonment, and selective abortion.

Fong takes a slightly different approach to understanding the effects of the one-child policy without diminishing the suffering experienced by many women. She notes that in urban areas where the cost of living is high and space restrictions are significant, resistance to the policy was relatively low. Fong's central thesis is that "urban daughters born under China's one child policy have benefited from the demographic pattern produced by that policy" (2002: 1099). Fong's data suggest that these daughters have an unprecedented power to challenge traditional gender roles in a way that will benefit them. An unintended consequence of the one-child policy has been to force parents to invest, both socially and economically, in their daughters when traditionally they would have invested in their sons.

Fong interviewed grandmothers, mothers, and singleton daughters to gain cross-generational perspectives on the position of women in society. Grandmothers told her that when they were young, they were unable to live with or provide financial and social support to their parents. Even if wage-paying jobs had been a possibility, as a result of having numerous children and a household to manage they would not have had the time to work outside the home. One grandmother explained how having to continually take time away from her factory job to have children hindered her ability to excel: "I got to work upstairs in the factory office because I had gone to school, but I couldn't take a position of responsibility because I always had to take time off when I got pregnant…. After my fourth child, my health was bad all the time, and I had to quit my job" (2002: 1101). The daughters of these women who gave birth to their own children in the one-child–policy era were able to work outside the home because of fewer child-rearing responsibilities. Because they were able to bring home a monthly wage, they were also able to provide financial support to their elderly parents, illustrating that they too could be as filial as sons: "As a junior high school student's mother told her husband when he complained that she was giving too much money to her parents, 'Why shouldn't I give them the money I've earned? You should be grateful that I don't give all my wages to them!'" (Fong 2002: 1102).

As a result of the changes in social status of their mothers and grandmothers, singleton daughters are better positioned to take advantage of opportunities that might not have been open to them if they had had to compete with brothers. Despite increased opportunities in school and the workplace, however, their lives continue to be subjected to the societal gender norms and roles that position them as secondary to men. Fong describes the experience of a student she had been tutoring who was waiting to hear her test results. On the one hand, this student was receiving the investment of time and money from her parents to excel at school. On the other, she had to continually prove her worth to her father:

> Although studious and well behaved, Ding Na was often criticized by her father, who liked to remind her that he had always wanted a son. He worried that she might not score high enough to get into a good four-year college, even though she usually ranked in the top 20 percent of her high school class on practice exams. "What will you do if you don't get into a good college?" he lamented. "If you were a boy, you could study abroad while supporting yourself as a laborer, but what can a girl do abroad besides sit around waiting for remittances I can't afford?" Although her mother praised her for being more willing to help with chores than most other teenagers, whenever Ding Na had trouble helping her father carry groceries or move furniture, he snapped, "Girls are so useless. A boy would have no trouble with this." On July 26, 1999, when Ding Na's college entrance exam scores were released, I began to see the relationship between Ding Na and her father in a different light…. She had scored higher than she had ever scored on a practice exam in high school, and well above the likely cutoff for her top-choice four-year college. She shouted with joy as we congratulated her. Her father beamed at her with tears in his eyes and said, "I was wrong to have wanted a son. A daughter like you is worth ten sons." (Fong 2002: 1098)

China remains a **patriarchal** society, with a socio-economic system structured by class and gender roles. Singleton daughters must negotiate gender roles in the family, as shown above, to prove they are as filial as sons, as well as in the workplace, where they are pressured to portray desired behaviors such as being more patient and meticulous than men. The ability of singleton daughters to "parody" the typical feminine gender role allows for social mobility and access while subsequently rejecting traditional roles, such as staying home to have numerous children and do all of the housework. Fong states that in some ways middle-class urban men have less social security than their female counterparts. While women face a "glass ceiling" that prohibits them from reaching the elite positions inhabited by men, they also have the protection of "marrying up," an option rarely available to men of the same social status. Urban middle-class males are experiencing a change in their position in society as a result of women's increased social mobility. Aside from having more competition in the workforce, they also explained that it was more difficult to find a wife. Now that singleton daughters are able to contribute to the purchase of an apartment, they have a greater choice of partners. Fong writes that

> a male vocational high school student told me that he could have gone to a college-prep high school if his parents, who ran a small shop, had spent all their savings on extra fees and bribes that would have gotten him in despite his low exam score. He said, "They gave me a choice. Either they could use their savings to send me to the college prep high school, or they could use it to buy an apartment for me so that I'll be able to get a wife when the time comes. I don't like to study, and I didn't think I could make it to college even if I went to a college prep school, so I chose the apartment." (2002: 1105)

The effects of a policy to curb national birth rate has had a substantial impact on all generations of a society that positions family as a central unit of support. Fong's analysis is a snapshot of the effects of the policy in a specific location, among a specific group of people. Her research cannot be generalized to all women in China, as it is specific only to urban women whose families had a very different experience with the one-child policy than those in rural areas. Her work illustrates the way in which politics and kinship intersect with gender roles, and how this has ignited a change in the urban-middle-class perception of the place of singleton daughters specifically, and women more generally, in society.

By looking cross-culturally at how gender is realized, we see that a holistic approach that considers kinship, the economy, and the political system highlights many key components that factor into how society perceives gender. Thorne and Pascoe situate their ethnographic studies within the education system, and focus specifically on the interactions of the students and teachers themselves. Fong, on the other hand, situates her study more generally in Chinese urban society. Both approaches illustrate the significance of gender to organizing the social world. We will now move on to our final ethnographic example, Serena Nanda's *Neither Man nor Woman*. By stepping far away from traditional binary gender roles, this research illustrates how the concept of gender is socially constructed.

Rejecting the Gender/Sex Dichotomy: Third Genders and Cross-Cultural Analysis

Our final ethnographic example of the chapter explores gender from a cross-cultural, **interpretive perspective** that considers how symbolism and religion create space in Indian society for an institutionalized third gender. Do people who identify outside of the mainstream gender categories have to contend with social rules and norms in the same way that men and women do? In what ways are their lives different from those who identify with the dichotomous gender systems of mainstream Western society? There are many societies in which a third gender exists, and by applying a cross-cultural approach we see that that gender is simply another social category that serves to organize rules, behaviors, and meanings for the people who exist within it. In this section, we move beyond the dichotomous gender roles of boys and girls, men and women, and consider the existence of a third gender role through a cross-cultural examination of the *hijras* of India.

Who are the hijras? This is a complicated question that many anthropologists have attempted to answer. Anthropologist Gayatri Reddy (2005: 2) provides this definition: "For the most part, hijras are phenotypic men who wear female clothing and, ideally, renounce sexual desire and practice by undergoing a sacrificial emasculation—that is, an excision of the penis and testicles—dedicated to the goddess Bedhraj Mata." The number of hijras in India varies drastically, depending on the source, with estimates ranging from 10,000 to two million (Reddy 2005). Hijra communities can be found throughout India, although they seem to be concentrated in the northern cities of Delhi and Lucknow, as well as in Hyderabad to the south.

Hijras are socially organized according to lineages and households, and from there they are further organized into a social hierarchy, with one senior hijra occupying a role of respect and dominance. The hijra community itself has further ways of distinguishing who is a hijra, including those who were "born" a hijra by virtue of having ambiguous genitals, those who are "made" a hijra through castration (Nanda 1999), and those who engage in activities deemed unauthentic, such as sex work or displaying sexual desire (Reddy 2005). While there have been a number of studies conducted with the hijra community over the last few decades, they are a highly secretive group, and gaining access to their communities is difficult. As a result, there remains much uncertainty around what the existence of the hijra community can tell us about Indian society and, on a grander scale, the story of human sexuality itself (Lai 1999).

The place of hijras in Indian society cannot be fully understood unless it is contextualized within historical and religious realms. While we do not have the space required to give a comprehensive explanation of this history here, ethnographies by

PLATE 8.2 Hijra

both Serena Nanda (1999) and Gayatri Reddy (2005) provide excellent overviews. Hijras have existed in Indian society for centuries and are described in scholarly and popular literature using an array of terms, including eunuchs, transgendered, homosexual, bisexual, inter-sexed, and hermaphrodites (Lai 1999).

While their historical role can be traced to the presence of eunuchs in the Muslim courts, their religious and spiritual role can be traced to the Hindu religion. The existence and legitimization of this third gender role is attributed to the presence of an array of alternative genders in Indian mythology and culture. Like other Indian **castes**, the origin of the hijras is told through a myth linking them to Hindu deities. This origin myth provides a link with Hinduism, thus not only validating a ritual place for hijras in society, but also linking their gender role with the deities and mythic figures of the religion (Nanda 1999: 13). Within Hindu and Indian mythology, there exist a number of examples of the combined power of men and women, among both deities and humans. These mythical figures are very well known among Indian society, allowing for the hijras not only to exist, but also to occupy a place of ritual significance (Nanda 1999: 20). For example, one of the most significant figures to the hijra community is that of Shiva. Shiva is "a deity who incorporates both male and female characteristics. Shiva is an ascetic—one who renounces sex—and yet appears in many erotic and provocative roles.... One of the most powerful forms of Shiva is that of *Ardhanarisvara*, or half man/half woman, which represents Shiva united with his shakti (female creative power). Hijras say that worshipers of Shiva give them special respect because of this close identification, and hijras often worship at Shiva temples" (1999: 20).

While situating the hijras within a historical and religious context is important, so too is understanding how contemporary hijras see themselves. This answer is extremely varied depending on to whom one speaks, where they live, their age, their social status, etc. It is important to remember that just as in any other community, its members each have their own story and identity. Nanda relays the story of four hijras in her ethnography, and their life stories include tales of how they came to join the hijra community, why they dress and perform the way they do, their working and religious life, and how their relationships, past and present, have informed who they are today. Reddy weaves the views of different hijras throughout her analysis and uses categories such as gender, religion, kinship, and class to structure her ethnography. Regardless of how their stories are represented, however, Reddy notes that it is important to remember that hijras do not see themselves solely as sexual beings. Rather, "they argue explicitly for the roles of kinship, religion, and class, among others, in their constructions of self-identity ... they provide a lens through which to examine the embeddedness of sexuality within other arenas of everyday life" (Reddy 2005: 33). While it can be tempting to isolate aspects of personhood into categories as a vehicle through which to better understand culture and society, one must stop and ask: "Is this how I view my own life? Do I see myself solely through one lens, whether it is ethnicity, age, sexuality or gender?" The likely answer is a resounding "no," as all of our lives are a mélange of experiences, categories, and relationships. This is what makes the individual so fascinating!

The role of hijras in Indian society is both multidimensional and ambiguous. Their formal role, and the way in which they earn social respect, is that of a ritual performer who bestows fertility blessings on newborn babies and new marriages. After the birth of a son, families will often throw a celebratory party where a group of hijras will be invited to perform their ritual dances. If compensated appropriately, the hijras will then bless the baby boy with the power of fertility. Weddings provide a similar scene, with hijras dancing and performing and expecting to be compensated for their time. Families willingly oblige, afraid that to disrespect the hijras will bring about infertility in their loved ones. It may appear somewhat of an odd choice to have impotent and emasculated men confer blessings on babies and newlyweds; these are not simply impotent men, however. Nanda explains that, "As ritual performers, they are viewed as vehicles of the divine power of the Mother Goddess, which transforms their impotence into the power of generativity.... The faith in the power of the hijras rests on the

Hindu belief in shakti—the potency of the dynamic female forces of creation that the hijras, as vehicles of the Mother Goddess, represent" (Nanda 1999: 5).

The income garnered from their formal role, however, is rarely enough for a hijra to live on, and many must make ends meet through other means, such as begging or prostitution. These practices are less socially desirable, and as a result their "true" role as a performer has been undermined. Many hijras themselves condemn prostitution, for it goes against the claims that hijras are ascetics, that is, that they have renounced sexual activity. At the same time, however, hijras must survive, and the wage they earn from prostitution supplements the small wage they earn as performers. As well, discussions with hijras illustrate that many freely admit to having sexual desire. Once again, we see a chasm between the official role and definition on the one hand, and the reality as it is lived in contemporary society on the other. The complex place that hijras occupy in Indian society and the contradictions that characterize their position require a holistic approach in order to gain a better understanding of their social role.

For our purposes here, we are interested in looking at how the existence of the hijras signifies a challenge to the dichotomous gender identities found in the West. Of course, not all Westerners ascribe to this dichotomy, and the prominence of trans people and their supporters has become increasingly strong over the last 20 years. From a Western perspective, it may be tempting to think of the hijras in terms of Western definitions of transsexuality or homosexuality. These identities, however, do not share the religious and ritual components that the hijra role in Indian society does. One of the central differences between trans people and the alternative gender roles found in other cultures is that "trans-sexualism has been defined in such a way as to reinforce our cultural construction of both sex and genders as invariably dichotomous" (Nanda 1999: 137). Trans people assert that while they are born with the genitalia of one sex, their gender identity, or "inner psychological conviction," is that of the other sex (1999: 137). The transitional status associated with a man becoming a woman, or a woman becoming a man, negates the possibility of a third gender and serves to reinforce the dichotomy of *either* man *or* woman that is so prominent in the Western world. While hijras are referred to as neither men nor women, the experienced gender identity of many hijras is, on first glance, as women. Can they really be a third gender if their gender identity is as women?

By discussing the deep-rooted place of hijras in Indian society, Nanda illustrates that there exists an institutionalized, or long-established, place in society for a third gender role. A gender role or identity does not mean the same thing for everyone—of the four hijras whose stories she tells, all have different conceptions of their own gender identity that is related to their personal experiences as a child, an adult, a woman, or a man. What they share, however, is a declaration that they are *not* men in either the physical sense, i.e., insofar as they are impotent and have undergone the religious obligation of emasculation, or in the behavioral sense, i.e., insofar as they do not have the sexual feelings and preferences of other men. As one hijra named Krishna states, "We are not men with the ordinary desires of men to get married and have families.

Otherwise, why would we choose to live this life?" (Nanda 1999: 16). Hijras wear their hair long, and most dress in women's clothing and take female names when they join the hijra community. They declare, however, that they are not women. Nanda describes how "their female dress and mannerisms are often exaggerations, almost to the point of caricature, and they act in sexually suggestive ways that would be considered inappropriate, and even outrageous, for ordinary women in their significant and traditional female roles as daughters, wives and mothers" (1999: 18). The most important detail that sets them apart from women is their inability to menstruate and have children. Thus, the lived gender identity that hijras experience as a group exists outside of the dichotomous gender system that structures mainstream society in Western countries.

Other anthropological research conducted with communities who do not ascribe to a dichotomous gender system illustrates the socially constructed reality of gender identity and behavior. Research among the kathoey of Thailand, the xanith of Oman, the berdache of Indigenous North America, and the f'afafine of Polynesia illustrates that a third gender is not a phenomenon limited to India and signifies the diversity of gender construction (Reddy 2005: 31). The work of Nanda, Reddy, and other anthropologists shows us that by looking cross-culturally at how gender roles are conceptualized and realized, the Western dichotomous approach to understanding gender (boy/girl, man/woman) is also a cultural construct, and only one way in a myriad of perspectives.

Theory Steering Perception

Thorne, Pascoe, and Fong approached the study of gender from a feminist perspective; however, their methodologies were very different and, as a result, they asked and answered very different research questions. While Thorne and Pascoe conducted participant observation and held interviews in two schools, Fong conducted participant observation, interviews, and surveys in a variety of locales (e.g., schools, homes). While Fong's approach allowed her to reach many more people than both Thorne and Pascoe, the issues that they were investigating would not have benefited from a survey, since the type of data yielded by that kind of data collection would not have enriched their understanding of gender and sexuality. Survey data, as used by Fong, were employed to recount *how* things happened—in this case, she wanted the perspectives of mothers and grandmothers concerning their past experiences as daughters, while observation is an interpretation of the immediate present. As well, Fong's scope of analysis included a discussion of the economic and political climate of the time, a necessary component to her understanding of how gender roles have transformed over time. Nanda employed an interpretive, cross-cultural approach that allowed her to consider the existence of third genders in societies across the world, and how these gender roles differed from or were similar to that of the hijras in India. Central to her analysis was a consideration of the symbolism, myth, and history of Indian culture, for an understanding of these components of society allowed her to conclude that the hijras did indeed occupy an "institutionalized" position within society. While all four researchers investigated gender, their approaches, methods, and theoretical perspectives led them to pose and answer very different questions.

Conclusion

Perhaps one of anthropology's greatest contributions is showing how difficult it is to arrive at conclusions about human nature without taking into account the full variety of human experience. Anthropologists do not deny that there is such a thing as human nature. Indeed, some anthropologists have been seriously engaged with finding out the common denominators that underlie the bewildering variety of cultural practices around the world. Seeking to find such a common denominator (if one exists) in constructions of sexuality or gender is but one example of this quest. In this chapter we have considered how constructions of gender contribute to the social organization of society by examining how it is experienced by children and teens in the American public education system, by singleton daughters in urban China, and by individuals who identify as belonging to a third gender in India. Anthropology, like the individuals who practice it, is situated in a specific time and place. It reflects the concerns of the society around it. In the same way that Franz Boas and Margaret Mead were interested in refuting racist ideology and discriminatory policies against immigrants, contemporary anthropologists concern themselves with social issues such as homophobia, the education of children, and women's rights. The aim of research is to bring about a better understanding of issues or questions that the public has deemed significant. Gender and sexuality are social constructs that are very much part of our daily lives, even if we do not think about them as distinct categories. The holistic approach embraced by anthropologists illustrates just how far-reaching these categories are, and also demonstrates the importance of gaining an understanding of how such categories are constructed, and why.

Study Questions

1   Explain what is meant by the phrase "we 'do' gender."
2   Summarize Thorne's research. How did her methods differ from a typical study of children? What did she discover about how roles are assigned and reinforced in the school environment?
3   Summarize what Pascoe discovered about hetero-masculinity and why she argues that homophobia is not just a matter of sexuality.
4   From a feminist theoretical perspective, why is it important to consider gender alongside other categories such as class, ethnicity, and age?

5   Explain how kinship and family relationships relate to social constructions of gender.

6   Compare and contrast the effect of China's one-child policy on urban and rural families. Outline the policy's generational influence on the economic situation of singleton daughters in urban communities.

7   Why is situating the hijras within a historical and religious context important to understanding their role in Indian society?

8   What does it mean to say that theory steers perception? Use examples from the chapter.

Discussion Questions

1   Consider the assertion that gender roles and behaviors are situational and fluid, meaning that they are likely to change depending on the company, the context, and one's age. Do you agree with this? Why or why not? Give an example from your own life experience to support your answer.

2   What value does a cross-cultural approach to studying gender and sexuality provide?

3   Consider your own experience growing up. What social cues, activities, policies, influences, rituals, rules, or expectations played a role in how you came to understand gender roles and sexuality?

4   Explain what is meant by the phrase "believing is seeing" in relation to gender behavior. In your experience, does this ring true?

CHAPTER 9

//

Race, Science, and Human Diversity

LEARNING OBJECTIVES

After reading this chapter, students should be able to

- understand the historical notion of race as both a biological and political concept;
- explain Darwin's theory of natural selection and his conclusions about the diversity of the human race;
- define *typological thinking* and *anthropometry* and discuss their historical significance;
- outline the history of the eugenics movement and historical attitudes toward "race mixing" and segregation;
- outline the Boasian argument against the connections of race, heredity, culture, and nation by racial nationalists;
- explain the historical circumstances that led to the genocide in Rwanda; and
- summarize the influence of genetics on anthropology's study of human diversity.

KEY TERMS

eugenics movement
genome

natural selection

typological thinking

Introduction

The problem of human diversity has always been central to anthropology, but physical differences bring that issue to focus in a particularly vivid way. Anyone can see that humanity comes in different flavors, but since all human populations are highly variable, the closer you look the more varieties you see. What are we to make of this? Are these superficial differences, or do they go deeper? What does their presence suggest about the history and future of our species? In this chapter we ask: What kind of a concept is "race"? Just what is it supposed to explain? Does it necessarily lead to "racism"? What is the relation between race, heredity, and culture? Why has it seemed so important to decouple them? In the spirit of the Boasian four-fields ideal, we also ask about the relation between cultural and physical anthropology, and of both to the biological sciences. How are developments in genetics and genomics leading to new forms of social identity and the revision of old ones?

We begin with a historical sketch of the problem and then turn to two historically important examples involving the concept of race. Thomas Jefferson (1743–1826) was the author of the American Declaration of Independence and president of the United States from 1800 to 1808; he also launched the Lewis and Clark expedition to the Pacific coast. In 1772, Jefferson married a local Virginia woman, and together they had a number of children, of whom two—both girls—survived to adulthood. But did he also father a *second* family through his relationship with an African-American domestic slave whose descendants are with us today? This question opens up the broader issue of how race was thought about in what was once a rigidly segregated society—of the social factors that influence how we think about human difference, and of how the lines are drawn between racial categories.

Our second example comes from Africa. Rwanda and Burundi are small land-locked countries in eastern Africa. In pre-colonial times, each was ruled by a king who came from an aristocratic cattle-keeping group of clans known as the Tutsi. Those they ruled over were farmers known as Hutu. Following the great land-grab by European powers, they came to be governed by Belgium. After independence in the early 1960s, internal conflict between segments of the population led to increasing violence, culminating in Rwanda in an attempt to wipe the Tutsi from the face of the earth. What was the role of the concept of "race" in the unfolding of this tragic event?

Finally, we'll consider how modern genetic technology is reshaping our concepts of race and social identity. This technology was influential in determining whether Thomas Jefferson did indeed father an African-American family. As always, first some background.

Understanding Diversity

By the early nineteenth century there had already been much speculation about the classification, nature, and origin of human races, accompanied by increasing knowledge about the actual range of human variability. But how did these differences arise? A number of schemes of racial classification were developed, along with theories to explain them. Perhaps physical differences—skin color for instance, or bodily stature—were influenced by the climate, or some other environmental factor. Perhaps the races were created separately in different parts of the world.

Charles Darwin (1809–82) didn't know what to make of human racial difference. And he thought about the question deeply, since variation within a species was key to his theory of evolution through **natural selection**. Natural selection works on variation, choosing variants with adaptive value and rejecting or ignoring those without it. In the long term those individuals with useful variations leave more offspring, and evolution moves on in the direction indicated by the selective process. Darwin thought of a race as an "incipient species." Species give rise to races—relatively minor variants—then to sub-species, and finally to true species that have lost the ability to interbreed with their cousins. As time goes by, the differences between the offspring of a common ancestor grow increasingly pronounced—and so we arrive at the classic image of evolution as a branching tree growing upward from its roots, but with some branches dropping off through extinction (see Plate 9.1 for a Victorian example of an evolutionary tree). What then of ourselves?

Darwin considered the various ways in which human races differ from one another and concluded that they are relatively superficial in comparison to what we have in common: "numerous points of resemblance are of much more importance than the amount of similarity or dissimilarity in a few points" (1998: 154). Thus, all humanity clearly belongs to one species. Put clothes on Fuegians and they're remarkably like Englishmen.[1] But racial difference still needed to be accounted for. Darwin's own theory—sexual selection—didn't attract many fans. He couldn't see that the distinctive racial traits have any selective value, and therefore turned to the notion that in the distant past they might have arisen out of local standards of beauty.

There were more plausible lines of argument. Maybe racial differences did (or once did) confer some hidden selective advantage. Perhaps natural selection isn't the only evolutionary mechanism. Perhaps the different human races separated from the common ancestral population at different times, or evolved on their own at different rates due to geographical separation after migration from wherever humanity originated.

With factors like these thrown in, it was still possible to talk about more or less "advanced" races while retaining the notion of common descent. On the other hand, if it could be shown that we all branched off from one another quite recently in evolutionary time and differ only in very minor ways, this would reinforce the argument for biological racial equality, and hence for social equality. Once again, scientific debates have moral and political implications. We've seen this already in the contrasting views of human nature held by Rousseau and Hobbes (see Chapter 1). Such debates persist, and general texts on paleoanthropology and human evolution contain the details.

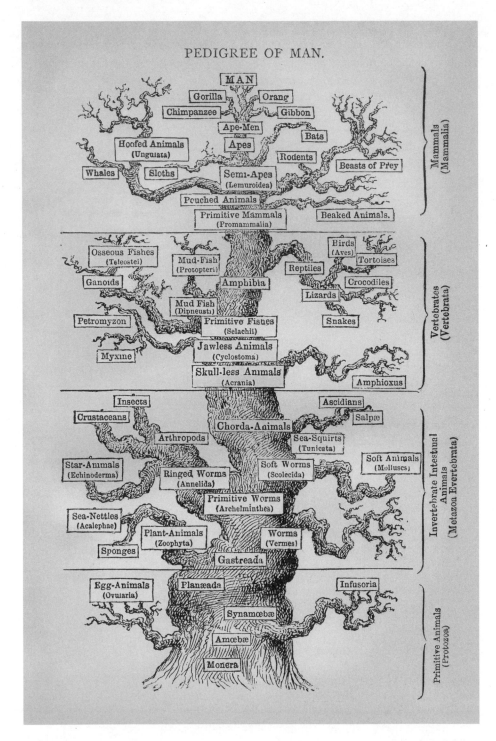

PLATE 9.1 Evolutionary Tree

The Urge to Classify

Here we want to highlight two related points. The first has to do with the way in which biological classification is carried out—slotting organisms into a common category on the basis of physical or genetic similarities and designating it as a species, sub-species, or merely a race. The criteria for doing so can be quite elaborate. The first modern system was devised in the eighteenth century by a Swede, Carl von Linné (or Linnaeus; 1707–78), in order to classify plants. He assigned them Latin names on the basis of similarities between their flowers. Thus we have *Primula vulgaris*, the common primrose, and so on. Linnaeus established the basis for the classification system still in use for all organisms, such as the two sub-species of the genus *Homo*: *Homo sapiens* ("Wise Man"), as distinguished from *Homo neanderthalensis* (extinct, and presumably less wise). Paleoanthropologists argue about whether their latest fossil discovery is sufficiently distinctive to be assigned to a species of its own or is merely a variant of one that's already been unearthed. There's always glory in a new discovery.

This is **typological thinking**, and racial thinking *is* typological thinking. The physical anthropologists of not so long ago classified humanity into a large number of types and sub-types, using criteria such as skull shape, skin color, hair texture, and eye configuration. Thus we get the big three: Caucasoid, Negroid, and Mongoloid, and sub-classes within each type. Each could be defined by a "pure" or ideal example, and actual people regarded as variations more or less close to it. Older textbooks in physical anthropology often feature photographs of individuals representing these idealized types. The skull was exceptionally important because of its accessibility and what it

Fig. 4. The Landmarks and Length and Height Measurements. gl = glabella; op = opisthocranium; na = nasion; sn = subnasale; gn = gnathion; eu = euryon; zy = zygion. Note that the euryon, zygion, and opisthocranium are not definite anatomical points like the nasion and subnasale, but are located wholly by measuring. 22

Fig. 5. Measuring Points and Measurements of Width. gl = glabella; na = nasion; sn = subnasale; gn = gnathion; eu = euryon; zy = zygion; al = alare. Note that the euryon, zygion, and alare are not definite anatomical points like the nasion and subnasale, but are located wholly by measuring. Note also that all the above measurements of width are maximum measurements. 23

PLATE 9.2 Anthropometry

19. *Teutonic types.* NORWAY. Pure blond. 20.

21. *Alpine type.* AUSTRIAN. Blue eyes, brown hair. Index 88. 22.

23. *Mediterranean type.* PALERMO, Sicily. Pure brunet. Index 77. 24.

THE THREE EUROPEAN RACIAL TYPES.

PLATE 9.3 Races of Europe (Ripley 1898)

contains, i.e., the brain. For example, through skull shape the European peoples were sorted into several major branches: the Mediterranean, the Alpine, and the Nordic (or Teutonic).

Such measurements were seen as being the key to racial history and to unpacking the composition of present-day populations—say the relative proportions of Celtic and Anglo-Saxon ancestry in the British Isles, or of Nordic and Alpine in Germany. Skull-measurement techniques were once standard items in the anthropology curriculum. But, given the internal variability of all populations, the findings arrived at in this manner were difficult to interpret, so some important statistical methods were invented to deal with such problems. Franz Boas, for example, took a keen interest in anthropometry (the science of human body measurement) and published extensively on his own anthropometric research.

The second point we want to emphasize is central to our story. "Race" as it's actually used in common speech is a fuzzy notion, and was even more so in the nineteenth and early twentieth centuries. It falls somewhere between "race" in a biological sense, and "people" or "nation" in a political sense. For example, it was possible to speak about belonging to "the British race" as something to be distinctly proud of, some essential quality of one's own being. This is the rhetoric of nineteenth-century nationalism. If race and nation are essentially the same, then national character is a reflection of the nation's racial makeup. Whereas we now tend to assume that national traits are a product of culture and history, racial nationalists claimed that race and culture are inextricably linked. Nazi racial ideology was an extreme version of that idea, as we see in the words of Adolf Hitler:

> All the human culture, all the results of art, science, and technology that we see before us today, are almost exclusively the creative product of the Aryan. If we were to divide mankind into three groups, the founders of culture, the bearers of culture, the destroyers of culture, only the Aryan could be considered as the representative of the first group. [The state] must set race in the center of all life. It must take care to keep it pure. (Hitler 1998: 292, 403)

The nature of heredity was poorly understood. There was a common and usually unspoken assumption that the historical experience of a nation, a people, or a race somehow gets imprinted on its hereditary material and is expressed over the generations in the behavior and capacities of individuals. Ethnic stereotypes reflect these assumptions: Italians are passionate, Irish are alcoholics, Jews are acquisitive, the French undependable, Germans solid, Negroes lecherous, Chinese crafty, and so on. Early in the twentieth century, a prominent writer on heredity and eugenics speculated what the impact of these new immigrants might be on the American character: "It appears certain that ... the population of the United States will, on account of the great influx of blood from South-eastern Europe, rapidly become darker in pigmentation, smaller in stature, more mercurial, more attached to music and art, more

given to crimes of larceny, kidnapping, assault, murder, rape and sex-immorality …"
(Davenport 1911: 219).

The Boasians took aim at this kind of thing. The concept of culture in its modern form was one response to the conscious and unconscious racism of the day. The context was an early-twentieth-century North America in the throes of radical social change brought about by a huge upsurge of internal and external migration. African-Americans were moving in large numbers from rural areas to the cities. Foreign immigration increasingly stemmed from sources outside northern Europe and the British Isles: Italy, Greece, the Balkans, Poland, and Russia, for example. Many Eastern European Jews came to North America as part of this wave. In the US, Canada, and Australia, Chinese immigration was discouraged by racial exclusion laws. Economic anxieties were one factor behind this; trade unionists believed that cheap Chinese labor would undercut their bargaining position. But there was also a general sense of racial incompatibility. Here's a Canadian example from 1902: "They come … with customs, habits and modes of life fixed and unalterable…. They form, on their arrival, a community within a community, separate and apart, a foreign substance within but not of our body politic, with no love for our laws or institutions; a people that cannot assimilate and become an integral part of our race and nation" (quoted in Anderson 1991: 73).

The problem of immigration was very much on the public mind when Boas began talking about race. Another factor was the rise of the **"eugenics" movement**. The term is derived from Greek and means "well born." It was coined by Charles Darwin's cousin, Francis Galton (1822–1911), who had become interested in the issue of heredity and racial "quality" with regard to the future of Great Britain. He believed that it should be possible to improve the British race, or at least to prevent it from degenerating due to the different birthrates between the upper and lower classes, between law-abiding citizens and the social problem groups: criminals, the insane, drug addicts, drunkards, prostitutes, the feeble-minded, and the welfare dependent. He therefore advocated social policies aimed at encouraging the upper classes to reproduce more enthusiastically and to discourage the lower orders from doing so.

The concept of "feeble-mindedness" turns out to be exceptionally significant, since it is related to the broader factor of innate intelligence. And that is related in turn to the rise of intelligence testing, a seemingly scientific way of judging the quality of individuals and groups. The IQ (intelligence quotient) test was originally devised by Alfred Binet (1857–1911) in France as a way of measuring the accomplishments of students in relation to the abilities of other children in their age group. An IQ of 100 was defined as the average; if students came in well under or well over that average, they might be recommended for remedial education or moved into a more advanced class.

But as time went on many, particularly in the United States, came to see IQ as reflecting an innate and possibly hereditary factor influencing intelligence and hence social capacity. If some group—a racial minority, say, or the poor—scored lower than the average, this could be seen as an expression of group heredity. In the early twentieth century the "feeble-minded" were seen as a social menace; if allowed to breed freely, it was thought, they would ultimately lead to the degeneration of the nation as a whole. If entire racial or national groups were judged of lesser or greater intelligence, this could be used to explain their level of relative cultural advancement (see Gould 1996).

The underlying assumption was that social class and national quality are largely facts of nature. We also owe the opposition between "nature" and "nurture" to Galton, who believed that the former is paramount in determining racial quality. What Galton said about eugenics in 1904 reflects the influence of his famous cousin:

> Eugenics co-operates with the workings of Nature by securing that humanity shall be represented by the fittest races. What Nature does blindly, slowly, and ruthlessly, man may do providently, quickly, and kindly. The improvement of our stock seems to me one of the highest objects that we can reasonably attempt. I see no impossibility in Eugenics becoming a religious dogma among mankind.... (Galton 1909: 42–43)

Some early feminists were interested in eugenics in addition to women's rights, and the planned-parenthood movement was one outcome—making contraception easily available to working-class women.[2]

Eugenics migrated to North America and became another element in the debate about the genetic future of the American and Canadian peoples. Unlike in Britain, this led to concrete social-policy initiatives, and a number of states and two Canadian provinces (Alberta and British Columbia) passed "eugenic sterilization" legislation aimed at the genetically "unfit"—usually people in state institutions or caught up in the welfare bureaucracy.[3] The National Socialist government in Germany took this further still, but eugenic legislation was also enacted in Scandinavia.[4] Many thousands were sterilized as a result, and in North America the fallout from these policies is still with us in the form of official apologies and financial compensation for the victims. Boas (1916: 478) had himself warned against the excesses of the eugenics movement: "Eugenics should not be allowed to deceive us into the belief that we should try to raise a race of supermen, nor that it should be our aim to eliminate all suffering and pain. Eugenics is not a panacea that will cure human ills; it is rather a dangerous sword that may turn its edge against those who rely on its strength."

We've noted that it was commonly thought that the character of a nation is determined by its racial composition. Anxiety about "race mixing" was therefore very much in the air as well, given the fact that North America seemed to be going through the greatest experiment of this kind that the world had ever seen. There were concerns about what would happen as the old social order lost its northern-European character and became increasingly "mongrelized." A number of influential studies investigated people of mixed-race background, for example in Canada, the Caribbean, and the German African colonies. It was thought that the greater the distance between two races, the more likely that crosses between them would be unstable in some way—less fertile perhaps, or morally unbalanced, a collection of discordant ethnic traits warring with one another. In South Africa and in the American South the fear of race mixing was addressed through "anti-miscegenation" legislation, to which we'll return shortly.

Franz Boas discussed all this in a lecture series that was published in 1911 as *The Mind of Primitive Man*, which we introduced in Chapter 2. It amounts to a Boasian manifesto—a statement of general principles that can be seen in his own writings and in those of his students for many years to come. In it Boas systematically tries to decouple race from culture, and presents the problem clearly in his introductory lecture:

> It appears that neither cultural achievement nor outer appearance is a safe basis on which to judge the mental aptitude of races. Added to this is the one-sided evaluation of our own racial type and of our modern civilization without any close inquiry into the mental processes of primitive races and cultures....
>
> The object of our inquiry is therefore an attempt to clear up the racial and cultural problems involved in these questions. Our globe is inhabited by many races, and a great diversity of cultural forms exists. The term "primitive" should not be applied indiscriminately to bodily build and the culture as though both belong together by necessity. It is rather one of the fundamental questions to be investigated whether the cultural character of a race is determined by its physical characteristics. The term race itself should be clearly understood before this question can be answered. If a close relation between race and culture should be shown to exist it would be necessary to study for each racial group separately the interaction between bodily build and mental and social life. If it should be proved not to exist, it will be permissible to treat mankind as a whole and to study cultural types regardless of race. (Boas 1963: 30–31; see also Boas 1969)

Boas set out to prove that there is in fact *no* close relation between race and culture, that "race" itself is an incoherent concept, and therefore that humankind can be studied as a whole "regardless of race" (see Stocking 1968). He set out to show that even skull shape is an unstable form and that it varies with changing environmental conditions. The task then becomes that of trying to understand individual cultural forms in all their complexity.

His students took on this challenge with enthusiasm, and some of them also wrote on the race issue. In 1942 Ruth Benedict and her colleague at Columbia University, Gene Weltfish (1902–80), drafted a pamphlet on *The Races of Mankind* that was intended for distribution to US troops. The military was still segregated; even the military blood supply was segregated (see Kenny 2006). Nazi propaganda didn't fail to point out the hypocritical element in a war that was supposedly being fought to defend democracy! Benedict and Weltfish stressed "the unity of the human race" and suggested organizing a racially integrated army division as a social experiment: "With America's great tradition of democracy, the United States should clean its own house and get ready for a better twenty-first century. Then it could stand unashamed before the Nazis and condemn, without confusion, their doctrines of a Master Race … sure that victory in this war will be in the name, not of one race or of another, but of the universal Human Race" (Benedict 1943: 192). The pamphlet was never distributed to the troops; Conservative congressmen thought it was subversive (Marks 2008: 245).[5] Nevertheless, segregation in the US armed forces was ended by presidential order in 1948.

But the most significant work coming from the Boasian group on the problem of race was *Man's Most Dangerous Myth: The Fallacy of Race* (1942). The author was Ashley Montagu (1905–99), an Englishman who had first studied anthropology in Britain and then immigrated to the United States where he did his Ph.D. under Ruth Benedict at Columbia. Montagu outlined the history of the traditional race concept, pointing out how superficial and dangerous it is given the true nature of human diversity being revealed by the geneticists. He concluded that "the so-called 'races' represent different kinds of temporary mixtures of genetic materials common to all mankind." For him the human varieties usually called "races" can be accurately described only in terms of gene frequency (Montagu 1942: 41). The problem then becomes determining what causes this variability.

Like the other Boasians, Montagu found no relationship whatsoever between "race" and "culture" or the capacity for culture. His stance was thoroughly relativistic, "by which I mean that all cultures must be judged in relation to their own history, and all individuals and groups in relation to their cultural history, and definitely not by the arbitrary standard of any single culture such … as our own" (1942: 147):

> What seemed to me wrong with the concept of "race" was that no one appears ever to have examined the presuppositions upon which it was based. Those preconceptions, which were taken for granted, even as axiomatic, were that an individual's race was determined by three conditions: (1) his physical characteristics, (2) his inherited mental capacities, and (3) the character of his group's cultural development. These three conditions were indissolubly linked with each other.… No one seemed to understand that there was really no biological connection between physical and mental characteristics or the ability to achieve a state of high civilization either for the individual or for the group. (quoted in Lieberman, Lyons, and Lyons 1995: 840)

Man's Most Dangerous Myth has never gone out of print, and it is currently in its sixth and much expanded edition. Montagu was also an instrumental figure in producing the influential UNESCO (United Nations Educational, Scientific, and Cultural Organization) *Statement on Race* (see Montagu 1972).[6]

The Rise of Genetics

The year 1900 was a big one for the understanding of human diversity: Gregor Mendel's (1822–84) breeding experiments with garden peas came to light again, and Karl Landsteiner (1868–1943) showed that hereditary factors in human blood are the source of harmful and sometimes fatal immune reactions during transfusion.

As mentioned, the nature of heredity was very poorly understood. This troubled Darwin, among others, because he knew that there had to be a mechanism for the preservation and transmission of useful variations; his theory wouldn't work otherwise. Mendel's experiments seemed to show that there are indeed hereditary unit traits that retain their identity and that are expressed in subsequent generations according to precise laws. Though the nature of this process wasn't known, it stood to reason that there had to be some biological factor with the capacity to preserve and transmit information of this kind. It was proposed to call it a "gene."

Landsteiner demonstrated that blood falls into groups—now called A, B, AB, and O—which, like the traits of pea plants, are passed on according to definite statistical rules. This discovery marked the beginning of human genetics as a science. It then turned out that these blood types are not evenly distributed across the globe, but have concentrations in certain regions. Type B, for example, has a peak in south-central Asia and India, while type O is virtually universal among the Native peoples of the Americas but is also common in northern Europe and Japan. Such findings gave rise to human population genetics, and to quite different questions than could be answered by skull measuring (Mourant 1983). It was now possible to talk about "gene frequencies" and to diagram them on charts that look a lot like old-fashioned weather maps—derived by connecting the dots for equal frequencies of the genetic trait of interest. The concept of "race" now seems very static; anthropologists and medical researchers turn instead to population genetics in order to explore evolutionary processes and historical connections between populations. We'll have more to say about this in the conclusion, but for now we turn to our case studies.

Red, White, and Black

Sex is one of the factors that serve to define community boundaries. Who is a legitimate mate? Who is in, and who is out? The traditional caste system of India provides a striking illustration: castes are theoretically endogamous; they only marry internally. Marriage and sex outside very narrow boundaries is considered polluting. "Honor killing" might well be the fate of someone—a woman particularly—who steps outside and brings shame upon her family.

But sex is hard to regulate. When Captain Cook reached Hawai'i he tried and failed to prevent his crews from associating with Hawaiian women and spreading venereal disease. When the English settled in Virginia in the early seventeenth century, there were soon liaisons between European men and Indigenous women. The mixed-race Métis population of Canada and the Mestizos of Mexico are results of this process. The most famous example is the "princess" Pocahontas (Smith 1966: 49). What happened between English captain John Smith (c. 1580–1631) and Pocahontas (c. 1595–1617) has become the stuff of myth. All we really know is what Smith himself tells us in his *History of Virginia*. Whether it's also a *true* story need not concern us. Smith says he was captured by the warriors of Tsenacommacah Chief Powhatan and brought before him, which provoked a debate about Smith's fate:

> The conclusion was, two great stones were brought before Powhatan; then as many could laid hands on [Smith], dragged him to them, and thereon laid his head, and being ready with their clubs, to beat out his braines, *Pocahontas* the Kings dearest daughter, when no intreaty could prevaile, got his head in her armes, and laid her owne upon his to save him from death: whereat the Emperor was contented he should live. (Smith 1966: 49)

It's all very romantic, and the names of John Smith and Pocahontas have been joined together ever since. But when it came to marriage she was not joined to Smith but to an English widower named John Rolfe (1585–1622)—"an honest Gentleman, and of good behavior" (Smith 1966: 113). There had been trouble between Powhatan's people and the English, and the marriage helped to smooth things over for the time being. Rolfe already had children by his first marriage, and with Pocahontas he had a son named Thomas (1615–80). He and Pocahontas, now named Rebecca, went to England and were introduced to King James, but she died as they were about to set sail back to America. John Rolfe's descendants by his first marriage came to be known as the "White Rolfes" and those through Pocahontas as the "Red Rolfes." Today some 100,000 people proudly claim "Red" descent.

That was a special case. As the English became more established in their new colony, a more familiar pattern set in. Conflict with Indigenous peoples led to open war, and war coupled with disease led to the destruction of the Native chiefdoms. As Jefferson said in his 1785 *Notes on the State of Virginia*, "spirituous liquors, the smallpox, war, and an abridgement of territory … had committed terrible havoc among them" (Jefferson 1964: 91).[7] With the realization that tobacco could be a valuable export, there was an increasing demand for labor; Africans were imported as early as 1620, and this in time led to the slave-based plantation system. But Indigenous people hadn't vanished, and poor rural communities of mixed white, black, and Indigenous ancestry took form that still retained a sense of their Indigenous identity.

Jefferson was interested in the Indians, and he engaged in a bit of local archaeology himself. Lewis and Clark were instructed to take detailed note of the Indigenous people they encountered along the way, and they did so—in part to explore the potential for trade (Wallace 1999: 101). Jefferson speculated about their ultimate origins:

Great question has arisen from whence came those aboriginals of America? ... The late discoveries of Captain Cook, coasting from Kamschatka to California, have proved that if the two continents of Asia and America are separated at all, it is only by a narrow strait.... The resemblance between the Indians of America and the eastern inhabitants of Asia, would induce us to conjecture, that the former are the descendants of the latter, or the latter of the former.... (1964: 96)

He was also concerned with the problem of slavery and the characteristics of blacks as a people. By his count there were in 1785 close to 300,000 free inhabitants in Virginia and about 270,000 slaves. In the American Declaration of Independence (1776) he had written, "We hold these truths to be self-evident, that all men are created equal, that they are endowed by their Creator with certain unalienable Rights." This document was hugely significant for the development of the concept of human rights. It was followed in the same century by the revolutionary French *Declaration of the Rights of Man* (1789) and the American *Bill of Rights* (1791), and more recently by the United Nations *Universal Declaration of Human Rights* (1948) and the Canadian *Charter of Rights and Freedoms* (1982). The UN declaration virtually quotes Jefferson in recognizing the "inherent dignity and the equal and inalienable rights of all members of the human family [as] the foundation of freedom, justice and peace in the world."

Yet Jefferson himself remained a slaveholder and was keenly aware of the inconsistency between his great words and the actual American situation—which he called a "blot" and a "great political and moral evil" that he hoped would one day lead to "a complete emancipation of human nature" once the public was ready for it (1964: 86). But he wondered whether black and white Americans could ever live together in peace or would somehow have to be separated (1964: 138–39).

Jefferson's personal circumstances remain obscure. Even while he was alive, rumors circulated about a relationship with a slave woman named Sarah (Sally) Hemings (1773–1835). As it happens, Sally was the half-sister of Jefferson's wife, Martha. Martha Wayles Skelton (1748–82) was a young widow when she married Jefferson in 1772. Her father, John Wayles, in addition to his white family had another family through Elizabeth Hemings, a slave and Sally's mother. Martha died in 1782 shortly after the birth of the last of their six children. Jefferson never married again, nor did he have a male legal heir. Only two daughters with Martha survived until adulthood. As can be seen, this all gets a little complicated.

Sally Hemings was a household servant. In 1785 she accompanied Jefferson and his daughters to Paris, where he served as American ambassador. She lived much of her life at Monticello, Jefferson's home and now a famous tourist attraction.[8] The historian of the Hemings family believes that Jefferson was the father of Sally's seven children—three boys and four girls—two of whom died in infancy (Gordon-Reed 2008). However, neither Jefferson nor Hemings left any account of the nature of their relationship; the evidence for it is mainly circumstantial. Jefferson granted freedom to all three of Sally's sons; other slaves were sold when he died to help pay off his debts. The genetics of the male line turned out to be an important factor in deciding "scientifically" whether Jefferson was indeed their ancestor (see below).

Jefferson died in 1826, and Sally Hemings in 1835. In the years that followed, the slavery issue finally led to the American Civil War. After the defeat of the South, slavery was abolished and constitutional amendments enacted that were aimed at protecting the civil rights of all citizens. Many of these gains were later reversed in the South by legislation restricting the rights of blacks. In Virginia the influence of the eugenics movement resulted in the 1924 *Act to Preserve Racial Integrity*, which declared that "it shall hereafter be unlawful for any white person in this State to marry any save a white person, or a person with no other admixture of blood than white and American Indian" (Kenny 2002: 272). Sixteen states—not all of them Southern—had similar laws.

Ashley Montagu ran through the list in his 1942 book on race. In California, marriage was prohibited with "Negroes, Mongolians, Mulattoes, or members of the Malay Race." In Florida, marriage was prohibited with "Any Negro" (person having one-eighth or more of negro blood)." Montana excluded "Negros or a person of negro blood or in part negro. Chinese person. Japanese person." The list goes on (Montagu 1942: 189–93). In Virginia, a "white person" was defined as having no known trace of non-white blood (including Asian)—*except* those who were one-sixteenth or less. This logic was based on a perception of who most people claiming Indigenous ancestry actually were. Given a long history of intermixture ("miscegenation") between white, Indigenous, and black communities, it was assumed that virtually all Indigenous peoples were legally black. The exceptions applied mainly to those with no record of black ancestry, who were clearly white in cultural terms, and who could demonstrate a line of descent leading back to Pocahontas.

What finally ended this form of discrimination was a case brought before the US Supreme Court in 1967. It was called *Loving versus Virginia*, and was on behalf of Richard and Mildred Loving. Richard (1933–75) was white and Mildred (1939–2008) was of mixed African-American and Rappahannock ancestry. The couple had married in Washington, DC, where interracial marriage was legal, but had taken up residence back in Virginia where they ran afoul of the Racial Integrity Act. The authorities learned of their status and had them arrested; the Lovings were convicted and sentenced to jail in 1959, but they were allowed to leave the state on the condition that they not return. The Virginia trial judge had said that "Almighty God created the races white, black, yellow, malay and red, and he placed them on separate continents…. The fact that he separated the races shows that he did not intend for the races to mix."[9] Some applied the same logic in defense of segregated schools: if schools were to be integrated, that would naturally lead to miscegenation, and finally to racial degeneration.

The Loving decision was appealed through the state system, but got nowhere. It was then brought before the US Supreme Court as a clear violation of the Lovings' civil rights. The Justices voted unanimously to overturn the Virginia decisions: "under our Constitution, the freedom to marry, or not marry, a person of another race resides with the individual and cannot be infringed by the State. These convictions must be reversed. It is so ordered."[10] And, legally speaking, that was the end of it.[11] These events are the subject of a very well received 2016 film called simply "Loving."

African Racism

When European explorers first reached the interior of East Africa in the 1860s, they were surprised to find centrally organized kingdoms. The largest of these was Buganda, first visited in 1864 by two British officers—John Hanning Speke (1827–64) and James Grant (1827–92). What motivated their trip was an attempt to find the source of the Nile, the Holy Grail of Victorian geography. Speke described his first sight of the royal court, near the present city of Kampala, the capital of Uganda:

> The palace or entrance quite surprised me by its extraordinary dimensions, and the neatness with which it was kept. The whole brow and sides of the hill on which we stood were covered with gigantic grass huts, thatched as neatly as so many heads dressed by a London barber, and fenced all round with the tall yellow reeds of the common Uganda tiger-grass; while within the enclosure, the lines of huts were joined together, or partitioned off into courts, with walls of the same grass. (Speke 1863: 287)

Speke and Grant were followed by the famous journalist and explorer Henry Stanley (1841–1904), who was impressed by the seemingly advanced nature of the Ganda kingdom. Royalty was something the Europeans understood and, as the British had done in India, local African rulers were incorporated into the structure of the colonial state by a kind of treaty arrangement: "A sharp line of separation was drawn between the royal family and commoners, and the blood royal was held to be most sacred" (Roscoe 1911: 187).

Speke records his reaction upon first meeting Kabaka Mtesa, the king: "A more theatrical sight I never saw. The king, a good-looking, well-figured, tall young man of 25, was sitting on a red blanket spread upon a square platform of royal grass, encased in tiger-grass reeds, scrupulously well dressed in a [bark-cloth toga]. A white dog, spear, shield, and woman [the symbols of Uganda] were by his side, as also a knot of staff officers, with whom he kept up a brisk conversation" (1863: 291). The king represented the nation; when a new king was installed he went through a ceremony in which he symbolically "ate Uganda." A rich oral tradition pointed back some 30 generations to the foundation of the kingdom. Though the royal clan was unique, it wasn't clear whether its power had arisen through conquest or had grown up organically from within (Kenny 1988). The economy was based on banana cultivation and fishing in Lake Victoria, with a lesser role for herding.

PLATE 9.4 Mtesa

The situation was quite different in the neighboring kingdoms to the southwest. Here society was divided up into caste-like groups, with a strongly defined contrast between cattle-keeping clans and the agriculturalists, whom the cattle-keepers were said to have conquered sometime in the distant past. The cattle-keepers dominated the farmers and extracted tribute from them in the form of grain, beer, and labor; but bonds of reciprocity were established by lending cattle to commoners—a form of feudalism. The entire system was held together through the person of the king, who was the symbolic and economic focus of the social order.

That is the situation that the Europeans found in Rwanda and Burundi. Cattle-keeping aristocrats, the Tutsi, dominated the agriculturalists, the Hutu, who were seen as their serfs. Relations between them were based on what Belgian anthropologist Jacques Maquet called "the premise of inequality"—the notion that categories of people are superior or inferior by nature, "the fundamental ... cultural premise underlying the social roles of the ruler and the subject" (Maquet 1961: 163–64). The Europeans saw Tutsi dominance as being based on their racial superiority, and this perception had a role in the Rwandan genocide.

As discussed above, all human populations are variable, and that's no less true in Rwanda and Burundi. Their populations had three components: Tutsi, Hutu, and a small minority of Twa—short-statured hunter-gatherers who had once made a living in the tropical forest. Maquet, who worked in Rwanda in the 1950s, outlined the local stereotypes of what these three groups are supposed to be like:

> The Twa are hunters, potters and iron-workers. Twa hunters are not numerous, as game is rare in most parts of Rwanda owing to the scarcity of forest. Some of them make a living as singers, dancers, and buffoons. The Hutu are agriculturalists and the Tutsi pastoralists. The statuses of the three groups are hierarchically ranked. The Tutsi group constitutes an aristocracy, the Hutu are commoners, and the Twa are said, half jokingly ... to be more akin to monkeys than human beings. A definite physical appearance is considered typical of each group. According to the socially accepted descriptions of the three stereotypes the typical Twa is short ... with a head low in the crown, face and nose flat, cheek-bones prominent, forehead bulging, eyes narrow and slightly oblique. Hutu characteristics are wooly hair, flat broad nose, thick lips ... and middle stature. Tutsi are very slender and tall. They often have a straight nose and a light brown skin color. (1961: 10)

From a European point of view, the physical and moral characteristics that seemed to separate Tutsi from Hutu were perfectly natural. They were the same qualities that separated aristocratic Europeans from their own working classes and peasantry. The Tutsi—tall, proud, and light of skin—were born to rule; they were thus people the colonial rulers could deal with. The theory was that their ancestors came from the Ethiopian highlands and were culturally and racially superior to those they came to rule over. The following appears in a 1925 Belgian colonial document:

> The Mututsi of good race has nothing of the negro, apart from his colour. He is usually very tall. He is very thin. His features are very fine: a high brow, thick nose and fine lips framing beautiful shining teeth. Batutsi women are usually lighter-skinned than their husbands, very slender and pretty in their youth .... Gifted with a vivacious intelligence, the Tutsi displays a refinement of feelings which is rare among primitive people. He is a natural-born leader, capable of extreme self-control and of calculated goodwill. (quoted in Prunier 1995: 6)

In practice it wasn't all that easy to tell Hutu and Tutsi apart: there has been a history of intermarriage; they fade into one another as physical types and speak the same Bantu language; they are not separate "tribes" but live in the same communities. Not all Tutsi kept cattle; not all Hutu were poor. So what happened?

PLATE 9.5 King of Rwanda

Rigid distinctions between Hutu and Tutsi were a creation of the colonial order itself. They were not so strongly defined before the coming of the Europeans, who imported their racial preconceptions along with them. There was certainly the "premise of inequality" that Maquet described, but it became increasingly rigid because the Belgian administration favored the Tutsi. People claiming Tutsi identity became a ruling class and virtually monopolized the positions of power that could be occupied by Africans within the framework of a white-ruled colonial state.[12]

> When the Belgians chased the Germans out of the territory in 1916, they discovered that two groups of people shared the land. The Tutsis, who were tall and quite light-skinned, herded cattle; the shorter, darker Hutus tended vegetable plots. The Belgians viewed the minority Tutsis as closer in kind to Europeans and elevated them to positions of power over the majority Hutu, which exacerbated the feudal state of peasant Hutus and overlord Tutsis. Enlisting the Tutsis allowed the Belgians to develop and exploit a vast network of coffee and tea plantations without the inconvenience of war or the expense of deploying a large colonial service. (Dallaire 2003: 47)

These developments set up the preconditions for the Rwandan genocide and similar conflicts in Burundi. Hutu politicians read Marx and Lenin and took aim at Tutsi class oppression. Class war became race war. A historian of the conflict in Burundi describes how such a thing could have happened in a part of Africa that originally seemed so promising: "From a society characterized by complex sociopolitical hierarchies, Burundi has now become greatly simplified, consisting of separate and mutually antagonistic ethnic aggregates. In time of crisis, Hutu and Tutsi emerge as the only relevant defining characteristic of group identities, reducing all other social roles to … marginal social significance" (Lemarchand 1996: 15).

Since Belgium left Rwanda and Burundi in the early 1960s, Tutsi have killed Hutu, and Hutu have killed Tutsi in both countries. In Rwanda the kingship was overthrown and many Tutsis became refugees in Uganda. Moderates on both sides were murdered or forced to flee. In short, the warring factions became racists. In the United States, a complex history of intermixture was boiled down to the opposition between "black" and "white"; in Rwanda and Burundi, an equally complex history was reduced to the distinction between "Tutsi" and "Hutu." But in Rwanda the outcome was attempted genocide, and 800,000 people died because of it—the result of a carefully orchestrated and politically motivated campaign of systematic murder, an African Holocaust. Canadian general Roméo Dallaire, who headed the UN peacekeeping mission in Rwanda, found himself unable to stop the genocide; instead, he was forced to witness it from the sidelines because of what he saw as the indifference and double-dealing of the outside world. But, he concluded: "Let there be no doubt: the Rwandan genocide was the ultimate responsibility of those Rwandans who planned, ordered, supervised and eventually conducted it. Their extremism was the seemingly indestructible and ugly harvest of years of power struggles and insecurity that had been deftly played upon by their former colonial rulers" (2003: 515). The failure of the UN mission broke General Dallaire's heart.

Genetic Identities

So far we've been dealing mainly with how "racial" identities are socially constructed—how they are products of history and politics, not biology. Critics of the race concept such as Boas, Benedict, and Montagu sought to demonstrate that there is no biologically rooted connection between race and culture. Their target was the racism of the day, and the notion that entire groups of people are superior or inferior because of their racial inheritance. The culture concept was a weapon in that struggle. But does this mean that biology is irrelevant to the study of human differences? No: human population genetics is a thriving field with many applications. It's clear that certain medical conditions are genetically caused and the statistical prevalence of many others influenced by genetic factors. If you look at contemporary medical journals you will see that research in these areas is a major growth industry.

Like blood groups, genetically related disorders have an uneven global distribution. Many examples could be cited: the frequency of sickle cell anemia found among African Americans, but also in the Mediterranean region and India; a number of inheritable disorders among Jews of eastern European descent; genetic disorders among Arab groups with a long history of cousin-marriage; the unusual frequency of iron-overload blood disorder and of cystic fibrosis in western Europe; diabetes among Native North Americans; and so on. Such tendencies can become the focus for political action, such as seeking targeted research funding (see Wailoo and Pemberton 2006).

By the 1990s it had become possible to speak of "molecular anthropology" based on "genomic" analysis. The term "**genome**" applies to the entirety of one's genetic heritage, that is, all the hereditary information one carries. It has a structure that reflects the deep history of one's family line. Technologies and analytical techniques have been developed that make it possible to assess the structure of particular genetic samples quickly and at increasingly low cost.[13] They make it possible to reconstruct one's past in genetic terms, and that of the groups with which one shares a common history.

These two applications of population genetics—medical and anthropological—came together in a controversial case involving the Nuu-chah-nulth of Vancouver Island. They became involved with medical genetics due to a high incidence of rheumatoid arthritis among them. Blood samples were gathered in the hope of getting at the root of this problem. No definite conclusions emerged, however, and it was later learned that these blood samples were used by the geneticist, who was then at the University of British Columbia, to aid another project for which consent had never been granted—genetically based research into the history of human settlement in the Americas:

> Leaders of the Nuu-chah-nulth ... describe the research as another example of exploitation of indigenous peoples. Some have demanded the return of the samples. The Nuu-chah-nulth problem came to the attention of UBC authorities after an indigenous peoples' newspaper reported tribal unrest over the use of their samples for non-arthritis research. [Policies have been introduced] that require researchers to obtain consent each time they wish to conduct new research on stored samples. (Dalton 2002: 111)

The timing and nature of human settlement in the Americas have been issues since Columbus's time. Columbus himself thought about it, as did Thomas Jefferson, Robert Fitzroy, and Charles Darwin. Boas and his group devoted much attention to the problem of cultural affiliations between the tribal peoples of the Northwest Coast and northeastern Russia.[14] The UBC researcher in this case used his samples to show "that the Nuu-chah-nulth contains lineage clusters that predate the colonization of the Americas"—in other words that they originated in Asia (Ward et al. 1991: 8723). Though he thanked them for their collaboration, evidently the Nuu-chah-nulth weren't informed that these samples might be used for a purpose other than the one that was originally intended.

Did this constitute a violation of professional ethics? No, probably not by the standards of the day. But standards change in response to cases like this. How you think about your "origin" is a matter of perspective: "To a Native American, origin might also signify the landscape feature or event where his or her people emerged or acquired their identity" (Lee et al. 2009: 39). The Nuu-chah-nulth sought the return of the blood samples in order to bury them with the bones of their ancestors.[15]

Family Histories

And so we come up against identity issues again. Some Native North Americans reject the "scientific" account of their origins and turn to their own stories instead. Others might well find genomics a useful tool in reconstructing the drama of how their ancestors settled the Americas. But probably all of us are interested in our family histories, in one way or another. There have been professional genealogists around for some time, and many families have members who make a hobby of it. Their activities are based on documentary evidence, birth and death records, immigration certificates, and so on. But new possibilities have appeared, enhanced by the power of the Internet.

One of the first practical uses of blood-typing was paternity testing. If paternity was in dispute, then a blood test could at least determine that Mr. X *wasn't* the father. Now the new genomic technologies make it possible to situate oneself relative to what has been called "deep time"—evolutionary time. Population genetics and genomics have led to a new form of identity-creation via the founding of genetic ancestry search services (Kenny 2009). This may prove especially appealing if there is really no other way to get a handle on one's past, say if one is African American and the African side of one's ancestry has been lost. The human genome research center at Howard University, a historically African-American school, has spun off a commercial enterprise called African Ancestry that aims at helping people recover that lost past:

> Do you know where you are from? Where you are really from? Not the town you were born in or the city you call home. Before the Middle Passage and the time of slavery in the Americas. The place where your bloodline originated and the roots of your family tree truly began. Many of us know we come from Africa but could not claim a specific ancestral homeland. That is, until now! With African Ancestry you can ... connect your ancestry to a specific country in Africa and often to a specific African ethnic group. Now you can know "where you are from" and redefine "who you are."[16]

This is also typological thinking, in that the focus is on essential identities, the core of selfhood. African Ancestry is now one of a number of services that use increasingly high-powered analysis to tell you about yourself, your near past, and your deep past all the way back to the origins of the human species in Africa. These services identify what ethnic groups you may be genetically affiliated with, about the movements of your ancestors long ago, and—by the way—give an estimate of your disease risks. Whatever you make of them, these services give us new ways of talking about ourselves and conceiving of our relations with others.

The simpler genetic tests they use focus on analysis of the Y-chromosome, or on mitochondrial DNA (mtDNA). You probably know that the Y-chromosome determines male sex (XY = male; XX = female). It can be transmitted only down the male line. Mitochondrial DNA is found in small structures in every cell and is essential for cellular energy production, but it is transmitted only down the female line. Both pass from generation to generation largely unchanged, and therefore the analysis of their structure points to processes and events that took place a very long time ago.

African Ancestry tells its potential subscribers that "there is no test for racial identification. Race is a social construct, not genetically determined. Similarly, ethnicity is more cultural than biological." This is certainly true, and yet some findings may have a considerable impact on the understanding of both your family's past and your own present circumstances. African Ancestry warns men interested in their service that it might turn out that their male line is derived from a European, not someone of African descent. As you've seen above, this would not be surprising given the history and nature of slavery. Conversely, in Brazil, which also has a multiracial history—white, black, and Indigenous peoples—it's been found that many who think of themselves as of European descent actually carry mtDNA derived from Africa or the Indigenous peoples of Brazil. The maternal ancestors of their lines were slaves or Indigenous, or both. The researchers who described these findings hoped that Brazilians, once aware of this complex biological history, "would tend to value the genetic diversity of their own country more and would build a more just and harmonious society" (Santos and Maio 2004: 371; see also Alves-Silva et al. 2000).

The controversy surrounding Thomas Jefferson's biracial family was given a new twist in 1998, when a team of geneticists announced in the journal *Nature* that "Jefferson fathered slave's last child" (Foster et al. 1998: 27–38). The child in question was Thomas Eston Hemings (1808–56), who is remembered as resembling Jefferson and having quite light skin (Gordon-Reed 2008: 271, 602). Jefferson's will stated that, upon his death, Eston should be given his freedom, which he was. He subsequently left Virginia, moved to the Midwest where he made his living as a musician, changed his name to Eston Hemings Jefferson, and in effect became "white."

How were the geneticists to get at the truth of this? Jefferson left no sons from his marriage. However, he had an uncle—Field Jefferson—whose male line, like Eston's, has continued on into our own day. Both were therefore available for Y-chromosome analysis. To make a long story short, there was a match between the two; other families suspected of having Jeffersonian ancestry showed no match and were thus excluded. Even that didn't *quite* settle the issue, but it was pretty close:

> We cannot completely rule out other explanations of our findings based on illegitimacy in various lines of descent. For example, a male-line descendant of Field Jefferson could possibly have illegitimately fathered an ancestor of the presumed male-line descendant of Eston. But in the absence of historical evidence to support such possibilities, we consider them to be unlikely. (Foster et al. 1998: 27–28)

The Thomas Jefferson Association, consisting of Jefferson's Euro-American descendants through his daughters, has invited the Hemings descendants to their meetings, and some from both sides appeared on the *Oprah Winfrey Show*. There have been joint gatherings at Jefferson's home, Monticello.

Conclusion

The concept of "race" has had a troubled career. From the beginning it was linked to the basic question of human origins and destiny, but also to the problem of how to interpret physical diversity. In the nineteenth century "race" became a key element in colonial discourse, and thus a projection of European political dominance. Caucasians were born to rule the colored races, if only to bring them up to the level where they could rule themselves. Colonized peoples have been paying the price for this assumption ever since. The ethical issues that have arisen within anthropology in recent years are one expression of that fact.

But "race" was an element in scientific discourse as well. The concept of evolution has, since Darwin's time, been a central factor in how human diversity is understood. This didn't necessarily work to the advantage of colonized peoples, since it was always possible to think of them as less "evolved." But race was a powerful factor within the European world as well, in that it was one expression of ethnic nationalism. Nevertheless, the evolutionary approach led to some challenging questions, and some very provocative answers, right down to our own time and the rise of "molecular anthropology." That story continues, and so we wonder if the career of race as an intellectually viable concept is coming to an end, or merely is in the process of changing into a new form driven by the circumstances of our time.

Notes

1   See Stepan (1982) and Stocking (1982) for background; see also Chapter 1.

2   For a general overview of the eugenics movement see Kevles (1995); for how it unfolded in the United States see Paul (1995), and in Canada, McLaren (1990).

3   See Carlson (2001).

4   We are speaking here only of what was done under the laws of these various states. In Nazi Germany much more was done "unofficially"—beginning with the mass killing of patients in mental institutions.

5   In the early 1950s, Gene Weltfish was investigated for suspected communist sympathies, and she lost her university job because of it.

6   The American Anthropological Association and the American Association of Physical Anthropologists have their own statements on race: http://www.aaanet.org/stmts/racepp.htm; http://www.physanth.org/association/position-statements/biological-aspects-of-race/.

7   See Wallace (1999: 74–101) for details of Jefferson's views and the fate of the Virginia Indians.

8   See http://www.monticello.org/.

9   Cited in 1967 US Supreme Court decision, http://supreme.justia.com/cases/federal/us/388/1/case.html.

10   See http://caselaw.lp.findlaw.com/scripts/getcase.pl?court=us&vol=388&invol=1.

11   As of June 26, 2015, the United States Supreme Court ruled that state-level bans on same-sex marriage are unconstitutional. Same-sex marriage is now legal in all states, Washington, DC, and all US territories except American Samoa (Liptak 2015). Canada has allowed same-sex marriage since 2006.

12   The American Anthropological Association Statement on Race points out that "ultimately 'race' became a strategy for dividing, ranking, and controlling colonized people used by colonial powers everywhere."

13   If you're interested in the details of how this is done, see Jobling, Hurles, and Tyler-Smith (2004).

14   To investigate this issue, Boas organized what was known as the Jesup North Pacific Expedition, which is remembered as "a research project of such scientific importance and geographical scope that it still ranks as the foremost expedition in the history of American anthropology" (Freed, Freed, and Williamson 1988: 7).

15   There are other cases of this sort. One involves the Yanomamo, who live in the borderlands between Venezuela and Brazil, from whom blood was taken in aid of a project on the population genetics of small tribal groups (see Couzin-Frankel 2010). Another relates to the Havasupai, a small tribe that lives in and around the Grand Canyon in Arizona, from whom blood samples were taken in the course of research undertaken to understand an unusual incidence of diabetes (Dalton 2004).

16   See http://www.africanancestry.com/home/.

Study Questions

1   Explain how the stories of Pocahontas and Thomas Jefferson illustrate our historical understanding of race as a biological and social concept.

2   What is eugenics? What did Galton mean when he said that "eugenics co-operates with the workings of Nature by securing that humanity shall be represented by the fittest races"?

3   Outline the Boasian stance on the relationship between culture and race using examples from the various scholars mentioned in the chapter.

4   Explain Benedict and Weltfish's argument against racial segregation in World War II.

5   How does the history of Thomas Jefferson and his descendants mirror how our understanding of race and identity has evolved over time?

6   Explain how Europeans perceived the relationship between the Hutu and the Tutsi in Rwanda and Burundi. How was this perception informed by the way

in which their own social classes were organized at home? What were the implications of their perceptions?

7 Explain the controversial case of the Nuu-chah-nulth of Vancouver Island and the geneticist from the University of British Columbia who took the blood samples. What does this case suggest about the ethics of genomic research?

Discussion Questions

1 How can cultural anthropology contribute to a better understanding of the way in which race is conceptualized? What questions can an anthropologist interested in studying race as a cultural construct pose?

2 Most anthropologists and other social scientists recognize that race is a socially constructed category, yet the concept of race persists in our culture. Why is this?

3 The rise of genetic ancestry search services such as African Ancestry reflects a desire among the public to learn about their genetic past. Why do you think this desire exists? In what ways does society contribute to the importance placed on genetic ancestry?

CHAPTER 10

//

The Politics of Culture

LEARNING OBJECTIVES

After reading this chapter, students should be able to

- understand the modern concept of culture and anthropology's role in developing it;
- discuss culture in terms of ownership and define the terms *cultural nationalism* and *revitalization movement*;
- discuss the Handsome Lake religion, the Whaler's Shrine, and the Makah whale hunt within the context of cultural ownership and revitalization;
- summarize Sproat's experience of the Indigenous peoples he helped to displace and his observations on private property and the potlatch;
- understand the circumstances that surrounded the Indigenous land claims in British Columbia and the significance of oral tradition in the Skeena River Valley case; and
- outline Satterfield's work on the culture of activism and her findings on the dispute over old-growth logging in Oregon.

KEY TERMS

activism	oral traditions	savage beast
essentialist	potlatch	treaty
noble savage	revitalization movement	

Introduction

The concept of "culture" in its modern form is probably anthropology's greatest contribution to human self-understanding, and is certainly its greatest contribution to the English language. As we've seen, it's also a notion that has political implications. The 1978 US Indian Child Welfare Act speaks of protecting "the unique values of Indian culture," and like all ideas, this particular concept has a history—and that takes us back once more to Franz Boas and his students.

Ruth Benedict declared that it's not race or common blood that binds people together; "what really binds men together is their culture, the ideas and the standards they have in common" (Benedict 1959: 14)—different ideas and standards, and therefore different cultures, each with its "unique values." As we explored in the last chapter, cultural identity is a truly complex thing. To us this may seem almost self-evident, which suggests how successful the Boasians were in getting this perspective across to the general public. It's a tolerant, relativistic, and hopeful worldview.

But that doesn't really tell us what culture itself is and how we should think about it. Benedict's approach was one possibility—by envisioning culture in terms of patterns, how its elements relate to one another. These patterns were to be seen as a product of history, and therefore subject to change. Similarly, Margaret Mead's *Coming of Age in Samoa* was an attempt to change North American attitudes about adolescence and sexuality.

Benedict's approach of envisioning culture in patterns owes much to Boas, and it reflects his own German heritage. Germany as we know it today is a relatively new country, first unified in 1870. Before that it was divided into states and principalities of greater or lesser size. But already before 1870 there was a sense of emerging unity. Philosophers, geographers, historians, linguists, and folklorists attempted to articulate it, and they discerned a common Germanic culture rooted in a common language, geographic locale, and historical experience. This called for seeing things holistically—in the round—motivated by "the desire to understand the phenomena and history of a country or of the whole earth" (Boas 1996: 16). Boas brought this attitude with him to North America, where it became a central feature of his anthropological research and teaching: "The culture of any given tribe ... can be fully explained only when we take into consideration its inner growth" (Boas 1963: 157).

Thus "culture" itself—which even Boas himself called "a vague term"—took shape as a distinct object, something good to "think with" (1963: 145). Indigenous peoples, who had been the traditional objects of anthropological research, began to see themselves in these terms as well. It became possible to speak about a culture in general terms, something to be preserved and defended—a site of resistance against colonial oppression. This process is related to the rise of advocacy groups that seek to speak for their peoples to protect a group identity in relation to national or regional governments. Michael Brown, an anthropologist who has studied the "cultural property" issue, observes that the culture concept originated as "a useful analytical device and nothing more. But in promoting the concept of culture anthropologists inadvertently spawned a creature that now has a life of its own. In public discourse, culture and such related concepts as 'tradition' and 'heritage' have become resources that groups own and defend from competing interests" (Brown 2003: 4).

Anthropologists have sometimes been seen as exploiters themselves, alien visitors engaged in cultural theft. This is a recipe for distrust and anger by the subjects of anthropological research, and then for self-examination by anthropologists themselves. In this chapter, we'll look at two episodes in which these issues came to the fore in controversies over land, identity, and cultural property. They are from the Pacific Northwest, an area of central importance in the development of North American anthropology. It also happens that we (your authors) live here and have a certain attachment to the region.

The first case study considers the controversy over possession of the "Whaler's Shrine," once an important ritual object among the Nootka (Nuu-chah-nulth) of western Vancouver Island, where Captain Cook made landfall in 1778. The shrine was purchased in 1904 by Franz Boas's ethnographic assistant, George Hunt, for the American Museum of Natural History in New York. The circumstances of that purchase are disputed, but—whatever the truth of the matter—the Muchalaht band of the Nuu-chah-nulth want it back. The question has arisen over whether whaling should be brought back as well, as it has been among the related Makah people of Washington State. The second example is an important Canadian land-claims case, in which anthropologists became advocates for the Native cause. It began in British Columbia but made its way to the Supreme Court of Canada and has a relevance well beyond that. The arguments turned on the validity of oral tradition and a confrontation between radically opposed visions about what pre-European Native society was actually like. Old controversies about savagery and civilization took a new form, shaped by the adversarial nature of the legal system. In a third and somewhat different example we consider the culture of environmental activism, and how two opposing groups engage with political discourse in ways that stand to engender support for their positions.

The Concept of Ownership

If culture is an important aspect of identity and self-respect, then a threat to it cuts very deep indeed. We've mentioned the forced immigration of the Cherokee to Oklahoma along the Trail of Tears, and their "continued loss of tribal knowledge and traditions." Anthropologists have long been concerned about what happens to a people under this kind of stress. Social and psychological breakdown is one possibility. Rebellion is another option, but the law of the stronger generally prevails. Effective resistance or accommodation may have to take another form.

Anthony F.C. Wallace (1923–2015), a Canadian-American anthropologist and historian, became interested in the psychological issues arising as a result of colonial domination. He charted the fate of the Iroquois from their position of strength in the early eighteenth century to their decline and fall as an independent people following the American Revolution (Wallace 1972). They were squeezed into small landholdings surrounded by ever-growing American settlements; their religious and political institutions were undercut by missionaries; alcoholism and other symptoms of social disintegration became widespread. Subsequently, an early-nineteenth-century Iroquois prophet—Handsome Lake (1735–1815)—preached a message that promised to lead his people back out of the cultural wilderness through a revival of Native practices, accompanied by a new moral code stressing order and self-discipline. His followers became known as "The People of the Longhouse"—the traditional structure in which their rituals are held. Stories were told of the coming of Columbus to the New World and of the "swarms" of white men who came afterwards bringing gambling, frivolous entertainment, and rum that would "turn their minds to foolishness and they will barter their country for baubles; then will this secret poison eat the life from their blood and crumble their bones" (Parker 1913). So the Creator took pity on his people and sent them prophets with instructions on how to set things right again.

The Handsome Lake religion is still practiced by some Iroquois on both sides of the US-Canada border. Wallace found the Handsome Lake religion as it was practiced in the 1950s to be a nostalgic "identification with Indianness itself, with the group of 'real' Iroquois people, as opposed to identification with white men and white-dominated organizations" (1972: 336–37). He generalized his findings to other colonial situations and hit on the term "**revitalization movement**" for what Handsome Lake and those like him had accomplished (Wallace 1956). This idea is central to the United Nations Declaration on the Rights of Indigenous Peoples, passed by the UN General Assembly in 2007:

> Indigenous peoples and individuals have the right not to be subjected to forced assimilation or destruction of their culture. Indigenous peoples have the right to practise and revitalize their cultural traditions and customs. This includes the right to maintain, protect and develop the past, present and future manifestations of their cultures, such as archaeological and historical sites, artefacts, designs, ceremonies, technologies and visual and performing arts and literature.
>
> States shall provide redress through effective mechanisms, which may include restitution, developed in conjunction with indigenous peoples, with respect to their cultural, intellectual, religious and spiritual property taken without their free, prior and informed consent or in violation of their laws, traditions and customs. (United Nations 2007)

One outcome of the tendencies expressed in the UN Declaration is the rise of what might be called "cultural nationalism." That said, we return to Vancouver Island and ask what became of the Whaler's Shrine.

HMS *Resolution* arrived off what is now Nootka Sound on Vancouver Island in March 1778. Captain Cook wrote that "we no sooner drew near the inlet than we found the coast to be inhabited and the people came off to the Ships in Canoes without showing the least mark of fear or distrust" (Cook 1967: 295). They began to trade with the English at once and kept at it vigorously until the visitors' departure a month later. Cook noted a tendency to theft, but relations between the parties were generally cordial. As always, he was a keen and generally sympathetic observer of the peoples he encountered, noting their great cedar-log canoes, their method of building houses of planks, and their extraordinary ceremonial masks.

Cook observed that "at the upper end of many apartments, were two large images, or statues placed abreast of each other and 3 or 4 feet asunder, they bore some resemblance to the human figure, but monsterous large. The men on some occasions wore Masks of which they have many and of various sorts such as the human face, the head of birds and other Animals, the most of them both well designed and executed" (1967: 314, 319). He also commented on their concepts of ownership, and early observations like his would play an important role in twentieth-century land-claims disputes: "I must observe that I have no where met with Indians who had such high notions of every thing the Country produced being their exclusive property as these; the very wood and water we took on board they at first wanted us to pay for" (1967: 306).

In the years that followed Cook's visit, the British, the Spanish, the Americans, and the Russians jostled for control and commercial advantage along the Northwest Coast.

PLATE 10.1 Nootka Village

PLATE 10.2 Nootka House

Cook's account of his voyage stimulated the trade in fur seal and sea-otter pelts. British settlement on Vancouver Island was stimulated by a desire to keep the Americans out (Johnston 1996). Native peoples were essential players in these early days, and that relationship had inevitable consequences.

Gilbert Malcolm Sproat (1834–1913) documented and lamented some of these changes. He was a Scot in the logging business, and in 1860 he established a camp at Port Alberni, which lies at the head of a long fjord leading into the interior of Vancouver Island from the sea. The British had declared themselves sovereign in the region and sold logging rights to Sproat's company. The local Indigenous people of course, knew nothing of this and were not pleased to hear about it: "These were the first savages I had ever seen, and they were probably at that time less known than any aboriginal people under British dominion" (Sproat 1868: 4). In his memoirs, Sproat recounts his initial conversation with a local chief:

> [I] explained to him that his tribe must move their encampment, as we had bought all the surrounding land from the Queen of England, and wished to occupy the site of the village…. He replied that the land belonged to themselves. "We do not wish to sell our land nor our water; let your friends stay in their own country. We don't care to do as the white men wish." "Whether or not," said I, "the white men will come. All your people know that they are your superiors." "We do not want the white man. He steals what we have. We wish to live as we are." (1868: 2, 4)

Sproat and his well-armed loggers moved in anyway. But he was curious about the people they were displacing, and over time he developed a greater sympathy for their predicament. He confirmed from his own experience what Cook had said 80 years earlier:

> While ... private property in land is not fully recognized among these people, each tribe maintains the exclusive right of its members to the tribal territory—including all lands periodically or occasionally occupied and used, sites for summer and winter encampments, fishing and hunting grounds and spots for burial—and would strongly resist encroachment upon these places. They believe that their villages existed and were occupied by birds and beasts even before the Indians themselves took human form. What Captain Cook said of this people ... is quite true of these tribes, as tribes. (1868: 80)

He also took note of the **potlatch**—a form of ceremonial gift-giving marking notable occasions such as a marriage, inheriting an important title, or erecting a totem pole: "The principal use ... of an accumulation of personal chattels is to distribute them periodically among invited guests, each of whom is expected to return the compliment by equivalent presents on like occasions" (Sproat 1868: 211). The etiquette of the potlatch—who sits where, who receives what and in what order—is quite elaborate and determined by the rank of the participants and the history of past exchanges (Adams 1973: 51–78).

In his famous essay *The Gift* (see Chapter 4), the French ethnologist Marcel Mauss used the ethnographical methods of Franz Boas and others to examine the potlatch and similar exchange systems.[1] The basic question he asked was, "How do such exchanges create and reinforce a moral bond between those engaged in them?" As noted above, in Chapter 4, Mauss had said that "in these 'total' social phenomena, as we propose calling them, all kinds of institutions are given expression at one and the same time—religious, juridical, and moral, which relate to both politics and the family; likewise economic ones, which suppose special forms of production and consumption ..." (Mauss 1990: 3).

Even though he was broadly sympathetic to Native society, Sproat, like Boas, later came to think that the potlatch had undergone a kind of inflationary process that led to "thrift-lessness ... inconsistent with all progress. It is not possible that the Indians can acquire property, or can become industrious with any good result, while under the influence of this mania" (quoted in Cole and Chaikin 1990: 15; see also LaViolette 1961). He encouraged the Canadian government to put a stop to it, and the potlatch was banned in 1884. This measure was a radical attempt to undermine an important social institution in order to set the Native peoples on the path to assimilation—to redirect their local economies from communal redistribution to individual accumulation (Loo 1992). The potlatch went underground, and Native people went to jail for practicing it. The ban was ended only in 1951.

Gilbert Sproat looked with some regret on the European seizure of Indigenous land and reflected on what gave them the right to do it:

> The whole question of the right of any people to intrude on another, and to dispossess them of their country, is one of those questions to which the answer is practically always the same.... The practical answer is given by the determination of intruders under any circumstances to keep what they have obtained; and this, without discussion, is what we, on the west coast of Vancouver Island, were all prepared to do. (1868: 8)

He documented some of the effects of this intrusion. Disease spread outward from the white settlements into Native communities. Missions were established but, in his opinion, accomplished little: "Their hunting and fishing places are intruded upon, their social customs disregarded, and their freedom curtailed, by the unwelcome presence, and often unseemly bearing, of those who are stronger than themselves. [The Indian] began soon to disregard his old pursuits, and tribal practices and ceremonies" (Sproat 1868: 278, 289). Sproat leaves us with a picture of a society caught between the old world and the new, fading away because it had lost the will to live. "There is, in my mind, little doubt that colonization on a large scale, by English colonists, practically means the displacing and extinction of the savage native population" (1868: 273).

That caught Charles Darwin's attention. He was in the process of finishing *The Descent of Man* (1871) when he came across Sproat's memoir. Extinction was an important topic, since Darwin was attempting to apply the insights he had developed in *The Origin of Species* to humanity itself. The subtitle of *The Origin* is "the preservation of favored races in the struggle for life." Given the astonishing human adaptability to all sorts of environmental conditions, Darwin concluded in *The Descent of Man* that "extinction follows chiefly from the competition of tribe with tribe, and race with race" (Darwin 1998: 189). The Vancouver Islanders were among the many who had lost out, and it looked to him like the Hawaiians were going to share their fate—a regrettable fact, but a fact nevertheless.

Whaler's Shrine

But this isn't what actually happened. As the British and Canadians consolidated their hold over what would become British Columbia, Native peoples were allotted land for reserves.[2] On the coast this often meant just the areas around their permanent villages. Most of the rest of the province was declared publicly owned *Crown land*—which could be leased to logging and mining interests. The way in which this allotment was carried out led to constitutional problems that we'll discuss shortly.

Franz Boas arrived in British Columbia in 1886, having already developed something of a reputation in Germany because of his ethnographic and geographical research on Baffin Island in the Canadian High Arctic. He had also become interested in Northwest Coast art and culture, and that would shape both his career and the general direction of anthropology in the United States and Canada (Cole 1999). His own ethnographic research was mainly among the Kwakiutl (Kwakwaka'wakw) people around Fort Rupert at the northeastern end of Vancouver Island. Ruth Benedict tapped his findings for the Northwest Coast chapter in *Patterns of Culture*, in which she stressed the dramatic nature of the Kwakiutl potlatch ceremonials.

Boas was involved with museums from the start. In 1896 he became Assistant Curator of Ethnology at the American Museum of Natural History in New York. Collecting Native artifacts and designing their display spaces became an important element in his career. He documented the ethnographic context of each item, often placing them in their natural settings, using realistic human figures in lifelike poses doing everyday things. The American Museum is proud of its Northwest Coast collection.[3] He traveled widely while conducting his linguistic and ethnographic research, and he employed research assistants to carry on in his absence. One of these was George Hunt (1854–1933), the son of an English Hudson's Bay Company employee and his Alaskan Tlingit wife. Hunt himself married into a Kwakiutl family, was proficient in the language, and became Boas's principal associate. It was this insider status that led him to the Nootka Whaler's Shrine.

PLATE 10.3 Nuu-chah-nulth Whaler's Shrine Figure

Such shrines belonged to high-ranking individuals with a hereditary connection to whaling, a dangerous and highly ritualized activity (Arima and Hoover 2011): "These rituals and the sites in which they were performed were closely guarded secrets known only to family members" (Jonaitis 1999: 5). They were houses of purification and prayer, in which the ancestors, whose skulls were kept in the shrine, were prayed to for their assistance in the hunt: "A whaler believed that a specific whale gave itself to him, through a mysterious power. Prayer and cleansing the mind and body made the whaler worthy of the great whale's gift of life" (Coté 2010: 34).

Boas had heard of the shrine and wished to acquire it for the American Museum. Though not a Nootka himself, Hunt was able to begin negotiations for purchasing the shrine by virtue of his status as a Kwakiutl shaman and his knowledge of sacred songs. The shrine was in a plank house, and, "as it turned out … the house was filled with human images, some ninety-five, with whale sculptures and human skulls" (Cole 1985: 161). Two chiefs claimed to own the shrine, and they dithered over the asking price (Jonaitis 1999: 62–65). In the end they divided $500, quite a substantial sum in those days: "Hunt had to promise to leave the house alone until all the people were away to the Bering Sea sealery and at the [salmon] canneries in New Westminster. He was to leave Nootka 'so as the Indians think I have not Bought to Keep things Quiet.' The two vendors promised 'that they will work to Bring it out in the night time'" (Cole 1985: 162). However, "the secret was not well kept and … Hunt learned that 'all the Indians is angry about their chief selling it to me.'" Nevertheless the shrine had already been shipped off to the American Museum, where it remains to this day in storage. The place where it once stood is now a Canadian National Historic Site.[4]

By fair means and foul, Native artifacts from everywhere made their way into the world's museums and private collections, abetted by a craze for "primitive art" (Price 2001). In fairness to ethnographic collectors like Boas, it should be said that their activities were also driven by the urgent sense that Native arts, languages, and cultures must be recorded and preserved before they were gone.

Many Indigenous peoples are now keen to defend what they still possess, reclaim what was once theirs, preserve their languages, and revive their artistic traditions. The same applies to human remains, which in the US are covered by the 1990 federal Native American Graves Protection and Repatriation Act. The shelves of American museums are full of Indigenous bones, dug up over the years by ordinary citizens, archaeologists, and physical anthropologists, including Boas (Cole 1985: 119–21). The Native American Graves Protection and Repatriation Act states that they should be returned to Indigenous communities if (a) they were found on reservation land and are known to be the lineal ancestors of Indigenous people presently living, or (b) claimed by "the Indian tribe that is recognized as aboriginally occupying the area in which the objects were discovered" (United States Congress 1990: Sec. 3C-1).[5] If the Whaler's Shrine had been situated in the US, the Act would certainly have applied to it. But this is a cross-border issue, and therefore a question to be settled between the American Museum and the Muchalaht Band. The Museum is unwilling to repatriate the Shrine until the Band has a proper place to safely display it, and the Band is trying to raise the money to build one—in part as an incentive for local tourism. However, "the community itself is divided over whether the shrine should return, and if it does, whether it should be open for public viewing or returned to its original status as a sacred place open only to its owners. Some people say that period in our history is over and we're moving forward. Other people say [the Shrine] is very powerful and should come back, and since it left the power of their community has suffered and if it is brought back the power will return" (Lee 2013). The dispute over the Whaler's Shrine was the subject of a 1994 National Film Board of Canada documentary film by anthropologist and filmmaker Hugh Brody. It is called *The Washing of Tears*, and cultural revitalization is the central theme. Brody was also expert witness in an important land-claim case to be discussed below.

As mentioned above, the Nuu-chah-nulth have also been involved in another repatriation fight, this one over the fate of blood samples that were collected from some of their people in the course of medical genetic research and ended up in England. That issue turns on the meaning of "informed consent," and we'll return to it in Chapter 10.

Traditional Practices, Contemporary Times

The Makah of Washington State are close linguistic and cultural relatives of the Nuu-chah-nulth. They reside around the town of Neah Bay near Cape Flattery at the southern entrance to the Straits of Juan de Fuca, and—like their kin on Vancouver Island—have been traditionally involved in whaling. They were guaranteed that right in the **treaty** they signed with the United States government in 1855 as part of the agreement to move onto their present reservation. Relations with their white neighbors have occasionally been tense, and the Makah have suffered from the same social problems as many other Indigenous communities.

Anthropologist Elizabeth Colson lived with them in the early 1940s and produced a still relevant ethnography that documents many aspects of their culture as it then was, including their relationship to the land: "For Makah and whites, the features of the landscape may seem to be the same; but so long as ... traditions are repeated and known, the two do not live in the same land; for they do not share a common background of symbolism and each reacts to the land in a different way" (Colson 1953: 49). She speaks of the "latent culture" of the Makah—gone in practice, but still remembered—and the role of oral tradition, which "helps to keep alive a feeling of belonging to a tradition other than the American" (1953: 184). In 1979 the Makah Cultural and Research Center (MCRC) was founded to serve the same end by more formal means—particularly the establishment of a museum:

> The MCRC expresses the Makah sense of continuity between contemporary identity and oral history, songs, objects, and landscape (both land and sea) ....
> The MCRC is an important means for the Makah people to continue to

vitalize their ways of knowing. It is also an important means to establish their knowledge as valid in the eyes of outsiders, as part of a self-determination process. The vitalization of their ways of knowing may take the forms of continuing to remember and honor ancestors … or remembering to care for objects as possessions of ancestors rather than simply as scientific artifacts. (Erikson 1999: 575)

Whaling came to an end in the early twentieth century following the commercial decimation of the whale population. However, the whales have now largely recovered and—with that recovery—the Makah expressed a desire to resume whaling for food and ceremonial purposes. That desire was put into practice in 1999 when—after long deliberation and public controversy—they exercised their treaty rights again and put to sea in a traditional canoe to kill—with a high-powered rifle rather than harpoons—a gray whale. The world's media were treated to the strange spectacle of a whale hunt being conducted in full public view, with the US Coast Guard protecting the Indigenous hunters from anti-whaling activists, some of them Canadian. Revitalization was a central motivation in bringing back the hunt—restoring the pattern of Makah culture: "Many of our tribal members feel that our health problems result from the loss of our traditional seafood and sea-mammal diet. We would like to restore the meat of the whale to that diet. We also believe that the problems that are troubling

PLATE 10.4 Makah Whaler

our young people stem from lack of discipline and pride and we hope that the restoration of whaling will help restore that. But we also want to fulfill the legacy of our forefathers and restore a part of our culture that was taken from us" (quoted in Erikson 1999: 563). Another member of the Makah tribe stated, "Whales are special. And they are wonderful and beautiful. My people do not deny this. And they have remained in our lives and cultures as sacred and respected animals, but they were also once an important food source. Our whaling tradition was and continues to be at the heart of our cultures, our spirituality, and our identities.... When we do harvest a whale, we will not only restore this missing link in our tradition but we will be truly be honoring the spirits of our whaling ancestors" (Coté 2010: 206–7).

And harvest one they did: an adolescent female gray whale. None have been officially hunted since then because of uncertainty over an environmental impact assessment. That story is still being played out. What will happen on Vancouver Island, where there were no treaties, also remains to be seen. Some Nuu-chah-nulth regard what the Makah did as a precedent.

Culture, Law, and the Role of the Anthropologist

The European occupation of North America was a complicated affair: the Spanish in the southeast and southwest, the French along the St. Lawrence River and interior fur-trade routes, the English expanding westward from their first settlements in Virginia and Massachusetts Bay. Given the strength of Indigenous nations such as the Iroquois, it became British policy to handle relations between them through treaties. The new American government undertook to honor the treaties the British had made, and began negotiating new ones of its own. In Canada the treaty-making process continued westward into what are now the prairie provinces of Manitoba, Saskatchewan, and Alberta.[6] But there it largely stopped. British Columbia was settled mainly from the other direction, eastward from the Pacific coast, and there was no organized treaty process at all. Instead, the province allocated reserves to Indigenous people according to its own estimation of what was required for their subsistence. This became a constitutional issue in our own time.

Indigenous peoples argued that the precedent established in the east should also have been followed in the far west, and that there is still a lot of unfinished business to do. The provincial government countered that Indigenous rights had been "extinguished" when the British Crown declared its sovereignty over the region. Court decisions at the federal level undercut that argument. This led to the initiation of an ongoing treaty process in British Columbia—very difficult and slow (and expensive) three-way negotiations between Canada, the province, and local Indigenous bands.[7]

That's the context of the case that concerns us here. In 1987 the Gitksan and Wet'suwet'en peoples launched an action in the Supreme Court of British Columbia seeking to gain title and governing authority over 22,000 square miles of territory surrounding the Skeena River Valley in the north central part of the province.[8] Both are interior groups, living along the Skeena and its tributaries, but both are coastal with regard to artistic traditions and social practices such as potlatching. The countryside above the rivers is remote and rugged.

So what does anthropology have to do with all this? First, the case turned on the relation between oral tradition and historical fact, a subject of long concern to anthropologists, biblical scholars, and folklorists.[9] Second, it involved a debate about concepts of ownership and the nature of government in tribal societies. Third, it revisited controversies that have been around since the seventeenth century about the nature of civilization, savagery, and social progress, and finally, several anthropologists spoke in support of the Indigenous claim. This case therefore also involves the role of anthropologists as advocates and the status of anthropology as an objective science.[10]

The success of the Indigenous case depended on convincing the court of the historical relevance of their **oral traditions**. The most important goal was to demonstrate that they did indeed have definite ideas about land ownership before the Europeans arrived—that tradition pointed to long-standing occupation and uninterrupted use of salmon streams and the resources in the mountains surrounding their river-valley settlements. "Occupation" and "use" are the keywords here; proof that they had existed since early times would back up the claim to collective title.

But it's misleading and ethnocentric to think about these matters in exclusively Western legal terms. Pre-European conceptions were aspects of a "total social phenomenon"—involving ecological relations, land, religious conceptions, the arts, social rank, and politically important exchange relationships between groups as expressed in the potlatch. As John Cove (1982: 7), an anthropologist who worked with the Gitksan during the 1970s and 1980s, points out, "A House was deemed to have title to a territory because it had merged its essence with a piece of land. That essence was its stock of supernatural powers acquired by ancestors of the House from spirits who had taken on physical forms to live in the same domain as humans." These encounters with spirits in animal form, as recited in songs and stories, are what gave a House the right to use specific carved images on its totem pole—symbolizing that group's claim to a particular piece of territory and the mythic stories that went with it. As we've seen, Gilbert Sproat had also remarked on this. Cove continues: "Resources on a House territory were not seen as 'things' merely there for its members use. Rather, a House had a special and exclusive relationship not only to its lands but to everything in or on them. A territory was a House's sacred space which it shared with other beings .... All having similar underlying form, consciousness, and varying degrees of power. Relations to them were not seen as unilateral and exploitative, but rather reciprocal and moral" (1982: 8).

Of course, many things had changed between the early days and the late 1980s when the Delgamuukw case began. Nevertheless, Cove found that "myths, names, crests, songs, feasts and Houses [remain] integral components of contemporary culture; as are traditional patterns of resource exploitation on House territories. Gitksan involvement in the land claims movement can be seen as an attempt to re-establish in a more complete way their relations to these territories" (1982: 14). The potlatch was certainly alive and well into modern times: "That the potlatch survives today in a state of considerable complexity is undoubtedly due to its value in the Natives' eyes as a means of furthering their land claims against the government. But it is also a touchstone of Indian identity in a world increasingly dominated by the Whiteman's values" (Adams 1973: 12). Traditional stories were family property, and the plaintiffs represented them at the trial as an essential part of the rituals validating chiefly titles and hence land-use rights. One Wet'suwet'en elder put it this way: "I always knew that the land that went with the chief's name would come to me some day. It isn't something I could just reach out and grab. It doesn't work that way. It isn't something that was made up. It was given to us and handed down in unwritten records, mouth to mouth. It was drilled into us around the campfires. It was drilled into our forefathers" (Mills 1994a: 119; see also Mills 1994b and Mills 2005).

The trial judge—Allan McEachern (1926–2008), Chief Justice of the British Columbia Supreme Court—viewed such evidence as largely "hearsay"; it also contained mythological elements, and therefore it was seen as an unreliable guide to what went on in real time. The claimants responded that these stories were recited at

PLATE 10.5 Gitksan Village

potlatches, and therefore validated on each occasion that a title was passed on. The community as a whole served as witness. Nevertheless the Justice concluded that

> the plaintiffs have a romantic view of their history which leads them to believe their remote ancestors were always in specific parts of the territory, in perfect harmony with natural forces, actually doing what the plaintiffs remembered their immediate ancestors were doing in the early years of [the twentieth] century. They believe the lands their grandparents used have been used by their ancestors from the beginning of time. When I come to consider events long past, I am driven to conclude on all the evidence, that much of the plaintiffs' historical evidence is not literally true. I am not able to find that the ancestors of the plaintiffs were using all of the territory for the length of time required for the creation of aboriginal rights. (McEachern 1991: 49)

He had a similar opinion concerning the general nature of pre-colonial Native society. A few quotations illustrate the stark contrast between the Gitksan view expressed in their opening statement at the trial and that of the judge in his final decision:

The Indigenous View (Wa and Delgam Uukw 1992)	The Crown's View (McEachern 1991)
"For us, the ownership of territory is a marriage of the Chief and the land. Each Chief has an ancestor who encountered and acknowledged the life of the land. From such encounters come power. The land, the plants, the animals and the people all have spirit—they all must be shown respect. That is the basis of our law."	"Aboriginal life … was far from stable and it stretches credulity to be believed that remote ancestors considered themselves bound to specific territories. They governed themselves in their villages and immediately surrounding areas to the extent necessary for communal living, eking out an aboriginal life."
"By following the law, the power flows from the land to the people through the chief; by using the wealth of the territory, the [matrilineal] House feasts its Chief so he can properly fulfill the law. This cycle has been repeated on my land for thousands of years."	"I am not persuaded their ancestors practiced universal or even uniform customs relating to land outside their villages. It cannot be said that they owned or governed such vast … tracts of land in any sense that would be recognized by the law."
"My power is carried in my House's histories, songs, dances and crests. It is recreated at the Feast when the histories are told, the songs and dances performed, and the crests displayed. With the wealth that comes from respectful use of the territory … the law, the Chief, the territory, and the Feast become one."	"The primitive condition of the natives described by early observers is not impressive. Being of a culture where everyone looked after himself or perished, the Indians knew how to survive (in most years). They became a conquered people, not by force of arms … but by an invading culture and a relentless energy.…"

Looking at these two versions of reality side by side is like contrasting Jean-Jacques Rousseau with Thomas Hobbes (see Chapter 1). Rousseau saw Indigenous America as more "virtuous" than corrupt old Europe—like the Garden of Eden from which the collective ancestors of the human race were expelled when they ate the forbidden fruit. These, of course, are images—but so were those of the lawyers and witnesses used to defend the province against the Native land claim. Justice McEachern believed that concepts of land ownership had once been very vague, but crystallized with the coming of the fur trade and the necessity to control trap-lines. He believed that Indigenous society was in a state of constant low-level war, and cited Hobbes himself (misspelling Hobbes's name) in his "Reasons for Judgment": "there is no doubt, to quote Hobbs [*sic*], that aboriginal life in the territory was, at best, 'nasty, brutish and short'" (McEachern 1991: 13).

He spoke about Native people living in a "communal" society but also about this being "a culture in which everyone looked after himself or perished." He used the phrase "eking out an aboriginal life," when the evidence shows that in fact these societies were generally capable of sustaining themselves in reasonable comfort and generating enough surplus for their potlatch system. If the Indigenous witnesses were inconsistent in their testimony about what lands were actually used, Justice McEachern was inconsistent in his views on the nature of pre-European society.

But the final judgment was unequivocal. The Gitksan and Wet'suwet'en would retain exactly the same rights they had before the case began, and no more—the use of traditional fishing sites, and the right to hunt and gather on otherwise unused Crown land. To participate in the modern economy, they would have to join it: "The plaintiff's claims for ownership of and jurisdiction over the territory, and for aboriginal rights in the territory are dismissed" (McEachern 1991: 297).[11]

The testimony of the anthropologists serving as expert witnesses for the First plaintiffs got the same treatment. There were three: Antonia Mills and Richard Daly, both of whom had lived and worked with the Gitksan and Wet'suwet'en; the third, Hugh Brody, had worked with groups in the north of the province, mapping trap lines and hunting territories. The result of Brody's research was a notable book—*Maps and Dreams*—that contrasted Western ideas about the land with those of the people he worked with (Brody 1981). As in the present case he found that Euro-Canadian concepts are utilitarian and individualistic; Indigenous concepts are spiritual and communal—a mystical relationship.

McEachern dismissed the testimony of all three because of supposed pro-Indigenous bias and lack of scientific objectivity. One was singled out because "he made it abundantly plain that he was very much on the side of the plaintiffs" (1991: 50). The statement of professional ethics of the American Anthropological Association became an issue here, and the Justice quoted it: "In research, anthropologists' paramount responsibility is to those they study. When there is a conflict of interest, these individuals must come first. Anthropologists must do everything in their power to protect the physical, social, and psychological welfare and to honor the dignity and privacy of those studied."[12]

The implication is that anthropologists can *never* give unbiased testimony if it goes against the interests of the people they've worked with; they must either distort the facts or hold their tongues. Justice McEachern concluded in sorrow that "it is always unfortunate when experts become too close to their clients" (1991: 51).

He expected his decision to be appealed, and it was—eventually making its way to the Supreme Court of Canada. This time there was a radical change in direction. Two major flaws were identified in the original judgment in the light of legal precedents at the federal level: devaluing the use of oral tradition as evidence and restricting Indigenous economic rights to traditional subsistence practices:

> The factual findings made at trial could not stand because of the trial judge's treatment of the various kinds of oral histories. The oral histories were used in an attempt to establish occupation and use for the disputed territory which is an essential requirement for aboriginal title.... Had the oral histories been correctly assessed, the conclusions on these issues of fact might have been very different.... The courts [must] come to terms with the oral histories of aboriginal societies, which, for many aboriginal nations, are the only record of their past.... Those histories play a crucial role in the litigation of aboriginal rights. (Persky 1998: 84, 75)

On the land issue, the Supreme Court concluded that the plaintiffs retained Indigenous title—a right to the land itself, and that its use does not have to be restricted to traditional subsistence practices. Its economic potential can be enhanced, though not in such a way as to "destroy" the land's value to the community as a whole. Such activities could include forestry, mining, and commercial fish farming, if conducted in an ecologically sensitive manner. In the Supreme Court's opinion, the original judgment had hopelessly stacked the deck against the Indigenous claimants and blocked their chance for economic progress as peoples—condemning them to live in rural ghettoes on the fringes of the white-dominated economy. The matter was sent back to the province for consideration, with the hope that these issues could be resolved through negotiation. This decision formed part of the background to still ongoing treaty negotiations.[13]

Cultural Survival

These are complex tales, typical of our times. They involve new concepts of human rights that have emerged slowly and painfully over the years—sometimes taking the form of declarations of general principles or legislation on a national level. Getting "rights" enshrined in law changes the nature of the debate. In Chapter 5 you saw how the Baby Veronica case has played out, and in this chapter we've described a similar process at work with regard to cultural property and land claims. A lot of money can be at stake, too, since identity issues are also economic issues. In western Canada much of the legal action has been aimed at providing rural Indigenous peoples with a viable economic base in the form of natural resources; in urban settings the goal is the acquisition of land for real estate and commercial development.

If we look elsewhere, Australia for example, the same tendencies are at work, and there have been legal actions similar to the ones described above. In the United States there are advantages in having official recognition as a tribe; federal benefits come with that status, as does exemption from local taxes (Clifford 1988). But these developments are all part of a bigger picture—the discourse of cultural survival and renewal. One sign of the times is the founding in 1972 of an organization called Cultural Survival and its journal *Cultural Survival Quarterly* by two Harvard anthropologists who worked in the Amazon region. The initial impetus was the effect of natural resource development on South American tribal peoples, a problem that is even more acute today. Cultural Survival has also become interested in "the much-needed revitalization of critically endangered Native American languages"—a serious concern among Indigenous peoples in Canada and Australia.[14]

The movement to reclaim cultural property has affected many museums with ethnographic collections, and formal procedures have been adopted to deal with such issues. The Department of Anthropology at the American Museum of Natural History, for example, has an office devoted to this problem.[15] As we have seen with the Whaler's Shrine and the Makah Museum, the establishment of such institutions on Native soil is in itself an important aspect of cultural preservation and revitalization.

Those with a skeptical take on such things have suggested that all this makes "culture" into a more solid object than it actually is, more like a brand or trademark (Brown 2003). Questions can also be raised about cultural "authenticity" and about who gets to decide what is authentic or not. And this applies to personal status as well. In the last chapter we raised questions about personal and national identity, and asked who is *really* anything? Who, for example, is *really* an Indigenous Australian, American, or Canadian, and therefore eligible for nationally recognized status as First Nations or Native American? In the next and final section of this chapter, we take a look at the culture concept from a slightly different angle. Instead of culture as a thing to possess or an identity one is born into, we consider the culture of activism, an identity that one chooses as a result of circumstance.

Analyzing a Conflict: Activism and Land Use

In this chapter we have considered how cultural symbols and meaning are embodied by things, spaces, and activities. When aspects of one's culture are threatened, the reaction is to push back. This pushback takes many forms, but no matter how we look at it, **activism** also brings people together. There is a common struggle, a perceived wrongdoing, and a motivation to enact change.

Anthropologist Terre Satterfield (2002) explores the culture of activism in the United States through an in-depth, ethnographic study of the intense dispute over old-growth logging and the protection of the northern spotted owl in Oregon's rain forests. Her research participants are two groups of opposing activists: the Forest Community Movement, consisting of small-scale loggers, and the Ancient Forest Movement, consisting of environmentalists. Satterfield explores how each group attempts to achieve its desire for a changed social world by engaging and manipulating political discourses, conceptions of morality, and symbolic tools. Satterfield is not concerned with who is right or wrong in this dispute; rather, she is interested in *how* each group expresses its agenda: "Rather than thinking of conflict as a contest of political, economic, and scientific forces (which it certainly is), I choose as my primary objective to draw attention to how these forces are expressed culturally in the impassioned wrangling of locally situated and politically committed loggers and environmentalists" (2002: 3).

While an individual's cultural identity is related to a host of categories, including ethnicity, gender, and age, an activist *chooses* to organize with others based on shared beliefs and solutions for dealing with a perceived threat or condition. Their shared position may be based on a shared ethnicity, for example, as is the case with Indigenous peoples who are actively engaged in movements for cultural repatriation. What sets them apart from others who share their ethnicity but do not identify as activists is their decision to unite and resist. Activists have organized in retaliation to a perceived threat to their right to exist, such as a threat to their livelihood, to their belief system, or to their right to expression. Examining a conflict illuminates how ideas and arguments (or discourse) are interpreted and embodied by the individuals involved. The identity they assume in terms of their activism is only one of many identities that these individuals embody: they are mothers and fathers, they work in the city or in the country, they are men and women, they are university graduates or have technical diplomas—the list goes on.

We are all familiar with the two groups engaged in the conflict, at least superficially. On the one hand are the "timber activists" or loggers—the popular image of these men (for it is almost always men) has changed over the last 50 years, from a wholesome and hard-working profession to one composed of unintelligent and rootless men. Cultural identity is not immune to the influences of changing political and economic forces, and the image of the logger certainly reflects the popularity of conservation. Loggers are rarely thought of as grassroots activists; however, the loggers whom Satterfield encountered strove to be taken seriously as legitimate activists wrongly portrayed in the media. Rather than dumb, careless men unconcerned for the future of the forests, they were men with families to feed and mortgages to pay who were simply trying to make a living in a dangerous, strenuous, and necessary profession. They were not big industry, but small business owners trying to make ends meet. One man described loggers as being "like eggs; tough on the outside, soft on the inside" (2002: 51).

The figure of the environmentalist evokes quite a different image. In contrast to loggers, popular conceptions of the environmentalists portray them as well-educated city dwellers who outfit themselves in Gore-Tex and hiking boots on the weekends.

We are very familiar with the environmentalist as activist, for the media have done a great job of documenting Greenpeace activists chaining themselves to trees or circling whaling boats off the coast of Russia. While many of the environmentalists that Satterfield spoke with and observed appeared to be sympathetic toward the loggers' plight (especially those who lived locally and counted the loggers as their neighbors), the protection of the trees and habitat was their primary concern.

While issues of class and gender are ever present within these two groups, they are not defining characteristics. Instead, it is their individual identities as loggers or environmentalists that unite them collectively. One way of understanding the worldview of each of these groups is to consider the types of discourse used by each to get their point across. Satterfield took note of the various slogans she encountered during her fieldwork. These messages appeared on bumper stickers, on posters, on signs stuck on the side of the road, on lawns, and in stores (keep in mind—this research was pre-Twitter and pre-Facebook!). These slogans provide an effective, if simplistic, summary of each side's position in the conflict. Decorating the side of the Forest Service Road, one sign read, "If environmentalists could have their way, we [timber activists, one assumes] would live from day-to-day. The spotted owl and the seal would thrive, and you and I could not survive" (2002: 42). Another bumper sticker jeered, "Do you have a job or are you an environmentalist?" At a Spirit of the Earth Activist Conference, large slogans adorned the walls. Posters read, "You may not like living with us now, but conservationists make great ancestors" and "We don't inherit the earth from our

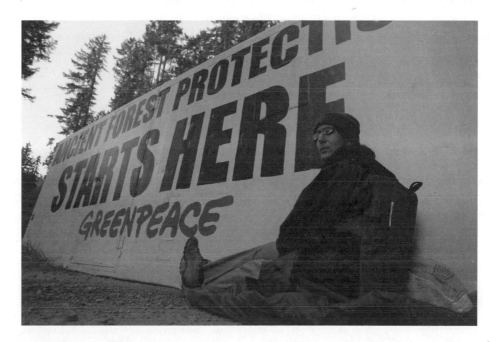

PLATE 10.6 Greenpeace Protester

ancestors, we borrow it from our children" (quoted in Satterfield 2002: 55). Here we see the two sides at work—timber activists embody the here and now. Their struggle has immediate consequences to their lives and those around them. Environmentalists, on the other hand, focus on the future. What we do today will have serious consequences for future generations.

Of particular interest to Satterfield were the ways in which these two opposing groups engaged with language and concerns as if the other group did not exist. She examined popular discussions and debates surrounding nature that both loggers and environmentalists drew from, and the ways in which the arguments and stance of each activist group interacted with one another. Both activist groups challenged and conformed to the dominant ideas of scientific, congressional, economic, or corporate bodies who were able to construct and impose their version of reality as seemingly "natural" (2002: 7). One body of discourse that both groups engaged with, albeit in very different ways, was the assumption of a shared vision of forest management with Indigenous groups. As we have already encountered during our examination of the Gitksan and Wet'suwet'en peoples' land-claim case and Justice Allan McEachern's ruling, the construction of Indigenous peoples by European explorers, philosophers, and politicians has not always been accurate or pleasant. Generally, this construction has taken the form of two interpretations: that of the "**noble savage**" and that of the "**savage beast**." Both constructions operate on **essentialist** understandings of Indigenous peoples' way of life, spirituality, and knowledge forms. The noble-savage construct refers to the notion that "there are simple people, living in an Edenic landscape and gentle climate, whose powers of reason and ability to live in harmony with nature ensure relief from the evils of civilization" (Satterfield 2002: 100). In contrast, the savage-beast construct portrays Indigenous peoples as living in a constant state of violence, disorganization, and chaos. While these two culturally constructed interpretations are based on outdated and racist understandings of human diversity, their use continues to be accepted by many non-Indigenous peoples as true understandings of the "nature" of Indigenous life.

Satterfield explores how the environmentalist movement has appropriated the "noble savage legacy" to legitimize its own cause. For many activists, drawing on Indigenous practices reflects their continued commitment to protecting the earth and adds a sense of "cultural authenticity to activists' imaginings of future land-use practices" (2002: 120). Because many environmentalists do not live in rural areas, nor do they work in forestry disciplines, their legitimacy is less substantiated than that of the loggers who live and work on the land. Their ability to align themselves with Indigenous peoples who, many believe, "effortlessly embody principles of Western conservation" adds authenticity to their argument (2002: 134).

Loggers are also in need of a means to validate their "right" to legitimacy over the land, and they often attempt to dismantle the notion of ecological nobility that environmentalists preach is at the heart of Indigenous relationships to the land. Loggers draw a parallel between Indigenous land use and knowledge with their own approach to maintaining the land, suggesting that they too deserve a level of public respect similar to what is afforded Indigenous peoples. Just as Indigenous claim that their use of the land is part of their "cultural" way of life, loggers argue that their way of life is also cultural. For example, many loggers argue that their way of forest management is simply another method that has evolved over time, and that Indigenous peoples themselves managed the forest using fire, a comparison that attempts to illustrate that the forest must be managed, and indeed always has been. The voices of the Indigenous peoples themselves are noticeably absent in both these instances: "Aboriginal peoples are caught up in a pro/anti dialogue not of their own making—a dialogue between competing White activists (loggers and environmentalists) that, at times, is ugly, racist and dehumanizing. It is a dialogue that reduces Aboriginal peoples to unidimensional strategic and counter-strategic implements caught in the crossfire of the struggle over Oregon's forests" (2002: 121).

While you may identify with the loggers, with the environmentalists, or with neither group, you may not find any relevance in this discussion to your own life. Regardless of your opinion, however, one cannot dispute that the environment is a hot political topic that transcends national borders and political parties. Politicians continually talk of their efforts to enact policies that will protect endangered species and vulnerable areas of land, while at the same time forging ahead with economic endeavors that are potentially disastrous for the environment. Celebrities endorse and create television shows and documentaries that aim to educate and stimulate young people to get involved in protecting the environment. The word "green" has been slapped onto anything that can be recycled, and magazines and newspapers are full of articles about how to minimize your "ecological footprint." So what are the discourses and ideologies that inform these debates? What images are continually relied upon in order to make a lasting and effective argument? How do issues of class, gender, and race come into play? By considering how one debate in a local, specific context was constructed and enacted, we have gained a better understanding of some of the popular discourses that surround all environmental debates in North America.

Conclusion

In this chapter we have focused mainly on the politics of culture in the Pacific Northwest, given the relevance of the cases we describe to the history of North American anthropology. However, cultural politics can be found everywhere and is easy enough to spot once you know what you're looking for. The question takes on added levels of complexity in multi-ethnic–multicultural societies where there are many alternative ways of living, being, and seeing, and it becomes increasingly difficult to find a common denominator among the competing voices. Just look around you.

Notes

1   Another such system was the *kula* exchanges of the Trobriands in the southwest Pacific, where Malinowski worked in the early years of the twentieth century (see Chapter 1).

2   Gilbert Sproat became a central figure in the allotment process in the southern interior of British Columbia. He attempted to allot land sufficient for the economic needs of local people and ran into trouble with white settlers because of it.

3   See http://www.amnh.org/exhibitions/permanent-exhibitions/human-origins-and-cultural-halls/hall-of-northwest-coast-indians.

4   See http://www.historicplaces.ca/en/rep-reg/place-lieu.aspx?id=17981. An overview of the history of the controversy and a detailed examination of the elements in the shrine can be found in Jonaitis (1999). Going back to the late eighteenth century, Jonaitis also looks at the ways in which the shrine has been represented by academic writers and the popular media.

5   This is Public Law 101–601: An Act to Provide for the Protection of Native American Graves. The Law also applies to native Hawaiian remains.

6   Whether these treaties were honored, or even properly understood when first signed, is another matter.

7   For historical background see Tennant (1990).

8   The case is known as "Delgamuukw v. The Queen." "Delgamuukw" is a clan title held by the original plaintiff in the case, a Gitksan elder named Ken Muldoe, who was acting on behalf of the Gitksan and Wet'suwet'en as a whole. "The Queen" means, in this instance, the province of British Columbia.

9   For a general introduction to the topic see Vansina (1985).

10 For the full details of the case and its anthropological relevance see Culhane (1998).

11 The proceedings lasted three years. The "Reasons for Judgment" document is itself 394 pages long, which is an indication of the importance attached to this case.

12 See http://www.aaanet.org/profdev/ethics/ (1971 Statement; amended 1986).

13 There is still no Gitksan treaty. Though one is being negotiated, it looks like the process has some way to go. See http://www.gov.bc.ca/arr/firstnation/gitxsan/.

14 See http://www.culturalsurvival.org/node/10279.

15 See http://anthropology.si.edu/repatriation/. The Canadian Museum of History has a detailed policy to deal with repatriation claims: http://www.civilization.ca/about-us/corporation/about-the-corporation/repatriation-policy.

Study Questions

1   How do Franz Boas and Ruth Benedict define culture?

2   Explain how places, things, and activities embody cultural meaning, using examples from the chapter.

3   Explain why Sproat encouraged the Canadian government to ban the potlatch.
4   Outline the history and controversy surrounding the Whaler's Shrine.
5   Explain why the Makah believed whaling was such an important part of their culture.
6   Compare and contrast Justice McEachern's ruling and the decision of the Supreme Court of Canada in the Skeena River Valley land claim.
7   What makes the culture of activism different from other social categories such as ethnicity, gender, and age?
8   How did both the environmentalists and the loggers studied by Satterfield associate their position with that of Indigenous peoples? What was wrong with this appropriation of Indigenous culture?

Discussion Questions

1   What is "cultural property," and what rules should apply to its ownership and control? Where do the museums stand in all this?
2   Justice McEachern dismissed the evidence put forth by the three anthropologists who testified as expert witnesses. What do you think about his decision? Should their testimonies have been allowed to stand? Why or why not?
3   Consider an activist group you are familiar with. What types of discourse do they utilize to get their message across? Is it effective? Why or why not?
4   How far are you willing to go in your toleration of foreign ways: does it extend to whaling, to female circumcision, to arranged marriages, to the wearing of prominent religious symbols, to the eating of dogs, dolphins, or chimpanzees, etc.? If there are limits, what are they and why?

///

CHAPTER 11

Anthropology, Cultural Change, and Globalization

LEARNING OBJECTIVES

After reading this chapter, students should be able to

- understand why studying globalization is important and why anthropology is well suited to understanding the processes of globalization;
- define the terms *change, progress*, and *modernization* using examples from the chapter;
- understand how globalization has created a shift in the relationship between culture and place;
- discuss how the movement of people and goods around the world has changed cultures and how we understand the concept of culture; and
- discuss how mass communication, technology, and global markets have changed both how and what anthropologists study.

KEY TERMS

change	globalization	modernization
cultural imperialism	isolationism	multi-site ethnography
de-territorialization	macro vs. micro levels	progress
economic migrant	migration	

Introduction

In this final chapter we will consider the issues of cultural change and globalization, and the place of anthropology, a discipline traditionally associated with the past, in our rapidly changing social world. We will consider a number of case studies that illustrate ways in which anthropological methods and research may lead to a better understanding of the complex processes of globalization on a local level. First, however, it is important that we define the terms used to describe these processes. In so doing, we will also examine some of the assumptions that are embedded in these seemingly neutral terms.

The Language We Use: Important Terms and Concepts

We continually hear of how the world is shrinking, how before long there will exist only one (Americanized?) culture, and that in a relatively short time the global political climate will look vastly different than the way it does today. The term **globalization** is used by politicians, activists, journalists, and everyday citizens. If asked to define globalization, what would you say? Would you focus on the economic processes? The negative effects of industrialization on the environment? The mass migration of people in search of wage labor and a better life? Or the increased ability to share information, art, ideas, and beliefs with people across the globe? These are all components of globalization and illustrate the all-encompassing manner in which the process of change affects aspects of life for people in very different ways. By this point in the book, we hope you have come to understand the importance of considering the impact of complex economic, political, and social processes on the individual person living in a specific community. Understanding the processes of globalization is no different; however, as the processes of globalization are not limited to activities occurring in specific communities and nation-states, the scope of analysis must be expanded.

In Kearney's words, globalization refers to "social, economic, cultural, and demographic processes that take place within nations but also transcend them, such that attention limited to local processes, identities, and units of analysis yields incomplete understanding of the local" (Kearney 1995: 548). This definition illustrates the complexity of globalization: while these processes and changes occur within the nation-state, they also travel beyond the seemingly well-defined borders of individual countries. While anthropologists specialize in focusing their lens on "the local," to limit their analysis to one geographic area would neglect the fact that these processes may very well have originated in a nation far removed from the one under study.

Culture and Place: A New Relationship

Cultural change is occurring at breakneck speed all over the world. The ability to communicate across vast geographical spaces in a manner that makes time nearly irrelevant has greatly changed the way many people live their lives. The Internet and other technological developments have introduced a new dimension to the concept of diffusion. While the diffusion of goods and ideas is nothing new—for example, tobacco first spread from the tropics of the Western hemisphere to North and South America, and then on to the rest of the world after 1492—the ways in which these ideas are moving, and the implications of such movement, are having profound effects on how we live our lives.

With the advent of mass communication systems, information is passed without the necessity of personal travel. And because not everyone has equal access (or any access at all) to these communication systems, information continues to circulate via word of mouth. Teenagers in China are infatuated with pop stars from Taiwan and Hong Kong, the elderly in Canada practice tai chi in community centers, and kids in the Philippines watch Disney cartoons in their living rooms. As anthropologists Jonathan Inda and Renato Rosaldo (2008: 11) state, "culture is highly mobile." Traditionally, we have thought of cultural practices and customs as tied to geographic locations. This is no longer the case: globalization has "weakened" the relationship between culture and place (Inda and Rosaldo 2008).

Despite the weakening of cultural ties to place, or the "**de-territorialization**" of culture, there will always exist an element of place within culture because people live and operate in local environments, and it is in these locations that culture moves, changes, and is experienced (Inda and Rosaldo 2008). The relationship between culture and place has changed with the increased movement of people across national boundaries and borders. We are familiar with the ease with which those with the financial means can travel across the world or speak with others in places far removed. But what about the "flow" of cultural ideas and goods—is this movement unidirectional? In other words, is one culture stronger and more pervasive than others?

The notion that the world is becoming smaller and more homogeneous (or the same) due to the processes of globalization is an often-repeated sentiment. Notions of the "one-world culture," "**cultural imperialism**" or "the West and the rest" imply that the cultural diversity of the world is in danger of extinction, and that as communication systems, travel, and modernization initiatives continue to flourish, it won't be long before everyone is wearing the same clothes, eating the same food, and living in the same style of houses. Western, or more specifically American, culture (both material goods and ideologies) appears to be absorbing the cultural diversity of the world. From an anthropological perspective, do you think that this is true, or even possible? When cultural traits are borrowed, they often undergo a major change in order to "fit" with local circumstances. People will always have their own cultural lens through which they see the world—this will not change just because they have access to Hollywood films or Nike shoes.

The notion that culture flows from the West to the rest of the world is simplistic. Consider the restaurants in your neighborhood or community—what cuisines are represented? Or the medical treatments that are available to you here in North

America—perhaps you have consulted a naturopath or an acupuncturist. The music that you listen to? The centers for worship in your city or town? While it may be true that Western cultural ideas and goods are well known in all corners of the globe, to say that the West is not a cultural *consumer* of other cultures is to imply that non-Westerners are only passive recipients of cultural knowledge and are not engaged in the sharing of information and ideas. Furthermore, the culture and population of the West are themselves extremely heterogeneous—consider Canada. How would you describe the culture of Canada without discussing the tremendous multiculturalism that the nation is well known for? The line that differentiates "the West from the rest" is no longer as clear as we once believed it to be, and as the movement of ideas and people continues to develop in new and exciting ways, it will become more blurred as technology surges forward.

The Meaning of Change

What examples come to mind when you hear the word **progress**? Do you think of technology? Industry? A way of thinking? Definitions of progress suggest a positive development, usually of a gradual move toward achieving a goal or reaching a higher standard. Definitions that consider progress in relation to people suggest the advancement of society toward "an improved or more advanced condition" (*Oxford English Dictionary*). This forward movement implies a positive change from one state to another, a leaving behind of something outdated to embracing something new. Now consider the term **change**. Change is a much broader concept that, on its own, has no direction or value—change is the result of action or thought, whether it is intentional, accidental, beneficial or harmful. Cultural change most often occurs in politically and economically stable societies in a gradual manner—cultural systems are, for the most part, stable systems. When change occurs in a rapid and abrupt manner, it often results in extreme modification to social relationships, particularly when beliefs and understandings of cultural values and institutions have been challenged.

Despite their difference in meaning, the words *progress* and *change* are often used interchangeably. To use the term progress to describe cultural change implies that this cultural change is for the better. Progress, however, is not a *cause* of cultural change but rather a particular way of describing such change. Change is an altering of the social and/or material world that may or may not be beneficial or welcome. This is an important distinction to keep in mind when discussing cultural change, particularly in the context of globalization. How can we judge whether or not a change has been positive? Must it be positive for all members of a society in order for it to be considered progress? Social change affects individuals in very different ways—what may be a positive change for some may result in a negative transformation for others. The experiences of cultural change are intricately entangled with social, political, and economic factors that bring about very different circumstances depending on where one is located in the social order of things.

The term **modernization** is often used to describe political, economic, and social changes. Like the notion of progress, modernization implies a value-laden transformation from antiquated to current, and usually includes material and technological progress and individual betterment. Modernization can be defined as the process of cultural and socio-economic change, and is often linked to urbanization, industrialization and the spread of education. The effects of modernization reach far beyond the economic systems of society—these changes creep into the social and political realms of everyday life. From a Western perspective, modernization brings with it many of the elements of social life that we hold dear, such as increased access to formal education, democratic political processes, and secularization; however, the effects of these changes often materialize in unexpected and unwelcome ways. Supporters of modernization assert that the benefits gleaned from the process make any inconveniences (whether they are social or environmental) worth the cost, while critics (including many anthropologists), state that the rapid cultural change brought about by modernization often leads to increased social inequality and environmental degradation.

An example of the unexpected consequences of modernization is evident in the case of the Skolt Lapps, a group who live in northern Finland and who traditionally supported themselves through fishing and herding reindeer. Reindeer were an integral part of the Skolt Lapp way of life—they provided meat and hides, were given as gifts, were a good to be traded or sold, and also provided a means for transportation, pulling sleds in the winter and packing in the summer. In the 1960s, the reindeer herders adopted the snowmobile, a move that was believed to make herding easier and more efficient. The unexpected consequences of this change, however, were enormous and far reaching. The cost of purchasing the snowmobiles and maintaining them is large, and this created a dependency on outside economic transactions, a dependency that had not existed to this extent before. As a result of the need for cash, the men were required to leave the village for wage work or depend on government assistance. Ironically, the adoption of the snowmobile contributed to a decline in reindeer herding—the number of deer in a herd fell drastically, from around 50 to 12. Not only is this number too small to maintain and receive any benefit from, but the deer are also constantly attempting to flee and join a larger herd. The relationship between the men and the deer drastically changed, for the deer are fearful and suspicious of the noisy and aggressive machines that the men ride (Pelto 1973).

The consequences of mechanized herding have been experienced in the economic sphere when men have been required to leave the village and enter into the cash-credit economy, as well as culturally, as herding and conceptions of manhood are deeply linked. While it would be correct to say that the Skolt Lapp economy has been modernized, it would be difficult to say that this change signified *progress* if we associate the word with a positive transformation.

The Flow of Goods

Another product of modernization is the increased flow of capital and goods across the world. Multinational corporations are companies that operate worldwide but are centrally controlled from one location. Motivated by profit, multinational corporations make decisions that will bring the highest return in the economic sector. At times, these decisions are made with little understanding of or regard for the impact on the interests and well-being of those who live where the product is sourced, manufactured, and distributed. While the presence of a manufacturing plant may bring numerous jobs to the area and circulate capital into the local communities for other services, such as restaurants, grocery stores, taxis, etc., the payment that workers receive is necessarily low in order for the corporation to benefit from setting up shop there. To keep costs low, the working conditions of many manufacturing plants are dismal, putting the lives of thousands at risk for the sake of profit. While some point fingers at the individuals who own these plants to ensure that their workers have safe conditions, others redirect this responsibility to the corporation, stating that plant owners have little choice but to pay their workers next to nothing in order to meet the demand for extremely cheap goods.

In April 2013, the Rana Plaza, a building housing garment workers in Savar, Bangladesh, went up in flames. Bars on the windows prevented people from escaping, and over 1,100 people perished when the eight-story building collapsed following the fire. The building was owned by a local businessman, who rented the space to two international clothing manufacturers. Bangladesh is a very poor country—43 per cent of residents live below the poverty line, and it ranks 146th out of 186 on the United Nations Development Index.[1] The garment industry is an extremely important source of income for the four million Bangladeshi textile workers, 40 per cent of whom are women. In response to this tragedy, clothing manufacturers have called upon the governments of their own nations and those of the host nation to enact stricter control on workplace conditions. It is yet to be seen whether any significant changes will occur, and what impact this will have upon the people who spend their days in the factories. This example illustrates the complexity of conducting business in a global economy, and how one decision made in a boardroom in the United States (or Canada, Spain, France, etc.) can have extreme consequences for thousands of people living in very precarious situations.

Anthropology is well suited, both theoretically and methodologically, to consider the impact that macro (or worldwide) processes have on individuals in communities all over the world, and how individuals respond in culturally informed ways. There are a number of anthropological studies that have considered the relationship between multinational corporations and the local communities where their goods are produced, such as Laetitia Cairoli's (2012) *Girls of the Factory: A Year with the Garment Workers of Morocco*, an ethnography that considers the lives of female garment workers in Fez, Morocco.

Understanding Processes of Change: An Anthropological Perspective

The value in anthropological research to understanding the processes of globalization lies in its ability to consider how global processes concerned with economics, politics, and the social world are experienced on a local and individual level: "[Anthropology] is preoccupied not just with mapping the shape taken by the particular flows of capital, people, goods, images and ideologies that crisscross the globe, but also with the experiences of people living in specific localities when more and more of their everyday lives are contingent on globally extensive social processes" (Inda and Rosaldo 2008: 5).

The methods that characterize anthropology as a social science position the voices and experiences of the individual as central to analysis. A researcher engages in participant observation, speaks with local citizens, and conducts interviews with those living in a specific place and time so as to understand how their daily lives are affected by the opening of a new manufacturing plant, the spread of cell phones, or access to the Internet. Anthropologists consider how individuals make sense of these processes through their own cultural lens. Globalization touches all aspects of life, and, as such, anthropologists have investigated how these processes have materialized in a diversity of social realms. Below, we take a brief look at how anthropologists have approached the study of globalization in terms of migration, international adoption, protest, economic aid, and the development of local economies.

Migration of People, Migration of Culture

The movement of people takes many forms and is motivated by a diversity of factors. There are those who move from rural environments to urban ones in search of wage labor and the desire for a better standard of living; students who travel across the world to continue their studies in different countries; families who are forced from their home because of the threat, or the actuality, of political, ethnic or religious violence; and men and women who cross national borders in order to earn a living as nannies, engineers, nurses, and maids. The movement of people is nothing new—pastoralists and foragers have always relocated regularly, and European expansion and exploration began hundreds of years ago. What characterizes the current state of migration as distinct, however, is the sheer *volume* of people who are no longer living in the nation in which they were born or raised, and the relative ease with which migrants can keep contact with their home country/community and the friends and family who remain there.

Migration is the movement of a person or people from one place to another. The movement of people has been a popular area of study for anthropologists, particularly in terms of *why* people decide to move, *how* they adapt to their new surroundings, and more recently, how this move affects their cultural and individual identity (which we explored in Chapter 10). Migration takes many forms. Perhaps the most common form is the movement of people within a nation from rural areas to urban centers.

PLATE 11.1 Burmese Refugees Waiting to Be Registered by a Thai Policeman

According to the "push-pull theory," because of the increase in population, rural environments are less able to support residents economically. As a result, people flock to urban centers with the hope of finding employment. The reality of this situation is often bleak—individuals are separated from their support networks and the fast pace of city life can be difficult to adjust to. Moreover, employment often comes in the form of low-paying and low-skilled work, such as cleaning or factory work, which may have grave psychological effects, as well as making it extremely difficult to make ends meet.

Migration has increased dramatically since the mid-1980s—it is estimated that nearly 2 per cent of the world's population lives abroad.[2] While rates of international migration are on the rise (a 37 per cent increase from 1990 to 2010), it is still relatively uncommon, with 9 out of every 10 people in the world living in their country of birth (United Nations, Department of Economic and Social Affairs 2010). Women make up approximately half of the population of international migrants, a relatively new trend over the last 50 years.

Immigration patterns have also changed. During the first part of the twentieth century, the majority of immigrants moving to countries such as Canada, the United States, and Australia were European, specifically from countries in western and northern Europe. The fact that these immigrants were coming from predominantly white nations was not coincidental—the receiving countries had strict immigration policies outlining who were and were not "desirable" populations. Australia, for instance, once had an explicitly "White Australia" policy. In Canada, the changing labor needs and a desire to improve the national image ignited a transformation and restructuring of these problematic immigration policies in the 1960s. In the last 20 years, Canada and the United States have experienced an increase in immigrants from Asia, Mexico, Latin America, and the Caribbean, as well as most recently from central and eastern Europe. It would be wrong, however, to say that migration is only happening from developing to developed countries—while 70 per cent of international migrants hail from the "South," roughly half of this population has migrated to other economically developing countries.[3]

Economic migrants, or individuals who relocate for a limited period of time in order to work, have no intention of making their move permanent. Asian women are the fastest-growing group of migrant workers—there are approximately 1.5 million Asian women working abroad. The majority of these women head to Saudi Arabia, Kuwait, Hong Kong, Singapore, and Japan and are employed primarily in the domestic service sector and professions such as nursing and teaching (Miller, Van Esterik, and Van Esterik 2001). Most of these individuals remain connected to their homeland and often send wages home to family. Indeed, remittances from migrants provide a major source of capital for many developing nations.[4] A number of anthropologists have investigated the complex experiences of migrant workers all over the world. In Canada, the Philippines became the nation's largest source of short- and long-term migrants in 2010. The edited collection *Filipinos in Canada: Disturbing Invisibility* (Coloma et al. 2012) explores how understandings of gender, youth, and identity intersect with migration and labor practices in Canada's Filipino community. In that volume, anthropologist Lisa Davidson investigates the experiences of Filipina women who travel to Canada to work as nannies under the Live-in Caregiver Program, a program designed to address shortages of child and elder care while offering permanent residence status to those workers who have stayed for two years.

Sharon Nagy (2006) explores the employment of transnational household workers in Doha, the capital city of Qatar, a small country on the Arabian Peninsula. The end of the twentieth century was a period of rapid urbanization in the Arabian Gulf. This transformation required an influx of workers in all sectors to meet building and development demands. While these workers were primarily international, village dwellers and Bedouin communities within Qatar also moved into Doha, establishing the city as a true mix of cultures and nationalities. During six years of fieldwork (1994–2000), Nagy considered the social interactions occurring in Doha along two lines: those between Qatari citizens and foreign nationals, and those between groups who share Qatari citizenry but who hail from very different cultural backgrounds. Nagy was interested in understanding how these social relationships and cultural understandings manifest in the spatial organization of the city. She describes how the impact of land and building grants, immigration laws, and employment regulations "facilitate residential isolation and limited interaction between groups. In addition, the way space is divided is linked to prevailing attitudes towards social differentiation and the existence of multiple ideologies of difference is reflected in multiple spatial phenomena" (2006: 135). Qataris prefer to live near those who are similar to themselves—this preference excludes non-Qataris, as well as Qataris who hail from different cultural, class, and religious backgrounds.

Nagy's research also explores the manner in which household relationships "reproduce" global hierarchies that are informed by ideas of gender and nationality. Within the relatively confined space of the household, Qatari women and children come into contact with foreigners whom they would not normally meet due to their restricted public movement. The domestic workers themselves, particularly the women, also have limited interactions with people outside of their house of employment. The household setting informs both employers' and employees' knowledge of the wider cultural backgrounds of each group (see Nagy 1998). Nagy's research illustrates that the processes involved in international economic migration are experienced on a multitude of levels—from the political and economic circumstances of sending and receiving countries, to the spatial organization of a city, to the individual households and lives of the employers and employees themselves.

Culture, Identity, and Citizenship: International Adoption

The act of adopting children across national borders has ignited heated debate among all sectors of society, from academics to politicians to families sitting around the dinner table. This practice touches on a number of issues that people tend to have very strong opinions about—the nature of family, the well-being of children born into poverty, the right of wealthy nations to adopt children from poorer ones, and the significance, if any, between biological origins and cultural identity. While there are a number of angles to this debate, we will focus our discussion on how the culture concept has been invoked on a number of levels in critiques of international adoption. Our discussion will consider how changes at the global and national levels altered the way that American citizens viewed their responsibility as a global super-power. This cultural transformation ignited the attention of American interest groups and citizens to the plight of children in war-torn or poverty-stricken situations, and the drive to offer assistance through adoption was set in motion. Sixty-five years later, adoption has become a legitimate method to create a family by those with the means to do so. Finally, at a more individual level, the practice by adoptive parents instilling a cultural education for children adopted across national borders is illustrative of an understanding of culture that is tied to biological traits.

Before we begin, however, it is important that we contextualize our discussion of adoption. As we have already seen in Chapter 5 the act of defining the family is a complex and culturally sensitive process. Definitions of who is family and who is not have far-reaching implications that are social, political, economic, and religious in nature. Clearly, this is not a process to be taken lightly. Western constructions of adoption operate on the premise that an orphan child is taken in by a nuclear-style family unit. The child becomes part of this family unit through a legal process rather than a biological one. This is but one understanding of both the orphan and adoption concepts, but it is far from universal. There has been extensive anthropological literature examining the practice of adoption and fostering and how it "fits in" to the larger concept of kinship.[5]

One example of this type of research is by anthropologist Jessica Leinaweaver (2007), who examines the practice of child-circulation in Ayacucho, a poverty-stricken area of Peru that witnessed political violence and upheaval in the 1980s and 1990s. In many cultures, such as Hawaiian and Chinese, the nuclear family unit is not the core unit and the act of caring for one's children often requires the cooperation of extended family and, at times, the larger community. In Ayacucho, Leinaweaver examined the practice of child-circulation, which involves the relocation of a child to a household of a family relative. This relocation is not regarded as permanent, and the child can move back and forth between the homes. Both parties involved stand to gain benefits, such as relief from feeding a child by the sending family and the additional help another set of hands can bring to the receiving household. As well, each party pays a price, such as incurring the cost of a new family member or the hardship of having one's child live somewhere else.

Leinaweaver (2007) describes how child-circulation serves the purpose of strengthening ties between families, allowing for better opportunities for children and assistance to adults. One Peruvian anthropologist declared that the concept of the orphan simply did not exist in Ayacucho as a relative would always be able to take in a child. This statement, however, refers only to the time before the political upheaval and violence that killed so many mothers and fathers. In 1983, the first orphanage was opened. Twenty years later, this institution has become a home to many children whose parents and relatives are *temporarily* unable to care for them. Most parents who leave their children here have every intention of taking them back once they are able to provide for them again.

Child rearing takes many forms, and the systems that govern kinship relations are subject to cultural worldviews and belief systems. Adoption, whether by those related by blood to a child or not, is a meaningful and legitimate act of creating a family. It is a process that challenges the assumption that blood kin are the only legitimate people who can raise a child. As we turn our lens toward international adoption, a process that crosses legal and cultural boundaries, it is important to consider the meanings of terms such as orphan, family, and adoption by all parties involved. Our focus in the next section is on the culture of adoption in North America, primarily from the perspective of the receiving nations and the adoptees.

As World War II came to an end in 1945, the United States was transformed from an **isolationist** nation to a major player on the international stage. American citizens had been awakened to the horrors of war as media reports circulated the globe, and over the next few decades, the US would increasingly become involved in international struggles. As a result of these political, economic, and social forces in the international realm, a cultural shift in the American public occurred. Perhaps most devastating to many Americans in the 1950s were accounts of innocent children who had been victims of war-related violence. While these reports would likely have caused concern at any time, the United States' new position of power seemed to ignite feelings of responsibility. Reports of children orphaned as a result of the atomic bombing of Hiroshima led to an outcry by Americans who wished to sponsor orphans and bring them to the United States where they could be adopted (Klein 2003). Liberal groups sought adoptive parents for those children fathered and left behind by American and European servicemen in the Philippines, Japan, China, Korea, and later Vietnam (Marre and Briggs 2009). Evangelical Christians believed it was their duty to spread the word of God and halt "godless communism." This movement inspired the creation of World Vision, a Christian organization still in operation today that facilitates the sponsoring of children in developing nations by those who send a monthly dollar amount. This religious movement inspired a number of Christian American families to make a further commitment by actually adopting children from Korea. It was not long before American-financed overseas orphanages and adoption services appeared (Marre and Briggs 2009).

PLATE 11.2 Korean Children with Their American Parents

As the culture of the United States was changing to reflect the nation's relatively new status, changes at home were having an impact on women's social position in society. Women were gaining higher social standing—their wages were creeping higher and professional opportunities previously closed to them were slowly opening. By the 1960s, fewer and fewer unwed mothers were putting their children up for adoption: "a combination of state supports for parents and rising wages and employment opportunities for women enabled them to keep their children. As soon as single mothers could afford to keep their children, they did" (Marre and Briggs 2009: 10). These social changes, alongside the legalization of birth control and abortion in the 1970s, led to a falling birth rate and far fewer babies being put up for adoption in North America.

These changes to the demography of American society, combined with social and religious movements, led many prospective adoptive parents to look overseas (Yngvesson 2009). The number of transnational adoptions has nearly doubled since the late 1980s, with the United States representing the largest receiving nation at 22,884 adoptions in 2004 (Selman 2009). In this same year, China, Russia, Guatemala, and South Korea were the largest sending nations. The process of adopting a child transnationally is lengthy, arduous, and, in most cases, expensive. Estimates put the cost of arranging a transnational adoption to Canada at approximately $35,000–$45,000,[6] ensuring that only those with economic means are able to engage in this type of adoption. While the sending nations as a whole are not necessarily poor, the families who tend to put children up for adoption are. This creates a highly unbalanced relationship, and many critics argue that the right of individuals from wealthy nations to adopt children from poorer nations is morally questionable. Tales of corruption, trafficking in children, and unwed mothers being forced to put their children in orphanages placed transnational adoption under international scrutiny. In 1993, the *Hague Convention on the Protection of Children and Co-operation in Respect of Intercountry Adoption* was signed, stating that countries must do whatever possible to keep the child within their own family, or to find a family for that child in their home country. Transnational adoption was to be the third option: "The convention insisted on a child's right to an identity and to the right to 'grow up in a family environment, in an atmosphere of happiness, love and understanding'" (Volkman 2005: 5).

Herein lies one of the major issues at the heart of international adoption. While considering the practice on a **macro** level, the act of wealthy nations adopting the children of poorer nations appears to be a band-aid solution to the problems of economic inequality in the world. When considered on a **micro** level, however, if an individual child who cannot be cared for by their kin can be spared a life of poverty by being adopted by a family from overseas, it is difficult to say that this process is corrupt. It is for this reason that the topic of international adoption ignites such passionate debate.

A shift in national cultural values, powerful religious movements, an increase in women's social position, and international legislation committed to protecting a child's right to a cultural identity have all contributed to establishing transnational adoption as a relatively accepted practice. The discourses employed to discuss this type of adoption have also changed over the last few decades. Originally, adoptive parents and the agencies that they went through assumed that an international adoption was a "closed" adoption—the child was adopted, brought to their new home, and raised as an American (or Canadian, Spaniard, etc.). Over time, however, the importance of cultural identity became a prominent topic of debate among those involved. Many adoptees began to challenge, question, and speak out about how transnational adoptions were carried out and discussed in mainstream society. It was not long before

> adoptees were expected, or at least invited, to explore their multiple identities: to retain a name, to imagine their birth families, to learn about "birth cultures," perhaps even to visit their birth countries and seek out relatives. Many Korean adoptees had grown up and had shaken off their sense of isolation as they met other adoptees like themselves. They began to speak forcefully, sometimes with anger and pain, about how they were not simply the white Minnesotans (or Swedes, or Californians) whom their parents and the culture as a whole had expected them to be. Some articulated their sense of dislocation, uncertainties about where they fit as they struggled to reconcile their outer appearance and inner sense of self, the ambiguities of simultaneously belonging and not belonging. (Volkman 2005: 5)

Many adoptive parents are now committed to providing a cultural education for their adopted children—language and cultural education classes, introducing children to adult role models of the same ethnicity, living in a diverse area, and traveling to the birth country have all become increasingly common. The Internet has an abundance of chat groups for adoptees and adoptive parents, providing virtual communities for those who have experienced adoption in one way or another. This desire for support and dialogue suggests that the realization of an individual's cultural identity is a complex process that touches on a number of issues, including kinship, geography, and appearance. Conceptualized in this way, identity is "associated with a root or ground of belonging that is inside the child (as 'blood,' 'primal connectedness,' and 'identity hunger') and is unchanging. But it is also outside the child in the sense that it is assumed to tie him or her to others whom he or she is like (as defined by skin color, hair texture, facial features, and so forth). Alienation from this source of likeness produces 'genealogical bewilderment' and a psychological need for the adopted child to return to where he or she 'really' belongs" (Yngvesson 2009: 26). If culture is indeed learned, does this move to associate the birth culture with transnationally adopted individuals raised in very different surroundings seem unusual, or do you believe that the notion of cultural origins is important for all individuals, whether they remember them or not?

Understanding culture is a complex undertaking, and it is not an easy task to create an environment where children are supported to foster aspects of their identity that they deem important. Through anthropological research, the voices of adopted children and their adoptive parents are increasingly being heard, and with them the challenges and successes of this complex approach to family making are better understood. Due to the circumstances of transnational adoption, however, the voices of the birth parents remain largely silent, a situation that reflects the power imbalance between those with the means to adopt children and those in the unfortunate situation of having to give up their children (Marre and Briggs 2009).

Protest

In the last days of 2010, the world watched as protests erupted across many parts of the Arab world, including Tunisia, Egypt, Libya, and Yemen, in a movement that became known as the Arab Spring. Protesters were rallying against repression, censorship, and violence from authorities, including governments and militia. While each protest took on a meaning of its own to reflect the situation in that nation, they shared a common approach of strikes, demonstrations, and marches and used social media such as Facebook to organize and communicate their cause. As a result of the protests, governments in Tunisia, Egypt, Libya, and Yemen fell, and other leaders announced their decision to step down at the end of their current terms.

In January 2011, Cairo, Egypt, took center stage as thousands of Egyptians occupied Tahrir Square to protest 30 years of power by President Hosni Mubarak. For weeks, television coverage documented the protests and protesters, from families spanning multiple generations to individual youth, united in their determination to bring about change. Anthropologist Lila Abu-Lughod watched the protests unfold from the living rooms of friends in a small Egyptian town south of Cairo where years earlier she had conducted ethnographic research. She was struck by the absence of footage or reporting from outside of Tahrir Square—what was happening in the countryside? How were the majority of Egyptians who lived *outside* of Cairo reacting to the revolution?

As an anthropologist, Abu-Lughod was interested in how the fight for democracy and freedom that was occurring on the streets of Cairo was experienced by the rural Egyptians living a life far removed from the busy metropolis. How were these momentous events affecting the daily lives of rural Egyptians? According to Abu-Lughod (2012: 25), "Affected by the same national policies and state institutions, each region and location experienced them through the specific problems they created for people locally. And each group that felt itself to be part of what these young men described as this 'glorious revolution' has taken up a different set of projects." Abu-Lughod had already established a trusting relationship with many individuals in the village, and because of this was able to observe and speak with people about their experiences of abuse and oppression at the hands of government authorities (police, councils, politicians). This small town was an important heritage site that attracted both local and international tourists, and because of this had sparked political and commercial interest. This interest was accompanied by corruption, and locals had been plagued with issues such as shortages of food and a lack of public services. Just as in Cairo, local youths used social media such as Facebook to come together to discuss local issues, as well as strategies to initiate improvements that would affect daily life, such as the distribution of bread and bottled cooking gas.

While differences in motivations existed in the country and the city, Abu-Lughod asserts that the acts of resistance she witnessed and that were described to her must be considered in the same vein as the protests occurring in Cairo, despite the fact that they were geographically removed and out of the spotlight of the international media. She describes how the language used to describe the struggle in the village was somewhat different from that used in Cairo, reflecting the importance of community and social responsibility: "The youth speak the moral language of responsibility, self-lessness and community welfare, the struggle against corruption and self-interest. It is a strong language of social morality, not of rights. They do not speak of democracy, but in tackling problems directly and personally; they are living it" (2012: 25).

Abu-Lughod's work illustrates the value of an anthropological approach to under-standing an event that gains international attention. Through observation and inter-views, the perspectives of those who are not included in the international media are given space to be heard, and through this discussion offer a more complete snapshot of the impact of such a significant event.

Economic Aid and Development

By this point in the book you should be comfortable with the fact that the processes of global exploration and expansion have existed since the time of James Cook. In the 1970s, anthropologists became very interested in the ways that institutions and organizations, rather than colonial explorers, led economic development initiatives. The unequal distribution of wealth among the world's nations, and the post-colonial legacy of political turmoil and economic uncertainty that characterizes much of the world's poorest nations, led to attempts by aid and development organizations to gen-erate economic activity and improve political stability with the hope that increased and more effective social services would follow. While many of these development initiatives are presented on humanitarian grounds, the motivations for these projects are often entrenched in political and economic issues. In the late 1990s, agencies such as the World Bank came under extreme criticism for failing to assist the poor in coun-tries where policies to improve economic security were being implemented. Instead, it was the economically developed nations that appeared to benefit, as their business investments resulted in profitable returns and thousands of jobs for the people in their employ, while populations in the receiving countries struggled to adapt to strict economic policies.

The job of the anthropologist in the early years of development projects was to make things operate as smoothly and efficiently as possible. As anthropologists were *employed* by these organizations, their loyalties were not to the local people but to the organizations themselves, who often had different objectives than the residents. Many of these development schemes had disastrous effects on the local people and their environment, and it wasn't long before the ethical involvement of anthropologists was called into question. Suddenly, anthropologists found themselves to be a very real part of the economic and development industry problem. This realization led to a shift in the role that the anthropologist assumed: "The question is not: What can we do to make this project successful? Instead, the anthropologist asks: Is this is a good project from the perspective of the target population?" (Miller, Van Esterik, and Van Esterik 2001: 421). (Indeed, the role of anthropology in development is a contentious and hot topic. For an in-depth and fascinating discussion of some of the difficulties associated with conducting fieldwork in the development and aid world, see the work of anthropologist David Mosse [2005; 2011], who has written extensively on the subject.)

Perhaps one of the best-known examples of an anthropologist playing an *effective* role in a development project is that of Gerald Murray (1987) in Haiti. While this example is now over 25 years old, it is an excellent case study to illustrate how anthropological knowledge can lead to the development of a more successful initiative, for both the organization supplying the funds and the local people. Murray exposed components of a multi-million-dollar reforestation project that were not compatible with the everyday realities of the farmers who were ultimately responsible for the success of the project.

MAP 11.1 Haiti

Haiti is one of the poorest nations in the Western hemisphere. It is located on the Caribbean island of Hispaniola, which it shares with the Dominican Republic. It has a long history of colonial rule in which both the French and the Spanish deforested the island to sell the wood for profit and plant cash crops that were in demand in Europe. After independence, foreign-owned lumber companies cleared most of the island of its valuable hardwoods. Haiti is now essentially deforested, and an increase in population has led to pressure on the land and a high demand for wood and charcoal in the cities.

Reforestation projects were failing miserably, in particular the USAID project that eventually employed Murray, an anthropologist who had just completed his dissertation on "the manner in which Haitian peasant land tenure had evolved in response to internal population growth" (Murray 1987: 225). The problem with the USAID approach lay in its inability to present a project that would allow the peasant farmers control of their land and of the trees that were being planted on it—as farmers, they were dependent on cleared land to plant cash crops and graze their goats. It did not make economic sense to plant the fruit trees that USAID supplied, as they were not meant to be cut down, thus further limiting the already scarce land available. It also made little economic sense to wait for an economic return on trees that would take years to mature. USAID was presenting the project from an ecological perspective—the intent was to aid in soil regeneration, not to offer farmers immediate economic profit. To the farmers who were trying to feed their families and maintain their land, however, the promise of improved conditions years down the road rang hollow in their ears.

After analyzing the shortcomings of the USAID project, Murray stated that it was not the attitudes of the peasants that were causing the project to fail, but instead one or two major flaws in the project plans. He jokingly stated that if he were given a jeep and access to a $50,000 checking account, he would be able to implement a program that would produce more trees in the ground than the current "multi-million-dollar charade" (Murray 1987: 226). Murray packed up his bags and left Haiti, only to receive a startling phone call some time later: "To my great disbelief, as I was correcting Anthro 101 exams some two years later, one of the program officers still in Haiti called to say that an Agroforestry Outreach Project (AOP) had been approved chapter and verse as I had recommended it; and that if I was interested in putting my life where my mouth had been and would leave the ivory tower to direct the project, my project bank account would have, not $50,000, but $4 million" (1987: 226).

Murray had suggested that, rather than providing fruit trees that were not to be cut, farmers be supplied with fast-growing trees, such as eucalyptus, that could be cut as early as four years after planting. The farmers were given full control over the trees—they could allow their goats to eat them (which is what had happened with the fruit tree seedlings), in which case they would not receive any more seedlings from the project; they could allow the trees to grow for four years and then clear the land and sell the wood for lumber and charcoal; or they could allow the trees to mature and provide coverage for their crops. The choice was theirs.

Initially, Murray had cautiously estimated that three million trees would be planted on the land of 6,000 farmers at the end of four years. By the end of the fourth year (by which time another anthropologist had taken over as director), the project had planted *20 million trees on the land of 75,000 farmers*. The project was an astounding success, primarily due to the compatibility of the project aims and the needs of the farmers themselves. The input of anthropological methods and theories greatly influenced the project throughout each stage of planning and implantation: "We are dealing, not with an ongoing project affected by anthropological input, but with a project whose very existence was rooted in anthropological research and whose very character was determined by ongoing anthropological direction and anthropologically informed managerial prodding" (Murray 1987: 235).

Unfortunately, the tumultuous political situation in Haiti has negated much of the positive benefits of the project. A military coup in 1986 disrupted civil society, including the cutting down of trees as an attempt by the military to exert power over the rural population. Since then, Haiti has seen two more military coups, the invasion and occupation by the United States in 1994 and again in 2004, extreme civil unrest, and the country's first democratically elected president, René Préval (b. 1943), who was elected both in 1996 and again in 2006. Perhaps most devastating, however, was the earthquake that struck on January 12, 2010. More than 220,000 people were killed, 300,000 injured, and more than one million made homeless. Three years later, the United Nations estimated that over one million people were still in need of humanitarian assistance.

Meeting Foreign Demand: Ecotourism and Mining

Anyone who has perused the glossy pages of a *National Geographic* or watched an episode of the reality television show *Survivor* knows the allure of a secluded tropical beach or pristine mountain range. Traveling to distant countries where the types of food eaten, the dress worn, and the language spoken are totally different from one's own is an exciting and at times terrifying experience. Encounters with different people, landscapes, and cultures can be a powerful tool for instilling a sense of social responsibility, particularly if the areas traveled to are at risk as a result of overuse, pollution or poor management. It is this sense of social conscience that travel agencies and tour groups hoped to tap into when the concept of ecotourism was developed.

As an industry, ecotourism is relatively new to the tourist trade. Becoming enormously popular in the 1990s and reaching its peak when the United Nations declared 2002 the "year of ecotourism," it was an approach that many believed would be beneficial for all involved: "The outcome of ecotourism ought to be win-win-win: ecotourists ought to win by getting to experience the 'natural areas' that attract them, people living alongside such 'natural areas' ought to win through opportunities for work enabled by the presence of wealthy outsiders in their midst, and those interested in the protection of these natural areas ought to win as everyone else involved becomes invested in the mission of conservation" (Walsh 2012: 51). Of course, not all great ideas translate into great products, and ecotourism has proven not to be the magic bullet it was thought to be. As we will see in anthropologist Andrew Walsh's ethnographic study of Madagascar, the reality for residents of this hot ecotourist destination was far from pristine.

The Ankarana region of Madagascar is home to an ecosystem unlike any other in the world. Ankarana National Park consists of 150-million-year-old limestone formations, caves, underground rivers, and sunken forests—as one can imagine, an awe-inspiring sight. It is also home to some very valuable natural resources, the most

MAP 11.2 Madagascar

sought-after being sapphires. Walsh's ethnography *Made in Madagascar: Sapphires, Ecotourism and the Global Bazaar* explores the emergence of two seemingly disparate trades in Madagascar: sapphire mining and ecotourism. While mining and environmentalism represent two vastly different approaches to development, Walsh illustrates that to the local people witnessing their region's inundation with outsiders (both foreign and from within the country), these two trades are fundamentally connected, and not simply because they are concerned with the natural resources of the area.

To the Antankarana people who live alongside the park, the Ankarana massif is a sacred site for instilling blessings related to prosperity, fertility, and health. During a ceremony known as "entry into the caves," hundreds of people from around the area gather to spend three days in the caves at the tombs of past rulers. There are stories, dances, and songs; blessings are sought for rain, for more children, for more cattle. Essentially, those seeking blessings are seeking a fertile and prosperous future, just as their ancestors have done for years before them. This site is not simply meaningful to the locals, however. Conservation agencies such as the World Wildlife Fund are also intent on protecting the area's ecosystem. Ecotourists flock here to see one of the world's largest population of lemurs, and over 100 bird species, 50 reptile species, and 10 frog species, as well as over 350 different species of plants.[7] Unfortunately, the goals of prosperity and fertility are quite different from—even opposed to—those of the conservation societies and ecotourists who have pledged to protect the area. While both groups want the area to thrive, their reasons for doing so are very different. As Walsh writes,

> For those who seek access to blessings inside the massif, success will be measured in new births, expanding herds, and increasing yields of rice and cash crops; the growth they desire will come to the local landscape in the form of new and bigger houses, more grazing cattle, and fields of newly planted sugar cane. As you can imagine, indications of growth such as these would not be signs of success to those whose goal is protecting Ankarana's distinctive biodiversity; in fact, the work of conservation is founded in an ethos that lends itself to quite dissimilar aspirations. As Keller puts it, "the conservation ethos" is one founded on the ideal of maintaining "equilibrium among the different species present on the planet" (2008: 251). And when the protection of biodiversity and the conservation of the present state of things is the goal, the kind of growth ensured by sacred sites like those to be found within the Ankarana massif will always represent a problem. (Walsh 2012: 13; Keller 2008: 251 as cited in Walsh 2012)

Walsh talked to individuals who made their living, in one way or another, through the ecotourism industry by acting as guides, entrepreneurs, drivers, and park guards. One guide in particular, Robert, had years of experience within and outside the Ankarana area working with researchers, individual tourists, and tourist groups.

Robert is a sought-after guide because of his agreeable personality, language abilities, and knowledge of the biodiversity in the park. Robert, like many other guides, does not come from the Ankarana area. For local individuals with little experience in guiding or dealing with tourists, the competition from experienced outsiders such as Robert has proven difficult.

The failure of the ecotourism industry to benefit those who live closest to the areas under protection is an accepted reality for many locals. The local perception in Ankarana is that ecotourism benefits outsiders much more than the local person, whether it is the conservation groups and ecotourists or the guides who move to the area to show these groups around. Alongside this resignation, Walsh began to uncover a great deal of speculation about why foreigners were willing to travel so far at such great expense to visit the park. One park employee told Walsh how an elderly relative could not believe his ears when she explained why foreigners were coming in droves to their home:

> There was an elder relative of mine [who] asked me, "Hey, my child, what is the reason for the visits of these *vazaha* ... why is it that they have come?" I laughed. "Do you want to know the reason for their visits? They come to see chameleons. They come to see lizards. Half of them come to see ants. Some come to see birds, and then there are some who come to see only trees." "IS that so!?!," he said. "Ya!" I said. "Haaa! Kakakakaka!" He almost fainted he was laughing so hard.... "Really my daughter!?! ... [He said,] I was thinking there were sapphires there, I thought there was gold there ... but that is all they are here to see?" [I answered] "Ya ... they come to see animals, to see snakes." He laughed and laughed. (2012: 66)

This was a common sentiment expressed by locals, Walsh states. Many locals also believe that foreigners are given access to valuable resources within the park that they themselves are restricted from, and that the purpose of the foreign conservation offices set up around the park is to ensure foreigners exclusive access while keeping locals out. The thought that people would travel from all over the world simply to observe animals, caves, and trees does not make sense to those who have been living among these objects their whole lives.

The realization that Ankarana's pristine biodiversity is also home to an enormous supply of sapphires has sparked the interest of an entirely different group of foreigners. Unfortunately, the goals of this group diverge from those of the local peoples much more starkly than in the case of the conservationists described above. Walsh notes that when he visited one small town in the area in 1995, there were a mere 400 people residing there. Two years later, this number had grown to an astounding 15,000 after word had circulated that foreigners were willing to pay a tremendous amount for the small blue stones that young children used as ammunition in their slingshots. Sapphires were a hot commodity, and everyone wanted a part.

Once again, speculation as to *why* sapphires were so valuable to foreigners was rampant in the local communities. Again, too, locals debated the real purpose of these stones: Were they used in the production of expensive electronics? Of watch faces? Of bullets and bombs? Walsh comments, "The idea that these foreigners were, as he [one local] and others in town had been assured by local conservation officials, tourists intent on 'taking nothing but pictures and leaving nothing but footprints' in Ankarana National Park was as hard to believe as the idea that the region's sapphires were being used in the manufacture of jewelry" (Walsh 2012: 48). What was widely accepted, however, was the understanding that while Madagascar had valuable resources that foreigners were willing to pay enormous amounts of money for, local people were simply not reaping the rewards.

While the mining industry is leaving its ugly mark on the pristine land that so many held so dear, it is also having an impact on traditional male roles in Madagascar culture. For most of these young men, earning a wage in the dangerous and risky mining industry has resulted in a shift in priorities—no longer is buying a house, supporting a family or providing for their parents a main concern. Rather, it is "*la vie!*," or living a lifestyle characterized by drinking, sex, and partying funded by the "hot money" earned in the pits. Not surprisingly, local Ankaranans (particularly the elderly) and conservationist groups alike have deemed the sapphire rush a "total fiasco," both for the damage imposed on the area by the rapid influx of people and for the ecological devastation brought on by mining practices. The environmental impact of this mining has taken a serious toll on the area, and Ankarana National Park saw a 50 per cent drop in visitors in one year. Most ecotourists are not interested in traveling to a park defaced with mining pits and shacks. One thing is for certain: "both [industries] stand to fall apart as soon as foreign consumers lose interest in what the region has to offer them" (2012: 72).

Walsh closes his ethnography by asking a question that has likely come into your own head at some point during your time reading this introductory text—*so what?* Why is this important? Why should I care? According to Walsh, these events are relative to all our lives because we are all *active* players in the "global bazaar," that very real marketplace where goods and services are traded from all over the world. If sapphires and ecotourism are not your thing, then perhaps coffee, tea or cell-phone batteries are. It is very difficult, if not impossible, to be a consumer in today's society without participating in this global bazaar. Through research and reporting, the public can become better informed consumers and can ignite change through their purchasing and travel practices.

The Globalization of Anthropology: Multi-Site Ethnographies and Virtual Worlds

We have seen how anthropologists have contributed to a better understanding of the processes of globalization, but we should also pause to consider how anthropology as a discipline has changed as a result of these same processes. One of the most interesting developments is in how the practice of fieldwork has changed over the last few decades. Anthropologists are increasingly embarking on **multi-site ethnographic studies**, where the focus is not one geographic location but a number of sites that share a common group of people, task, or ideology. For example, anthropologist Christina Garsten (1994) explored the organizational culture of Apple Computer in the Silicon Valley, Paris, and Stockholm, while Ulf Hannerz (2003) explored the social world of foreign news correspondents in Jerusalem, Tokyo, and South Africa.

A key component of multi-site ethnography involves identifying and exploring the links or relationships between the various sites—these anthropologists are not simply comparing a handful of locales, but are instead examining a group of sites that are in some way related. In Garsten's ethnography, she explores the ways in which company culture is influenced by national culture, as well as the difference between the center of the company (Silicon Valley) and its peripheral sites. For his part, Hannerz examines the relationship between correspondents and the news agency for which they work, as well their relationship to other news agencies with correspondents in the field. Interviews or focus groups often play a predominant role in data collection, for there is less time to spend on participant observation when an anthropologist has a number of field sites.

Another change in fieldwork practices can be seen in the case of anthropologists who are focusing their research on the virtual world. Tom Boellstorff explores the culture of Second Life in his ethnography *Coming of Age in Second Life*, "a virtual world owned and managed by a company, Linden Lab, where by the end of my fieldwork tens of thousands of persons who might live on separate continents spent part of their lives online" (Boellstorff 2008: 4). Created in 2003, Second Life is one of many online virtual worlds where, as of this writing, millions of people have created communities, bought and sold virtual goods, attended social activities, and discovered friendship and love. News of the thriving actual economy of Second Life attracted world media coverage when it was reported that US$1 million of economic activity occurred daily.

Boellstorff is a professor of anthropology at the University of California, Irvine, and an ethnographer who has published extensively on his research studying gay cultures in Indonesia. In *Coming of Age in Second Life*, Boellstorff was interested in exploring what anthropology could contribute to understanding culture in a virtual world. He wanted to investigate the notion of a "virtual worldview": "What might the set of assumptions and practices that make up Second Life culture teach us about such a virtual worldview?" (2008: 24). Boellstorff conducted fieldwork within Second Life between June 2004 and January 2007 as Tom Bukowski, an avatar or character that exists within the environment of Second Life. Unlike Cathy Small's research at AnyU discussed in Chapter 3, Boellstorff fully disclosed his anthropologist status in his profile and openly discussed his research with other residents of Second Life.

You may recognize the similarity in title with another ethnography that we discussed in this book—that of Margaret Mead's *Coming of Age in Samoa*. The similarity in title is indeed intentional—like Margaret Mead 70 years before him, Boellstorff uses traditional anthropological methods such as participant observation and interviewing to explore a cultural world that seems strange and foreign to many who do not live there. He notes the importance of participant observation in particular, explaining that by engaging with one's surroundings, the anthropologist does not rely on individuals to explain their culture, but instead watches and participates in how a culture unfolds. Participant observation considers how all aspects of a culture relate to one another: it is "useful for gaining a conceptual handle on cultural assumptions that may not be overtly discussed…. Participant observation can illuminate debates and issues of which the researcher was unaware prior to the research, and so could not have thought to include on a list of interview questions or survey form" (Boellstorff 2008: 76). Boellstorff also notes the importance of recognizing that his fieldwork and the resulting ethnography constitute a specific snapshot of a two-and-a-half-year period in this world. While this is an important reminder for readers of all ethnographies, the point is particularly pertinent in this case due to the rapid and constant technological updates in the environment under study.

While Boellstorff employed traditional anthropological methods to embark on an untraditional approach to fieldwork, he did have some unique methodological decisions to make. Boellstorff was faced with deciding whether or not to engage with participants in the *actual* world. While many researchers studying virtual worlds have done so, Boellstorff decided to restrict his research to events and individuals who existed within the virtual world, as this was the culture that he was interested in investigating: "I made no attempt to meet Second Life residents in the actual world or learn their actual-world identities, though both happened on occasion. I took their activities and words as legitimate data about culture in a virtual world. For instance, if during my research I was talking to a woman, I was not concerned to determine if she was 'really' a man in the actual world, or even if two different people were taking turns controlling her" (2008: 61).

Boellstorff's ethnography offers a detailed analysis of this virtual world, exploring place and time as they exist in Second Life, as well as concepts of personhood, relationships, and community. Also included are the topics of economy, politics, governance, and issues of inequality, much as one would see in ethnographies where the fieldwork took place in the actual world. Rather than focusing on a specific aspect of Second Life culture, Boellstorff instead chose to present the culture as an interrelated whole, examining how aspects of this culture relate to one another. Because of this holistic approach, Boellstorff was required to be somewhat brief in his discussion of the social world. This book is therefore as much an ethnography of Second Life as it is a discussion of anthropology's role in understanding virtual worlds more broadly.

Boellstorff (2008: 238) concludes that "virtual worlds are distinct domains of human being, deserving of study in their own right" and not simply as a product of technology produced in the actual world (Boellstorff 2008: 238). While traditional anthropological methods are effective for gathering data in order to understand the virtual world, this is a culture that is distinct and separate from the actual world. Boellstorff argues that while virtual worlds are relatively new, "being virtual" in the way that humans have always been able to imagine themselves in different settings and locales, including those they have never been to or may not even exist, is part of human culture: "online worlds draw upon a capacity for the virtual that is as old as humanity itself" (2008: 238). We will no doubt see more ethnographies exploring the virtual world in the years to come, and they will likely take very different forms than what Boellstorff has offered, due in large part to the rapidly changing context in which they are set.

Conclusion

Our discussion of globalization tells us that we must consider the economic, political, and social processes on both a macro and micro—or national/international and local—level in order to fully understand the all-encompassing nature of global change. Anthropology is well suited to investigating how individuals negotiate these changes, changes that very well may have been initiated thousands of miles away but that are experienced in the day-to-day activities of local citizens. As we have seen, cultural change does not necessarily imply progress, nor does modernization necessarily imply an improvement in the quality of life. The use of these value-laden terms without consideration for what they imply perpetuates the notion that the "West" is what all other nations should strive to imitate.

We have considered a number of prominent issues connected with global change: political and social protest, the transnational flow of people, and development and ecotourism. The anthropologists who spent time dealing with these issues illustrate that while the processes of globalization have far-reaching implications, the manner in which individuals experience these processes in their daily lives requires important consideration. As a discipline, anthropology has also been changed, most notably in its methodology, as we see with the increase in multi-site ethnography and research conducted in the virtual world. While the discipline will continue to change and adapt its methods and approaches to better understand the ways in which we live, the focus on the individual experience will always remain.

Notes

1   See http://www.cbc.ca/news/business/story/2013/06/17/f-vp-evans-bangladesh-women.html.

2   See http://www.un.org/esa/population/migration/Akhtar_Sweden_Feb_2013_FIN.pdf.

3   See http://www.un.org/esa/population/migration/Akhtar_Sweden_Feb_2013_FIN.pdf.

4   See http://www.unfpa.org/pds/migration.html.

5   See Weismantel (1995) on Zumbagua, Ecuador; Howell (2003) on Norway; and Aptekar (1988) on Colombia.

6   See http://www.theglobeandmail.com/life/parenting/the-painful-new-realities-of-international-adoption/article547159/?page=all.

7   See http://www.travelmadagascar.org/PARKS/Ankarana-National-Park.html.

Study Questions

1   Drawing on the tragedy in Bangladesh, explain how the increased flow of capital and goods has local and international implications.

2   Compare and contrast the concepts of *change* and *progress* using examples from the chapter.

3   Identify the benefits and challenges associated with modernization, using the Skolt Lapps as an example.

4   Explain the processes of migration and outline the effects of economic migration across the world in general, and specifically in Qatar.

5   Outline the history of international adoption in the West and explain why the practice has a profound effect on cultures at both the macro and micro levels.

6   Outline the problems facing the failed USAID reforestation program in Haiti and explain how Gerald Murray used an anthropological approach to craft a successful program.

7   Outline Walsh's work in Madagascar and explain why the goals of local residents are inconsistent with the foreign demands of mining and tourism. Why is it important for those living outside of Madagascar to understand how the processes of globalization have an impact upon those living there?

8   Explain the difference between traditional ethnography and multi-site ethnography, using examples from the chapter.

9   Outline Boellstorff's ethnographic study *Coming of Age in Second Life*, including his methodological choices, his findings, and what his work suggests about the future of cultural anthropology.

Discussion Questions

1   Discuss the practical value anthropology can offer us in understanding our globalized world. How are the processes of globalization influencing fieldwork?

2   Consider the ethnographic examples put forth in this chapter. Identify how the processes of globalization have influenced citizens of these locales. Are these consequences positive or negative? Are the ramifications cultural, political, economic?

3   Why is the notion of cultural imperialism too simplistic to explain the processes of globalization? Use examples from the text and from your own experience in your discussion.

4   Do the benefits of globalization outweigh the harms? Should modernization be abandoned to protect cultures (e.g., should the Lapps eschew snowmobiles)? How can anthropology help places and cultures find a middle ground?

Conclusion

Anthropologists are storytellers. In this book we have looked at many stories that reflect the circumstances of their time and place. We hope you can see how anthropology arose as a discipline and the topics that have engaged our attention at various points in the history of the subject. As we've noted a number of times, the world changes, and anthropology changes along with it. Nevertheless, we think it's possible to identify persistent themes and questions that transcend particular historical circumstances. The emergence of a distinctive anthropological method—ethnography—is another unifying factor. As for persistent themes, we might consider the following:

Nature and Culture: the light that comparative anthropological research can shed on the problem of what basic human nature is, as opposed to what culture and circumstances lead us to be.

The Dynamics and Direction of History: the central problem of social evolutionary thought, and one of the reasons why so-called primitive peoples have proved so fascinating as a "natural laboratory" of human possibility.

The Bonds of Community: how we come together in groups, whether they be families, tribes, nations, or the transnational communities made possible by social media and the Internet. This includes the symbolism and rituals of group identity.

Collective Visions: The process of imposing meaning on experience; how culture and social life steer our understandings of how the world works—our cosmologies, our religions, our interpretations of why things happen the way they do, our very selves.

Anthropologists engage in "fieldwork" to get at a problem that is seen as significant given the current state of the discipline. In earlier times much research was exploratory—aimed at documenting the range of human diversity. But usually there is some theoretical motivation as well, for example looking at how global processes affect local activities and perceptions. The usual output is an academic paper, addressed to other scholars as part of the normal give-and-take of any discipline. Sometimes the product is more substantial: a book on some specific theme, perhaps, or a full-scale ethnography. Such work falls somewhere between science and literature, and in recent times anthropologists have devoted considerable attention to the nature of the creative process itself—ethnographic writing as an art.

Occasionally such work attracts a wider audience because it addresses something of public concern, such as hunger, human rights, sexuality, or the environment. Of course, prominent figures such as Margaret Mead are rare; nevertheless, you've seen that anthropologists are out there in the "real world" as advocates, working in applied

265

settings, and commenting on social issues. You've also seen that small-scale societies often far removed from the Western world were once the focus of most anthropologists' attention. But today anthropologists are just as likely to be engaged in researching a public school, a scientific laboratory, an IVF clinic, a video gaming parlor, sporting events, a religious community, a business organization, or a political movement. A common denominator is actually *being there*—participant observation. Though disciplinary boundaries are seldom clear-cut, this approach distinguishes anthropology from the other social sciences.

And here we must stop. We encourage you to reflect on how what you've read in this book can be applied to your own experience and understanding of local and global events. Remember that anthropology is a way of seeing.

Glossary

Activism: action in pursuit of a political or social goal

Applied medical anthropology: one of two dominant approaches in the field of medical anthropology that operates with the goal of improving the health outcomes of a group, usually in collaboration with biomedical health practitioners

Archaeology: the study of the material remains of past and present cultures

Bio-cultural approach: a theoretical approach that investigates the complex relationship between biology, culture, ecology, and history. Bio-cultural anthropologists view human biological variability as a function of adaptation to the environment with a specific focus on how socio-cultural environments shape this adaptation

Biological determinism: the notion that there is a direct correlation between cultural characteristics regarding categories such as gender, race, or class with biological traits

Bride-service: the situation where a man works for his in-laws in return for their daughter

Bridewealth: valuable property transferred from the family of the man to that of his prospective bride

Cartesian dualism: a system of thought whereby something is conceptually divided into two separate entities, such as the mind and body

Caste: "an explicitly hierarchical social system based on hereditary, endogamous groups, in which each is characterized by a specific status, occupation, mode of life, and pattern of customary interactions with other such groups" (Winthrop 1991: 27)

Change: the result of action or thought, whether it is intentional, accidental, beneficial or harmful, with no particular direction or value

Comparative method: how a particular theory fares when applied cross-culturally

Critical approach: considers how illness, as described by those in a particular context, serves to represent or misrepresent power relations within society to serve the interests of those in power

Cultural ecology: a term coined by anthropologist Julian Steward in order to outline the nature of economic and political systems in their full environmental and historical contexts

Cultural imperialism: the imposition of a powerful country's culture on another country or group of people

Cultural relativism: the idea that one should suspend moral judgment and assumptions in order to appreciate and understand a culture on its own terms, rather than in comparison to one's own

Culture: the complex whole that includes knowledge, belief, art, morals, law, custom, and any other capabilities and habits acquired by humans as a member of society

Culture shock: refers to the feelings of confusion and insecurity that arise from living in a new culture or surroundings

Descent: the connection an individual has to their ancestors

De-territorialization: moving away from social, political, or cultural ties to Native geographic entities or populations

Diffusion: the spread of tools, practices or other features from one culture to another

Division of labor: how tasks are allocated within society by gender, age, and specialization

Dowry: property that accompanies a woman into the marriage relationship—a kind of pre-inheritance that in an ideal world would be passed on to her offspring

Economic migrant: an individual who relocates for a limited period of time in order to work, and who has no intention of making their move permanent

Endogamy: marriage within a group, as opposed to exogamy, marriage outside a group

Epistemology: the theory of the scope and nature of knowledge

Essentialism: the belief that a group of people possess a set of inherent characteristics often used in discussions related to race, gender, class, and sexuality

Ethnocentrism: the act of judging other cultures by the standards and values of one's own

Ethnography: a theoretically informed description and explanation of a way of life

Ethnology: a branch of anthropology that compares and analyzes the characteristics of different peoples and the relationship between them

Eugenics movement: social policies aimed at encouraging the upper classes to reproduce more enthusiastically and to discourage the lower orders from doing so

Exchange: a form of interaction involving reciprocal social relations

Feminist theoretical perspective: an approach whose central tenet is that all social relations and the knowledge of these relations are gendered; this approach highlights the role of patriarchy in maintaining the oppression of women in society

Gender: "the socially constructed roles, behaviors, activities, and attributes that a given society considers appropriate for men and women" (World Health Organization, Western Pacific Region 2017)

Gender roles: the seemingly different sets of actions and behaviors associated with girls and boys, men and women, that a society deems appropriate

Genome: the entirety of one's genetic heritage

Gift: an ambiguous form of exchange implying the necessity for immediate or delayed reciprocity. The topic of a famous essay by French ethnologist, Marcel Mauss, who examined the function of gift-giving in creating and maintaining social bonds

Globalization: "social, economic, cultural, and demographic processes that take place within nations but also transcend them, such that attention limited to local processes, identities, and units of analysis yields incomplete understanding of the local" (Kearney 1995: 548)

Habitus: the meaningful yet unconscious activity that pervades our daily lives

Hetero-masculinity: the cultural pressure exerted on males to be masculine in traits and heterosexual in orientation or else be viewed as feminine and socially unacceptable (Theodore and Bason 2000)

Historical particularism: an approach to understanding society whereby the unique history of each culture is considered influential and central to understanding the present

Holistic approach: involves looking at the complete picture rather than individual parts

Hunter-gatherers: a non-agricultural form of primary food resource exploitation. There are many variants depending on local conditions

Indigenous: "Indigenous communities, peoples and nations are those which, having a historical continuity with pre-invasion and pre-colonial societies that developed on their territories, consider themselves distinct from other sectors of the societies now prevailing on those territories, or parts of them. Despite their cultural differences, indigenous peoples from around the world share common problems related to the protection of their rights as distinct peoples."–Indigenous Peoples as the UN.

Inductive approach: starting from specific ideas or observations and moving into broader theories of thought

Interpretation: the process of creating meaning out of experience

Interpretive approach: a theoretical perspective that considers how cultural symbols, beliefs, and perceptions influence people's health and treatment of illness

Interpretive perspective: an approach that considers the meaning that social actors give to what they and others do

Isolationism: a foreign-policy approach advocating non-involvement in other nations' affairs on the premise that this will best serve one's own national interests

Kinship: relationship by blood or marriage

Kinship systems: how kinship relations are organized into structured wholes

Kula: a ceremonial form of delayed gift-exchange found in the island groups adjacent to the north coast of New Guinea

Linguistic anthropology: the study of the relationship between culture and language

Macro vs. micro levels: the macro level of analysis considers social structures and institutions, while the micro level occurs at the individual, face-to-face level

Mana: the distinguishing characteristic of any sacred being

the Market: both a place and a process, where value is established and reinforced in acts of exchange. There is a large anthropological literature on markets (e.g., as in Redfield's Topoztlan; or the New York Stock Exchange)

Marriage: a legally recognized relationship between people who intend to live together as sexual and domestic partners

Matrilineage: the transmission of all titles, rights, and property in the female line

Meaning: a complex concept, difficult to define. A "culture" can be thought of as a system of symbolic communication in which "meaning" emerges out of the manner in which cultural elements are related to one another—as in a spoken language, a ritual, or art form. The anthropologist's goal is to "interpret" and understand such things

Medical anthropology: employs anthropological theory and method in exploring understandings of health and health care from a cross-cultural perspective

Medicalization: the process by which human conditions and social problems come to be treated as illness

Migration: the movement of a person or people from one place to another

Mode of production: a term associated with the writings of Karl Marx, involving analysis of the relationship between technology, the labor process, and the distribution of power in society

Modernization: the process of cultural and socio-economic change, often linked to urbanization, industrialization, and the spread of education

Money: symbols representing stored wealth used to mediate the process of exchange

Multi-site ethnography: identifying and exploring the links, or relationships, of various study sites that are in some way related

Natural selection: the selection by natural processes of genetic variants with adaptive value and the rejection of those without it; in the long term those individuals with useful variations leave more offspring, and evolution moves on in the direction indicated by the selective process

Noble savage: refers to the notion that "there are simple people, living in an Edenic landscape and gentle climate, whose powers of reason and ability to live in harmony with nature ensure relief from the evils of civilization" (Satterfield 2002: 100)

Oral traditions: "the means by which knowledge is reproduced, preserved and conveyed from generation to generation. Oral traditions form the foundation of Indigenous societies, connecting speaker and listener in communal experience and uniting past and present in memory" (Hulan and Eigenbrod 2008: 7)

Paradigm: a model or framework about how a group of ideas relate to one another

Participant observation: joining and engaging in the culture and customs of the people who are the focus of one's study over an extended period of time

Patriarchy: a system of power in society whereby relationships are organized to maintain male supremacy

Patrilineage: kin who define their relationship through male descent—father to son, etc.

Physical anthropology: the study of human variation, adaptation, and change

Polygyny: the custom of being married to more than one wife at a time

Potlatch: a form of ceremonial gift-giving found on the Northwest Coast, used to mark important social occasions, such as assuming an important title, erecting a ceremonial pole, and other significant collective events

Primitive communism: The notion that there was once, and in some places still is, a form of human society characterized by equality of wealth and status and the absence of private property

Progress: a gradual move toward achieving a goal or reaching a higher standard.

Definitions that consider progress in relation to people suggest the advancement of society toward a state of greater civilization; this forward movement implies a positive change from one state to another, a leaving behind of something outdated in order to embrace something new

Purposeful sampling: a method whereby research participants are selected based on having certain characteristics that the researcher deems necessary for inclusion

Qualitative research: aims to understand the why and how of human behavior through methods such as participant observation and interviews

Queer theory: a paradigm that does not lend itself easily to a simple definition or explanation, as it has been conceptualized by those who engage with it in a diversity of ways. While there is no one definition of queer theory, in the broadest sense queer theory is a "theoretical perspective from which to challenge the normative" (Goldman 1996: 170), or a "radical questioning of social and cultural norms, notions of gender, reproductive sexuality, and the family" (Smith 1996: 280)

Reciprocity: the "Golden Rule" in action: "Do unto others as you would have them do unto you." Implying a balancing of the books, and not necessarily a friendly relationship—as is reciprocal murder in the course of a feud

Reflexive thinking: how our personal opinions and beliefs influence the ways in which we see the people and activities around us

Revitalization movement: an organized effort by members of a society or group to construct a more satisfying culture (Wallace 1956: 265)

Rite of passage: a ritual marking and celebrating of a change in social status, such as a birth, marriage, graduation, or funeral

Savage beast: a construct that portrays Indigenous peoples as living in a constant state of violence, disorganization, and chaos

Social evolution: the transformation of one social form into another, as for example the "evolution" of organized states out of previously tribal societies. In nineteenth-century thought, this was seen as the emergence of complexity out of simpler modes of organization

Social memory: how social life affects the processes of memory and forgetting, whether on an individual psychological level or in terms of how groups think of their collective history

Sociocentric theory: an approach to understanding society that looks internally for causes, rather than to impersonal notions such as fate or physical causality

Socio-cultural anthropology: the study of human culture, social organization, and behavior

State of Nature: a term used by early social and political theorists for the imagined condition of humankind before the rise of civilization

Structural functionalism: an approach to understanding society whereby the major structures of society are comparable to the organs of a biological organism

Theoretical medical anthropology: one of two dominant approaches in the field of medical anthropology that aims to understand the how and why of medical systems in a particular context

Trans: "GATE—Global Action for Trans* Equality—defines Trans* as the following: Trans* people includes those people who have a gender identity which is different to the gender assigned at birth and/or those people who feel they have to, prefer to or choose to—whether by clothing, accessories, cosmetics or body modification—present themselves differently to the expectations of the gender role assigned to them at birth. This includes, among many others, transsexual and transgender people, transvestites, travesti, cross dressers, no gender and gender queer people. The term Trans* should be seen as a place-holder for many identities, most of which are specific to local cultures and times in history, describing people who broaden and expand a binary understanding of gender" (Devor 2014: ix)

Treaty: an agreement made under law; in the context of Indigenous land, it is a contract between an Indigenous people and another governing body

Typological thinking: the idea that aspects of our world can be sorted into groups based on natural resemblances—for example the various species of plants and animals. Racial thinking is of this sort in that it supposes that humankind can be categorized into groups based upon common features such as skin color, skull shape, hair texture, and so on

Universal health care: health care system that provides care and financial protection to all citizens of a particular country. It is organized around providing a specified package of benefits to all members of a society with the end goal of providing financial risk protection, improved access to health services, and improved health outcomes

Value: what something is "worth"—either intrinsically (as with some sacred object), or in exchange for something else (as in trade)—often determined by market interactions

References

Chapter 1

Beaglehole, J.C. 1974. *The Life of Captain James Cook*. Stanford: Stanford University Press.

Burrow, J.W. 1968. *Evolution and Society: A Study in Victorian Social Theory*. Cambridge: Cambridge University Press.

Connerton, Paul. 1989. *How Societies Remember*. Cambridge: Cambridge University Press; https://doi.org/10.1017/CBO9780511628061.

Cook, James. 1967. The Journals of Captain James Cook on His Voyages of Discovery. Vol. III: *The Voyage of the* Resolution *and* Discovery *1776–1780,* part one, ed. J.C. Beaglehole. Cambridge: Cambridge University Press.

Cook, James. 1968. *The Voyage of the* Endeavour *1768–1771*, ed. J.G. Beaglehole. Cambridge: Cambridge University Press.

Darwin, Charles. 1966. *Narrative of the Surveying Voyages of His Majesty's Ships* Adventure *and* Beagle, vol. 3. New York: AMS Press.

Darwin, Charles. 1998. *The Descent of Man*. Amherst, NY: Prometheus Books.

Desmond, Adrian, and James Moore. 2009. *Darwin's Sacred Cause: Race, Slavery and the Quest for Human Origins*. London: Allen Lane.

Engels, Friedrich. 1972. *The Origin of the Family, Private Property and the State*. Harmondsworth: Penguin Books.

Fentress, James, and Chris Wickham. 1992. *Social Memory*. Oxford: Basil Blackwell.

Fitzroy, Robert. 1966. *Narrative of the Surveying Voyages of His Majesty's Ships* Adventure *and* Beagle, vols. 1 & 2. New York: AMS Press.

Fraser, Simon. 1960. *The Letters and Journals of Simon Fraser*. Toronto: Macmillan.

Hobbes, Thomas. 1962. *Leviathan*. New York: Collier Books.

Marx, Karl. 1965. *Pre-Capitalist Economic Formations*. Trans. Jack Cohen. New York: International Publishers.

Morgan, Lewis Henry. 1851. *The League of the Ho-de-no-sau-nee, or Iroquois*. Rochester: Sage & Brothers.

Morgan, Lewis Henry. 1877. *Ancient Society*. New York: Henry Holt & Co.

Rousseau, Jean-Jacques. 1992. *Discourse on the Origins of Inequality (Second Discourse), Polemics, and Political Economy*. Trans. Judith Bush, Roger Masters, Christopher Kelly, and Terence Marshall. Hanover: Dartmouth College Press.

Stocking, George W. 1987. *Victorian Anthropology*. New York: Free Press.

Trautmann, Thomas R. 1987. *Lewis Henry Morgan and the Invention of Kinship*. Berkeley: University of California Press.

Tylor, E.B. 1903. *Primitive Culture*. London: John Murray.

Wickwire, Wendy. 1994. "To See Ourselves as the Other's Other: *Mlaka'pamux* Contact Narratives." *Canadian Historical Review* 75 (1): 1–20. https://doi.org/10.3138/CHR-075-01-01.

Williams, Glyn. 2008. *The Death of Captain Cook: A Hero Made and Unmade.* Cambridge, MA: Harvard University Press.

Chapter 2

Aberle, David F. 1982. *The Peyote Religion among the Navaho.* Chicago: University of Chicago Press.

Barrett, Stanley. 2000. *Anthropology: A Student's Guide to Theory and Method.* Toronto: University of Toronto Press.

Boas, Franz. 1911. *The Mind of Primitive Man.* New York: Macmillan.

Boas, Franz. 1966. *Kwakiutl Ethnography.* Ed. Helen Codere. Chicago: University of Chicago Press.

Cole, F.-C., and Fred Eggan. 1959. "Robert Redfield, 1897–1958." *American Anthropologist* 61 (4): 652–62. https://doi.org/10.1525/aa.1959.61.4.02a00110.

Cole, Douglas. 1999. *Franz Boas: The Early Years, 1858–1906.* Vancouver: Douglas & McIntyre.

Darnell, Regna. 1990. *Edward Sapir: Linguist, Anthropologist, Humanist.* Berkeley: University of California Press.

Darnell, Regna. 1998. *And Along Came Boas: Continuity and Revolution in Americanist Anthropology.* Amsterdam: John Benjamins Publishing Co.

Feinberg, R. 1988. "Margaret Mead and Samoa: *Coming of Age* in Fact and Fiction." *American Anthropologist* 90 (3): 656–63. https://doi.org/10.1525/aa.1988.90.3.02a00080.

Freeman, Derek. 1983. *Margaret Mead and Samoa: The Making and Unmaking of an Anthropological Myth.* Cambridge, MA: Harvard University Press.

Gilliam, A. 1993. "Symbolic Subordination and the Representation of Power in Margaret Mead and Samoa." *Visual Anthropology Review* 9 (1): 105–15. https://doi.org/10.1525/var.1993.9.1.105.

Kenyatta, Jomo. 1979. *Facing Mount Kenya: The Traditional Life of the Gikuyu.* London: Heinemann.

Lewis, H.S. 2001. "The Passion of Franz Boas." *American Anthropologist* 103 (2): 447–67. https://doi.org/10.1525/aa.2001.103.2.447.

Lewis, Oscar. 1951. *Life in a Mexican Village: Tepoztlan Restudied.* Urbana: University of Illinois Press.

Malinowski, Bronislaw. 1944. *A Scientific Theory of Culture.* Chapel Hill: University of North Carolina Press.

Malinowski, Bronislaw. 1984. *Argonauts of the Western Pacific.* Long Grove, IL: Waveland Press.

Mead, Margaret. 2001. *Coming of Age in Samoa: A Psychological Study of Primitive Youth for Western Civilization.* New York: Harper Perennial.

Mooney, James. 1973. *The Ghost-Dance Religion and the Sioux Outbreak of 1890.* New York: Dover Publications.

Moses, L.G. 1984. *The Indian Man: A Biography of James Mooney*. Urbana: University of Illinois Press.

Mukhopadhyay, C.C., and Y.T. Moses. 1997. "Reestablishing 'Race' in Anthropological Discourse." *American Anthropologist* 99 (3): 517–33. https://doi.org/10.1525/aa.1997.99.3.517.

Powell, John Wesley. 1881. *First Annual Report of the Bureau of Ethnology*. Washington, DC: Smithsonian Institution.

Radcliffe-Brown, A.R. 1957. *A Natural Science of Society*. Glencoe: Free Press.

Redfield, Robert. 1930. *Tepoztlan, a Mexican Village: A Study of Folk Life*. Chicago: University of Chicago Press.

Redfield, Robert. 1960. *The Little Community*. Chicago: University of Chicago Press.

Richards, Audrey I. 1939. *Land, Labour and Diet in Northern Rhodesia: An Economic Study of the Bemba Tribe*. London: Oxford University Press.

Richards, Audrey I. 1948. *Hunger and Work in a Savage Tribe: A Functional Study of Nutrition among the Southern Bantu*. Glencoe: Free Press.

Richards, Audrey I. 1956. *Chisungu: A Girl's Initiation Ceremony among the Bemba of Northern Rhodesia*. London: Faber & Faber.

Stocking, George W. 1984. *Functionalism Historicized: Essays on British Social Anthropology*. Madison: University of Wisconsin Press.

Stocking, George W. 1995. *After Tylor: British Social Anthropology, 1888–1951*. Madison: University of Wisconsin Press.

Chapter 3

Amit, Vered. 2000. "Introduction: Constructing the Field." In *Constructing the Field: Ethnographic Fieldwork in the Contemporary World*, 1–18. New York: Routledge.

Barrett, Stanley R. 2000. *Anthropology: A Student's Guide to Theory and Method*. Toronto: University of Toronto Press.

Caputo, Virginia. 1995. "Anthropology's Silent 'Others': A Consideration of Some Conceptual and Methodological Issues for the Study of Youth and Children's Cultures." In *Youth Cultures: A Cross-Cultural Perspective*, ed. Vered Amit-Talai and Helena Wulff, 19–42. London, New York: Routledge.

Dyck, Noel. 2000. "Introduction." In *Games, Sport and Cultures*, 1–9. Oxford, New York: Berg.

Fernea, Elizabeth Warnock. 1969. *Guests of the Sheik: An Ethnography of an Iraqi Village*. Garden City, NY: Anchor Books.

Fernea, Robert. 1970. *Shaykh and Effendi: Changing Patterns of Authority among the El Shabana of Southern Iraq*. Cambridge, MA: Harvard University Press.

Geertz, Clifford. 1973. *The Interpretation of Cultures*. New York: Basic Books.

Gluckman, Max. 1958. *Analysis of a Social Situation in Modern Zululand*. Manchester: Manchester University Press.

Hassan, Fayza. 2001. "Elizabeth Warnock Fernea: Part of It All." *Al Ahram Weekly Online* 527 (19 March–4 April). http://weekly.ahram.org.eg/Archive/2001/527/profile.htm.

Malinowski, Bronislaw. 1922. *Argonauts of the Western Pacific*. London: Routledge & Kegan Paul.

Malinowski, Bronislaw. 1966. *Coral Gardens and Their Magic*. London: Allen & Unwin.

Malinowski, Bronislaw. 1967. *A Diary in the Strict Sense of the Term*. Trans. Norbert Guterman. New York: Harcourt Brace & World.

McGee, R.J., and R.L. Warms. 1996. *Anthropological Theory: An Introductory History*. London: Mayfield Publishing.

Narayan, Kirin. 1993. "How Native Is a 'Native' Anthropologist?" *American Anthropologist* 95 (3): 671-86. https://doi.org/10.1525/aa.1993.95.3.02a00070.

Nathan, Rebekah. 2005. *My Freshman Year: What a Professor Learned by Becoming a Student*. Ithaca, NY and London: Cornell University Press.

Rhode, David. 2007. "Army Enlists Anthropology in War Zones." *New York Times*, October 5. http://www.nytimes.com/2007/10/05/world/asia/05afghan.html?pagewanted=all&_r=0.

Stocking, George. 1995. *After Tylor: British Social Anthropology 1885–1951*. Madison: University of Wisconsin Press.

Young, Michael W. 2004. *Malinowski: Odyssey of an Anthropologist 1884–1920*. New Haven, CT: Yale University Press.

Chapter 4

Boas, Franz. 1966. *Kwakiutl Ethnography*. Ed. Helen Codere. Chicago: University of Chicago Press.

Boehm, Christopher. 2012. *Moral Origins: The Evolution of Virtue, Altruism, and Shame*. New York: Basic Books.

Clemmer, R.O., L.D. Myers, and M.E. Rudden. 1999. *Julian Steward and the Great Basin: The Making of an Anthropologist*. Salt Lake City: University of Utah Press.

Cole, D., and I. Chaikin. 1990. *An Iron Hand upon the People: The Law Against the Potlatch on the Northwest Coast*. Vancouver, Toronto: Douglas & McIntyre.

Dahlberg, Frances, ed. 1981. *Woman the Gatherer*. New Haven: Yale University Press.

Darwin, Charles. 1998. *The Descent of Man*. Amherst, NY: Prometheus Books.

Geismar, Haidy. 2001. "What's in a Price? An Ethnography of Tribal Art at Auction." *Journal of Material Culture* 6 (1): 25–47. https://doi.org/10.1177/135918350100600102.

Gomberg-Muñoz, Ruth. 2016. "Criminalized Workers: Introduction to the Special Issue on Migrant Labor and Mass Deportation." *Anthropology of Work Review* 37 (1): 3–10. https://doi.org/10.1111/awr.12080.

Guenther, Mathias. 1976. "From Hunters to Squatters: Social and Cultural Change among the Farm San of Ghanzi, Botswana." In *Kalahari Hunter-Gatherers: Studies of the !Kung San and Their Neighbors*, ed. Richard B. Lee and Ervin DeVore, 121–33. Cambridge, MA: Harvard University Press. https://doi.org/10.4159/harvard.9780674430600.c8.

Horton, Sarah B. 2016. "Ghost Workers: The Implications of Governing Immigration through Crime for Migrant Workplaces." *Anthropology of Work Review* 37 (1): 11–23. https://doi.org/10.1111/awr.12081.

LaViolette, Forrest E. 1961. *The Struggle for Survival: Indian Cultures and the Protestant Ethic in British Columbia*. Toronto: University of Toronto Press.

Lee, Richard B. 1968. "What Hunters Do for a Living: Or, How to Make Out on Scarce Resources." In *Man the Hunter*, ed. Richard B. Lee and Ervin DeVore, 30–48. Chicago: Aldine.

Loo, Tina. 1992. "Dan Cranmer's Potlatch: Law as Coercion, Symbol, and Rhetoric in British Columbia 1884–1951." *Canadian Historical Review* 73 (2): 125–65. https://doi.org/10.3138/CHR-073-02-01.

Malinowski, Bronislaw. 1984. *Argonauts of the Western Pacific.* Long Grove, IL: Waveland Press.

Marlowe, Frank W. 2010. *The Hadza: Hunter-Gatherers of Tanzania.* Berkeley: University of California Press.

Mauss, Marcel. 1990. *The Gift: The Form and Reason for Exchange in Archaic Societies.* Trans. W.D. Halls. New York: Routledge.

Price, Sally. 1989. *Primitive Art in Civilized Places.* Chicago: University of Chicago Press.

Rodkey, Evin. 2016. "Disposable Labor, Repurposed: Outsourcing Deportees in the Call Center Industry." *Anthropology of Work Review* 37 (1): 34–43. https://doi.org/10.1111/awr.12083.

Steward, Julian H. 1972. *Theory of Culture Change: The Methodology of Multilinear Evolution.* Urbana: University of Illinois Press.

Washburn, Sherwood L. 1976. "Foreword." In *Kalahari Hunter-Gatherers: Studies of the !Kung San and Their Neighbors*, ed. Richard B. Lee and Ervin DeVore, xv-xvii. Cambridge, MA: Harvard University Press.

Woodburn, James. 1968. "An Introduction to Hadza Ecology." In *Man the Hunter*, ed. Richard B. Lee and Ervin Devore, 49–55. Chicago: Aldine.

Chapter 5

Eggan, Fred, ed. 1955. *Social Anthropology of North American Tribes.* Chicago: University of Chicago Press.

Evans-Pritchard, E.E. 1940. *The Nuer.* Oxford: Oxford University Press.

Evans-Pritchard, E.E. 1951. *Kinship and Marriage among the Nuer.* Oxford: Clarendon Press.

Fortes, Meyer. 1969. *Kinship and the Social Order.* Chicago: Aldine.

Fox, Robin. 1967. *Kinship and Marriage: An Anthropological Perspective.* Harmondsworth: Penguin Books.

Franklin, Sarah, and Susan McKinnon, eds. 2001. *Relative Values: Reconfiguring Kinship Studies.* Durham, NC: Duke University Press.

Lafitau, Joseph François. 1974. *Customs of the American Indians Compared with the Customs of Primitive Times*, vol. 1. Trans. William Fenton and Elizabeth Moore. Toronto: The Champlain Society.

Malinowski, Bronislaw. 1954. *Magic, Science and Religion.* Garden City, NY: Doubleday.

Mauss, Marcel. 1990. *The Gift: The Form and Reason for Exchange in Archaic Societies.* Trans. W.D. Halls. London: Routledge.

Miller, James Rodger. 1996. *Shingwauk's Vision: A History of Native Residential Schools.* Toronto: University of Toronto Press.

Morgan, Lewis Henry. 1851. *The League of the Ho-de-no-sau-nee, or Iroquois.* Rochester, NY: Sage & Brothers.

Morgan, Lewis Henry. 1871. *Systems of Consanguinity and Affinity of the Human Family.* Washington, DC: Smithsonian Institution.

REFERENCES

Morgan, Lewis Henry. 1877. *Ancient Society*. New York: Henry Holt & Co.

Nanda, Serena. 2000. "Arranging a Marriage in India." In *Stumbling toward Truth: Anthropologists at Work*, ed. Philip R. Devita, 196–204. Long Grove, IL: Waveland Press.

Perdue, Theda, and Michael D. Green. 2005. *The Cherokee Removal: A Brief History with Documents*. 2nd ed. Boston: Bedford/St. Martin's.

Perdue, Theda, and Michael D. Green. 2007. *The Cherokee Nation and the Trail of Tears*. New York: Viking.

Proctor, Robert N. 1988. *Racial Hygiene: Medicine under the Nazis*. Cambridge, MA: Harvard University Press.

Radcliffe-Brown, A.R. 1950. "Introduction." In *African Systems of Kinship and Marriage*, ed. A.R. Radcliffe-Brown and C. Daryll Forde, 1–85. London: Oxford University Press.

Radcliffe-Brown, A.R. 1952. *Structure and Function in Primitive Society*. London: Routledge and Kegan Paul.

Richards, Audrey. 1950. "Some Types of Family Structure amongst the Central Bantu." In *African Systems of Kinship and Marriage*, ed. A.R. Radcliffe-Brown and C. Daryll Forde, 207–51. London: Oxford University Press.

Sahlins, Marshall. 2013. *What Kinship Is—And Is Not*. Chicago: University of Chicago Press. https://doi.org/10.7208/chicago/9780226925134.001.0001.

Schneider, David M. 1980. *American Kinship: A Cultural Account*. 2nd ed. Chicago: University of Chicago Press.

Schneider, David M. 1984. *A Critique of the Study of Kinship*. Ann Arbor: University of Michigan Press. https://doi.org/10.3998/mpub.7203.

Schneider, David M., and Kathleen Gough, eds. 1962. *Matrilineal Kinship*. Berkeley: University of California Press.

Smith, John. 1624. *The General Historie of Virginia, New-England, and the Summer Isles*. Facsimile edition. London: Michael Sparkes.

Strathern, Marilyn. 1992. *Reproducing the Future: Essays on Anthropology, Kinship, and the New Reproductive Technologies*. Manchester: Manchester University Press.

Chapter 6

Benedict, Ruth. 1959. *Patterns of Culture*. Boston: Houghton Mifflin.

Benedict, Ruth. 2005. *The Chrysanthemum and the Sword: Patterns of Japanese Culture*. Boston: Houghton Mifflin.

Bourdieu, Pierre. 1977. *Outline of a Theory of Practice*. Trans. Richard Nice. Cambridge: Cambridge University Press. https://doi.org/10.1017/CBO9780511812507.

Darnell, Regna. 2001. *Invisible Genealogies: A History of Americanist Anthropology*. Lincoln: University of Nebraska Press.

Daws, Gavan. 1968. *Shoal of Time: A History of the Hawaiian Islands*. Honolulu: University of Hawaii Press.

Durkheim, Émile. 1995. *The Elementary Forms of Religious Life*. Trans. Karen E. Fields. New York: Free Press.

Durkheim, Émile, and Marcel Mauss. 1965. *Primitive Classification*. Trans. Rodney Needham. Chicago: University of Chicago Press.

Evans-Pritchard, E.E. 1937. *Witchcraft, Oracles and Magic among the Azande*. Oxford: Clarendon Press.

Foucault, Michel. 1988. *The Care of the Self*. Vol. 3 of *The History of Sexuality*, trans. Robert Hurley. New York: Vintage Books.

Foucault, Michel. 1990. *An Introduction*. Vol. 1 of *The History of Sexuality*, trans. Robert Hurley. New York: Vintage Books.

Geertz, Clifford. 1973. *The Interpretation of Cultures*. New York: Basic Books.

Hall, Edward. 1959. *The Silent Language*. Garden City, NY: Doubleday.

Hall, Edward. 1966. *The Hidden Dimension*. Garden City, NY: Doubleday.

Kuhn, Thomas. 1970. *The Structure of Scientific Revolutions*. 2nd ed. Chicago: University of Chicago Press.

Lévi-Strauss, C. 1969. *The Elementary Structures of Kinship*. Boston: Beacon Press.

Luhrmann, Tanya. 2012. *When God Talks Back: Understanding the American Evangelical Relationship with God*. New York: Vintage Books.

Luhrmann, Tanya. 2013. "Belief Is the Least Part of Faith." *New York Times*, May 29. http://www.nytimes.com/2013/05/30/opinion/luhrmann-belief-is-the-least-part-of-faith.html.

Malinowski, Bronislaw. 1947. "The Problem of Meaning in Primitive Languages." In *The Meaning of Meaning*, ed. C.K. Ogden and I.A. Richards, 296–336. New York: Harcourt, Brace.

Mauss, Marcel. 2006. "Techniques of the Body." In *Techniques, Technology and Civilization*, ed. Nathan Schlanger, 77–95. New York: Berghahn.

Post, Emily. 1922. *Etiquette in Society, in Business, in Politics and at Home*. New York: Funk & Wagnalls.

Sacks, Oliver. 1995. *An Anthropologist on Mars*. Toronto: Vintage Canada.

Sahlins, Marshall. 1985. *Islands of History*. Chicago: University of Chicago Press.

Sahlins, Marshall. 1995. *How "Natives" Think: About Captain Cook for Example*. Chicago: University of Chicago Press. https://doi.org/10.7208/chicago/9780226733715.001.0001.

Satterfield, Terre. 2002. *Anatomy of a Conflict: Identity, Knowledge, and Emotion in Old-Growth Forests*. Vancouver: UBC Press.

Stanner, W.E.H. 1979. *White Man Got No Dreaming: Essays 1938–1973*. Canberra: Australian National University Press.

Stocking, George. 1995. *After Tylor: British Social Anthropology 1888–1951*. Madison: University of Wisconsin Press.

Tylor, E.B. 1903. *Primitive Culture*. London: John Murray.

Wilson, Bryan, ed. 1970. *Rationality*. Oxford: Blackwell.

Wright, Susan. 1998. "The Politicization of 'Culture.'" *Anthropology Today* 14 (1): 7–15. https://doi.org/10.2307/2783092.

Yengoyan, Aram A. 1986. "Theory in Anthropology: On the Demise of the Concept of Culture." *Comparative Studies in Society and History* 28 (2): 368–74.

Chapter 7

Allan, B., and J. Smylie. 2015. *First Peoples, Second Class Treatment: The Role of Racism in the Health and Well-being of Indigenous Peoples in Canada*. Toronto: The Wellesley Institute.

REFERENCES

Attaran, A., Donald R. Roberts, Chris F. Curtis, and Wenceslaus L. Kilama. 2000. "Balancing Risks on the Backs of the Poor." *Nature Medicine* 6 (7): 729–31. https://doi.org/10.1038/77438.

Behague, D., C. Tawiah, M. Rosato, T. Some, and J. Morrison. 2009. "Evidence Based Policy-Making: The Implications of Globally-Applicable Research for Context-Specific Problem-Solving in Developing Countries." *Social Science & Medicine* 69 (10): 1539–46. https://doi.org/10.1016/j.socscimed.2009.08.006.

Biehl, J., and A. Petryna. 2013. "Critical Global Health." In *When People Come First: Critical Studies in Global Health*, ed. João Biehl and Adriana Peteryna, 1–22. Princeton University Press.

Briggs, C.L., and C. Mantini-Briggs. 2002. *Stories in the Time of Cholera: Racial Profiling during a Medical Nightmare*. Berkely: University of California Press.

Cashdan, E. 1989. "Hunters and Gatherers: Economic Behavior in Bands." In *Economic Anthropology*, ed. S. Plattner, 21–48. Stanford, CA: Stanford University Press.

Centers for Disease Control and Prevention. 2017. "Malaria: Frequently Asked Questions." Last modified April 21, 2017. https://www.cdc.gov/malaria/about/faqs.html.

Farmer, P., and B.J. Good. 1991. 'Illness Representations in Medical Anthropology: A Critical Review and a Case Study of the Representation of AIDS in Haiti'. In *Mental Representation in Health and Illness*, ed. J.A. Skelton and R.T. Croyle, 132–162. New York: Springer-Verlag.

Fugh-Berman, Adriane. 1998. "Alternative Healing." In *The Reader's Companion to U.S. Women's History*, ed. Gwendolyn Mink, Marysa Navarro, Wilma Mankiller, Barbara Smith, and Gloria Steinem, 26: 26–27. Boston: Houghton Mifflin.

Hahn, R.A., and M. Inhorn. 2009. "Introduction." In *Anthropology and Public Health: Bridging Differences in Culture and Society*, ed. Robert A. Hahn and Marcia C. Inhorn, 1–31. Oxford, New York: Oxford University Press. https://doi.org/10.1093/acprof:oso/9780195374643.003.0001.

Janes, C., and K. Corbett. 2009. "Anthropology and Global Health." *Annual Review of Anthropology* 38 (1): 167–83. https://doi.org/10.1146/annurev-anthro-091908-164314.

Joralemon, D. 2016. *Exploring Medical Anthropology*. New York: Routledge.

Kamat, Vinay. 2009. "The Anthropology of Childhood Malaria in Tanzania." In *Anthropology and Public Health: Bridging Differences in Culture and Society*, ed. Robert A. Hahn and Marcia C. Inhorn, 35–64. Oxford, New York: Oxford University Press.

Khongsdier, R. 2007. "Bio-Cultural Approach: The Essence of Anthropological Study in the 21st Century." In *Anthropology Today: Trends, Scope and Applications*, Anthropologist Special Volume, ed. V. Bhasin and M.K. Bhasin, 3: 39–50. New Delhi: Kamla-Raj Enterprises.

Maines, Rachel P. 1998. *The Technology of Orgasm: "Hysteria," the Vibrator, and Women's Sexual Satisfaction*. Baltimore: Johns Hopkins University Press.

Maslove, D., A. Mnyusiwalla, E. Mills, J. McGowan, A. Attaran, and K. Wilson. 2009. "Barriers to the Effective Treatment and Prevention of Malaria in Africa: A Systematic Review of Qualitative Studies." *BMC International Health and Human Rights* 9 (26): n.p. http://dx.doi.org/10.1186/1472–698X-9–26.

Mayo Clinic. 2016. "Sickle Cell Anemia." December 29. http://www.mayoclinic.org/diseases-conditions/sickle-cell-anemia/home/ovc-20303267. Accessed on June 3, 2017.

McCoy, D., J. Kembhavi, J. Patel, and A. Luintel. 2009. "The Bill & Melinda Gates Foundation's Grant-Making Programme for Global Health." *Lancet* 373 (9675): 1645–53. https://doi.org/10.1016/S0140-6736(09)60571-7.

Muela, Susanna Hausmann, Joan Muela Ribera, and Marcel Tanner. 1998. "Fake Malaria and Hidden Parasites—The Ambiguity of Malaria." *Anthropology & Medicine* 5 (1): 43–61. https://doi.org/10.1080/13648470.1998.9964548.

Pfaffe, J.F. 2003. "The Ju/'hoansi People." The Peoples of the World Foundation. Accessed February 5, 2017. http://www.peoplesoftheworld.org/hosted/juhoansi/.

Pool, R., and W. Geissler. 2005. *Medical Anthropology*. Berkshire, UK: Open University Press.

Public Health Agency of Canada. 2014. *HIV/AIDS Epi Updates—October 2014, Chapter 1: National HIV Prevalence and Incidence Estimates for 2011*. Last modified November 28. Centre for Communicable Diseases and Infection Control, Public Health Agency of Canada. http://www.phac-aspc.gc.ca/aids-sida/publication/epi/2010/1-eng.php.

Quilo, Queenie S., Mary Antoinette T. Mabini, Mincie Pale O. Tamiroy, Myrma Jean A. Mendoza, Sulpecia L. Ponce, and Liwayway S. Viloria. 2015. "Indigenous Knowledge and Practices: Approach to Understanding Disaster." Special Issue, *Philippine Sociological Review* 63: 105–29.

Scheper-Hughes, N., and M.M. Lock. 1987. "The Mindful Body: A Prolegomenon to Future Work in Medical Anthropology." *Medical Anthropology Quarterly* 1 (1): 6–41. https://doi.org/10.1525/maq.1987.1.1.02a00020.

Singer, M., and P.I. Erickson. 2011. "Introduction." In *Wiley Blackwell Companions to Anthropology: Companion to Medical Anthropology*, ed. Merrill Singer and Pamela I. Erickson, 1–6. Chichester, UK: Wiley Blackwell. https://doi.org/10.1002/9781444395303.

Sobo, E.J. 2011. "Medical Anthropology in Disciplinary Context: Definitional Struggles and Key Debates (or Answering the Cri Du Coeur)." In *Wiley Blackwell Companions to Anthropology: Companion to Medical Anthropology*, ed. Merrill Singer and Pamela I. Erickson, 7–28. Chichester, UK: Wiley Blackwell. https://doi.org/10.1002/9781444395303.

Society for Medical Anthropology. Accessed February 19, 2017. http://www.medanthro.net/9/.

Vitzthum V.J., A.G. Fix, and A. Livingstone. 2006. "The Four-Field Anthropology and Multi-Faceted Life of Frank B. Livingstone." *Retrospectives: Works and Lives of Michigan Anthropologists* 16 (1): 136–74. Ann Arbor, MI: MPublishing, University of Michigan Library.

Woelk, G., K. Daniels, J. Cliff, S. Lewin, E. Sevene, B. Fernandes, and A. Mariano et al. 2009. "Translating Research into Policy: Lessons Learned from Eclampsia Treatment and Malaria Control in Three Southern African Countries." *Health Research Policy and Systems* 7 (31): n.p. http://dx.doi.org/10.1186/1478-4505-7-31.

World Health Organization. 2008. "Key Facts, Figures and Strategies: The Global Malaria Action Plan." Geneva: Roll Back Malaria Partnership. http://archiverbm.rollbackmalaria.org/gmap/GMAP_Advocacy-ENG-web.pdf.

World Health Organization. 2010. "The World Health Report: Health Systems Financing; The Path to Universal Coverage." November 22, 2010. Geneva: World Health Organization. http://www.who.int/whr/2010/en/.

World Health Organization. 2015. "General Information: Malaria." Last modified April 28, 2015. http://www.paho.org/hq/index.php?option=com_content&view=article&id=257 3%3A2010-general-information-malaria&catid=1233%3Amalaria-program&Itemid=2060&lang=en.

World Health Organization. 2016. "Cholera: Fact Sheet." Last modified October 2016. http://www.who.int/mediacentre/factsheets/fs107/en/.

Chapter 8

Caputo, Virginia. 1995. "Anthropology's Silent 'Others': A Consideration of Some Conceptual and Methodological Issues for the Study of Youth and Children's Cultures." In *Youth Cultures: A Cross-Cultural Perspective*, ed. Vered Amit-Talai and Helena Wulff, 19–41. London, New York: Routledge.

Fabes, Richard A., Carol Lynn Martin, and Laura D. Hanish. 2003. "Young Children's Play Qualities in Same-, Other-, and Mixed-Sex Peer Groups." *Child Development* 74 (3): 921–32. https://doi.org/10.1111/1467-8624.00576.

Fong, Vanessa L. 2002. "China's One-Child Policy and Empowerment of Urban Daughters." *American Anthropologist* 104 (4): 1098–1109. https://doi.org/10.1525/aa.2002.104.4.1098.

Hoffmann, Melissa L., and Kimberly K. Powlishta. 2001. "Gender Segregation in Childhood: A Test of the Interaction Style Theory." *Journal of Genetic Psychology* 162 (3): 298–313. https://doi.org/10.1080/00221320109597485.

James, Allison, and Alan Prout. 1997. *Constructing and Reconstructing Childhood: Contemporary Issues in the Sociological Study of Childhood*. 2nd ed. London: Routledge.

Lai, Vinay. 1999. "Not This, Not That: The Hijras of India and the Cultural Politics of Sexuality." *Social Text* 61: 17(4): 119–40.

Liptak, Adam. 2015. "Supreme Court Ruling Markes Same-Sex Marriage a Right Nationwide." *The New York Times*, June 26. https://www.nytimes.com/2015/06/27/us/supreme-court-same-sex-marriage.html?_r=0.

Maccoby, Eleanor E. 1998. *The Two Sexes: Growing Up Apart, Coming Together*. Reprint ed. Cambridge, MA: Belknap Press.

Maccoby, Eleanor E., and Carol Nagy Jacklin. 1987. "Gender Segregation in Childhood." *Advances in Child Development and Behavior* 20: 239–87. https://doi.org/10.1016/S0065-2407(08)60404-8.

Miller, Barbara D., Penny Van Esterik, and John Van Esterik. 2001. *Cultural Anthropology*. Canadian Edition. Toronto: Pearson Education Canada.

Nanda, Serena. 1999. *Neither Man nor Woman*. Toronto: Wadsworth Publishing.

Pascoe, C.J. 2007. *Dude, You're a Fag: Masculinity and Sexuality in High School*. Los Angeles: University of California Press.

Pascoe, C.J. 2011. *Dude, You're a Fag: Masculinity and Sexuality in High School*. 2nd ed. Los Angeles: University of California Press.

Pellegrini, Anthony D. 2009. *The Role of Play in Human Development*. New York: Oxford University Press. https://doi.org/10.1093/acprof:oso/9780195367324.001.0001.

Phillips, Katie. 2011. "Conservative Media vs. J. CREW: The Battle of the Pink Toenails." *Forbes*. http://www.forbes.com/sites/shenegotiates/2011/04/13/conservative-media-vs-j-crew-the-battle-of-the-pink-toenails/.

Reddy, Gayatri. 2005. *With Respect to Sex: Negotiating Hijra Identity in South India*. Chicago, London: University of Chicago Press. https://doi.org/10.7208/chicago/9780226707549.001.0001/ 9780226707549.001.0001.

Thorne, Barrie. 1994. *Gender Play: Girls and Boys in School*. New Brunswick, NJ: Rutgers University Press.

Chapter 9

Alves-Silva, Juliana, M. da Silva Santos, P. Guimaraes, A. Ferreira, H. Bandelt, S. Pena, and V. Prado. 2000. "The Ancestry of Brazilian mtDNA Lineages." *American Journal of Human Genetics* 67 (2): 444–61. https://doi.org/10.1086/303004.

Anderson, Kay J. 1991. *Vancouver's Chinatown: Racial Discourse in Canada, 1875–1980*. Montreal, Kingston: McGill-Queen's University Press.

Benedict, Ruth. 1943. *Race: Science and Politics*. New York: Viking Press.

Boas, Franz. 1916. "Eugenics." *Scientific Monthly* 3 (5): 471–78.

Boas, Franz. 1963. *The Mind of Primitive Man*. New York: Free Press.

Boas, Franz. 1969. *Race and Democratic Society*. New York: Biblo and Tannen.

Carlson, Elof Axel. 2001. *The Unfit: A History of a Bad Idea*. Cold Spring Harbor, NY: Cold Spring Harbor Laboratory Press.

Couzin-Frankel, Jennifer. 2010. "Researchers to Return Blood Samples to the Yanomamö." *Science* 328 (5983): 1218. https://doi.org/10.1126/science.328.5983.1218.

Dallaire, Roméo. 2003. *Shake Hands with the Devil: The Failure of Humanity in Rwanda*. Toronto: Random House Canada.

Dalton, Rex. 2002. "Tribe Blasts 'Exploitation' of Blood Samples." *Nature* 420 (6912): 111. https://doi.org/10.1038/420111a.

Dalton, Rex. 2004. "When Two Tribes Go to War." *Nature* 430 (6999): 500–2. https://doi.org/10.1038/430500a.

Darwin, Charles. 1998. *The Descent of Man*. Amherst, NY: Prometheus Books.

Davenport, Charles Benedict. 1911. *Heredity in Relation to Eugenics*. New York: Henry Holt. https://doi.org/10.5962/bhl.title.29389.

Foster, Eugene, M.A. Jobling, P.G. Taylor, P. Donnelly, P. de Knijff, Rene Mieremet, T. Zerjal et al. 1998. "Jefferson Fathered Slave's Last Child." *Nature* 396 (6706): 27–28. https://doi.org/10.1038/23835.

Freed, Stanley A., Ruth S. Freed, and Laila Williamson. 1988. "Capitalist Philanthropy and Russian Revolutionaries: The Jesup North Pacific Expedition (1897–1902)." *American Anthropologist* 90 (1): 7–24. https://doi.org/10.1525/aa.1988.90.1.02a00010.

Galton, Sir Francis. 1909. *Essays in Eugenics*. London: Eugenics Education Society.

Gordon-Reed, Annette. 2008. *The Hemingses of Monticello: An American family*. New York: W.W. Norton.

Gould, Stephen Jay. 1996. *The Mismeasure of Man*. New York: W.W. Norton.

Hitler, Adolf. 1998. *Mein Kampf* [My Struggle]. Trans. Ralph Manheim. Boston: Houghton Mifflin.

Jefferson, Thomas. 1964. *Notes on the State of Virginia*. New York: Harper Torchbooks.

Jobling, Mark A., with Matthew Hurles and Chris Tyler-Smith. 2004. *Human Evolutionary Genetics: Origins, Peoples & Disease*. New York: Garland Science.

Kenny, Michael G. 1988. "Mutesa's Crime: Hubris and the Control of African Kings." *Comparative Studies in Society and History* 30 (4): 595–612. https://doi.org/10.1017/S0010417500015450.

Kenny, Michael G. 2002. "Toward a Racial Abyss: Eugenics, Wickliffe Draper, and the Origin of the Pioneer Fund." *Journal of the History of the Behavioral Sciences* 38 (3): 259–83. https://doi.org/10.1002/jhbs.10063.

Kenny, Michael G. 2006. "A Question of Blood, Race, and Politics." *Journal of the History of Medicine* 61: 456–91.

Kenny, Michael G. 2009. "Genomics, Genetic Identity, and the Refiguration of 'Race.'" In *Race and Science: Scientific Challenges to Racism in Modern America*, ed. Paul Farber and Hamilton Cravens, 212–27. Corvallis: Oregon State University Press.

Kevles, Daniel J. 1995. *In the Name of Eugenics: Genetics and the Uses of Human Heredity*. Cambridge, MA: Harvard University Press.

Lee, Sandra Soo-Jin, Deborah Bolnick, Troy Duster, Pilar Ossorio, and Kimberly TallBear. 2009. "The Illusive Gold Standard in Genetic Ancestry Testing." *Science* 325 (5936): 38–39. https://doi.org/10.1126/science.1173038.

Lemarchand, René. 1996. *Burundi: Ethnic Conflict and Genocide*. Cambridge: Cambridge University Press.

Lieberman, Arthur, Andrew Lyons, and Harriet Lyons. 1995. "An Interview with Ashley Montagu." *Current Anthropology* 36 (5): 835–44. https://doi.org/10.1086/204440.

Maquet, Jacques. 1961. *The Premise of Inequality in Ruanda*. London: Oxford University Press.

Marks, Johnathan. 2008. "Race across the Physical-Cultural Divide in American Anthropology." In *A New History of Anthropology*, ed. Henrika Kuklick, 242–58. Oxford: Blackwell Publishing.

McLaren, Angus. 1990. *Our Own Master Race: The Eugenic Crusade in Canada*. Toronto: McClelland & Stewart. https://doi.org/10.3138/9781442623316.

Montagu, M.F. Ashley. 1942. *Man's Most Dangerous Myth: The Fallacy of Race*. New York: Columbia University Press.

Montagu, M.F. Ashley. 1972. *Statement on Race: An Annotated Elaboration and Exposition of the Four Statements on Race Issued by the United Nations Educational, Scientific, and Cultural Organization*. New York: Oxford University Press.

Mourant, A.E. 1983. *Blood Relations: Blood Groups and Anthropology*. London: Oxford University Press.

Paul, Diane. 1995. *Controlling Human Heredity, 1865 to the Present*. Atlantic Highlands, NJ: Humanities Press.

Prunier, Gérard. 1995. *The Rwanda Crisis: History of a Genocide*. New York: Columbia University Press.

Ripley, William Z. 1898. *The Races of Europe: A Sociological Study*. London: Kegan Paul, Trench, Trubner.

Roscoe, John. 1911. *The Baganda*. London: Macmillan.

Santos, Ricardo Ventura, and Marcos Chor Maio. 2004. "Race, Genomics, Identities and Politics in Contemporary Brazil." *Critique of Anthropology* 24 (4): 347–78. https://doi.org/10.1177/0308275X04047841.

Smith, John. 1966. *The Generall Historie of Virginia, New-England, and the Summer Isles*. Facsimile edition. London: Michael Sparkes.

Speke, John Hanning. 1863. *Journal of the Discovery of the Source of the Nile*. Edinburgh: William Blackwood and Sons.

Stepan, Nancy. 1982. *The Idea of Race in Science: Great Britain, 1800–1960*. London: McMillan. https://doi.org/10.1007/978-1-349-05452-7.

Stocking, George. 1968. "The Critique of Racial Formalism." In *Race, Culture, and Evolution: Essays in the History of Anthropology*, 160–94. Chicago: University of Chicago Press.

Stocking, George. 1982. *Victorian Anthropology*. New York: Free Press.

Wailoo, Keith, and Stephen Pemberton. 2006. *The Troubled Dream of Genetic Medicine*. Baltimore: Johns Hopkins University Press.

Wallace, Anthony F.C. 1999. *Jefferson and the Indians: The Tragic Fate of the First Americans*. Cambridge, MA: Harvard University Press.

Ward, R.H., Barbara Frazier, Kerry Dew-Jager, and Svante Pääbo. 1991. "Extensive Mitochondrial Diversity within a Single Amerindian Tribe." *Proceedings of the National Academy of Sciences* 88: 8720–24. https://doi.org/10.1073/pnas.88.19.8720.

Chapter 10

Adams, John W. 1973. *The Gitksan Potlatch: Population Flux, Resource Ownership and Reciprocity*. Toronto: Holt, Rinehart & Winston of Canada.

Arima, Eugene, and Allan Hoover. 2011. *The Whaling People of the West Coast of Vancouver Island and Cape Flattery*. Victoria: Royal BC Museum.

Benedict, Ruth. 1959. *Patterns of Culture*. Boston: Houghton Mifflin.

Boas, Franz. 1963. *The Mind of Primitive Man*. 4th ed. New York: Free Press.

Boas, Franz. 1996. "The Study of Geography." In *Volksgeist as Method and Ethic: Essays on Boasian Ethnography and the German Anthropological Tradition*, ed. George W. Stocking, 3 16. Madison: University of Wisconsin Press.

Brody, Hugh. 1981. *Maps and Dreams: Indians and the British Columbia Frontier*. Vancouver: Douglas & McIntyre.

Brown, Michael F. 2003. *Who Owns Native Culture?* Cambridge, MA: Harvard University Press.

Clifford, James. 1988. *The Predicament of Culture: Twentieth-Century Ethnography, Literature, and Art*. Cambridge, MA: Harvard University Press.

Cole, Douglas. 1985. *Captured Heritage: The Scramble for Northwest Coast Artifacts*. Vancouver, Toronto: Douglas & McIntyre.

Cole, Douglas. 1999. *Franz Boas: The Early Years, 1858–1906*. Vancouver, Toronto: Douglas & McIntyre.

Cole, Douglas, and Ira Chaikin. 1990. *An Iron Hand upon the People: The Law against the Potlatch on the Northwest Coast*. Vancouver, Toronto: Douglas & McIntyre.

Colson, Elizabeth. 1953. *The Makah Indians: A Study of an Indian Tribe in Modern American Society*. Minneapolis: University of Minnesota Press.

Cook, James. 1967. *The Voyage of the* Resolution *and* Discovery *1776–1780*. Ed. J.G. Beaglehole. Cambridge: Cambridge University Press.

Coté, Charlotte. 2010. *Spirits of Our Whaling Ancestors: Revitalizing Makah & Nuu-chah-nulth Traditions*. Seattle: University of Washington Press.

Cove, John J. 1982. "The Gitksan Traditional Concept of Land Ownership." *Anthropologica* 24 (1): 3–17. https://doi.org/10.2307/25605083.

Culhane, Dara. 1998. *The Pleasure of the Crown: Anthropology, Law and First Nations*. Burnaby, BC: Talonbooks.

Darwin, Charles. 1998. *The Descent of Man*. Amherst, NY: Prometheus Books.

Erikson, Patricia Pierce. 1999. "A-Whaling We Will Go: Encounters of Knowledge and Memory at the Makah Cultural and Research Center." *Cultural Anthropology* 14 (4): 556–83. https://doi.org/10.1525/can.1999.14.4.556.

Freed, Stanley, Ruth S. Freed, and Laila Williamson. 1988. "Capitalist Philanthropy and Russian Revolutionaries: The Jesup North Pacific Expedition (1897–1902)." *American Anthropologist* 90 (1): 7–24. https://doi.org/10.1525/aa.1988.90.1.02a00010.

Johnston, Hugh M., ed. 1996. *The Pacific Province: A History of British Columbia*. Vancouver, Toronto: Douglas & McIntyre.

Jonaitis, Aldona. 1999. *The Yuquot Whaler's Shrine*. Seattle: University of Washington Press.

LaViolette, F. 1961. *The Struggle for Survival: Indian Cultures and the Protestant Ethic in British Columbia*. Toronto: University of Toronto Press.

Lee, Jeff. 2013. "Muchalaht Wrestle with Emotions Caused by Loss of Shrine." *Vancouver Sun*, April 15.

Loo, Tina. 1992. "Dan Cranmer's Potlatch: Law as Coercion, Symbol, and Rhetoric in British Columbia, 1884–1951." *Canadian Historical Review* 73 (2): 125–65. https://doi.org/10.3138/CHR-073-02-01.

Mauss, Marcel. 1990. *The Gift: The Form and Reason for Exchange in Archaic Societies*. Trans. W.D. Halls. London: Routledge.

McEachern, Allan. 1991. *Reasons for Judgment* [in the Delgamuukw Case]. Vancouver: Criminal Court Registry Office.

Mills, Antonia. 1994a. *Eagle Down is Our Law: Witsu'wit'en Law, Feasts, and Land Claims*. Vancouver: University of British Columbia Press.

Mills, Antonia. 1994b. "Rebirth and Identity: Three Gitksan Cases of Pierced-Ear Birth-Marks." In *Amerindian Rebirth: Reincarnation Beliefs among North American Indians and Inuit*, ed. A. Mills and Richard Slobodin, 211–41. Toronto: University of Toronto Press.

Mills, Antonia, ed. 2005. *Hang Onto Those Words: Johnny David's Evidence*. Toronto: University of Toronto Press.

Parker, Arthur C. 1913. *The Code of Handsome Lake, the Seneca Prophet*. Albany: University of the State of New York.

Persky, Stan. 1998. *Delgamuukw: The Supreme Court of Canada Decision on Aboriginal Title*. Vancouver: Greystone Books.

Price, Sally. 2001. *Primitive Art in Civilized Places*. 2nd ed. Chicago: University of Chicago Press.

Satterfield, Terre. 2002. *Anatomy of a Conflict: Identity, Knowledge, and Emotion in Old-Growth Forests*. Vancouver, Toronto: UBC Press.

Sproat, Gilbert Malcolm. 1868. *Scenes and Studies of Savage Life*. London: Smith, Elder & Co.

Tennant, Paul. 1990. *Aboriginal Peoples and Politics: The Indian Land Question in British Columbia, 1849–1989*. Vancouver: University of British Columbia Press.

United Nations. 2007. *United Nations Declaration on the Rights of Indigenous Peoples (Resolution 61/295)*. New York: United Nations. http://www.un.org/esa/socdev/unpfii/documents/DRIPS_en.pdf.

United States Congress. 1990. *An Act to Provide for the Protection of Native American Graves (Public Law 101–601)*. Washington, DC: Government Printing Office.

Vansina, Jan. 1985. *Oral Tradition as History*. Madison: University of Wisconsin Press.

Wa, Gisday, and Delgam Uukw. 1992. *The Spirit in the Land: Statements of the Gitksan and Wet'suwet'en Hereditary Chiefs in the Supreme Court of British Columbia, 1987–1990*. Gabriola Island, BC: Reflections.

Wallace, Anthony F.C. 1956. "Revitalization Movements." *American Anthropologist* 58 (2): 264–81. https://doi.org/10.1525/aa.1956.58.2.02a00040.

Wallace, Anthony F.C. 1972. *The Death and Rebirth of the Seneca*. New York: Vintage.

Chapter 11

Abu-Lughod, Lila. 2012. "Living the 'Revolution' in an Egyptian Village: Moral Action in a National Space." *American Ethnologist* 39 (1): 21–25. https://doi.org/10.1111/j.1548-1425.2011.01341.x.

Aptekar, Lewis. 1988. *Street Children of Cali*. Durham, NC: Duke University Press.

Boellstorff, Tom. 2008. *Coming of Age in Second Life: An Anthropologist Explores the Virtually Human*. Princeton, NJ: Princeton University Press.

Cairoli, M. Laetitia. 2012. *Girls of the Factory: A Year with the Garment Workers of Morocco*. Gainsville: University Press of Florida.

Coloma, Sintos Roland, Bonnie McElhinny, Ethel Tungohan, John Paul C. Catungal, and Lisa M. Davidson, eds. 2012. *Filipinos in Canada: Disturbing Invisibility*. Toronto: University of Toronto Press.

Garsten, Christina. 1994. *Apple World: Core and Periphery in a Transnational Organizational Culture, Stockholm Studies in Social Anthropology 33*. Stockholm: Almqvist & Wiksell International.

Hannerz, Ulf. 2003. "Being There ... and There ... and There! Reflections on Multi-Site Ethnography." *Ethnography* 4 (2): 201–16. https://doi.org/10.1177/14661381030042003.

Howell, Signe. 2003. "Kinning: The Creation of Life Trajectories in Transnational Adoptive Families." *Journal of the Royal Anthropological Institute* 9 (3): 465–84. https://doi.org/10.1111/1467-9655.00159.

Inda, Jonathan Xavier, and Renato Rosaldo, eds. 2008. "Introduction: A World in Motion." *The Anthropology of Globalization: A Reader*. Malden, MA: Blackwell Publishing.

Kearney, Michael. 1995. "The Local and the Global: The Anthropology of Globalization and Transnationalism." *Annual Review of Anthropology* 24 (1): 547–65. https://doi.org/10.1146/annurev.an.24.100195.002555.

Keller, Eva. 2008. "The Banana Plant and the Moon: Conservation and the Malagasy Ethos of Life in Masoala, Madagascar." *American Ethnologist* 35 (4): 650–64. https://doi.org/10.1111/j.1548-1425.2008.00103.x.

Klein, C. 2003. *Cold-War Orientalism.* Berkeley: University of California Press.

Leinaweaver, Jessica. 2007. "On Moving Children: The Social Implications of Andean Child Circulation." *American Ethnologist* 34 (1): 163–80. https://doi.org/10.1525/ae.2007.34.1.163.

Marre, D., and L. Briggs, eds. 2009. "Introduction: The Circulation of Children." In *International Adoption: Global Inequalities and the Circulation of Children*, 1–28. New York: New York University Press. https://doi.org/10.18574/nyu/9780814791011.003.0001.

Miller, Barbara D., Penny Van Esterik, and John Van Esterik. 2001. *Cultural Anthropology.* Canadian Edition. Toronto: Pearson Education Canada.

Mosse, David. 2005. *Cultivating Development: An Ethnography of Aid Policy and Practice.* London and Ann Arbor, MI: Pluto Press.

Mosse, David, ed. 2011. *Adventures in Aidland: The Anthropology of Professionals in International Development.* Studies in Applied and Public Anthropology, vol. 6. New York, Oxford: Berghahn Press.

Murray, Gerald. 1987. "The Domestication of Wood in Haiti: A Case Study in Applied Evolution." In *Anthropological Praxis Translating Knowledge into Action*, ed. Robert M. Wulff and Shirley J. Fiske, 223–40. Boulder, CO: Westview Press.

Nagy, Sharon. 1998. "'This Time I Think I'll Try a Filipina:' Global and Local Influences on Relations between Foreign Household Workers and Their Employers in Doha, Qatar." *City & Society* 10 (1): 83–103. https://doi.org/10.1525/city.1998.10.1.83.

Nagy, Sharon. 2006. "Making Room for Migrants, Making Sense of Difference: Spatial and Ideological Expressions of Social Diversity in Urban Qatar." *Urban Studies* 43 (1): 119–37. https://doi.org/10.1080/00420980500409300.

Pelto, Pertti J. 1973. *The Snowmobile Revolution: Technology and Social Change in the Arctic.* Menlo Park, CA: Cummings.

Selman, P. 2009. "The Movement of Children for International Adoption: Developments and Trends in Receiving States and States of Origins, 1998–2004." In *International Adoption: Global Inequalities and the Circulation of Children*, ed. D. Marre and L. Briggs, 32–51. New York, London: New York University Press. https://doi.org/10.18574/nyu/9780814791011.003.0002.

United Nations, Department of Economic and Social Affairs. 2010. *The World's Women: 2010 Trends and Statistics.* New York: United Nations. http://unstats.un.org/unsd/demographic/products/Worldswomen/WW2010pub.htm.

Volkman, Toby Alice, ed. 2005. "Introduction: New Geographies of Kinship." In *Cultures of Transnational Adoption*, 1–22. Durham, NC and London: Duke University Press. https://doi.org/10.1215/9780822386926-001.

Walsh, Andrew. 2012. *Made in Madagascar: Sapphires, Ecotourism, and the Global Bazaar.* Toronto: University of Toronto Press.

Weismantel, Mary. November 1995. "Making Kin: Kinship Theory and Zumbagua Adoptions." *American Ethnologist* 22 (4): 685–704. https://doi.org/10.1525/ae.1995.22.4.02a00010.

Yngvesson, B. 2009. "Refiguring Kinship in the Space of Adoption." In *International Adoption: Global Inequalities and the Circulation of Children*, ed. D. Marre and L. Briggs, 103–18. New York, London: New York University Press. https://doi.org/10.18574/nyu/9780814791011.003.0006.

Glossary

Devor, Aaron H. 2014. *The Transgender Archives: Foundations for the Future*. Victoria, BC: University of Victoria Chair in Transgender Studies. http://www.uvic.ca/library/about/ul/publications/documents/Devor_Foundations_2016_2ndEd.pdf.

Goldman, Ruth. 1996. "Who is That *Queer* Queer? Exploring Norms around Sexuality, Race and Class in Queer Theory." In *Queer Studies: A Lesbian, Gay, Bisexual and Transgender Anthology*, ed. Brett Beemyn and Mickey Eliason, 169–83. New York, London: New York University Press.

Hulan, Renee, and Renate Eigenbrod, eds. 2008. *Aboriginal Oral Traditions: Theory, Practice, Ethics*. Halifax: Fernwood Publishing.

Kearney, Michael. 1995. "The Local and the Global: The Anthropology of Globalization and Transnationalism." *Annual Review of Anthropology* 24 (1): 547–65. https://doi.org/10.1146/annurev.an.24.100195.002555.

Satterfield, Terre. 2002. *Anatomy of a Conflict: Identity, Knowledge, and Emotion in Old-Growth Forests*. Vancouver: UBC Press.

Smith, C. 1996. "What Is This Thing Call Queer?" In *The Material Queer: A LesBiGay Cultural Studies Reader*, ed. D. Morton, 277–85. Boulder, CO: Westview Press.

Theodore, P.S., and S.A. Bason. 2000. "Heterosexual Masculinity and Homophobia: A Reaction to the Self?" *Journal of Homosexuality* 40 (2): 31–48.

Wallace, Anthony F.C. 1956. "Revitalization Movements." *American Anthropologist* 58 (2): 264–81. https://doi.org/10.1525/aa.1956.58.2.02a00040.

Winthrop, Robert H. 1991. *Dictionary of Concepts in Cultural Anthropology*. New York: Greenwood Press.

World Health Organization, Western Pacific Region. 2017. "Health Topics: Gender." Accessed June 2, 2017. http://www.wpro.who.int/topics/gender_issues/en/.

Sources

Plates

1.2   James Teit and Lucy Antko, Image #11686, American Museum of Natural History Library.

1.3   Charles Darwin, 1840 (w/c on paper), by George Richmond. Down House, Downe, Kent, UK / © Historic England / Bridgeman Images.

1.4   Vice Admiral Robert Fitzroy (1805–65), Royal Naval College, Greenwich, London, UK / Bridgeman Images.

1.5   A native of Tierra del Fuego, from *Narrative of the Surveying Voyages of His Majesty's Ships Adventure and Beagle* (1839). © British Library Board / Robana / Art Resource, NY.

1.6   Captain Cook's Landing at Botany, A.D. 1770. National Library of Australia, 2141 #S4470.

1.7   Lewis Henry Morgan, National Anthropological Archives, Smithsonian Institution, INV 02863100, Photo Lot 33. Reproduced by permission.

2.1   "Malinowski with Trobriand Islanders during fieldwork, 1918," Image MALINOWS-KI/3/18/2, reproduced by permission of the Library of the London School of Economics & Political Science.

2.3   Margaret Mead with Manus mother and child, 1953. © Bettmann / CORBIS.

3.1   Film still from *Black Mountain* (2008); Charlotte Whitby-Coles undertaking her Ph.D. research in India, at pilgrimage site of Kalo Dungar, Rann of Kutch, Gujarat. Photographer: Amin Hajee. Reproduced by permission of the Royal Anthropological Institute. https://www.therai.org.uk.

5.1   Cave of the Patriarchs, from the south, Hebron, Israel. Image courtesy of Djampa, CC BY SA 4.0.

5.2   A.R. Radcliffe-Brown, reproduced by permission of the Institute of Social and Cultural Anthropology, Oxford.

5.3   Trail of Tears sign, Bartlett, TN. Image courtesy of Thomas R. Machnitzki, CC BY SA 3.0.

6.1   Professor Marcel Mauss with Georges Duchemin, 1936–1937. Photo by Henri Lehmann. Print on baryta paper, 12.3 x 17.8 cm. Musée du Quai Branly / Scala / Art Resource, NY.

6.2   A characteristic Dinka attitude, Terrakekka to Aweil, Sudan, 1925 (1927). Artist: Thomas A Glover. HIP / Art Resource, NY.

6.4   US President Barack Obama (L) bows as he shakes hands with Japanese Emperor Akihito (C) and as Empress Michiko (R) looks on upon Obama's arrival at the Imperial Palace in Tokyo on November 14, 2009. Mandel Ngan / AFP / Getty Images.

6.5   E.E. Evans-Pritchard with Azande boys, by unknown photographer. © Pitt Rivers Museum, University of Oxford, PRM 1998.341.576.

6.6   Portrait of Emile Durkheim (1858–1917) (b/w photo), French Photographer / Bibliothèque Nationale, Paris, France / Bridgeman Images.

8.1   Children in gender specific Halloween costumes, Frederic J. Brown / AFP / Getty Images.

8.2   Hijra, image courtesy of Mike Garten, CC BY 3.0.

9.4   Mutara III Rudahigwa, Mwami (King) of Rwanda (1931–1959). Portrait photo, 1957. akg-images / Paul Almasy.

10.1   Habitations in Nootka Sound, from drawings executed by John Webber during the Third Voyage of Captain Cook 1777–1779. © British Library Board / Robana / Art Resource, NY.

10.2   Nootka Group in Interior of House, Nootka Sound, British Columbia, from *Atlas to Accompany A Voyage of Discovery of the North Pacific Ocean and Round the World*, 1784. Washington State Historical Society / Art Resource, NY.

10.3   Whale shrine figure, Nuu-chah-nulth Indians (Nootka), Catalog #16/9902, Division of Anthropology, American Museum of Natural History.

10.4   Makah whaler, University of Washington Libraries, Special Collections, Asahel Curtis, photographer, NA740. Reproduced by permission.

10.5   Gitskan Village (Hazelton Indian Village), Image E-08391, courtesy of Royal BC Museum and Archives.

10.6   Logging road blockade, Oregon, USA. Greenpeace activist Jennifer Kirby locks herself to a large yellow container blockading a logging road at the site of the Soukow Timber Sale in the Medford Bureau of Land Management District in southwest Oregon. © Greenpeace / Dang Ngo.

11.1   Burmese refugees waiting to be registered by a Thai policeman, Thierry Falise / LightRocket via Getty Images.

11.2   Korean children with their American parents, © Bettmann / CORBIS.

Maps

1.1   Cook's third voyage, image courtesy of Phirosiberia, CC BY SA 3.0.

7.1   Venezuela, from Charles L. Briggs, with Clara Mantini-Briggs, *Stories in the Time of Cholera: Racial Profiling during a Medical Nightmare*, © 2003 by The Regents of the University of California. Reproduced by permission of the University of California Press.

Index